# The Emotional Life of Postmodern Film

*Emotion* and *Postmodernism*: is it possible to imagine an odder couple, stranger bedfellows, less bad company? *The Emotional Life of Postmodern Film* brings this unlikely pair into sustained dialogue, arguing that the interdisciplinary body of scholarship currently emerging under the rubric of "affect theory" may be unexpectedly enriched by an encounter with the field that has become its critical other. Across a series of radical re-reappraisals of canonical postmodern texts, from Fredric Jameson's *Postmodernism* to David Cronenberg's *Crash*, Duncan shows that the same postmodern archive that has proven resistant to strongly subject-based and object-oriented emotions, like anger and sadness, proves all too congenial to a series of idiosyncratic, borderline emotions, from knowingness, fascination and bewilderment to boredom and euphoria. The analysis of these emotions, in turn, promises to shake up scholarly consensus on two key counts. On the one hand, it will restructure our sense of the place and role of emotion in a critical enterprise that has long cast it as the stodgy, subjective sister of a supposedly more critically interesting and politically productive *affect*. On the other, it will transform our perception of postmodernism as a now-historical aesthetic and theoretical moment, teaching us to acknowledge more explicitly and to name more clearly the emotional life that energizes it.

**Pansy Duncan** is Lecturer in the School of English and Media Studies at Massey University, Auckland, New Zealand, where she writes on media affect and aesthetics. Her articles have been published in a range of venues, including *PMLA*, *Cultural Critique*, *Textual Practice*, *Screen* and *Film Quarterly*.

# Routledge Research in Cultural and Media Studies

For a full list of titles in this series, please visit www.routledge.com.

50 **A Social History of Contemporary Democratic Media**
*Jesse Drew*

51 **Digital Media Sport**
Technology, Power and Culture in the Network Society
*Edited by Brett Hutchins and David Rowe*

52 **Barthes' *Mythologies* Today**
Readings of Contemporary Culture
*Edited by Pete Bennett and Julian McDougall*

53 **Beauty, Violence, Representation**
*Edited by Lisa A. Dickson and Maryna Romanets*

54 **Public Media Management for the Twenty-First Century**
Creativity, Innovation, and Interaction
*Edited by Michał Głowacki and Lizzie Jackson*

55 **Transnational Horror Across Visual Media**
Fragmented Bodies
*Edited by Dana Och and Kirsten Strayer*

56 **International Perspectives on Chicana/o Studies**
"This World is My Place"
*Edited by Catherine Leen and Niamh Thornton*

57 **Comics and the Senses**
A Multisensory Approach to Comics and Graphic Novels
*Ian Hague*

58 **Popular Culture in Africa**
The Episteme of the Everyday
*Edited by Stephanie Newell and Onookome Okome*

59 **Transgender Experience**
Place, Ethnicity, and Visibility
*Edited by Chantal Zabus and David Coad*

60 **Radio's Digital Dilemma**
Broadcasting in the Twenty-First Century
*John Nathan Anderson*

61 **Documentary's Awkward Turn**
Cringe Comedy and Media Spectatorship
*Jason Middleton*

62 **Serialization in Popular Culture**
*Edited by Rob Allen and Thijs van den Berg*

63 **Gender and Humor**
Interdisciplinary and International Perspectives
*Edited by Delia Chiaro and Raffaella Baccolini*

64 **Studies of Video Practices**
Video at Work
*Edited by Mathias Broth, Eric Laurier, and Lorenza Mondada*

65 **The Memory of Sound**
Preserving the Sonic Past
*Seán Street*

66 **American Representations of Post-Communism**
Television, Travel Sites, and Post-Cold War Narratives
*Andaluna Borcila*

67 **Media and the Ecological Crisis**
*Edited by Richard Maxwell, Jon Raundalen, and Nina Lager Vestberg*

68 **Representing Multiculturalism in Comics and Graphic Novels**
*Edited by Carolene Ayaka and Ian Hague*

69 **Media Independence**
Working with Freedom or Working for Free?
*Edited by James Bennett and Niki Strange*

70 **Neuroscience and Media**
New Understandings and Representations
*Edited by Michael Grabowski*

71 **American Media and the Memory of World War II**
*Debra Ramsay*

72 **International Perspectives on Shojo and Shojo Manga**
The Influence of Girl Culture
*Edited by Masami Toku*

73 **The Borders of Subculture**
Resistance and the Mainstream
*Edited by Alexander Dhoest, Steven Malliet, Barbara Segaert, and Jacques Haers*

74 **Media Education for a Digital Generation**
*Edited by Julie Frechette and Rob Williams*

75 **Spanish-Language Television in the United States**
Fifty Years of Development
*Kenton T. Wilkinson*

76 **Embodied Metaphors in Film, Television, and Video Games**
Cognitive Approaches
*Edited by Kathrin Fahlenbrach*

77 **Critical Animal and Media Studies**
Communication for Nonhuman Animal Advocacy
*Edited by Núria Almiron, Matthew Cole, and Carrie P. Freeman*

78 **The Middle Class in Emerging Societies**
Consumers, Lifestyles and Markets
*Edited by Leslie L. Marsh and Hongmei Li*

79 **A Cultural Approach to Emotional Disorders**
Psychological and Aesthetic Interpretations
*E. Deidre Pribram*

80 **Biopolitical Media**
Catastrophe, Immunity and Bare Life
*Allen Meek*

81 **The Emotional Life of Postmodern Film**
Affect Theory's Other
*Pansy Duncan*

# The Emotional Life of Postmodern Film
Affect Theory's Other

Pansy Duncan

NEW YORK AND LONDON

First published 2016
by Routledge
711 Third Avenue, New York, NY 10017

and by Routledge
2 Park Square, Milton Park, Abingdon, Oxon OX14 4RN

Routledge is an imprint of the Taylor & Francis Group, an informa business

© 2016 Taylor & Francis

The right of Pansy Duncan to be identified as author of this work has been asserted by her in accordance with sections 77 and 78 of the Copyright, Designs and Patents Act 1988.

All rights reserved. No part of this book may be reprinted or reproduced or utilised in any form or by any electronic, mechanical, or other means, now known or hereafter invented, including photocopying and recording, or in any information storage or retrieval system, without permission in writing from the publishers.

Trademark notice: Product or corporate names may be trademarks or registered trademarks, and are used only for identification and explanation without intent to infringe.

*Library of Congress Cataloging-in-Publication Data*

Duncan, Pansy.
The emotional life of postmodern film: affect theory's other / by Pansy Duncan.
   pages cm. — (Routledge research in cultural and media studies; 81)
Includes bibliographical references and index.
   1. Emotions in motion pictures. 2. Postmodernism—Social aspects.
   I. Title.
PN1995.9.E46D88 2015
791.43'653—dc23          2015028273

ISBN: 978-1-138-95506-6 (hbk)
ISBN: 978-1-315-66661-7 (ebk)

Typeset in Sabon
by codeMantra

Printed and bound in Great Britain by
TJ International Ltd, Padstow, Cornwall

# Contents

| | |
|---|---|
| *List of Figures* | ix |
| *Acknowledgments* | xi |
| | |
| Introduction: Postmodernism and Emotion | 1 |
| 1   Euphoria, Ecstasy, Sublimity: The Emotional Life of Postmodern Theory | 38 |
| 2   Fascination: Between the Rough and the Glossy | 77 |
| 3   Fear: Dead Subjects and Living Dolls | 108 |
| 4   Bewilderment: The Ravaged Face of Postmodern Theory and Aesthetics | 134 |
| 5   Boredom: Avant-Garde and Trash | 165 |
| 6   Knowingness: Feeling Theory and its Other | 187 |
| Restlessness: A Coda | 217 |
| | |
| *References* | 225 |
| *Index* | 239 |

# List of Figures

| | | |
|---|---|---|
| 2.1 | The rough and the glossy. | 79 |
| 2.2 | The gleaming bent steel of the opening credits. | 80 |
| 2.3 | Catherine runs her hand over James's scars. | 81 |
| 2.4 | Catherine's fascination with the gleaming surface. | 86 |
| 2.5 | James runs his hand over his wife's dented side panel. | 93 |
| 2.6 | The scar comes into relief against the gleaming side panel of a car. | 98 |
| 3.1 | *Scream*'s publicity poster. | 109 |
| 3.2 | Casey's screaming face is mapped onto Ghostface's latex "scream" mask. | 127 |
| 4.1 | The face of the "Terrifying Bum." | 135 |
| 4.2 | Harring's face initially functions to secure the suture. | 146 |
| 4.3 | The bewildered face seems to theatricalize the mechanisms of suture. | 146 |
| 4.4 | The ruined face of Diane Selwyn. | 150 |
| 4.5 | Harring grasps her face as if to keep it in place. | 151 |
| 5.1 | *Gummo*'s frames are filled with junk. | 165 |
| 6.1 | "Did somebody say my name?" | 197 |
| 6.2 | The deepened grin of gratified knowingness. | 197 |

# Acknowledgments

That the niggly, irksome emotions I write about in this book are not among the cluster emotions I associate with writing it is testament to the grace of the many people who have helped usher it through to publication. Annamarie Jagose was there from the first, and her theoretical and editorial interventions leave their mark on every sentence of this book that manages to communicate some kind of sense. It is a pleasure to be beholden to a figure who continues to set for me an example of a life that seamlessly weds passionate engagement to professional commitment. Colleagues at the University of Auckland, especially Misha Kavka, Eluned Summers-Bremner and Katherine Sender, as well as those farther afield, like Lee Wallace, Sianne Ngai and Meaghan Morris, have been generous in ways that far exceed the bounds of any professional obligation. Their readiness to respond gracefully and efficiently to calls on their time, even when panicky, last-minute or ill-advised, impresses me the more I come to understand the many other obligations that besiege the work-life of senior academics. More recently, my colleagues at Massey University—especially Erin Mercer, Rand Hazou and Jeremi Szaniawski—have made my workplace far more fun than any salaried position should be allowed to be. As Head of School, Joe Grixti has been a model of professional support and personal sweetness. I will always be grateful to Frances and Bill van Dammen for the tolerance they showed in welcoming into their family someone whose prospects, both professional and culinary, must often have seemed less than promising—and grateful, too, for raising a son, Tim, whose love I will always be happily unworthy of. Finally, I could not have begun—let alone completed—this book without the support of my parents, Robyn Hawkesby and Grant Duncan. Their unwavering and often unjustified faith in the value of doctoral study, despite the prolonged financial infantilism it has entailed, has been galvanizing in every possible way. This book is dedicated to them.

An earlier version of Chapter 2 initially appeared in *PMLA* as "Taking the Smooth with the Rough: Texture, Emotion and the Other Postmodernism" (*PMLA* 129.2 [2014]: 2-4-222), and Chapter 5 began its print career as "Bored and Boringer: Avant-Garde and Trash in Harmony Korine's *Gummo*" in *Textual Practice* 29.4 (2015): 717–743, available on http://www.tandfonline.com. I am grateful to the editors of both these journals for permission to republish that material here.

# Introduction
## Postmodernism and Emotion

### I

"Emotion" and "Postmodernism": is it possible to imagine an odder couple, stranger bedfellows, less bad company? Whereas "emotion" rolls readily off the critical tongue, "postmodernism" sticks stubbornly in the critical throat—and we don't have to look far to account for the two terms' strikingly different scholarly receptions. For if it is now a matter of record that the past two decades have witnessed an explosion of scholarship on affect and emotion still widely dubbed the "affective turn," it is equally a matter of record that the turn toward affect and emotion is a turn *away* from postmodern aesthetics and theory.[1] Ann Pellegrini and Jasbir Puar's 2009 survey of the resurgence of "critical interest in the cultural politics and claims of affect" is only one example of what now seems a ubiquitous if unspoken critical imperative: that the celebration of new work on emotion and affect go hand in hand with the denunciation of an older postmodern critical and aesthetic apparatus.[2] Blithely taking Fredric Jameson's now-notorious adage about a postmodern "waning of affect" as an index of postmodernism's hostility to emotional and affective analysis, Pellegrini and Puar no less blithely take the "growing centrality of theories of affect" as a sign that postmodernism has had its critical and cultural day.[3] As they put it, "some thirty years after Jameson's first exploration of these questions [of feeling], it is *postmodernism* that has ceased to be sounded as a term of, and for, critical analysis."[4] The writers are quick, of course, to note that Jameson's proclamations about the "waning of affect" in postmodernism are matched by a series of seemingly contradictory proclamations about the simultaneous emergence of free-floating, non-cognitive entities he calls "intensities."[5] Despite the interpretative nuance this might be expected to introduce, however, Pellegrini and Puar persist in representing the rise of theories of affect and emotion as a straightforward impeachment both of Jameson himself and of the chronologically dated and critically moribund postmodernism that he has come to represent.

Pellegrini and Puar are not alone in insisting that where the critical stocks of affect and emotion are on the ascendant, those of postmodern theory and aesthetics must be on the wane. In her 1994 contribution to a cluster of work not yet formalized enough to be called a corpus, Kathleen Woodward

## 2 Introduction

argued that the "excitement" of recent "research on the emotions" lay in the extent to which "it has not been underwritten by major theoretical developments such as Foucauldian genealogy or Derridean deconstruction," developments often annexed to the postmodern turn in criticism.[6] Eight years later, by the time Brian Massumi released his watershed *Parables for the Virtual,* this argument was so well established that it could be compressed into a casual, dismissive dig: "Fredric Jameson notwithstanding, belief has waned for many, but not affect. If anything, our condition is characterized by a surfeit of it."[7] And by 2014, the opening gambit of Eugenie Brinkema's *The Forms of the Affects*—"Must one even begin an argument anymore by refuting Fredric Jameson's infamous description of the 'waning of affect' in postmodernity?"—suggests that what was once a critical claim has hardened into critical cliché.[8] Yet even if one were to overlook what theorists of feeling have to say about postmodern theory, it would be harder to overlook what they fail to say—to discount, that is, the conspicuous absence of postmodern concepts from contemporary accounts of emotion. While the forms of economic, social and cultural speculation associated with postmodern thinking could conceivably supply a valuable conceptual scaffold for theories of affect and emotion, postmodernism is almost never explicitly invoked or deployed in these analyses.[9] Though the hard critical times on which the term "postmodernism" has fallen across the academy cannot be imputed exclusively to its perceived lack of fit with the "affective turn," it is surely no accident that the promotion of "affect" and "emotion" to the status of critical buzzwords coincides with the demotion of "postmodernism" to the status of critical pariah, and its subsequent displacement as a figure for the roughly contemporary by terms such as "globalization," "hypermodernity," "metamodernism," or even—as if out of a desire to efface the very memory of postmodern theory—a suddenly sprightly, undead "modernity."[10] Lacking both the vintage patina of the genuinely historical and the glossy luster of the bracingly current, too recent to be wholly forgotten but too old to be fully respectable, the term "postmodernism" has simply dropped off the critical docket altogether.

In many respects, of course, some of the burden of this polarization of postmodernism and emotion rests with postmodern theory itself, in which doom-laden claims about emotion's demise have sounded an insistent and influential refrain.[11] Jean Baudrillard's suggestion that "the cold and cool universe" has eclipsed "desire, passion, seduction ... expression and competition, [which] are the games of the hot universe," identifies the emergence of digital technology and media with the onset of a kind of emotional ice age; David Harvey recruits a "withdraw[al] into a kind of shell-shocked, blasé or exhausted silence" as the first line of defense against the social, political, technological and economic changes that his thinking outlines; while Jameson's notorious—and endlessly cited and circulated—adage the "waning of affect" casts the cultural conditions of postmodernism as the backdrop for a wholesale affective extinction.[12] But even setting these statements aside,

*Introduction* 3

finding conceptual quarter for emotion within the theoretical and aesthetic co-ordinates of the postmodern poses a seemingly insurmountable challenge. From Jean-Francois Lyotard's proclamations about the end of meta-narrative to Baudrillard's statements about the demise of the real, theories of the postmodern tend to be energized by what Catherine Constable has called "a logic of negation," in which the subjective, social and hermeneutic structures that sustain our long- and still-dominant "cognitive-appraisal" models of emotion are deconstructed where they are not thoroughly demonized.[13] Cognitive-appraisal theory casts emotion as the sign and expression of a subject, yet in postmodernism the subject is dead; cognitive-appraisal theory construes emotion as interpretative, yet in postmodernism, the hermeneutic depth models that once enshrined the promise of stable meaning have collapsed; cognitive-appraisal theory affords emotion a visceral, physiological aspect, yet postmodernism has been seen as inaugurating an age of disembodied indifference. At a pinch, some theorists have suggested that, if indisputably hostile to "emotion," postmodern theory may be more immediately hospitable to "affect"—a mobile, organic and nonsubjective model of feeling that has secured wide critical currency in the wake of work by Lauren Berlant, Brian Massumi, Eve Kosofksy Sedgwick and Nigel Thrift and whose seeming freedom from the shackles of subjectivity and hermeneutics makes it unusually compatible with the tenets of postmodernism.[14] Reconciling postmodern theory's critique of the subject and hermeneutics with the subjective and interpretative phenomenon still denoted by the term "emotion," however, seems a lost cause.

Yet if postmodern theory should be held at least partly responsible for the apparent polarization of "emotion" and "postmodernism," the field that I will henceforth refer to as "feeling theory"—in order to encompass both work on affect and work on emotion—must also shoulder some of the blame. For while "emotion" holds a nominal place in feeling theory, it is "affect" that has been the main terminological medium through which critics identified with the field have sought to carry out its critical mandates. Enthusiastically hailed by critics as "the way forward," "affect" has so fully monopolized feeling theory's revisionist energies that, more by default than by deliberation, "emotion" has tended to remain under the sway of older subjective and interpretative "cognitive-appraisal" models of feeling—despite the valiant reinterpretative efforts of critics such as Sianne Ngai and Rei Terada.[15] This is not, of course, to say that scholars in feeling theory have left the cognitive-appraisal paradigm critically unchallenged. On the contrary, this model of emotion has been repeatedly taken to task, both for its neglect of the physiological dimensions of feeling and for its complicity with existing socio-linguistic regimes.[16] Yet because this critique is less often taken as a platform to rethink our understanding of "emotion," than it is used as a pretext for shifting attention to an ostensibly more critically interesting and politically productive "affect," these models of emotion have tended to remain intact, if only as a kind of historical artifact or critical

## 4   Introduction

whipping boy. Massumi's construction of affect as a mobile, nonsubjective and asignifying potentiality, for example, asks an emotion figured as the "capture," "closure" and "mastery" of affect to bear the full weight of the ideological captivity that affect is said to escape.[17] Shaviro's contention that "emotion is affect captured by a subject, or tamed and reduced to the extent that it becomes commensurate with that subject," effectively consolidates the very subjective models of emotion he means "affect" to resist.[18] And in Sedgwick and Adam Frank's now-classic account of Silvan Tomkins' model of affect, the term "emotion" is kept in play only as long as it takes the pair to skewer "commonsense" cognitive-appraisal models of emotion, as if these models entirely exhausted emotion's critical potential or interest.[19] While clearly a key term within feeling theory, then, "emotion" has not benefitted from any of feeling theory's transformative critical power. On the contrary, it remains suspended within a now somewhat superannuated cognitive-appraisal frame whose postulates square poorly with key postmodern themes like the "death of the subject" and "new superficiality or depthlessness." Given feeling theory's persistent if slightly grudging investment in emotion, then, it should come as little surprise that critics continue to preface "new" work in the field with a ritual vanquishing of an "old" postmodernism.

It is this book's contention, however, that this gesture flies in the face of feeling theory's avowed commitment to what Ann Cvetkovich has called "the richness of emotional experience."[20] To write off an entire aesthetic and theoretical archive with one stroke is potentially to disregard a treasury of theoretical possibility. And if, as Terada puts it, "there is no such thing as the absence of emotion," it is my hunch that moments of apparent emotional absence might actually yield the richest reserves to draw on in rethinking emotion—reserves, moreover, that the theoretically undernourished specter of "emotion" now haunting the margins of feeling theory reminds us we cannot afford not to tap.[21] *The Emotional Life of Postmodern Film*, then, turns on the argument that both feeling theory in general, and its model of emotion in particular, may be unexpectedly enriched by an engagement with the corpus that has become feeling theory's critical and disciplinary other. While its primary theoretical affiliations are with feeling theory, this book argues that the best way to honor feeling theory's commitment to "the richness of emotional experience" is to bring feeling theory and postmodernism into dialogue. Through close re-readings of a cluster of canonical postmodern theoretical and filmic texts, from Fredric Jameson's *Postmodernism* to David Cronenberg's *Crash* (1996), *The Emotional Life of Postmodern Film* maps the idiosyncratic emotional life of an aesthetic and theoretical field that, while hostile to the "vehement passions" like anger, grief or fear that ratify our familiar cognitive-appraisal models of emotion, is very far from frigid, icy or emotion-free.[22] As the book shows, postmodern aesthetic and theoretical forms are encrusted by a series of ghostly, borderline emotions, from knowingness, fascination, bewilderment and boredom, to ecstasy and euphoria, that incorporate as their enabling conditions the very hermeneutic and subjective crises that would initially appear to foreclose emotional response. Emerging, paradoxically, out of the scene of emotion's problematization, absence or even failure, these unique emotional formations have a decidedly unorthodox relation to bodily animation, facial expression, meaning, subjectivity and intentionality. Their analysis, in turn, has the capacity to reshape not just some of the key precepts of feeling theory, but our apprehension of postmodernism as a now-historical aesthetic and theoretical moment.

As this summary suggests, the aims of this book are decidedly dual. On the one hand, I turn to postmodernism as a means of enriching feeling theory. My efforts to smoke out emotion in this least likely of places will have radical consequences not just for feeling theory's conception of emotion, long cast as the stodgy, subjective sister of a mobile, promiscuous and liberatory "affect," but for its understanding of its own practice, terminology, and genealogy. On the other hand, I turn to emotion as a means of renewing our understanding of postmodernism. A model of postmodern aesthetics and theory sensitized to the emotional formations that organize and encrust it allows us not only to reconcile postmodernism with recent work in feeling theory, but to recast that work as one of postmodernism's key symptoms. The buzz that now surrounds thinking about affect and emotion, of course, means that this book's implications for feeling theory will inevitably find readier critical uptake. Yet its implications for postmodernism should not be overlooked either. Indeed, one of the book's gambits is that, just as modernism has metamorphosed under the "fresh eyes and ears" of the "new modernist studies," so postmodernism may be ripe for an analogous reassessment.[23]

Realizing these twin aims will involve a total transformation of our received understanding of both emotion and postmodernism. That the emotions I broach in this study bear little resemblance to the strongly object-directed and subject-borne emotions that have become the linchpins of conventional, "cognitive-appraisal" models of emotion should be already be apparent. For more than simply devoid of the powerfully exemplary status of the "anger, grief and fear" Fisher champions as the "core vehement states," they seem to lack even the immediately recognizable emotional credentials of the "envy, irritation, paranoia" reviewed in Ngai's dazzling bestiary of marginal or minor emotions, *Ugly Feelings*.[24] In crystallizing not around "canonically major forms and genres" but around a set of postmodern aesthetic practices long assumed to foreclose the very possibility of emotion, these peculiarly postmodern emotional formations are each touched by a certain ghostliness or negativity.[25] Less what Sally Markowitz calls "meta-responses," responses to a response, than compensatory responses to our *failure* to respond with the kind of immediacy and legibility we conventionally attribute to emotion, boredom is a restless, irritable emotional registration of emotion's lack or absence; fascination projects the figure of an other who feels intensely in order to compensate for and resolve its

## 6  *Introduction*

own emotional paucity; fear is an emotion that emerges in proximity to the spectacle of another's emotional deficiency; and bewilderment pivots on the complete collapse of the subjective and epistemic platforms that conventionally underpin emotion.[26] These are emotions, in other words, that both materialize at and revolve around the scene of emotion's crisis or demise. Indeed, their adhesion to the spectacle of emotional lack at the level of object routinely registers in a similar contiguity to emotional lack at the level of physical effect. Whereas "animation" or "arousal" is often adduced as a precondition of emotion, boredom, for example, is marked by fatigue and lethargy; fascination by a kind of physiological paralysis; bewilderment by facial "blankness"; and knowingness by a smug insouciance.[27] Of course, while all bearing the physiological seal of their origin in and proximity to emotional deficiency, these emotions are far from homogenous in form. Knowingness is a mobile, social emotion that must be conferred upon us by others; bewilderment pivots on a chiasmus in which the respective attributes of subject and object are felt to be inverted; and euphoria is an internally contradictory emotion animated by the (mis)recognition that "emotion" has been displaced by "affect" in postmodern aesthetics. What these emotions share, however, is that in taking the emotional measure of postmodern aesthetic practices like self-reflexivity, allusion, disruption and depthlessness that have been strongly coded as hostile to the very possibility of emotion, they are each stamped by a certain spectral or vampiric relation to the kind of "strong, violent or primary passions" that continue to dominate our emotional imaginary.[28]

Yet if the critical interest of these emotions lies in their adjacency to the scene of emotional lack, their critical power lies in the fact that they nevertheless fulfill a certain minimal criterion of emotion—the fact that they are, in Terada's words, "psychological, at least minimally interpretive experiences."[29] For, *as* emotions, they pose a powerful challenge to the emotional edicts of the cognitive-appraisal paradigm. Where cognitive-appraisal theories predicate emotion on depth hermeneutic judgment, fascination cleaves to postmodernism's flat or depthless surfaces; where cognitive-appraisal theory construes facial signs as an expression of emotion, knowingness is a metaleptic effect of its own facial display; where cognitive-appraisal theory places the passions "at the farthest remove from irony," the peculiarly postmodern, recursive species of fear I examine here arises against the backdrop of the postmodern text's endless self-reflexivity; and where cognitive-appraisal theory assumes a binary show-down between emotion and its absence, between emotional "arousal" and non-emotional homeostasis, these emotions all turn this distinction into no distinction at all.[30] Indeed, in their radical divergence from cognitive-appraisal theory's conceptual co-ordinates, these emotions effectively destabilize the subjective, ethical and hermeneutic norms that cognitive-appraisal models are so often called upon to anchor. To take just two examples, where emotion has conventionally functioned as "proof of the human subject," bewilderment is the

Introduction 7

hallmark of a subject collapsed into an object, a subject stripped of his identity, self-presence and cognitive faculties.[31] Likewise, where emotion has long been grounded in an ideal of "individual decisions" that spur "action," fascination marks both judgment's suspension and its triangulation through an ostensibly omniscient other and action's displacement by paralysis.[32] Far from what Massumi calls "old surprises to which we have become more or less accustomed," then, these strange, posthumous emotions defy our commonsense emotional scripts. In putting pressure on the values that cognitive-appraisal models of emotion both draw upon and sustain, they not only provide ample affordances to feeling theory's efforts to rethink feeling's relation to subjecthood, embodiment, sociality and politics, but call into question some of the key precepts and practices of feeling theory itself.[33]

Yet if the vision of emotion called up by the figure of an emotional post-modernism is an idiosyncratic one, the vision of postmodernism called up by these postmodern emotions is no less idiosyncratic. As it has become customary to announce in inaugurating an account of the postmodern, postmodern theory is by no means a unified or coherent field. On the contrary, even the most perfunctory overview reveals that profiles of the postmodern run the gamut from Linda Hutcheon's picture of postmodern "doubleness" or duplicity, to Peter Sloterdijk's analysis of postmodern cynicism or "enlightened false consciousness"; from Brian McHale's vision of the postmodern "ontological dominant" to Jameson's melancholic failures of temporality, subjecthood and hermeneutic depth; and from Lyotard's crisis of meta-narratives, to Baudrillard's hallucinatory meditations on reversibility, ecstasy and the obscene in a universe marked by the triumph of the simulacrum over an expired real—to say nothing of more recent reflections on the transformation of sociality and textuality in the age of the Internet.[34] When these cultural and social shifts are translated to the aesthetic and formal register, as they often are, "the postmodern" seems no less fragmented. On the one hand, postmodern aesthetics involves a new self-reflexivity that amplifies the self-reflexive tendency in modernism; on the other, it marks a return to the representational practices that had been snubbed by an anti-representational modernism. On the one hand, postmodernism is nostalgia and pastiche, a freewheeling riffle through the dustbin of historical style; on the other, it expresses a discontent with the disintegration of modernist stylistics, and an effort to revivify the project of radical innovation initiated with high modernism. On the one hand, postmodernism is subversive de-doxifying critique; on the other, it's a philistine reveling in the commodified thrill of the cinematic blockbuster. The same theoretical diversity that marks these speculations about postmodern aesthetic shifts also marks speculation about the technological and economic shifts that ostensibly animate them. From Jameson's argument that postmodern aesthetics is an instance of "the cultural logic of late capitalism," to Harvey's conceptualization of late capitalism's time-space compression, and from Lyotard's emphasis on new types of information, knowledge and technology, to Baudrillard's

## 8   Introduction

intuition that we have undergone a transition from an economy dominated by industry and production to one fueled by the circulation of signs and images—theories of postmodernism are manifold and various, where they are not entirely contradictory.[35]

Rather than try to distil this rich stew of observation, polemic and speculation, however, this book exploits postmodern theory's *lack* of consistency to create a space for thinking newly about emotion and postmodernism. In my chapter on fascination, for example, I show that the binary logic of surface/depth that organizes much postmodern aesthetic analysis can be complicated by the fact that this logic is so often encrypted in the language of surface texture. Similarly, in my chapter on fear, I argue that the postmodern specter of the end of emotion is destabilized by that specter's long and vigorous critical life, suggesting that postmodern fear is in some sense bound up with the spectacle of its own demise. Yet this book does not only *not* provide a consistent vision of postmodernism. More radically, it entirely brackets debate about whether "postmodernism, post-modernism or postmodernity" could be a property of any text, period or mood whatever in the first place, suspending the question of whether these terms name an actually existing entity or whether, as John Frow contends, "the word can be taken as designating nothing more and nothing less than a genre of theoretical writing."[36] Working, rather, within the ambit of a small set of filmic and theoretical texts that are already widely considered to be postmodern in specifiable ways, my more modest aim is to show how, though not always positively valorized, or even always explicitly acknowledged, emotion has been central to the development of key postmodern figures and gestures—as rhetorical tool, as theoretical lynchpin and as subject matter.[37] This book, in other words, examines postmodernism's ecstatic reversibility rather than its mere indeterminacy; postmodernism's fascinatingly glossy surfaces rather than its mere depthlessness; postmodernism's bewildering fragmentation of the human face rather than its mere epistemic and ontological uncertainty; postmodernism's smugly knowing smiles rather than its purely cerebral practices of decoding; and postmodernism's tedious or terrifying affective voids rather than its mere emotional vacancies. Far from irrelevant to recent thinking about emotion and affect, it argues, postmodern theory and aesthetics becomes a valuable platform through which to engage it.

Yet if this is one of this book's primary lines of arguments, it is a line that very quickly forks in two. On the one hand, I will be arguing that feeling theory can learn a great deal from postmodernism, not just about emotion's capacity to transform in the face of threats to experience, biology, selfhood and embodiment, but about its own practice, terminology and origins. On the other, however, I will be arguing that feeling theory may *already* have learned more from postmodern theory and aesthetics than it avows, and that, as Hilary Chute maintains, if the term postmodernism has suffered a reduction in "taxonomic urgenc[y]," this is simply because the practice of postmodernism has so successfully made its mark on our critical range and critical style.[38] Indeed, I will suggest that the strongest evidence that postmodernism's signature critical and aesthetic gestures have left a lasting impression on our critical imaginary lies precisely in the new body of literature I am identifying as "feeling theory"—a project that is better understood as a continuation than as a termination of the postmodern enterprise. Seen in this light, then, postmodern aesthetics and theory may not only be amenable to, but may actually prefigure, aspects of the kinds of feeling-oriented analyses currently enjoying a critical vogue.

## II

While this book's archive and aims are decidedly dual, encompassing both feeling theory and postmodern aesthetics, it should be clear by now that—despite my resistance to some of its assumptions about both emotion and postmodernism—this book's primary allegiances lie with the former. But what are the core critical imperatives of the field I have been calling "feeling theory"? While often represented as a relatively new development that can be credited to the landmark essays of Massumi and Sedgwick in 1995, feeling theory also marks a coalescence of older trends, owing a significant debt, for example, both to certain strands of feminist and queer scholarship, and to the explosion of scholarly work on historical trauma in the 1990s.[39] Yet feeling theory is also fed by genealogical currents outside the mainstream of critical theory or cultural studies. Influences as diverse as the work of psychologist Silvan S. Tomkins, the philosophers Henri Bergson, Gilles Deleuze and Felix Guattari and Benedict de Spinoza, and the neuro-scientist Antonio Damasio, attest not just to feeling theory's own interdisciplinary impulse but to its sense of its *object*'s capacity to cross boundaries and frontiers, as an entity that is both social and physiological, both human and non-human, both constructed and natural.[40] As Melissa Gregg and Gregory J. Seigworth put it, "affect is found in those intensities that pass body to body (human, non-human, part-body and otherwise), in those resonances that circulate about, between and sometimes stick to bodies and worlds, and in the very passages or variations between these intensities and resonances themselves."[41] While diverse and interdisciplinary, however, feeling theory is not without a common impetus. What unifies the study of feeling in the critical humanities is a conviction, shared by this writer, that much earlier criticism has, as Ruth Leys puts it, "given too flat or unlayered or disembodied" an account of subjectivation, politics, ideology and the social, and thus that these critical practices must be supplemented by an understanding of the work of feeling in shaping textual, social and political life.[42]

In this connection, one of feeling theory's primary projects involves tracing the relation between feeling and the political, social and economic worlds that have been the more conventional objects of critical analysis. Within the conceptual constraints of more traditional cognitive-appraisal theories of emotion, of course, feeling is an exclusively subjective, personal

10  *Introduction*

phenomenon, and the predominance of this paradigm in the critical humanities and social sciences has long licensed feeling's marginalization, pathol-
ogization, moralization or dismissal. For feeling theory, by contrast, feeling
emerges in, indexes, and encrusts the political, even as its capacity to catalyze political action remains moot. Feeling theory, in other words, has set
out to document the various dynamics of diagnosis, response, resistance,
formation or failure that mark the fraught relation between feeling and
political, social and economic life.[43] A range of work might be cited here,
from Jonathan Flatley's work on "melancholia," cast less as a mood than as
a practice that might "produce its own kind of knowledge"; to Sara Ahmed's
work on the sociality of emotions, in which she contends that "it is through
emotions that [the] surfaces or boundaries" of both collective and individual
life are formed; to Lauren Berlant's work on the affectively charged "inti-
mate publics" central to American popular political culture; and Michael
Hardt and Antonio Negri's work on affective labour as part of the ensemble
of "immaterial labour" forms that "ha[ve] come to have an increasingly
crucial role in the organization of neoliberal, globalised capitalism."[44] More
than merely limning the relationship between politics and feeling, however,
these theorists have sought to reassess what *counts* as political feeling in the
context of a contemporary moment in which faith in the potentially transformative agency of activism and critique has dropped rapidly away. While
powerful emotions like "anger," "fear" and "pride" have long carried political weight, scholarship in feeling theory—from Ngai's work on anxiety,
irritation and envy, to Heather Love's work on shame and depression and
FeelTank Chicago's work on political depression—calls on a number of less
illustrious feelings to play their part in a newly expanded political field.[45]

Yet what differentiates "feeling theory" from other fields of scholarly
endeavor is at least as much a difference of methodology as it is of object
or argument. Theories of feeling participate in a move away from a practice
of ideology critique long locked into the task of exposing hidden (political,
racial, sexual, class or gender) violence. Emphasizing instead what Clare
Hemmings calls "the unexpected, the singular or the quirky over the generally applicable," and what Nigel Thrift dubs "the little, the messy and
the jerry rigged," they propose a richer descriptive and phenomenological
account of our experience of texts and world.[46] This insistence that the
text be read not as a "symptom to be denounced, but as a problem to be
explained, described and understood" has been schematized in a number of
new theories of reading, from Rita Felski's account of the "new phenomenology," to Francois Dosse's efforts to stake out "a third way between the
prevalence of pure lived experience and the priority of conceptualization,"
to Eve Kosofsky Sedgwick's blueprint for "reparative reading," an approach
to interpretation motivated not by paranoia but by pleasure and interest.[47]
These methodological tendencies in feeling theory are clearly reflected in
*The Emotional Life of Postmodern Film.* In mobilizing film texts to make
an argument about the significance of emotion in postmodern discourse,

*Introduction* 11

I rely heavily on the capacity of the filmic building blocks of editing, camera movement, lighting, *mise-en-scene* and colour to supply resources for resisting some of the more familiar truisms about postmodern aesthetics. This reliance on the gloss and grain of textual experience is redoubled where the emotions my arguments bring into play remain under-theorized, and thus demand a kind of phenomenological "fleshing out." In its commitment to close reading, this book carries the implication that it may be precisely ideology critique's tendency to flatten the reading of texts into paraphrase and précis that has obscured the unique contours of postmodern emotion.

Yet while this book is indebted to many of the concepts and themes developed within feeling theory, perhaps the scholar to whom it owes most is Rei Terada, whose bold *Feeling in Theory* offers a paradigm not just for thinking about feeling in contemporary culture, but for thinking about feeling in dialectical tension with a model of contemporary critical and aesthetic practice that seems to militate against it. Where *The Emotional Life of Postmodern Film* addresses the relation between emotion and postmodern theory, Terada focuses on the analogous relation between emotion and poststructuralist theory, a field of analysis that is not only one of postmodernism's clearest symptoms, but that, like postmodernism, has been "widely criticized because its emphasis on the death of the subject seems to preclude dealing with emotion."[48] Terada's gambit, however, is that "poststructuralism's destroying the illusion of subjectivity does not destroy emotion."[49] On the contrary, she argues, "emotion is the sign of the absence of that illusion."[50] Elaborating this argument across a series of close analyses of texts by Paul de Man, Jacques Derrida and Gilles Deleuze, she demonstrates that poststructuralist theory can be shown to offer a consistent theory of emotion as a nonsubjective (but still interpretative and psychological) phenomenon, characterized by a process of self-difference between a sense of origin and the work of rhetorical projection. Crucially, Terada's effort to think two ostensibly opposed terms in conjunction—like, I hope, my own—can be distinguished from other projects whose efforts to yoke "emotion" to "postmodernism" fail to fully transform either term. Kimberly Chabot Davis's *Postmodern Texts and Emotional Audiences*, for example, argues that

> Poststructuralist theory discredited depth models as illusions and replaced the belief in inner depth and essences with a fragmentation of the subject and a play of surfaces. Jameson wrongly concludes, however, that a postmodernist fragmented subjectivity precludes the expression of real emotion ... Jameson simply ignores that affective depth-models—sentimentality and melodrama—can still be found in postmodern culture.[51]

Instead of interrogating the rigidly subjective and hermeneutic model of emotion that underwrites the claim that postmodernism's "fragmentation of the subject and a play of surfaces" is incompatible with emotion, Davis

## 12  *Introduction*

merely argues that contemporary culture is *unevenly* postmodern, and that while some texts have fallen victim to postmodern "fragmentation," others remain readable through "affective depth-models."[52] I do not dispute her claim that traditional aesthetic and emotional formations persist in some postmodern texts. I do, however, contend that this claim fails to take up fully the challenge postmodernism poses to our thinking about emotion. This is the challenge of establishing a necessary rather than merely contingent relation between emotion and postmodernism; of tracing the visible and manifest emotional contours of postmodern aesthetic strategies, rather than straining to read, between the lines, the emotional residue of vestigial modernist forms.

Relying heavily on the term "feeling," this foregoing account of feeling theory's key critical co-ordinates has cast the field in a relatively neutral register. Yet as I have already suggested, reference to the fuzzy, encompassing concept of "feeling" belies the deep terminological division that sees many critics in feeling theory pit "affect" on the one hand against "emotion" on the other. For most scholars associated with feeling theory, that is, the critical project detailed above takes place almost exclusively under the sign of "affect," a term widely promoted as the progressive, liberatory counterpart to a stodgy, conservative and prosaically subjective "emotion." This book is a bid to problematize the terms of this opposition. But what exactly are these terms? What, in other words, is the terminological orthodoxy I am seeking to trouble? While I have already suggested that the models of "affect" and "emotion" dominant in feeling theory today accord the two terms diametrically opposite relations to subjectivity, meaning, and narrative, it is now time to clarify the logic of this distinction—and of this book's relation to it—in greater detail. As we have seen, the model of emotion that holds sway in feeling theory is largely borrowed from the body of scholarship on emotion that I have been calling "cognitive-appraisal theory." While its basic conceptual co-ordinates date back as far as the classical stoics, the "cognitive-appraisal" model of emotion only came to prominence in its current form in the early 1960s, in the wake of experiment-based research by Stanley Schachter, who found that it is conscious judgments or "appraisals," not phsiological changes, that do the primary work of characterizing and differentiating emotions.[53] But whereas Schacter assumes a baseline level of arousal that is only retroactively coloured by interpretation, later work was to dial up the role of appraisal or judgment in order to grant it a causal rather than merely differentiating function. As Gerald L. Clore and Andrew Ortony were to put it, "Emotions *depend on* the perceived meaning or significance of situations" in the world.[54] And this notion that emotion is an intentional state directed toward an object or situation in the world and regulated by our beliefs, cognitions, and desires, has since been installed throughout the sciences and social sciences as what Eve Sedgwick calls our "commonsense model of emotion," sounding across work in philosophy by Robert Solomon, Amelie Rorty and Martha Nussbaum and Ronald de

Sousa, in psychology by Richard Lazarus, Andrew Ortony, Gerald L. Clore, and in the social sciences by David R. Heise and Theodor Kemper, to name just a few.[55] Within this consensus, of course, positions vary. While more radical pundits like Nussbaum and Solomon argue that judgment is fully sufficient for emotion, others contend that physiological arousal is also necessary; while some insist that emotion comes complete with a specific propositional judgment about an object, others simply require that emotion have a basic, intentional "aboutness" or "orientation toward" the world; while some allow for the possibility of unconscious judgment, others identify judgment with the conscious and the rational; while some attribute the evaluative judgments underpinning emotion to an autonomous, unified, monadic subject, others emphasize the role of social norms in shaping emotions' evaluative content. Yet despite these themes and variations, the same basic physiological, intentional and cognitive features recur again and again across the corpus.

What seems most significant for our purposes, however, is that the particular instantiation of the cognitive-appraisal model adopted—and impugned—by feeling theory falls at the stronger rather than weaker end of the spectrum, projecting a fundamentally subjective and intentional entity that rests on conscious individual judgment and precipitates unproblematized ethical action. Is feeling theory's model of "emotion" geared primarily toward affording "affect" a critical foil? However we choose to answer this, it is perhaps unsurprising that while "emotion" understood in these rigidly cognitive terms does make the occasional cameo in feeling theory, for most scholars identified with the field, it is "affect" that is given the starring role. Clearly differentiated from "emotion" along the lines of its distinctive relation to subjectivity, meaning, and narrative, "affect" now names a distinct and legible phenomenon. According to Massumi, for example, whose pioneering 1996 essay "The Autonomy of Affect" laid the foundations for much recent thinking on the subject, whereas emotion is subjective and interpretative—"a subjective content, the socio-linguistic fixing of the quality of an experience which is from that point onward defined as personal"—affect is a prepersonal, asignifying "intensity," or, as he puts it, "irreducibly bodily and autonomic."[56] Drawing both on Deleuze's model of affect as the passage from one bodily state to another and Tomkins' model of affect's autonomy from the drives, Massumi sets an autonomous, organic and pre-personal "affect" up against a subjective and interpretative "emotion" understood to be fully embedded in and wedded to social and cultural regimes of meaning.[57] More recent critical work on feeling by scholars across the critical humanities have echoed and extended this gesture, with Eric Shouse, for example, insisting that "affect is a non-conscious experience of intensity; it is a moment of unformed and unstructured potential."[58] To say that affect operates at an autonomic and organic level is not, of course, to say that it is not *responsive* to both cognitive judgment and to the social and cultural environment in which cognition is embedded, nor

14    *Introduction*

that it doesn't *feed into* cognitive judgment. Rather, it is to say that the plane on which these affective responses take place is inaccessible to the conscious mind, meaning that our cognitions can no more directly regulate or condition affect than they can avoid being regulated and conditioned *by* affect.

And it is here that the critical value of "affect" for an enterprise like feeling theory comes into sharp focus. For attending to affect allows scholars to paint a far richer and more textured picture of the ways in which aesthetic, political and social systems operate and are sustained than older accounts that shackle feeling to cognitive judgment or evaluation have ever been able to deliver. Massumi's work is exemplary here in its anatomy of the ways in which many of the political and ideological effects associated with Ronald Reagan's presidency were fomented at an affective level below conscious awareness and control, through his manipulation of affect to "produce ideological effects by nonideological means," and Massumi's arguments have since been expanded in important work by Berlant, William E. Connolly, Deborah Gould, Eric Shouse, Sedgwick and Nigel Thrift.[59] Yet this emphasis on affect's ability to enrich our account of ideological regimes is matched by a similar emphasis on affect's capacity to escape these regimes. For if affect—as a phenomenon that "exceed[s] the context of [its] emergence, as the excess of ongoing process," and that is marked by a "vitality ... sense of aliveness [and] changeability"—can be mobilized to ideological end, its fundamental "autonomy" also holds out the utopian possibility of eluding the clutches of established ideological and social norms.[60] It should come as little surprise, then, that, especially after its institutional enshrinement in Gregg and Seigworth's aegis-defining 2010 collection *The Affect Theory Reader*, affect has been widely touted as the embodied promise of "freedom from social constraint."[61] Its mobility and flexibility, its availability to social and political analysis, and its capacity to evade ideological norms without requiring anchorage in an essentialized subject, make "affect" immediately instrumental to the effort to rethink and transform the relation between feeling and the political that lies at feeling theory's heart.[62] Emotion, meanwhile, is merely something that critics risk "ending up with" if they're not careful to avoid falling into the twin traps of subjectivism and meaning.[63]

This, then, is where my book intervenes. Turning its attention to the spectral, borderline emotions that veneer postmodern aesthetic and theoretical forms, *The Emotional Life of Postmodern Film* shows that "emotion" may prove quite as valuable a resource as "affect" in advancing feeling theory's aims. Indeed, more than demonstrating emotion's expediency to feeling theory's existing social and political agenda, this book suggests that tracking emotion's characterization and instantiation across the postmodern aesthetic and theoretical field can pose a powerful challenge to that agenda, sparking questions about feeling theory's conception of and engagement with affect; about the role of feeling in critical analysis; and about feeling theory's own disciplinary provenance. Re-conceptualizing emotion's form and structure, of course, is hardly a new project for feeling theory, whose efforts to counter older subjective, intentional and cognitive models of feeling have not been entirely engrossed by "affect." Rei Terada's incisive *Feeling in Theory* sets against the "expressive hypothesis" that underwrites most cognitive-appraisal models a nonsubjective model of emotion that casts emotion as a rhetorical effort to resolve epistemic uncertainty into subjectivity stability; Sianne Ngai's *Ugly Feelings* eschews the stronger emotions that anchor cognitive-appraisal models of emotion in favor of a series of critically unprestigious and socially devalued emotions that are conspicuously effete in their relation to intentionality and action; while Kathleen Woodward's *Statistical Panic* examines a series of "new" emotions, from "statistical panic" to "bureaucratic rage" that "register emerging shifts in social and cultural formations."[64] Yet where emotion retains its reputation as affect's crusty, conservative cousin, and postmodernism, in turn, retains its status as feeling's anathema, it is clear that we continue to be guided by cognitive-appraisal theory's emotional script. Nor is it difficult to account for this model's lingering hold over the theoretical imaginary. While the weak and "ugly" emotions that Ngai takes on in *Ugly Feelings* occupy the far end of the emotional spectrum opened up by the cognitive-appraisal paradigm, they don't necessarily challenge the paradigm itself; while successfully combatting cognitive-appraisal's expressive mandates, Terada's work is less interested in pressing up against emotion's intentional, interpretative and psychological limits, a fact indexed in her reliance on fear as her go-to example; and while Woodward's work offers enlightening analyses of a series of "'new' feelings ... associated with changes in the culture," it doesn't actually adjust the lens through which emotion is viewed.[65]

In *The Emotional Life of Postmodern Film*, then, I turn to the ghostly, idiosyncratic bevy of emotions that emerge in the postmodern archive in the hope of opening up feeling theory's models of emotion beyond cognitive-appraisal theory's limited explanatory horizon.[66] In doing so, of course, I do not mean to argue that the cognitive-appraisal paradigm has no descriptive purchase on, say, certain instantiations or modes of anger, grief or fear.[67] Instead, writing in an additive rather than critical register, I mean to enrich and expand our models of emotion to account for the less conventional contours of a series of marginal emotions that Philip Fisher might dismissively call "provincial."[68] Nor do I mean to argue that the strange, vampiric emotions I have chosen to examine thoroughly relinquish all relation to the figures of cognition, subjectivity, physical arousal, hermeneutic depth and immediacy that sustain the cognitive-appraisal paradigm. Instead, I will show how, materializing in the scrim of an often hostile and refractory postmodern field, these emotions let go of just one, two, or three of the numerous structural scaffolds on which cognitive-appraisal models of emotion tend to rest. Where cognitive-appraisal theory has reified judgment or interpretation as the primary ingredient in emotion, postmodern aesthetics delivers emotions that depend on judgment's suspension, failure or triangulation; where cognitive-appraisal theory has reified the subject as

## 16  *Introduction*

source and vessel of emotion, postmodern aesthetics engenders emotions that coalesce around the subject-as-object; where cognitive-appraisal theory has reified the figure of an intentional object, postmodern aesthetics points to the recursive mental and social structures through which emotion can take itself as its object; where cognitive-appraisal theory has reified the trope of emotional expression as an entity "lifted from a depth to a surface," postmodern aesthetics forces us to examine emotions that are felt as the retroactive effect of their own "expressive" signs; and where cognitive-appraisal theory has reified the "action readiness" inherent in strong or intense emotions, postmodern aesthetics reveals the political efficacy of weak, recursive emotions like boredom.[69] But given the mobility and flexibility of these models, can we still be said to be talking about emotion rather than affect? This book's answer is yes, but the question cannot be resolved here once and for all. Indeed, one of the tasks of this book will be to determine how far it is possible to take emotion from its conventional moorings in subjectivity, intentionality, cognition and interpretation without sacrificing the dialectical relation to these terms that differentiates emotion from affect.

## III

But why cinema? This book's turn to film texts in the effort to bring postmodern theory and aesthetics into dialogue with feeling theory finds its most powerful justification in the longstanding cultural affinity between cinema and emotion.[70] Steven Shaviro has memorably described movies as "machines for generating affect," and this striking claim is echoed across the critical board: for Thomas Elsaesser and Malte Hagener, "cinema is inherently linked to the body and the senses"; for Greg M. Smith, "everyone agrees that eliciting emotions is a primary concern for most films"; while for Linda Williams, the pathos of melodrama is "the fundamental mode of popular American moving pictures."[71] Indeed, in the wake of recent work associated with film theory's own "affective turn," the emotional and affective dimension of cinematic experience has acquired a new critical polish, with many film scholars rushing to down the psychoanalytic apparatus developed for an analysis of "identification," "desire" and "lack" in favor of a new set of critical tools more suited to the analysis of affect and emotion.[72] While often figured as a singular, monolithic development, of course, film theory's own "affective turn" is as multiple and fragmented as the homonymous "turn" taking place more across critical theory and cultural studies. Indeed, the scholarship now appearing under this rubric can be broken down into four quite distinct bodies of work. Perhaps the most prominent of these clusters comprises work by Steven Shaviro, Marco Abel, Giuliana Bruno, Lisa Cartwright and Patricia Pisters, whose debt to a Deleuzean model of "affect" is encrypted in their reliance on the vocabulary of "violence," "force," "pulsion," "energy" and "movement."[73] Yet this affect-oriented approach is not the only, nor even the most influential, among approaches

Introduction   17

to feeling. A coterie of critics emerging out of the shadow of classical, psychoanalytically inspired film apparatus theories, such as Linda Williams, Christine Gledhill and Steve Neale, have turned to the "corporealized spectator" in an attempt to combat the perceived Cartesianism of psychoanalytic film theory's masterful, singular, disembodied "gaze."[74] In a battery of work informed by existential phenomenology, meanwhile, critics like Jennifer Barker, Vivian Sobchack, Laura U. Marks, Greg Singh, and Tarja Laine have sought to reground cinematic spectatorship in a corporealized, embodied conceptualization of vision and consciousness.[75] And, fourth and finally, theorists influenced by "cognitive" work in philosophy and psychology, including Noel Carroll, Torben Grodal, Berys Gaut, Carol R. Plantinga and Greg M. Smith, have begun to analyze the cognitive underpinnings of cinematic emotional formations like sadness, empathy, fear and arousal.[76] While diverse in both their aims and their archives, these distinct bodies of work coalesce around a shared resistance to the theoretical edicts of the "apparatus" theories that dominated the 1970s and 1980s, a period now cast as a kind of theoretical dark age in which a cerebral "semiotics" tyrannized over the corporeal "stuff" of everyday experience.

In many ways, of course, *The Emotional Life of Postmodern Film* is very much a function and effect of this "affective turn" in film studies. Yet the fact that it cannot be readily aligned with any one of the specific theoretical subfields identified above attests to the fact that, more than merely a part of that turn, it also seeks to compensate for some of its limitations. In keeping with more recent work by Eugenie Brinkema, Diedre Reber, and Rachel Greenwald Smith, that is, this book feeds into what Brinkema identifies as "the newest turn in the theoretical humanities," "a meta-turn" that has seen a range of critics, both inside and outside feeling theory, reassess some of that field's foundational verities.[77] In the case of this book, that reassessment is motivated not by a sense that the rich and necessary work associated with film theory's "affective turn" is without value, but a sense that the account of *emotion* that circulates across the field remains severely proscribed. The reasons for this proscription vary, of course. In the case of critics more inclined to a Deleuzian model of "affect," emotion—understood as a feeling underpinned at least minimally by some kind of psychological dimension—is simply not on the table, cast aside in favour of a vision of "forces," "pulsions," "movements" and "violences" in which, as Eugenie Brinkema has noted, bossy calls for attention to feeling in general often seem to take priority over attention to any feeling in particular.[78] Yet the same failure to broach cinematic emotion head-on characterizes other approaches to feeling too. In the case of more phenomenologically oriented film theorists, for example, specific emotional states are routinely overlooked in favor of generalizing statements about emotion, feeling, perception and sensation *per se*. It is not, of course, that phenomenological film critics are *un*-invested in specificity. On the contrary, work in the phemomenological vein is deeply preoccupied by the critics' own felt pressures and stirrings in the particular

18    *Introduction*

cinematic encounter, from Laura U. Marks's descriptions of the forms of "haptic visuality" facilitated by the video art of Leslie Peters and Phyllis Baldino, to Anne Rutherford's paeans to the "energetic charge" given off by the "texture of the segmented exoskeleton of a locust" in a sequence from Terence Malick's *Days of Heaven,* to Jennifer Barker's sensitive account of the "skin to skin contact" between her spectatorial body and the "film body" in Andrei Tarkovsky's *Mirror.*[79] Yet one of the paradoxes of this commitment to the ineffable, unnameable specificity of the sensual experience yielded by this or that filmic moment is that it routinely gives way to an equally extreme generality. For example, in refusing to generalize her "heightened awareness" before the locust through reference to a particular emotion—for "How can you claim an emotional response to the texture of the segmented exoskeleton of a locus?"—Anne Rutherford's account of that experience culminates in the most generalized claim of all, namely that "a sensory-affective encounter." In this odd oscillation between close-up specificity and wide-angle generality, the intermediate term—emotion—is routinely overlooked.[80] And yet emotion remains the key cultural rubric through which particular cinematic encounters are most often codified and, indeed, experienced. Bracketing emotion, of course, has the benefit of enabling phenomenological critics to stand clear of the messy, tangled complexities of questions of language, culture and meaning in which emotional formations are invariably enmeshed, allowing them to veer, instead, between the minutely descriptive and the vaguely speculative.[81] Yet the effect of this bracketing has been to impoverish film-phenomenology's grasp of a cinematic experience that is always both organic and cultural, both bodily and linguistic.

Tarja Laine's recent contribution to the field, *Feeling Cinema,* is an exception to this rule in its willingness to bring a phenomenological approach to bear on distinct, culturally codified emotional formations like shame, horror and love.[82] Yet Laine's work also brings clearly into relief a problem associated with those critics who, unlike the majority of phenomenological film theorists, *do* broach emotion directly. This is that they remain thoroughly in thrall to the "handful of classic emotions" identified with popular feeling-oriented genres, from the "fear" or "disgust" of horror film, to the "pleasure" of porn, to the "sadness" of melodrama.[83] This limited emotional lexicon is immediately apparent in the work of critics affiliated with cognitive theories of film emotion: Noel Carroll's most famous work focuses on the mechanics of fear in the horror genre, Berys Gaut's attends to general questions of empathy and identification, while Carl Plantinga's zeroes in on the solicitation of pity in the weepie.[84] These critics' remarkably circumscribed emotional range is a function of their subscription to cognitive appraisal models of emotion, where the assumption that emotions "have an intentional object," incorporate some kind of "evaluative thought," and "provide a motivating force" for action makes strong, object-oriented emotions like sadness, fear and arousal more conceptually congenial than more diffuse or borderline states.[85] Yet even those critics whose investment in cinematic feeling arises from feminist and

*Introduction* 19

Foucauldian commitments seem reluctant to look beyond this familiar emotional palette, with Neale's psychoanalytic account of melodrama and tears, Williams's Foucauldian analysis of the affective organization of hard core pornography, and Carol Clover's fascinating excursions into the masochistic thrills of the slasher genre no less circumscribed by the overt sensational appeals of standard genre formations. Both groups, of course, deliver a series of rich and valuable accounts of the specific emotional formations they choose to analyse. Yet neither those critics associated with the cognitive school, nor those whose work owes more to Michel Foucault, offer an emotional vocabulary adequate to the full range of cinematic experience—to those experiences of cinema that, while not quite captured by these classic genre formations, neither quite scatter into the ineffable realm of affective "force" or "intensity." While certainly not as cosily familiar as what Carroll calls the "garden-variety emotions, like anger, fear, hatred, sorrow and so on," these experiences are not only recognizable and nameable, but virtually ubiquitous in discussions of postmodern aesthetics.[86] From the "bewilderment" that critics and spectators regularly claim to feel in encounters with some of the more narratively and formally adventurous examples of postmodern cinema, to the "knowingness" that seems to hover in the vicinity of postmodern "pastiche," postmodern cinema is bound up with a series of emotions that are as pervasive in our popular discourses about postmodernism as they are marginalized from critical discourses about cinematic feeling. In seeking to broaden film theory's emotional lexicon, then, *The Emotional Life of Postmodern Film* delivers an individuated account of these idiosyncratic, borderline emotions. Indeed, in rewriting our conception of film emotion and postmodernism, this account may prove equally useful in mapping the emotional geography of a contemporary cinematic landscape that, transformed by recent developments in digital technology, has given rise to analogous anxieties about the "material and technological crisis of the flesh."[87]

Yet I should note here that while the implications of this argument bear most fully on film theory, its influences and inspirations lie with a quite different critical corpus. Critics such as Berlant, Sasha Torres and Amy Villarejo, all working outside the purview of film theory, have sought to elucidate the emotional labour not of overtly emotive genres like pornography, melodrama or horror, but of less manifestly sensational forms, such as the "independent" filmmaking of Gregg Araki, the politically "relevant" feature, and the cinematic scene of coming out respectively.[88] In exploring the muted, displaced or underperformed feelings thrown up by a textual corpus not usually associated with feeling, then, the work of Berlant, Marks, Torres and Villarejo provides a valuable template for this book's effort to trace the emotional profile of a theoretical and aesthetic framework resistant to conventional emotional configurations—to consider how, as Thrift puts it, "we are being made susceptible in new ways."[89]

Of course, while cinema's enduring relationship with emotion supplies one rationale for this book's textual choices, its equally long and vigorous

20    *Introduction*

relationship with the theories and aesthetics of postmodernism supplies another. Identifying cinema as "the predominant instrument for exploring social reality" in postmodernism, Jameson's *Postmodernism, or the Cultural Logic of Late Capitalism* turned film texts like George Lucas's *American Graffiti* (1973) and Roman Polanski's *Chinatown* (1974) into theoretical touchstones for accounts of postmodern pastiche, the loss of history and the nostalgia mode, and his later *Signatures of the Visible* only consolidated cinema's status as an exemplary textual foundation for the analysis of postmodern culture.[90] As Constable has suggested, while an "icon of modernity," cinema is also a "symbol of the postmodern," the hallucinatory gloss of its surfaces providing a crystallizing figure for postmodernism's visually oriented epistemology.[91] Certainly, cinema is neither "postmodernity's" dominant nor its most representative media platform. It is neither ubiquitous in, nor a clear manifestation of, the social, political and economic conditions limned in postmodern theory, and Shaviro's contention, in 2010, that "film gave way to television as a cultural dominant a long time ago, in the mid-twentieth century, and television in turn has given way in recent years to computer-and network based, and digitally generated, 'new media,'" held as much water in the 1990s when the majority of the films this book will examine were released as it does now.[92] Yet perhaps because of its distance from the technological, economic and social changes parsed by postmodern theory, cinema has delivered some of the most concise inscriptions of postmodern form. From Brian de Palma's hysterical pastiches of Hitchcock, to Quentin Tarantino's relentless verbal and visual allusions, to the loss of historicity of *Back to the Future* (Robert Zemeckis, 1985) and the hypnotic depthlessness of *Crash* (David Cronenberg, 1996), cinema yields generous resources for postmodern analysis.

The introduction of postmodern aesthetic theory into the study of postmodern film, however, has had some less than fortunate side-effects. At stake here is not just the almost routine way in which critics characterize postmodern cinema as a dazzling mesh of allusions and references, a cinema of "depthless pastiche," a "layering of cinematic references and in-jokes," nor just the equally routine way in which the postmodern spectator is celebrated for her "encyclopedic film competence," her ability to "draw on a repertoire of codes and references," and her "mastery of the process of decoding/deciphering."[93] Rather, it is that these aesthetic and social claims are more often than not laminated to an emotional claim: that postmodern cinema is "vacant," "empty" and branded by a peculiar dearth of affect.[94] Attributing to postmodern cinema a kind of "hyperconscious intertextuality," Jim Collins, for example, paints postmodern spectatorship in a vocabulary so austere and cerebral that it evokes not people watching a movie but machines processing information: "[the spectator] engages in a process of retrieval, drawing on a reservoir of images that constitutes the past."[95] In portraying postmodern textuality as a "paramount laboratory for semiotic research in textual strategies," meanwhile, influential semiotician and postmodernist Umberto Eco transforms the experience of watching post-modern film into a quasi-scientific practice of deciphering, reading, sorting and decoding.[96] The logic of these gestures becomes all too clear in Cristina Degli-Eposti's definition of the postmodern film as a "text that use strategies of disruption like self-reflexivity, inter-textuality, bricolage, multiplicity and simulation through parody and pastiche"—a definition that, while rightly identifying the key aesthetic strategies of postmodern film, problematically reduces these strategies *en masse* to strategies of disruption, and disruption, in turn, to "an intellectual game ... that implies various levels of spectatorial competence."[97] Geared primarily toward "disrupting" the more positive operation of traditional filmic strategies rather than toward promoting any substantive effects of their own, postmodern film and postmodern spectatorship become a purely critical, cognitive, or, in Constable's sense, "negative" phenomenon.[98] One of the ongoing legacies of this reading, however, is that the question of exactly why spectators would flock to see these films—what kind of basic emotional magnetism these ostensibly dry and cerebral exercises exert—remains entirely up for grabs.

In developing answers to this and other questions, then, this book will argue that postmodern film is rich with a strange, ghostly form of emotion that is not the emotional residue of older aesthetic strategies but a direct adjunct of the postmodern aesthetic strategies that initially seem so hostile to it. From Wes Craven's *Scream* (1996), David Lynch's *Mulholland Drive* (2001) and Harmony Korine's *Gummo* (1997), to David Cronenberg's *Crash* (1996) and Wes Anderson's *Rushmore* (1998), the film texts I will broach are a relatively representative sample from what many critics eagerly identified as the "postmodern" movement in cinema. While hardly the first properly "postmodern" films—as Jameson's theoretical reliance on a cluster of film texts from the 1970s across the body of *Postmodernism* makes only too clear—they nevertheless hail from an era in which the term postmodernism was gaining wide popular and critical currency as what Jesse Fox Mayshark calls a "cultural tide of pop postmodernism ... reached [its] peak."[99] On the one hand, the films' self-reflexive, postmodern occupation of their various generic categories perpetuate unique, displaced versions of traditional cinematic emotions that are all the more powerful for being "postmodern," as my account of the strange, recursive species of fear that circulates through the postmodern neo-slasher archive will attest. On the other, they spawn emotions new to the cinematic repertoire, like bewilderment, boredom, knowingness and fascination, whose ghostliness and negativity affords them a certain rapport with the "disruptive" aesthetic strategies long identified with postmodern film.

Yet in writing of "postmodern emotion," where exactly in the cinematic machinery do I locate these emotions? Are we talking about emotion as represented on screen, as felt by spectators, or as recollected in the critical and journalistic literature? Differing markedly in their account of just *what* we mean when we talk about feeling, the various sub-strands of thinking

## 22 Introduction

about film feeling equally differ in their sense of just *where* cinematic feeling is to be found. Critics of a psychoanalytic bent, like Linda Williams and Carol Clover, tend to zero in on emotion as it is represented, detailing the screams, cries and ecstasies of on-screen bodies; cognitive critics, like Noel Carroll and Berys Gaut, focus on the emotional cues provided by dialogue, action and narrative; while phenomenologically oriented critics tend to reify spectatorial feeling, offering extended inventories of their own corporeal quivers and vibrations against the backdrop of scenes and images from the text itself. More recently, critics such as Laine, Rutherford and Brinkema, however, have argued that the cinematic text itself is structured like a feeling, and thus that the text's formal and material properties should be the primary object for—or at the very least central to—the study of cinematic feeling. For Laine, for example, "All films have an operational, intentional structure of their own that I call the emotional core of the film," a core that is understood as "an affective quality that is immanent to the film and inseparable from the spectator's aesthetic experience," while Brinkema's rousing call for a focus on the "formal dimension of affect" invites us to "treat[] affects as structures that work through formal means, as consisting in their formal dimensions (as line, light, color, rhythm, and so on) of passionate structures."[100] *The Emotional Life of Postmodern Film* shares Laine and Brinkema's intuition—an intuition long enshrined in the conventional critical idiom of "tone" or "mood"—that an emotion inherent in the text itself can be read directly off formal and stylistic strategies like editing, lighting and mise-en-scene. This book, then, shows how each of the emotional formations on its roster crystallize around a formal or visual motif central to the film under discussion: the glossy surface, in the case of fascination; the numb subject, in the case of postmodern fear; the fragmented face of failed suture, in the case of bewilderment; discarded consumer kitsch, in the case of boredom; and the wry smile, in the case of knowingness. Yet *The Emotional Life of Postmodern Film* seeks to balance this attention to the way emotion inscribes itself textually with attention to emotion's diffusion through spectatorial experience and discursive analysis. Drawing on film theory, critical reception, and my own experience, as well as on intense close analysis of the individual films, I seek to create a composite portrait of each emotion by tracking it across a range of venues.

While film remains my primary textual touchstone, and while my account of the postmodern will be articulated primarily through a discussion of film texts, my first chapter, "Euphoria, Ecstasy, Sublimity," provides a broader conceptual context for my argument by grappling directly with three figures who are widely recognized as the key thinkers of postmodernism: Baudrillard, Jameson and Lyotard. Secondary commentators often infer that, in their commitment to interrogating time-honored categories like truth, value and subjectivity, figures like Jean Baudrillard, Fredric Jameson and Jean-Francois Lyotard must be equally committed to a glacial and emotion-free vision of postmodernism. Yet in re-reading Jameson's work on "euphoric intensities,"

*Introduction* 23

Baudrillard's work on "ecstasy" and Lyotard's work on the "sublime" as nuanced and idiosyncratic theories of emotion, this chapter demonstrates not only that emotion is central to postmodern theory, but that the models of emotion enshrined in postmodern theory can both enrich and interrogate feeling theory's own. Jameson's model of postmodernism plays host to a series of recursive "euphoric intensities" that ultimately serve as a kind of proleptic critic of current critical investments in "affect." Baudrillard's panegyrics to "ecstasy," an emotion that structurally approximates the state of "reversibility" he identifies with advanced capitalist societies, demands a reassessment of our understanding of feeling theory's own critical origins. Lyotard's influential analyses of the sublime, meanwhile, develop a picture of the "sublime sentiment" as a kind of meta-emotion that has the capacity to reflect on and critique some of feeling theory's guiding assumptions about emotion.[101] Together, these theorists muster complex, dialectical models of emotion that paradoxically feed off the subjective and hermeneutic instabilities that might seem to foreclose emotion altogether.

In keeping with the dialectical procedure established in this chapter, each of the five subsequent film-based chapters sets a postmodern aesthetic strategy that has been thought to preclude feeling altogether in snug relation to a specific "postmodern" emotion. Taking a cue from the compelling, highly variegated textural world of David Cronenberg's controversial psycho-sexual thriller *Crash*, my second chapter, "Fascination: Between the Rough and the Glossy" limns the not-so-hidden emotional life of the depthless, recumbent postmodern surface. Routinely marshaled to ratify the so-called postmodern "waning of affect," the opposition surface/depth remains the chief optic through which critics have read the hermeneutic and emotional consequences of postmodern aesthetics. Without contesting the proposition that postmodern aesthetics involves a striking decay of hermeneutic depth, however, this chapter points out that, more remarkable than that surface's lack of depth is its rich textural excess. From Baudrillard's glossy simulacra to Jameson's fragments, and from Cronenberg's satiny car bonnets to his grotesque wounds and contusions, postmodern aesthetics and theory is shot through with a textural rubric that complicates our understanding of the relation between surface and depth, between true emotion and false, and between the strangely spectral state of fascination and the "vehement passions" we more readily cluster the rubric of emotion.[102]

Chapter 3, "Fear: Dead Subjects and Living Dolls," considers the operation of fear in Wes Craven's "postmodern" horror classic, *Scream*, a telling example of a conventionally emotion-orientated genre whose ruling emotion is subjected to postmodern reassessment. With its striking convergence of horrific violence and comic affective cues delivering an unusually stark inscription of the then-critically ubiquitous figure of the numb, affectless viewer, *Scream* seemed to bear out the notion, then on high cultural and critical rotate, that postmodern cinema was a harbinger of a general decay of feeling. This chapter, however, resists this conclusion through a revisionist

## 24 *Introduction*

analysis of Sigmund Freud's "The Uncanny," arguing that one of that essay's key intertexts, Ernst Jenstch's "On the Feeling of the Uncanny," offers a kind of proto-postmodern model of fear as an emotion that revolves around the spectacle of emotional bankruptcy—a model of fear at once suppressed and exemplified by Freud's own argument. In describing the ways in which Jentsch's model of fear is borne out in *Scream*'s form, narrative and reception, this chapter argues that the figure of the fearful, feeling subject, whose expiry the film appears to consolidate, is inextricable from the paradigmatically numb, affectless postmodern subject that is its apparent antithesis. Like the fabled slasher himself, continually extinguished and just as continually resurrected, emotion contrives to reappear in displaced form just when it seems to have been killed off altogether.

The fourth chapter, "Bewilderment: The Face of Postmodern Aesthetics and Theory," addresses an emotion that arises, paradoxically, out of the suspension or disruption of the mechanisms of filmic "suture" that are conventionally thought to predicate spectatorial emotional involvement. As I will show, bewilderment's special affinity with postmodern aesthetic and social co-ordinates has afforded the emotion a certain critical cachet across postmodern theory and aesthetics as a kind of privileged signifier of postmodern experience. Yet in *Mulholland Drive* (David Lynch, 2001), as elsewhere, bewilderment's filmic and spectatorial circulation relies on the collapse, inversion or distortion of the on-screen face that has long served as the cornerstone of theories of suture. While celebrated as an eloquent bodily symptom of the "actual" subjective and epistemic conditions of postmodernity, then, bewilderment is also an extreme emotion whose destabilizing effects find their apotheosis in the form of a range of grotesque violences visited upon the face of the bewildered subject. It should come as no surprise, then, that the emotion is all too routinely quarantined to the body of the social and sexual "other," in this case, the *noir*-ish, bewildered lesbian *femme fatale*. Tracking the cultural and theoretical career of bewilderment across both *Mulholland Drive* and a coterie of key postmodern theoretical texts, this chapter will argue that the critical and aesthetic valorization of bewilderment offers a glimpse into some of the more debilitating and sadistic tendencies of postmodern theory and practice.

Chapter 5, "Boredom: Avant-Garde and Trash," addresses another emotion that has acquired a certain critical currency in postmodern aesthetics: boredom. As I will show, while clearly establishing itself in the tradition of the cinematic "avant-garde," *Gummo* favours over the "shock" or "anger" that traditionally animates avant-garde cinema an insistent boredom that saturates the film's form, content and reception. Where boredom remains the morally and politically devalued signature emotion of the consumer culture that the modernist avant-garde has conventionally defined itself against, *Gummo* was, all too predictably, heralded as an avant-garde failure. Observing, however, that postmodern aesthetics has effected a drastic shift in the status of shock, this chapter argues that far from an emotional accessory to consumer culture, boredom has become the emotional economy's affective waste product, its emotional "trash." In this light, it becomes possible to construe *Gummo*'s engagement with boredom not as an index of the film's avant-garde failure but as part of an effort to repurpose the avant-garde for changed aesthetic co-ordinates. Exploring the convergence of emotional and literal trash through a semiotic analysis of the film's junk-filled, over-stuffed frames, I argue that precisely *as* a trivial, vacuous and a-political feeling—as our emotional trash—boredom possesses an unexpected utility in a newly configured avant-garde project.

Whereas earlier chapters argue for the persistence of emotion in postmodernism, the sixth chapter, "Knowingness: Feeling Theory and its Other," argues for the persistence of postmodernism through the emotion of knowingness. As I will show, knowingness's unique union of epistemic instability and cultural hyper-competence has seen it repeatedly yoked to, even identified with, postmodern textual and critical practices. It thus comes as little surprise that the emergence of feeling theory—a critical field unified, at least in part, by its repudiation of "postmodern" methodological and conceptual habits—has been coterminous with the widespread critical condemnation and censure of "knowingness." This chapter contends, however, that the notion that feeling-orientated criticism has relinquished postmodernism's characteristic "knowing" aesthetic and critical posture depends on a rigidly restrictive and narrow model of the emotion. As I will demonstrate, knowingness is less an inherent quality of an isolatable textual or critical strategy, than the effect of social feedback, and as such, remains far more mobile and insidious than the proposal that we might simply "surrender" it allows. This argument is advanced through a close reading of Wes Anderson's *Rushmore*, a film whose critical status as the cinematic avatar of a "New Sincerity" places it in a relation to filmic postmodernism that is roughly analogous to feeling theory's relation to critical postmodernism.[103] Contending that *Rushmore*'s efforts to sever itself from circuits of knowingness merely amplifies its implication in them, I suggest that a similar inevitability attends knowingness's function in much recent feeling-orientated criticism, where that knowingness—and thus the postmodernism it laminates—possesses a continuing if unacknowledged power.

This book takes up residence in the space opened up by Grossberg's contention that postmodern aesthetic, sociological and historical discourses are predicated not on the demise of emotion but "on the perception that something 'feels' different."[104] For Grossberg, then—as for *The Emotional Life of Postmodern Film*—the intellectual and artistic labour that has taken place under the aegis of postmodern theory and aesthetics is animated not by a sense of emotional lack but by a sense of emotional transformation. To say that postmodern aesthetics and theory has an emotional compass of its own, of course, is not to say that that the specter of "the waning of affect" has no sway over the postmodern imaginary; on the contrary, the shadow of emotion's possible or potential demise falls upon every one of the emotions

## 26  Introduction

this book broaches, informing boredom's restless search for distraction and diversion just as it informs bewilderment's collapse of the subjective and facial platforms on which emotion has conventionally rested. Tightly bound up with moments of irony, critical self-reflexivity, allusion and fragmentation, these emotions are shot through with their own absence and structured around their own negation, and thus bear less resemblance to what Greg Singh calls "the feeling of having a feeling" than to what one might dub the feeling of *not* having a feeling.[105] My gambit in *The Emotional Life of Postmodern Film*, however, is not only that these emotions may help strengthen our grasp of feeling theory's practice, origins and terminology, but that their ability to do so derives precisely from their strange gestation in an archive that initially seems "affectively neutral."[106] This book's argument does not bear on feeling theory alone, of course. In bringing postmodernism and feeling theory into dialogue, I seek to revivify not just our thinking about emotion but our thinking about postmodernism. If, from postmodernism, feeling theory can learn to think emotion in more supple and flexible ways, from feeling theory, in turn, our accounts of postmodernism's critical legacy may learn to acknowledge more explicitly and to name more clearly the emotional life that energizes it.

## Notes

1. The phrase "the affective turn" first entered critical circulation with Patricia Clough, *The Affective Turn: Theorizing the Social* (Durham, NC: Duke University Press, 2007), 1. While Glossophilia focuses primarily on the impact of the "affective turn" on the critical humanities, this "turn" is a broadly interdisciplinary phenomenon that penetrates far beyond the text-based disciplines.
2. Ann Pellegrini and Jasbir Puar, "Affect," *Social Text* 27.3 (2009): 36.
3. Fredric Jameson, "Postmodernism, or, the Cultural Logic of Late Capitalism," *New Left Review* 146 (1984): 53–94; Pellegrini and Puar, "Affect," 36. Jameson's article was to yield the bulk of the pilot chapter of Jameson's 1990 book of the same name. (Fredric Jameson, *Postmodernism, or, the Cultural Logic of Late Capitalism* [Durham, NC: Duke University Press, 1990.])
4. Pellegrini and Puar, "Affect," 36.
5. Pellegrini and Puar, "Affect," 36.
6. Kathleen Woodward, "Global Cooling and Academic Warming: Long-Term Shifts in Emotional Weather," *American Literary History* 8.4 (Winter, 1996): 761.
7. Brian Massumi, *Parables for the Virtual: Movement, Affect, Sensation* (Durham, NC: Duke University Press, 2002), 27. According to Massumi, whose work on affect has yielded some of the affective turn's founding texts, critical theory's failure to account for this "surfeit" derives from the fact that its "entire vocabulary has derived from theories of signification that are still wedded to structure even across irreconcilable differences"—theories he identifies with poststructuralism, one of postmodernism's key manifestations. (Massumi, *Parables for the Virtual*, 27.)
8. Eugenie Brinkema, *The Forms of the Affects* (Durham, NC: Duke University Press, 2014), xi. For other examples of this tendency, see Cameron McCarthy

*Introduction* 27

*et al*'s work on race and affect, which argues that far from being "overwhelmingly marked by a certain exhaustion or waning of affect," "contemporary life [is] … marked by a powerful concentration of affect"; Elspeth Probyn's endorsement of "a new nexus of research on affect," which is preceded by an extended critique of a monolithic "theory" she identifies with " 'poststructuralism' or 'post-modernism'"; and Eve Kosofsky Sedgwick and Adam Frank's groundbreaking 1995 essay on Silvan Tomkin's "formidably rich phenomenology of emotions," in which the writers sought to clear the ground for their proposed turn to affect by dismissing many of the "things theory [currently] kn[ew]"—"things" that included classic postmodern gestures like the critique of Western culture's "bipolar, transitive relations of subject to object, self to other, and active to passive." (Cameron McCarthy et al, "Danger in the Safety Zone: Notes on Race, Resentment and the Discourse of Crime, Violence and Suburban Security," *Cultural Studies* 11.2 [1997]: 274; Elspeth Probyn, "Teaching Bodies: Affects in the Classroom," *Body and Society* 10.4 [December 2004]: 23, 25, 24; Sedgwick and Frank, "Shame in the Cybernetic Fold," *Critical Inquiry*, 21.2 (Winter 1995) 497, 496). For examples of theorists of feeling who pit the study of feeling not against postmodernism per se but against the poststructuralist theories and methodologies often associated with it, see Ann Cvetkovich, introduction to Political Emotions, ed. Janet Staiger, Ann Cvetkovich and Ann Reynolds (New York, 2010), 4–7; Heather Love, "Feeling Bad in 1963," in *Political Emotions*, ed. Janet Staiger, Ann Cvetkovich and Ann Reynolds (New York, 2010), 112–133; Simon O'Sullivan, "The Aesthetics of Affect: Thinking Art Beyond Representation," *Angelaki* 6.3 (2001): 26.

9. The claim that postmodernism has been stripped of its critical prestige is best borne out by its absence from two important recent reference volumes for American cultural and literary studies, neither of which gave "postmodernism" an entry: Bruce Barrett and Glenn Hendler's *Keywords for American Cultural Studies* (New York: New York University Press, 2007) and Greil Marcus and Werner Sollers' *A New Literary History of America* (Cambridge, MA: Harvard University Press, 2012). The claim finds further corroboration in the more recent work of some of postmodernism's own most vocal early champions. While the nominalism of Brian McHale's account of postmodernism would seem to preclude anything as positivist as an announcement of its end, his recent retrospective consideration of his own work, entitled, significantly enough, "What Was Postmodernism?" offers just that. Pointing to the events of 9/11 as the mark of a significant historical break with postmodernism, McHale speculates that "Maybe on 9/11 history finally caught up with our postmodern imagination of disaster, and we are now living in the aftermath of postmodernism." (Brian McHale, "What Was Postmodernism?" *Electronic Book Review*, December 20, 2007, accessed September 3, 2011, www.electronicbookreview.com/thread/fictionspresent/tense.) Even Linda Hutcheon, whose work throughout the eighties and nineties amounted to a lovingly exhaustive profile of the postmodern, and whose *The Politics of Postmodernism* provided a template for a wealth of thinking on the subject, declares, in a new introduction to that book, that "the postmodern moment has passed, even if its discursive strategies and its ideological critique continue to live on." (Linda Hutcheon, *The Politics of Postmodernism* [New York: Routledge, 2002], xi.) While it's not quite clear what postmodernism consists in if not "discursive

28  *Introduction*

strategies and ideological critique," Hutcheon's statement constitutes a fairly unambiguous assertion of postmodernism's demise. Similarly, Steven Connor, whose 1989 work *Postmodernist Culture* offered a wide-ranging series of accounts of the changes inaugurated by the advent of postmodernism in literature, popular culture, architecture and art, suggests in his 2004 introduction to the *Cambridge Companion to Postmodernism* that we occupy the "dissipation" period of postmodernism, the terminal stage of the epoch's rise and fall. (Steven Connor, *Postmodernist Culture: An Introduction to Theories of the Contemporary* [Oxford: Blackwell, 1989]; Steven Connor, introduction to *Cambridge Companion to Postmodernism*, ed. Steven Connor [Cambridge: Cambridge University Press, 2004], 1.) The sense that something "else" has emerged to displace postmodernism is thus endemic, not only among those committed to forms of thinking seemingly incompatible with postmodernism, but among postmodernism's former advocates.

10. Fredric Jameson and Masao Miyoshi, *The Cultures of Globalization* (Durham, NC: Duke University Press, 1998); Gilles Lipovetsky, *Hypermodern Times* (Cambridge: Polity Press, 2005), 11; Timotheus Vermeulen and Robin van den Akker, "Metamodernism," *Journal of Aesthetics and Culture* 2 (2010), 6. With specific regard to the recent rise of a newly expansive "modernity" as a loose synonym for the "present," and of a new modernist studies, Jason Gladstone and Daniel Worden note, "the category of modernism has become quite elastic in recent scholarship. Modernist critics have ... Pushed modernism ... forward into the late twentieth century." (Jason Gladstone and Daniel Worden, "Introduction: Postmodernism, Then," *Twentieth Century Literature* 57.3–4 [2011]: 294). Some examples of recent work that embodies this tendency—that is, that casts the post-1945 moment as a continuation or even realization of modernism, rather than a break with it—include Amy Hungerford's essay "On the Period Formerly Known as Contemporary," *American Literary History* 20.1–2 (2008): 410–419; Mark McGurl, *The Program Era: Postwar Fiction and the Rise of Creative Writing* (Cambridge, MA: Harvard University Press, 2009); and Walter Benn Michaels' *The Shape of the Signifier* (Princeton, NJ: Princeton University Press, 2004).

11. Steven Shaviro offers a nice summation of this popular argument: The argument goes something like this: "Thanks to the new electronic technologies, the world has become a single global marketplace. Universal commodity fetishism has colonized lived experience. The real has been murdered by its representations. Every object has been absorbed into its own image. There is no longer (if there ever was) any such thing as a single, stable self. Subjectivity has broken into multiple fragments, and the high modernist endeavor to totalize these fragments, to redeem them, to bring them back together again, is a futile and meaningless exercise. The death of emotion is concomitant with all these other losses." (Steven Shaviro, "The Life, After Death of Postmodern Emotion," *Criticism* [Winter 2004]: 5.).

12. Jean Baudrillard, *The Ecstasy of Communication* (New York: Autonomedia, 1988), 26; David Harvey, *The Condition of Postmodernity: An Inquiry Into The Origins of Cultural Change* (Oxford: Blackwell, 1990), 351; Fredric Jameson, *Postmodernism, or, The Cultural Logic of Late Capitalism* (London: Verso, 1990), 8.

13. Catherine Constable, "Postmodernism and Film," in *The Cambridge Companion to Postmodernism*, ed. Steven Connor (Cambridge: Cambridge University Press, 2004), 54. Still the dominant scholarly framework for understanding

Introduction 29

emotion (as opposed to affect), cognitive-appraisal theory represents emotion as a subjective intentional state directed toward an object and regulated by our beliefs, cognitions, and desires. Martha Nussbaum, a leading exponent of the theory, is exemplary in her emphasis on the specifically propositional component of emotion, arguing that "emotions involve judgments about the salience for our well-being of ... external objects, judgments in which the mind of the judge is projected unstably outwards into a world of objects." (Martha Nussbaum, *Upheavals of Thought: The Intelligence of Emotions* [Cambridge, 2003], 2.) I offer a more detailed account of cognitive-appraisal theories of emotion later in the introduction.

14. Lauren Berlant, *Cruel Optimism* (Durham, NC: Duke University Press, 2011); Brian Massumi, "The Autonomy of Affect," *Cultural Critique* 31 (Fall 1995); Eve Kosofsky Sedgwick, *Touching Feeling: Affect, Pedagogy, Performativity* (Durham, NC: Duke University Press, 2003); Nigel J. Thrift, *Non-Representational Theory: Space, Politics, Affect* (New York: Routledge, 2008).

15. Claire Hemmings, "Invoking Affect: Cultural Theory and the Ontological Turn," *Cultural Studies* 19.5 (September 2005): 550; Sianne Ngai, *Ugly Feelings* (Cambridge, MA: Harvard University Press, 2005); Rei Terada, *Feeling in Theory: Emotion After the "Death of the Subject"* (Cambridge, MA: Harvard University Press, 2002).

16. Critiques of cognitive-appraisal theory have focussed on two key perceived weaknesses. First, that cognitive-appraisal models of feeling elide the physiological dimension of affect and thus fail to "locate in the body some important part of the difference among different emotions." (Sedgwick, *Touching Feeling*, 113.) Second, that it fails to "think the relation between the psychic and the social." (Cvetkovich, introduction to *Political Emotions*, 5.).

17. Massumi, *Parables for the Virtual*, 35, 35, 17.

18. Shaviro, *Post-Cinematic Affect*, 3.

19. Sedgwick and Frank, "Shame in the Cybernetic Fold: Reading Silvan Tomkins," 18. Patricia Clough provides another example of this tendency to dismiss emotion in the process of reifying affect, observing regretfully that "many of the critics and theorists who turned to affect often focused on the circuit from affect to emotion, ending up with subjectively felt states of emotion—a return to the subject as the subject of emotion." (Patricia T. Clough, "The Affective Turn: Political Economy, Biomedia, and Bodies," in *The Affect Theory Reader*, ed. Melissa Gregg and Gregory Seigworth [Durham, NC: Duke University Press, 2010], Kindle Edition.).

20. Ann Cvetkovich, introduction to *Political Emotions*, ed. Janet Staiger, Ann Cvetkovich and Ann Reynolds (New York: Routledge, 2010), 6.

21. Terada, *Feeling in Theory*, 13.

22. Phillip Fisher, *The Vehement Passions* (Princeton, NJ: Princeton University Press, 2001), 26. While I quote Fisher's phrase "the vehement passions" because it so evocatively conjures the particular brand of feeling that cognitive-appraisal arguments lean on, namely strongly subject-based and object-directed emotions, the reliance on a circumscribed coterie of negative emotions (especially fear, anger, grief and disgust) to provide the blueprint for the whole spectrum of emotional experience is standard across the field.

23. Douglas Mao and Rebecca Walkowitz, "The New Modernist Studies," *PMLA* 123.3 (May, 2008): 738, 737.

## 30 Introduction

24. Fisher, *The Vehement Passions*, 26; Ngai, *Ugly Feelings*, cover blurb.
25. Ngai, *Ugly Feelings*, 10.
26. Terada, *Feeling in Theory*, 4; Sally Markowitz, "Guilty Pleasures: Aesthetic Meta-Response and Fiction," *Journal of Aesthetics and Art Criticism* 50 (1992), 307. See also Susan Feagin, "The Pleasures of Tragedy," *American Philosophical Quarterly* 20 (1983): 95–104.
27. Nico Frijda, *The Emotions* (Cambridge: Cambridge University Press, 1984), 249; Ngai, *Ugly Feelings*, 91. Frija's argument that "emotional experience, in its most prototypical form, is a complex of the three kinds of awareness: situational meaning structure, arousal, and action readiness" is representative of work across the entire cognitive-appraisal spectrum in its sense that a base level of emotional "arousal" is a condition of emotion (Frijda, *The Emotions*, 249). And while in many ways Ngai's brilliant *Ugly Feelings* seeks to test the limits of this model, her suggestion that "The affective state of being 'animated' seems to imply the most basic or minimal of all affective conditions: that of being, in one way or another, 'moved,'" suggests her subscription to one, at least, of its presuppositions (Ngai, *Ugly Feelings*, 91).
28. Fisher, *The Vehement Passions*, 115.
29. Terada, *Feeling in Theory*, 4.
30. Fisher, *The Vehement Passions*, 44; Mick Power and Tim Dalgleish, "Cognitive Theories of Emotion," in *Cognition and Emotion: From Order to Disorder* (Hove: Psychology Press, 2008), 85.
31. Terada, *Feeling in Theory*, 5.
32. Daniel M. Gross, *The Secret History of Emotion: From Aristotle's Rhetoric to Modern Brain Science* (Chicago: University of Chicago Press, 2006), 3.
33. Massumi, *Parables for the Virtual*, 220–1.
34. Linda Hutcheon, *The Politics of Postmodernism* (New York: Routledge, 1989), 15; Peter Sloterdijk, *Critique of Cynical Reason* (Minneapolis: University of Minnesota Press, 1987); Brian McHale, *Postmodernist Fiction* (New York: Routledge, 1987); Jameson, *Postmodernism*, 7–54; Jean-Francois Lyotard, *The Postmodern Condition: A Report on Knowledge* (Minneapolis: University of Minnesota Press, 1984); Jean Baudrillard, *Jean Baudrillard: Selected Writings*, ed. Mark Poster (Stanford: Stanford University Press, 1988); George P. Landow, *Hyper/Text/Theory* (Baltimore: Johns Hopkins University Press, 1994); Allucquere Rosanne Stone, *The War of Desire and Technology at the Close of the Mechanical Age* (Cambridge, MA: MIT Press, 1995).
35. Jameson, *Postmodernism*, 3; Harvey, *The Condition of Postmodernity*, 147; Jean-Francois Lyotard, *The Inhuman: Reflections on Time* (Stanford, CA: Stanford University Press, 1991); Jean Baudrillard, *For a Critique of the Political Economy of the Sign* (St Louis, MO: Telos Press, 1981).
36. John Frow, *Time and Commodity Culture: Essays in Cultural Theory and Post-modernity* (Oxford: Oxford University Press, 1998), 15. Dana Polan makes a similar claim, contending that postmodernism is simply a "machine for generating discourse." (Dana Polan, Postmodernism and Cultural Analysis Today," in E. Ann Kaplan [ed], *Postmodernism and Its Discontents: Theories, Practices* [London: Verso, 1988], 57.)
37. The term "ecstasy," for example, recurs continually throughout Baudrillard's discussions of the simulacrum, yet its specifically affective charge—as opposed to its function as an empty conceptual designator—has been largely suppressed

*Introduction* 31

or overlooked in discussions of his work. In Jameson's work, the feeling of "euphoria" is persistently used as an example of what he calls postmodern "intensities," which, while often identified with floating, de-subjectivised affects, might more properly be understood as emotions. In Lyotard's work, conversely, while the affective weight of his theorization of the feeling of the "sublime" been fully credited, its lamination to a model of the postmodern "inhuman" has been overlooked. My first chapter will discuss these examples in detail.

38. Hilary Chute, "The Popularity of Postmodernism," *Twentieth Century Literature* 57, 3–4 (2011): 356.

39. Brian Massumi, "The Autonomy of Affect," *Cultural Critique* 31 (Fall 1995): 83–109; Eve Kosofsky Sedgwick and Adam Frank, "Shame in the Cybernetic Fold: Reading Silvan Tomkins," in *Shame and its Sisters: A Silvan Tomkins Reader*, ed. Eve Kosofsky Sedgwick, Adam Frank and Irving E. Alexander (Durham, NC: Duke University Press, 1995), 1–28.

40. Silvan S. Tomkins, *Affect, Imagery, Consciousness, Volume 1: The Positive Affects* (New York: Springer Publishing Company, 2008); Aristotle, *Nicomachean Ethics* (Chicago, IL: University of Chicago Press, 2011); Henri Bergson, *Laughter: An Essay on the Meaning of the Comic*, trans. Cloudesely Brereton and Fred Rothwell (Rockville, ML: Arc Manor, 2008); Gilles Deleuze and Felix Guattari, *A Thousand Plateaus: Capitalism and Schizophrenia* (London: Continuum, 2004); Benedict de Spinoza, *Ethics*, trans. Edwin Curley (London: Penguin Books, 1996); Damasio, *Descartes' Error*. As Hardt puts it, the "challenge of the perspective of the affects resides primarily in the syntheses it requires. This is, in the first place, because affects refer equally to the body and the mind; and, in the second, because they involve both reason and the passions ... [Affects] illuminate, in other words, both our power to affect the world around us and our power to be affected by it, along with the relationship between these two powers." (Hardt, foreword to Patricia Clough, ed., *The Affective Turn: Theorizing the Social*, [Durham, NC: Duke University Press, 2007], xi.)

41. Melissa Gregg and Gregory J. Seigworth, *The Affect Theory Reader* (Durham, NC: Duke University Press, 2010), 1.

42. Ruth Leys, "The Turn to Affect: A Critique," *Critical Inquiry* 37.3 (Spring 2011): 436.

43. As Heather Love puts it, "The tension or even contradiction between emotion and politics has energized a new body of scholarship." (Heather Love, "Feeling Bad in 1963," in *Political Emotions*, ed. Janet Staiger, Ann Cvetkovich and Ann Reynolds [New York: Routledge, 2010], 112.).

44. Jonathan Flatley, *Affective Mapping: Melancholia and the Politics of Modernism* (Cambridge, MA: Harvard University Press, 2008), 2; Sara Ahmed, *The Cultural Politics of Emotion* (London: Routledge, 2004), 10–11; Lauren Berlant, *The Queen of America Goes to Washington City: Essays on Sex and Citizenship* (Durham, NC: Duke University Press, 1997); Michael Hardt and Antonio Negri, *Reflections on Empire* (Cambridge: Polity Press, 2008), 62. See also Hardt's work on love, in which he defends the possibility of "a love that unites eros and agape, that brings together the personal and the political" against exclusively private and personal models of love. (Michael Hardt, "About Love," [paper presented at European Graduate School, Pennine Alps, Switzerland, 2007], accessed October 20, 2011, http://www.youtube.com/watch?v=ndnkjnMxxLc&feature=relmfu.)

## 32  Introduction

45. Ngai's work addresses "ugly feelings" like anxiety and envy, feelings characterized by "obstructed agency," in order to argue that their overt symptomatization of art's powerlessness paradoxically affords them a certain critical reach; Heather Love suggests that the "backward" affects of shame and depression that underpin queer marginalization should become available for political identification, alongside the positive affects of pride and solidarity that propel queer entitlement; while FeelTank Chicago calls on "political depression," as well as "detachment, numbness, vagueness, confusion, bravado, exhaustion, apathy, discontent, coolness, hopelessness and ambivalence." (Ngai, *Ugly Feelings*, 32; Love, *Feeling Backwards*, 1–5; Lauren Berlant, Vanalyne Greene, Debbie Gould, Mary Patten and Rebecca Zorach, "What is FeelTank?" *Feel Tank Chicago*, last updated, May 9, 2011, accessed October 5, 2011, http://feeltankchicago.net/.)
46. Clare Hemmings, "Invoking Affect," *Cultural Studies* 19.5 (2005): 548; Thrift, *Non-Representational Theory*, 197. In accounting for those elements shaping individual and political life that are neither subsumed by, nor resistant to, a repressive norm, Cvetkovich thus advises "going slowly, noticing the details of the moment or the object without demanding that it instantly give rise to a reading or a political efficacy, or without having to choose between art and politics." (Cvetkovich, introduction to *Political Emotions*, 11.)
47. Love, "Feeling Bad in 1963," 113; Rita Felski, *The Uses of Literature* (Boston: Blackwell, 2008); François Dosse, *Empire of Meaning: The Humanization of the Social Sciences,* trans. Hassan Melehy (Minneapolis: University of Minnesota Press, 1999), xvii; Eve Kosofsky Sedgwick, *Touching Feeling: Affect, Pedagogy, Performativity* (Durham, NC: Duke University Press, 2003), 123–52. Feeling theory's turn away from critique reflects analogous methodological shifts across the critical humanities, exemplified by Sharon Marcus and Stephen Best's notion of "surface reading"; Franco Moretti's call for a "distant reading" practice that would revolve around units both far larger and far smaller than the individual work; and Bruno Latour's suggestion that the demise of "critique" demands we turn our attention to "matters of concern." (Stephen Best and Sharon Marcus, "Surface Reading: An Introduction," *Representations* 108.1 [2009]: 1–21; Franco Moretti, *Graphs, Maps, Trees: Abstract Models for Literary History* [New York: Verso, 2007]; Bruno Latour, "Why Critique Has Run out of Steam: From Matters of Fact to Matters of Concern," *Critical Inquiry* 30 [Winter, 2004]: 225–48.)
48. Charles Altieri, "Constructing Emotion in Deconstruction," *Contemporary Literature* 43.3 (Autumn 2002): 606.
49. Terada, *Feeling in Theory*, 157.
50. Ibid.
51. Kimberly Chabot Davis, *Postmodern Texts and Emotional Audiences: Identity and the Politics of Feeling* (West Lafayette, IN: Purdue University Press, 2007), 21.
52. In arguing this, Davis's work can be aligned with the work of a number of critics, such as Susan Best and Michael L. Schwalbe, who attack the allegation that there is no feeling in postmodern aesthetics but who fail to interrogate the logic on which this allegation most often rests. (Susan Best, *Visualizing Feeling: Affect and the Feminine Avant-Garde* [London: I. B. Tauris and Co., 2011]; Michael L. Schwalbe, "Goffman Against Postmodernism: Emotion and the Reality of the Self," *Symbolic Interaction* 16.4 [Winter, 1993]: 333–350.).

Introduction 33

53. Stanley Schachter, "The Interaction of Cognitive and Physiological Determinants of Emotional State," in *Advances in Experimental Social Psychology*, ed. L. Berkowitz (New York: Academic Press, 1964), 49–79. Cognitive-appraisal models resonate strongly with—where they do not draw heavily on—the work of Aristotle, who figures emotion as an important component of the engaged political life. (Aristotle, *Nicomachean Ethics* [Chicago: University of Chicago Press, 2011].)

54. Gerald L. Clore and Andrew Ortony, "Cognition in Emotion: Always, Sometimes, or Never?" in *Cognitive Neuroscience of Emotion* (Oxford: Oxford University Press, 2000), 25. My italics.

55. For influential philosophical work in a cognitive-appraisal vein, see Roland de Sousa, *The Rationality of Emotion* (Cambridge, MA: MIT Press, 1990); Martha Nussbaum, *Upheavals of Thought: The Intelligence of Emotions* (Cambridge: Cambridge University Press, 2001); Amelie Rorty, *Explaining Emotions* (Berkeley: University of California Press, 1980). Robert Solomon, *The Passions: Emotions and the Meaning of Life* (New York: Doubleday, 1976); for key work in psychology and cognitive science that works with a similar template see Richard Lazarus and Susan Folkman, *Stress, Appraisal and Coping* (New York: Springer Publishing Company, 1984); Andrew Ortony, Gerald L. Clore and Allan Collins, *The Cognitive Structure of Emotions* (Cambridge: Cambridge University Press, 1988); Richard D Lane and Lynn Nadel, *Cognitive Neuroscience of Emotion* (Oxford: Oxford University Press, 2000); and for sociological approaches that draw on this model see Theodore D. Kemper, *Research Agendas in the Sociology of Emotion*; Jan E. Stets and Jonathan H Turner, *Handbook of the Sociology of Emotions* (New York: Springer, 2007); David R. Heise, *Understanding Events: Affect and the Construction of Social Action* (New York: Cambridge University Press, 1979).

56. Massumi, *Parables for the Virtual*, 28.

57. See also the work of Lawrence Grossberg, who shares Massumi's position on the relation between affect and emotion, arguing that, "unlike emotions, affective states are neither structured narratively nor organized in response to our interpretations of situations." (Lawrence Grossberg, *We Gotta Get Out of This Place: Popular Conservativism and Postmodern Culture* [New York: Routledge, 1992], 8.)

58. Eric Shouse, "Feeling, Emotion, Affect," *M/C Journal* 8 (December 2005), 5.

59. See also Eric Shouse's claim that "the importance of affect rests upon the fact that in many cases the message consciously received may be of less importance to the receiver of that message than his or her nonconscious affective resonances with the source of the message." (Eric Shouse, "Feeling, Emotion, Affect," *M/C Journal* 8 (December 2005); or, alternatively, William Connolly's contention that "culutre involves practices in which the porosity of argument is inhabited by more noise, unstated habit and differentia intensities of affect than adamant rationalists acknowlegde." (William E. Connolly, *Neuropolitics: Thinking, Culture, Speed* (Minneapolis: Minnesota University Press, 2002), pp. 44.

60. Gregg and Seigworth, *The Affect Theory Reader*, 5; Hemmings, "Invoking Affect," For a skeptical overview of the critical tendency to fetishize affect as the embodied promise of "freedom from social constraint," see Claire Hemmings, "Invoking Affect: Cultural Theory and the Ontological Turn," *Cultural Studies* 19.5 (September 2005): 548–567.

34  *Introduction*

61. Hemmings, "Invoking Affect," 550.
62. Gregg and Seigworth, *The Affect Theory Reader*.
63. Patricia Clough, "The Affective Turn: Political Economy, Biomedia, and Bodies," *The Affect Theory Reader*, ed. Melissa and Gregg and Gregory J. Seigworth (Durham, NC: Duke University Press, 2010), 207. The quote runs, in full, "many of the critics and theorists who turned to affect often focused on the circuit from affect to emotion, ending up with subjectively felt states of emotion—a return to the subject as the subject of emotion."
64. Terada, *Feeling in Theory*, 11; Sianne Ngai, *Ugly Feelings*, Woodward, *Statistical Panic*, 7.
65. Woodward, *Statistical Panic*, 7.
66. The readiest answer in assessing the character of some of these feelings, of course, is that they are not emotions at all, but affects—and indeed, a number of critics, Shaviro included, have sought to take on the challenge of thinking feeling in postmodernism by arguing for the significance of affect in postmodernism. Yet where the provocation of postmodern theory and aesthetics for theories of feeling lies in its call to think feeling after the problematization of subject, object, depth, intention and certainty, the introduction of a noninterpretative, desubjectivized, pre-cultural "affect" does not really answer that challenge. Rather than attempting to reconceive the relation between feeling and subjectivity, intentionality, cognition and meaning in order to accommodate emotion in postmodernism, affect theory simply removes subjectivity, intentionality, cognition and meaning from the equation.
67. The problem, that is, is not with the cognitive-appraisal model itself, but with the way it has been universalized under the sign of the assumption that *all emotions must work in the same way all the time*. This assumption has had a deleterious effect on thinking about emotion, not only in spawning redundant definitional squabbles within cognitive-appraisal theory, but in playing into feeling theory's tendency to charicature emotion. This assumption is indexed in Diana Fritz Cates' anxious summary of current disagreements between various cognitive-appraisal theorists: "Do thoughts cause emotions, which are themselves something other than thoughts? Do thoughts cause and partly constitute emotions? Do thoughts alone constitute emotions?" (Diana Fritz Cates, "Conceiving Emotions: Martha Nussbaum's *Upheavals of Thought*," *Journal of Religious Ethics* 31.2 [Summer 2003]: 326.).
68. In championing the study of the strong, vehement states of anger and grief, Fisher condemns psychoanalytic theory's neglect of these states in favor of what he calls "provincial" emotions like avarice and jealousy. (Fisher, *The Vehement Passions*, 26.)
69. Nico H. Frijda, *The Emotions* (Cambridge: Cambridge University Press, 1986), 72.
70. Shaviro, *Post-Cinematic Affect*, 3.
71. Thomas Elsaesser and Malte Hagener, *Film Theory: An Introduction Through the Senses* (New York: Routledge, 2010), 173; Greg M. Smith, *Film Structure and the Emotion System* (Cambridge: Cambridge University Press, 2003), 4; Linda Williams, "Melodrama Revised," in *Refiguring American Film Genres: Theory and History*, ed. Nick Browne (Berkeley: University of California Press, 1998), 42.
72. While film studies' turn to feeling is often represented as a new development, Janet Staiger has argued that the alliance between cinema and feeling runs so

Introduction   35

deep that, in many ways, thinking about feeling has never really been off the film theoretical agenda. For Staiger, in other words, the recent proliferation of work on cinematic feeling merely lays bare an investment in emotion that has shadowed film theory's entire history, a history that has seen "theorists of cinema ... consider emotion within nearly every type of ontological or epistemological proposition." (Janet Staiger, introduction to "Political Emotions and Public Feelings," *Political Emotions*, ed. Janet Staiger, Ann Cvetkovich, Ann Reynolds [New York: Routledge, 2010], 2). By this light, Siegfried Kracauer's work on the reactionary cult of cinematic "distraction" and Walter Benjamin's insistence on the emancipatory power of the cinematic "shock effect," to say nothing of later psychoanalytic theories of cinematic fantasy, desire and identification, can be seen to prefigure modern-day theories of filmic emotion and affect. (Siegfried Kracauer, *The Mass Ornament: Weimar Essays*, trans. Thomas Y. Levine [Cambridge: Harvard University Press, 1995], 328; Walter Benjamin, *Illuminations: Essays and Reflections*, ed. Hannah Arendt [New York: Vintage Digital, 2011], Kindle Edition, "The Work of Art in the Age of Mechanical Reproduction.") Reference to this tradition both belies the persistent refrain that earlier instantiations of film theory had disregarded feeling, and reminds us why cinema might be a valuable resource for extending our grasp of the phenomenon.

73. Affect-oriented work: Marco Abel, *Violent Affect: Literature, Cinema and Critique after Representation* (Lincoln, NE: University of Nebraska Press, 2007); Lisa Cartwright, *Moral Spectatorship: Technologies of Voice and Affect in Postwar Representations of the Child* (Durham, NC: Duke University Press, 2008); Patricia Pisters, *The Matrix of Visual Culture* (Stanford, CA: Stanford University Press, 2003); Steven Shaviro, *The Cinematic Body* (Minneapolis: University of Minnesota Press, 1994); Steven Shaviro, *Post-Cinematic Affect* (Hants: O-Books, 2010.

74. For work that, under the influence of Foucault, seeks to "flesh out" the spectator at the heart of apparatus theory, see Christine Gledhill, introduction to *Home is Where the Heart Is: Studies in Melodrama and the Woman's Film*, ed. Christine Gledhill (London: British Film Institute, 1987); Linda Williams, "Film Bodies: Gender, Genre and Excess," *Film Quarterly* 44.4 (Summer 1992): 3; Williams, *Hard Core: Power, Pleasure and the Frenzy of the Visible* (Berkeley: University of California Press, 1989); and Rick Altman, "Dickens, Griffith and Film Theory Today," *South Atlantic Quarterly* 88 (1989): 321–59.

75. For phenomenological work, see Jennifer Barker, *The Tactile Eye: Touch and the Cinematic Experience* (Berkeley: University of California Press, 2009); Tarja Laine, *Feeling Cinema: Emotional Dynamics in Film Studies* (London: Bloomsbury Academic, 2013); Laura U. Marks, *Touch: Sensuous Theory and Multisensory Media* (Minneapolis: University of Minnesota Press, 2002); Ann Rutherford, *What Makes a Film Tick? Cinematic Affect, Materiality and Mimetic Innervation* (New York: Peter Lang, 2011); Greg Singh, *Feeling Cinema: Affect and Authenticity in Popular Cinema* (London: Routledge, 2014); Vivian Sobchack, *Carnal Thoughts: Embodiment and Moving Image Culture* (Berkeley: University of California Press, 2002).

76. Cognitive work in the field includes Noel Carroll, *The Philosophy of Horror, or, Paradoxes of the Heart* (London: Routledge, 1990); Carol R. Plantinga and Greg M. Smith, *Passionate Views: Film, Cognition and Emotion* (Baltimore:

36  *Introduction*

Johns Hopkins University Press, 1999); and Torben Grodal, *Moving Pictures: A New Theory of Film Genres, Feelings and Cognition* (Oxford: Oxford University Press, 1999).

77. Brinkema, *The Forms of the Affects*, xi; Diedre Reber, "Headless Capitalism: Affect as Free-Market Episteme," *differences: A Journal of Feminist Cultural Studies* 32.1 (2012): 66–100; Rachel Greenwald-Smith, *Affect and American literature in the Age of Neo-Liberalism* (Cambridge: Cambridge University Press, 2015).

78. Brinkema, *The Forms of the Affects*.

79. Marks, *Touch*, 10; Rutherford, *What Makes a Film Tick?* 28–9; Barker, *Tactile Eye*, 12.

80. Beginning, as Sobchack makes clear, with a "particular experience," with the aim of "describ[ing] and explicat[ing] the general or possible structures and meanings that inform the experience and make it potentially resonant and inhabitable for others." (Sobchack, *Carnal Thoughts*, 5.)

81. Singh, *Feeling Film*, 3; Marks, *Touch*, 2; Barker, *The Tactile Eye*, 21.

82. Laine, *Feeling Cinema*.

83. Steve Neale, "Melodrama and Tears," *Screen* 27.6 (1986): 6–23; Williams, *Hard Core*.

84. Carroll, The Philosophy of Horror; Berys Gaut, "Empathy and Identification in Cinema," *Midwest Studies in Philosophy* 34.1 (2010): 136–157.

85. Noel Carroll, 23; Berys Gaut, *A Philosophy of Cinematic Art*, 244–245.

86. Noel Carroll, "Film, Emotion, and Genre," in Philosophy of Film and Motion Pictures, 218.

87. Vivian Sobchack, *Carnal Thoughts: Embodiment and Moving Image Culture* (Berkeley: University of California Press, 2004), 161. Writing of new cinematic technologies, including the displacement of film stock by a dispersed and seemingly disembodied digital technology, Sobchack argues that "the electronic [media] is phenomenologically experienced not as a discrete, intentional, body-centered mediation and projection in space but rather as a simultaneous, dispersed, and insubstantial transmission across a network or web that is constituted spatially more as a materially flimsy latticework of nodal points than as the stable ground of embodied experience" (Sobchack, *Carnal Thoughts*, 154). This move, in turn, has met with a barrage of recuperative criticism insisting that the incipient obsolescence of the material technology on which classic theories of cinema are based has not evacuated our experience of movies of visceral power, and that in "the era of digital cinema, the body and the senses are, if anything, even more central for an understanding of the film experience." (Elsaesser and Hagener, *Film Theory: An Introduction Through the Senses*, 171.) For another example of this argument, see Shaviro, whose *Post-Cinematic Affect* offers a stunning series of analyses of the "structures of feeling" that emerge in a "computer- and network-based, and digitally generated, 'new media.'" (Shaviro, *Post-Cinematic Affect*, 2.)

88. Lauren Berlant, "Structures of Unfeeling: *Mysterious Skin*" (paper presented at Sydney Gay and Lesbian Mardis Gras Queer Thinking at the University of Sydney, Australia, February 19, 2011); Sasha Torres, "Televising Guantanamo: Transmissions of Feeling During the Bush Years," in *Political Emotions*, ed. Janet Staiger, Ann Cvetkovich and Ann Reynolds (New York: Routledge: 2010), 45–65; Amy Villarejo, "The Halting Grammar of Intimacy: Watching *An American Family*'s Final Episode," in *Political Emotions*, ed. Janet Staiger, Ann Cvetkovich and Ann Reynolds, (New York: Routledge: 2010), 193–214.

*Introduction*   37

89. Thrift, *Non-Representational Theory*, viii.
90. Jameson, *Signatures of the Visible*.
91. Constable, "Postmodernism and Film," 43.
92. Steven Shaviro, *Post-Cinematic Affect*, 2.
93. Peter Brooker and Will Brooker, Introduction to Peter Brooker and Will Brooker, eds., *Postmodern After-Images: A Reader in Film, Television and Video*, (London: Arnold, 1997), 6; Jim Collins, "Genericity in the Nineties," in *Film Theory Goes to the Movies*, ed. Collins, H. Radner and A. Preacher Collins (London: Routledge, 1993), 248; Umberto Eco, "*Casablanca*: Cult Movies and Intertextual Collage," *Substance* 14.2, Issue 47 (1985):11; Jonathan Bignell, *Postmodern Media Culture* (Edinburgh: Edinburgh University Press, 2000), 52; Andrew Ross, *No Respect: Intellectuals and Popular Culture* (London: Routledge, 1989), 59.
94. James Wood, *Guardian*, 19 November, 1988; Brooker and Brooker, *Postmodern After-Images*, 95.
95. Collins, "Genericity in the 90s," 250.
96. Eco, "*Casablanca*": 3.
97. Cristina Degli-Esposti, introduction to Cristina Degli-Esposti, ed., *Postmodernism in the Cinema*, (London: Berghahn, 1998), 6, 4. Also exemplary here is the work of Fred Pfeil, "Revolting Yet Conserved: Family Noir in Blue Velvet and Terminator," *Postmodern Culture* 2.3 (May 1992).
98. Constable, "Postmodernism and Film," 54.
99. Jesse Fox Mayshark, *Post-Pop Cinema: The Search for Meaning in New American Films* (Westport, CT: Praeger Publishers, 2007), 1–2.
100. Laine, *Feeling Cinema*, 3.
101. Ibid.
102. Fisher, *Vehement Passions*, 11.
103. The phrase "New Sincerity" has been on high rotate in newspapers, magazines and blogs in recent years, but its origins probably lie in Jim Collins's influential 1993 essay, "Genericity in the 90s: Eclectic Irony and the New Sincerity." (Collins, "Genericity in the 90s," 262.).
104. Lawrence Grossberg, "Postmodernity and Affect: All Dressed Up with no Place to Go," *Communication* 10.3–4 (1988): 277.
105. Singh, *Feeling Film*, 27.
106. Thrift, *Non-Representational Theory*, 228. See also Sara Ahmed's claim that even the apparent absence of emotion in the figure of the "hard" or aloofly resistant body is "not the absence of emotion, but a different emotional orientation." (Sara Ahmed, *The Cultural Politics of Emotion* [London: Routledge, 2004], 4).

# 1 Euphoria, Ecstasy, Sublimity
## The Emotional Life of Postmodern Theory

**I**

If feeling theory's familiar map of our emotional life has taken its bearings from feelings like anger, fear, sadness and love, the emotions that surface in postmodern theory—emotions like ecstasy, euphoria and "the sublime sentiment"—demand a radical redrawing of that map.[1] Through a series of up-close encounters with the work of the three theorists whose hold over our understanding of the postmodern seems most enduring, this chapter seeks to set that cartographic project in motion. Fredric Jameson, Jean Baudrillard and Jean-Francois Lyotard: each of these theorists delivers a compelling critique of the subjective, social and hermeneutic platforms that have conventionally underpinned emotion. Each, in turn, has been cast as the proponent of a frigid and emotionless postmodernism wholly incompatible with the rich, interdisciplinary body of work generated across the past two decades under the auspices of the so-called "affective turn." Yet these theorists can also be shown to traffic in flexible and idiosyncratic models of emotion that, far from irrelevant to feeling theory, may help re-energize the field, shaking up the sediment that has begun to form around feeling theory's existing explanatory paradigms. Jameson's work on postmodernism, for example, across both the 1984 essay "Postmodernism, or the Cultural Logic of Late Capitalism," and the landmark 1989 book of the same name, promotes a model of emotion as a recursive, self-contradictory "intensity"—an emotion that paradoxically takes the expiry of emotion, and the birth of affect, as its object. Baudrillard's recurrent yet little-remarked recourse to the term "ecstasy," meanwhile, elevates emotion to the status of a metaphysical principle, drawing on ecstasy's unusual oscillating structure—as an emotion that slides definitionally between subject and object, inside and outside, animal and mechanical—to approximate the phenomenological climate of an advanced capitalist society in which "reversibility" rather than semiotic fixity is the name of the game. Lyotard's influential anatomy of the sublime, finally, develops a picture of the "sublime sentiment" as a kind of meta-emotion that internalizes and dramatizes feeling theory's stock understanding of the relationship between affect and emotion as its very essence.[2] As this chapter will show, the analysis of these emotions affords us a new critical lens not just on postmodern theory itself but on the affect- and emotion-oriented analytic that so often claims to displace it.

## II

While Jameson did not originate the term "postmodernism," his groundbreaking efforts to yoke the aesthetic and cultural developments earlier identified with the term to a series of historically coeval economic and political developments effectively "redrew the whole map of the postmodern at one stroke."[3] Indeed, it is in large part thanks to the authority and influence of the book *Postmodernism* that the term "postmodernism" came by its status as a conceptual anchor for so much critical thought during the decade after its publication. Yet of all the claims made in that volume, none has enjoyed quite the glittering critical career of Jameson's announcement that postmodernism is marked by "the waning of affect"—a theoretical catch-phrase that, achieving totemic status in the 1990s as a condensation of critical anxieties about what we *were*, remains no less totemic for critics today in its supposed condensation of what are *no longer*.[4] According to Jameson, while ultimately pursuant to shifts in practices of consumption and production that mark "late" or "multinational" capitalism, the "waning of affect" in postmodernism can be most immediately traced to two interlocking cultural shifts.[5] On the one hand, Jameson ascribes the waning of affect to the demise of the hermeneutic models of meaning embodied in the oppositions surface/depth, inside/outside and appearance/reality, a demise that results in a "new kind of flatness or depthlessness, a new kind of superficiality in the most literal sense."[6] Where emotion is typically understood as turning on some kind of hermeneutic interpretation, or what Martha Nussbaum calls "judgments about the salience for our well-being of ... external objects," this "new depthlessness" rebuffs emotion's advances at every point.[7] On the other, Jameson attributes the waning of affect to the demise of the subject, the figure of the centered and unified individual that had been the cornerstone of political and social theory, and that is traditionally thought to be the "source" of emotion. As Jameson puts it, "the liberation, in contemporary society, from the older anomie of the centered subject may also mean ... a liberation from ... feeling as well, since there is no longer a self to do the feeling."[8]

Yet despite the confidence with which critics have cited and circulated the slogan—and despite Jameson's own seemingly straightforward account of its meaning—the significance and implications of "the waning of affect" remain ambiguous. For while "the waning of affect" has an immediate ring of truth if *affect* is treated as a synonym for *emotion*, it echoes rather hollowly if *affect* is read through the terminological lens supplied by current scholarship on feeling. Unlike emotion, still tethered in the critical imagination to notions of subjectivity and hermeneutic interpretation, affect is widely identified across feeling theory as "a-signifying," as "not ownable or recognizable," and as "irreducibly bodily and autonomic."[9] It is thus unclear why affect should *not* find quarter in a postmodern moment whose defining social and cultural attribute is the failure of subjective and hermeneutic depth. On the contrary, this failure seems to furnish a perversely congenial

## 40  *Euphoria, Ecstasy, Sublimity*

set of social and cultural co-ordinates for feelings of a non-subjective and non-interpretative order—an intuition distilled in Brian Massumi's oft-cited insistence that, rather than lacking in affect, "if anything, [postmodernism] is characterized by a surfeit of it."[10] Only compounding this terminological instability, Jameson repeatedly offsets his now-notorious maxim "the waning of affect" with proclamations about the emergence of what—borrowing a term from the work of Jean-Francois Lyotard, who had himself appropriated it from Gilles Deleuze—he calls "intensities."[11] According to Jameson, to announce the demise of affect "is not to say that the cultural products of the postmodern era are entirely devoid of feeling." Rather, it is to suggest "that such feelings—which it may be better and more accurate, following J.F. Lyotard, to call intensities—are now free-floating and impersonal and tend to be dominated by a peculiar kind of euphoria."[12] From this angle, Jameson's work seems to broadcast less the sunset of feeling than the dawn of what he refers to as "a whole new type of emotional ground tone."[13] Unfortunately, however, his effort to assign a form and structure to these incipient "intensities" only further confuses his reader, since the "free-floating and impersonal" phenomena he outlines bear an unmistakable resemblance to the simultaneously trans-personal and pre-personal entities we now call "affects"—the very phenomena that the phrase "the waning of affect" seems already to have consigned to a moribund modernism.[14] On a superficial overview, then, Jameson's position on feeling remains curiously unresolved.

Given these striking terminological ambiguities, it should come as no surprise that the reception of *Postmodernism* among critics identified with feeling theory has been decidedly mixed—although of the two interpretative camps that have formed around the volume, by far the most vocal and influential voices belong to those who dismiss *Postmodernism* as a dated jeremiad against feeling. From Brian Massumi's derisive dig in the watershed *Parables for the Virtual* ("Fredric Jameson notwithstanding, belief has waned for many, but not affect"), to Lauren Berlant's announcement that "we witness, here, then, not 'the waning of affect,' but the waning of genre," to Lawrence Grossberg's insistence that "postmodernity" is not, "as Jameson has claimed, a waning of affect," a contemptuous riff on "the waning of affect" has become something of a critical meme in feeling theory, with each new iteration of the expression marking another step in its evolution from a sound-bite-sized signifier of what postmodernism *was*, to an equally cogent token of what contemporary theories of affect and emotion are *not*.[15] Admittedly, these critics' tendency to treat "the waning of affect" as if its meaning were at once entirely self-evident and entirely exhaustive of Jameson's position on feeling raises numerous methodological red flags. Yet in many respects their scorn seems readily justified. First, there's the logical anomaly remarked above: far from necessitating the expiry of affect, the parallel crises suffered in postmodernism by the subject, on the one hand, and hermeneutic models of meaning, on the other, should logically

*Euphoria, Ecstasy, Sublimity*  41

entail not the demise but the proliferation of an "affect" construed as an impersonal, desubjectivized and noncognitive entity. Reinforcing this logical anomaly, however, is an empirical one. The flourishing of affect in contemporary social and political life—to say nothing of the burgeoning of theories of affect in contemporary scholarly life—leaves the charge that "affect" is "waning" in postmodernity looking decidedly anachronistic. These logical and empirical objections to "the waning of affect," however, are both amplified by Jameson's choice of the term "affect." With some notable exceptions, it is "affect" that most critics working in feeling theory today favour in seeking to unsettle our established conceptions of feeling's relation to individual and collective life.[16] Critically and theoretically problematic, then, Jameson's claim that *affect*, in particular, is on the decline is also terminologically problematic, in jettisoning from the province of the postmodern a term that many critics in feeling theory have enthusiastically hailed as "the way forward." [17]

Yet if Grossberg and Massumi appoint Jameson as an enemy of the work currently taking place under the banner of "affect theory," Ian Buchanan's powerful historicist reconsideration of Jameson's work heralds Jameson as an unusually far-sighted forebear of that work. In *Fredric Jameson: Live Theory*, in fact, Buchanan shows that the critical tendency to identify Jameson's famously waning "affect" with the model of "affect" that dominates the current scholarly literature on feeling rests on a surprisingly simple terminological misunderstanding. As Buchanan shows, Jameson characterizes "affect" as a phenomenon grounded in the subject and directed at an object—a "wordless pain within the [individual] monad" that is at the same time "expressed by projection outward" onto a hermeneutic object.[18] Yet the contours of this model of "affect" map not onto the impersonal, organic, a-signifying model of "affect" valorized by Massumi and Grossberg, but onto conventional cognitive-appraisal models of emotion, which cinch emotion to both a subjective source and an interpretative object. Far from banishing "affect" from postmodernism, then, in Buchanan's reading, it is "emotion" (which Jameson, somewhat idiosyncratically, *refers to* as "affect") that Jameson relegates to a superseded historical moment. Recasting Jameson's postmodernism as anti-emotion rather than anti-affect, Buchanan concludes that "What Jameson means by 'affect' then is the emotion of the individual subject, understood as a self-enclosed ego or monad. It does not survive into postmodernity because its precondition does not."[19] This striking reinterpretation is afforded further weight as the discussion moves from "the waning of affect" to Jameson's other statements about feeling—in particular, his account of the euphoric "intensity." According to Buchanan, whereas Jameson uses "affect" to refer to an older feeling-formation eroded by the failure of subjectivity and hermeneutics, he uses "euphoric intensity," in turn, to refer to the new feeling-formation that emerges in the wake of these twin failures. In Jameson's own words, one of "the constitutive features of the postmodern" is "a whole new type of emotional ground tone—what

## 42 *Euphoria, Ecstasy, Sublimity*

I will call 'intensities,'" which are defined as "free-floating and impersonal and ... dominated by a peculiar kind of euphoria." [20] The crucial point for Buchanan, however, is that these mostly impersonal, euphoric "intensities" closely approximate the a-signifying, non-subjective phenomena that we are now accustomed to calling "affects." In this sense, then, far from hostile to the model of "affect" that prevails in feeling theory today, Jameson's vision of postmodernism includes a prescient early model of affect. Unsurprisingly, the impact of this argument on the critical estimation of Jameson's work has been immense, with more recent scholarship on feeling, by critics such as Steven Shaviro, earmarking Jameson approvingly as one of "affect theory's" unexpected allies.[21]

As should already be clear, then, Jameson's reception in feeling theory is a remarkably bifurcated one. If some critics are condemnatory, casting Jameson as affect theory's theoretical antagonist, others are recuperatory, claiming him as an unwitting progenitor of current theories of affect. Whereas Massumi and Grossberg's critique of Jameson seems limited by its fixation on the slogan-like proclamation "the waning of affect" at the expense of Jameson's claims about intensities, Buchanan's work is welcome both for historicizing our understanding of Jameson's notion of "affect" and for recovering the significance of Jameson's "intensities." In what follows, however, I will argue that while more cogent and considered than that of Massumi and Grossberg, Buchanan's reading falls into a similar trap, in too hastily assimilating Jameson's understanding of intensities to pre-established models of feeling. While he is incisive in his initial observation that in Jameson's vocabulary "affect" is a synonym for a traditional model of emotion, his subsequent equation of Jameson's "intensities" with a Massumian "affect" is the effect of a false choice, in which it is assumed that intensities must be aligned either with an "emotion" burdened with all the weight of outmoded humanist thinking or with an "affect" understood as completely non-interpretative, pre-personal and free-floating. Indeed, while clearly seeking to reclaim *Postmodernism* for feeling theory, Buchanan has inadvertently condemned him to a marginal status within the field by ensuring that he functions less as a dynamic interlocutor than as an affable adherent. In what follows, however, I will use a close, detailed reading of a key passage in *Postmodernism* to show that Jameson's fabled euphoric "intensity" is homologous neither with a Massumian model of affect, nor with the orthodox appraisal paradigms that still monopolize our understanding of emotion. Framing intensities not as a theoretical blueprint for the models of affect currently in critical circulation, but as a unique, idiosyncratic variant of emotion, I will argue that Jameson's account of these intensities yields both a transformed understanding of *emotion* and a kind of proleptic critique of our current critical investments in *affect*. In this light, I will suggest, *Postmodernism* can join the ranks of recent work by Eugenie Brinkema, Claire Hemmings, Ruth Leys and Dierdra Reber in inviting us to reflect, whether from inside or outside feeling theory, on the

Euphoria, Ecstasy, Sublimity 43

theoretical orthodoxies that have begun to crystallize across the so-called "affective turn."[22]

Jameson's most sustained analysis of the workings of "that euphoria or those intensities which seem so often to characterize the newer cultural experience" takes place in the course of a description of the practices of two equally, if very differently, paradigmatic postmodern artists. Doug Bond's work is radically anti-anthropomorphic, characterized by desolate, evacuated spaces (Jameson, for example, speaks of "the empty bathrooms of Doug Bond's work").[23] Duane Hanson's work, meanwhile, takes anthropomorphism to an extreme, in a series of "polyester figures"—most famously his life-size, eerily convincing simulacra of Hawaiian shirt-clad tourists—who appear strikingly out of place in the high-culture cathedral of the gallery spaces in which they are shown.[24] Yet while in many respects the artistic practices of Doug Bond and Duane Hanson could not be more different, taken together, their work brings the hermeneutic crisis that marks postmodern art into striking relief. For Bond's focus on space without figure and Hanson's focus on figures without space suggest two halves of a never-to-be-completed whole.[25] In this, they starkly illustrate Jameson's suggestion that "the representation of space itself has come to be felt as incompatible with the representation of the human body," such that space is "radically anti-anthropomorphic" and the human body, in turn, radically isolated. Whereas classical realist painting's trademark dialectic of figure and ground binds the two terms together, with the subject metonymically representing the space and the space, in turn, expressing the subject, these quintessentially postmodern pieces rest on a radical incommensurability between ground and figure. More than a simple gap between signifier and signified, at stake here is something closer to what Jameson, drawing on Lacan's work on schizophrenia, calls the full-scale "breakdown of the signifying chain."[26] As Jameson puts it, "when the links of the signifying chain snap, then we have schizophrenia in the form of a rubble of distinct and unrelated signifiers," as figure and ground are irretrievably dissociated, unable to be reconciled into a seamless signifying sequence.[27] In their rubbery, synthetic resistance to a hermeneutics of depth, then, "Bathroom," "Museum Guard" and "Tourist II" seem like lightning-rods for the supposedly affect-like "intensities" that Buchanan assiduously tracks through Jameson's work.

Yet as Jameson's glancing description of the works themselves gives way to a fuller delineation of the feelings that coalesce around them, the passage itself at once invokes and rules out the possibility that "affect" is what is at play here. According to Jameson, the disintegration of signifying relations embodied in the work of Bond and Hanson results in an experience of "doubt and hesitation," which in turn sees "the world ... momentarily lose[] its depth and threaten[] to become a glossy skin, a stereoscopic illusion, a rush of filmic images without density."[28] Phrases like "stereoscopic illusion" and a "rush of filmic images without density" are strongly reminiscent of the

## 44 *Euphoria, Ecstasy, Sublimity*

model of affect conjured by Melissa Gregg and Gregory J. Seigworth in their evocation of "visceral forces beneath, alongside, or generally other than conscious knowing, vital forces insisting beyond emotion that can serve to drive us toward movement, toward thought and extension," and their recurrence throughout the passage consequently invites us to imagine a world thrillingly suffused with a-signifying, organic and non-subjective affect.[29] In tying this "rush of filmic images without density" to the hermeneutic crisis incarnated in the work of Hanson and Bond, then, Jameson appears to limn a direct, causal relation between semiotic collapse and the emergence of intensities. In doing so, he seems to validate Buchanan's suggestion that the "intensities" that Jameson appoints as postmodernism's signature feeling formation are analogous to Massumi's "affect."

Yet a finer-grained analysis of the passage at both the syntactic and semantic levels quickly undermines this reading. For far from actually *entailing* a "world … become a glossy skin, a stereoscopic illusion, a rush of filmic images without density," the significatory malfunction these works embody merely "threatens" such a world—a threat, moreover, that is mediated by the cognitive states of "doubt and hesitation." In bodying forth, then, the non-relation between signifier and signified, human content and cued response, world and meaning, the works under discussion are tasked less with *indexing* a feeling-world released from the interpretative strictures that constrain emotion, than with *dramatizing* that world as a possibility. At the heart of this encounter, it seems, is not affect *per se* but the idea of affect. Whereas Buchanan reads Jameson as arguing that postmodern texts attract a nimbus of detached, impersonal, a-signifying affect, in fact, Jameson calls on affect here only as the preliminary cognitive object for a larger structure of (doubtful and hesitant) response to the postmodern text. And that is not all. For far from concluding his analysis, Jameson's account of the spectator's vision of affect—as a "rush of filmic images without density"—is merely the preface to a further feeling-oriented inquiry: "Is this now a terrifying or exhilarating experience?"[30] As we already know, Jameson tends toward the latter, pinpointing the postmodern moment as the victory of euphoric exhilaration over terror, as the "end of the psychopathologies of the ego" and the advent of new "euphoric intensities."[31] Yet the answer to the question is of less significance here than the fact of the question. A rhetorical appeal to the reader's judgment effectively encodes this euphoric response as the effect of an evaluative judgment about an object (where the "object" in question is emotion's displacement by affect as the postmodern's definitive "structure of feeling").[32] The theoretical implications of this seemingly throwaway moment are far-reaching. Where cognitive-appraisal theories of emotion conventionally associate emotion with intentionality and judgment, and where theories of affect, in turn, scrupulously limit the role of intentionality and judgment, to yoke euphoria to intentionality and judgment is to make it a dead ringer for emotion. Predicated on a judgment, Jameson's euphoric "intensities" thus seem to have more in common with emotions than with affects.

Perhaps unsurprisingly, though, Jameson's "euphoric intensity" can no more be absorbed into the definitional confines of familiar cognitive-appraisal models of emotion than it can be identified with familiar models of affect. For while euphoria's relation to judgment is exemplary in its adherence to cognitive-appraisal theory, the judgment at play here is a judgment of a very unusual kind, in that it revolves less around an object in the world (the breakdown of signification) than around this object's implications for feeling itself (the dawn of affect, as inscribed in the vision of a world "become a glossy skin, a stereoscopic illusion, a rush of filmic images without density"). Taking the breakdown of signification as a sign that a diagnostic, evaluative emotion has ceded its place to an a-signifying affect ("a rush of filmic images without density"), euphoria takes this substitution, in turn, as an occasion for ecstatic excitement. Intensities like euphoria, then, are posthumous emotions, emotions whose uniquely recursive structure transfigures the death of emotion into their paradoxical emotional license. Indeed, it is just this recursive, vampiric or spectral aspect of emotion that Jameson adumbrates in his description of Andy Warhol's *Diamond Dust Shoes*, a series of silk-screen prints taken from photographic negatives of ladies' shoes whose submission to the double-exposure of both photograph and silkscreen trap them under the shimmering surface of their new status as kitsch. As Jameson shows, *Shoes'* reliance on the negative rather than the photograph as its base effects a kind of critique of the emotive allure of the commodity by revealing the deadly materiality that underpins commodification.

> The external and colored surface of things ... has been stripped away to reveal the deathly black and white substratum of the photographic negative which subtends them. [33]

At one level, then, *Shoes* thwarts the fascinating charm of the commodity by exposing the twin materialities of production and reproduction that sustains it. Yet the paradox on which Jameson's analysis rests is that despite—or perhaps because of—its attempts to "strip away" the charm of the commodity image to its "black and white substratum" in order to quash all emotion, *Shoes* engenders even more emotion, if in a "compensatory, decorative" form:

> There is a kind of return of the repressed in *Diamond Dust Shoes*, a strange, compensatory, decorative exhilaration, explicitly designated by the title itself, which is, of course, the glitter of gold dust, the spangling of gilt sand that seals the surface of the painting and yet continues to glint at us. [34]

In being crushed to "dust," what these diamonds lose in ontological stability—and exchange value—they gain in ubiquity, as "that spangling of gilt sand that seals the surface of the painting and yet continues to glint at us"; in just the same way, an emotion quashed by self-reflexive critique is

## 46  Euphoria, Ecstasy, Sublimity

at once demoted from the status of emotion and at the same time dispersed and diffused across the text as a whole to persist in an undead, eternally regenerating state. Indeed, in converting the hermeneutic and subjective crises that might seem to preclude emotion into emotion's enabling condition, Jameson's euphoric emotion seems paradoxically *more* tenacious than affect. "Filled with motion, vibratory motion, resonation," and unstoppable in its dynamism and relationality, affect is incompatible with the death of the bodily organism, whose "capacities to act and be acted upon" it marks; the dissolution of the subjective and hermeneutic scaffolding that has traditionally sustained emotion, by contrast, merely heralds a shift in emotion's intentional focus, from an object in the world to the (euphoric) fact of its own displacement by affect.[35]

These euphoric or exhilarating intensities allow us to imagine a different order of emotion—an order of emotion that pivots precisely on the hallucinatory spectacle of affect's displacement of "older" interpretative and subjective registers of feeling. But what are the broader theoretical consequences of accepting Jameson's suggestion that certain species of emotion possess a recursive or spectral structure, and that "affect" might be conceived not as an actual phenomenon, but as the specular object of this unique, recursive brand of emotion? In what follows, I will trace three distinct sets of implications for contemporary thinking about feeling, where the first bears specifically on our prevailing conception of emotion; the second on our collective investments in affect; and the third on the very distinction between emotion and affect that continues to structure so much of our thinking about feeling.

First, and perhaps most obviously, to attribute this recursive structure to Jameson's euphoric intensities is to invite a reassessment of the appraisal paradigm that—more by default than deliberation—still governs feeling theory's conceptualization of emotion. Thoroughly subject-based and object-oriented, appraisal theory's picture of emotion as a subjective phenomenon that "depend[s] on [the] perceived meaning or significance of situations" in the world actually shores up norms of personhood, individuality, animation and embodiment that feeling theory aims to unsettle—leaving it unclear what positive or substantial role *emotion* could possibly serve in a critical enterprise, like feeling theory, committed to rethinking feeling's relation to subjectivity and the social.[36] In turning his attention to a series of euphoric intensities whose strange, posthumous status defies our familiar emotional scripts, then, Jameson not only opens up new way of thinking about emotion, but opens up a host of new critical uses for emotion. Far from an "old surprise[] to which we have become more or less accustomed," the euphoric intensity is stamped by a spectral or vampiric relation to the kind of "strong, violent or primary passions" that dominate our emotional imaginary.[37] Fully equipped to meet the challenge of the hermeneutic and subjective crises that the postmodern moment takes as its insignia, euphoric intensities suggest that emotion may prove quite as valuable a resource as affect in advancing feeling theory's aims.

But there is another, perhaps more urgent, set of consequences that we might tease out of Jameson's model of euphoria—consequences that bear less on any potential revaluation of emotion, than on feeling theory's existing valuation of affect. For as an emotion that crystallizes specifically around a mistaken belief in affect's triumph, Jameson's model of euphoria helps sensitize us to the kinds of euphoric critical circuits that form around affect as a critical object, which is to say, to the unacknowledged emotional fringe-benefits that thinking about affect might yield for its most invested theorists. It's not hard to identify currents of euphoric emotion in contemporary work on affect. According to Massumi, for example, whereas affect is "outside expectation and adaptation, as disconnected from meaningful sequencing, from narration, as it is from vital function" and "escapes confinement in the particular body," emotion is linear, cultural and bound by convention, its "formed, qualified, situated perceptions and cognitions fulfilling functions of actual connection or blockage ... the capture and closure of affect."[38] In its breathless reveries of escape, flight and evasion, Massumi's espousal of affect exhibits precisely the euphoric fantasy of emotion's demise that Jameson so clearly dissects in his descriptions of euphoric intensities. To the extent that a similar euphoria can be "discovered" in a great deal of intellectual work, of course, the revelation that a pulse of euphoria quivers through feeling theory hardly amounts to a devastating critique. It does, however, speak to the tension between theory and practice inherent in a field where a decidedly proprietary and personal emotional experience—euphoria—takes an a-signifying, impersonal affect as its object.

Indeed, in impelling us to acknowledge the kind of emotional fringe-benefits that thinking about affect might offer its most invested theorists, Jameson's analysis of euphoria equally asks us to query our identification of certain experiences as "affect" in the first place. More than just an emotion that takes the (idea of the) ascendence of affect as its object, euphoria is an emotion that by definition *misrecognizes itself as an affect*. As must already be clear, euphoria's status as an emotion (a feeling underpinned by a judgment) is fundamentally at odds with the propositional content of that judgment (the idea that in postmodernism feeling has been released from the bounds of judgment). In this sense, euphoria rests on a classic performative contradiction, in which form and content, the fact of the emotion and the belief in emotion's expiry that grounds it, are in direct conflict. In order to elide this gap, the euphoric subject must undertake a further interpretative movement, suppressing her feeling's intentional, object-oriented status, and (mis)reading the euphoria she feels as an *example* of the triumph of affect that it in fact takes as its (entirely mental) *object*. To the extent, then, that the emotion of euphoria will always by definition be experienced as an affect, euphoria is profoundly marked by misrecognition—a misrecognition that may account not just for Jameson's repeated negative evaluation of the phenomenon as "hallucinatory," but for the emotion's more general cultural status as an inherently "exaggerated" emotion, even a "potential symptom that should be assessed."[39]

## 48   Euphoria, Ecstasy, Sublimity

It is precisely Jameson's sense of euphoria's peculiarly self-reflexive and self-cancelling character that prompts his next suggestion, namely that the "new emotional ground tone" exemplified by euphoric intensities "can best be grasped by a return to older theories of the sublime."[40] Widely cited in contemporary critical theory, Immanuel Kant's formulation of the sublime, which Jameson rehearses here, is now well known: in it, the subject finds compensation for her incapacity to *grasp* nature's infinite breadth through the faculty of imagination, in her positive capacity to *comprehend* that infinite breadth through the faculty of reason.[41] Converting a sense of powerlessness before infinity itself into a sense of pleasurable triumph before the concept of infinity, that is, the feeling of the sublime "makes intuitable the superiority of the rational vocation of our cognitive powers over the greatest power of sensibility."[42] The parallels with Jameson's euphoria should already be clear. An emotion paradoxically predicated on the idea of the supreme power of ideas, the sublime, like the euphoric intensity, strategically disavows and misrecognizes its own emotional infrastructure: just as the sublime's powerful emotional ballast flies in the face of its abiding conviction that emotion has been trumped by reason, so euphoria's powerful emotional ballast flies in the face of its conviction that emotion has been trumped by affect. What is valuable about this model of euphoria for our purposes, I suggest, is its quiet, insidious quality, its capacity to transmute every pulse of feeling identified as an "affect" into a (potentially) misrecognized emotion. In doing so, it compels us to consider the extent to which theories of affect recapitulate the disavowals and misrecognitions at the heart of euphoria itself. To what extent, that is, is Buchanan's reading of euphoria as an affect implicated in the misrecognition that Jameson identifies as internal to euphoria itself? To what extent, for that matter, is all work in affect theory implicated in such a misrecognition?

Jameson does not answer this question, of course, yet he does deepen our understanding of euphoria's "misrecognition" by characterizing both his textual examples, and the intensities he identifies as their primary spectatorial effect, in very specific ways. As we have already seen, the intensities Jameson describes "tend to be dominated by a peculiar kind of euphoria."[43] And as we have also seen, while insisting on the fact that the glossy, commodified "form" of these texts prevents their "content" from functioning representationally or symbolically, Jameson repeatedly calls attention to the *kind* of content that is crossed out or neutralized: from the "dead stock" of Andy Warhol's deathly *Diamond Dust Shoes* and the mournful social satire of Hanson's *Tourist II* to an anonymous assembly of photorealist images described by Jameson as depicting "automobile wrecks," a city "deteriorated or disintegrated," "urban squalor" and "an unparalleled leap in the alienation of daily life," the artworks Jameson selects all traffic in imagery of death, decay and loss.[44] In appointing this uniquely depressing bevy of texts as the focal point for his uniquely euphoric intensities, I suggest, Jameson encodes a striking claim about euphoria's operation. Specifically, he implies

Euphoria, Ecstasy, Sublimity 49

that the euphoric viewer's mistaken belief that the texts' representational "breakdown" entails the rise of "affect" rests on a fantasy of affective autonomy from the "squalor" and "alienation" that the texts emblematize. If intensities are understood as affects, of course, Jameson's insistence on both the texts' gloomy content and the intensities' "euphoric" content seems unnecessary, or even wrong-headed—since affect is by definition incalculable and asignifying, unbound by social and cultural meaning. Reading the euphoric intensity as a (mis)interpretative emotion, however, brings this insistence into sharper focus. The more unpleasant the content of the texts at issue, the more euphoric the spectator feels in sensing—mistakenly—that her feelings escape determination by the hermeneutic protocols that govern emotion. Ironically, it is precisely this seeming disparity between feeling response and textual content that, for Massumi, substantiates and corroborates the projection of an incalculable, non-subjective, a-signifying "affect." Drawing on a series of laboratory experiments on childrens' audio-visual spectatorship, in which scientists observed a gap between the "sad" affect of the on-screen content and the subjects' rating of their affective experience of this content as "pleasant," Massumi infers that "the strength or duration of an image's effect is not logically connected to the content in any straightforward way," and that feeling must, therefor, take place on a plane completely independent of signification.[45] Yet for Jameson—echoing a long line of thinkers, from Aristotle on tragic catharsis forward—the claim that there is a "mismatch" between emotional response and the significance of the textual source does not solidify readily into the conclusion that the relation between feeling and object is non-interpretative. For Jameson, on the contrary, the hermeneutic connection between the emotion and the textual object *lies precisely in its incongruity*. Energized by the belief that the breakdown of signification has released the subject from the interpretative strictures of emotion, euphoria is only intensified by the recognition that the significatory "content" it transcends is so potentially painful. And in casting euphoric intensities' investment in affect as a function of our desire to escape the "urban squalor" and "alienation" around us, Jameson hints that our critical investment in affect may hinge on an analogous desire—the desire to imagine ourselves into a feeling formation unfettered by the painful realities of a socius that Lauren Berlant characterizes in the language of "overwhelming and impending crises of life-building and expectation."[46]

Yet this account of euphoria's provenance does more, I suggest, than simply "explain" the euphoric intensity. More powerfully, it suggests that euphoria may ultimately defy the distinction *between* affect and emotion, between a subjective and interpretative order of feeling on the one hand, and an organic, asignifying, presubjective order of feeling on the other. In the grip of the euphoric intensity, our interpretative response to a "deteriorated or disintegrated" world consists in casting off the harrowing interpretative burden it places on us in favour of euphoria's enchanted embrace. An interpretative index of historical-material reality to the precise extent that

## 50 *Euphoria, Ecstasy, Sublimity*

it breaks with that reality, the "euphoric intensity" suggests that we may be at our most responsive and sensitive as registrars of the social at the very moment that we are most disconnected from it. Moving beyond the rigid binary logic that demands that we claim feeling either for the subjective and interpretative, or for the prepersonal, mobile and organic, euphoria's unique, binocular structure makes it at once "a break ... in the social" and an "engagement with the nature of the social" at once "escape and excess" and continual social "capture."[47]

Where not dismissed as affect theory's theoretical antagonist, Jameson has tended to be cast as affect theory's elder statesman. This section, however, has argued that Jameson's relation to the cluster of work on affect and emotion that has recently crystallized into a full-scale "affective turn" is both far more ambivalent, and far more potentially productive, than either of these readings would suggest. As I have shown, Jameson's model of euphoria has a host of important consequences for the critical consensus that has formed around the status and meaning of both *affect* and *emotion*. First, in figuring emotion as an irreducible, ever-renewable resource that paradoxically feeds off the spectacle of its own displacement by a mobile, promiscuous and non-subjective "affect," Jameson's euphoric intensity serves to transform our understanding of emotion—transfiguring affect's stodgy, subjective sister into a strange and estranging phenomenon that may prove unexpectedly useful to feeling theory's efforts to rethink feeling's relation to politics, sociality and subjectivity. Second, the euphoric intensity stages a kind of proleptic critique of affect, and hence of the theoretical apparatus now congealed around the term. In euphoria's unique constellation of self-reflexivity and misrecognition, "affect" registers not as an "autonomic, bodily reaction[]" occurring ... outside consciousness," but as an effect of a euphoric misrecognition in which we compulsively mistake the mental object of our feeling for its structure.[48] And in the light or shadow of this reading, we are forced to re-read our investment in and assumptions about affect as a critical object. To what extent is the weighty theoretical machinery that has formed around "affect" underpinned by a euphoric misrecognition? And to what extent might this misrecognition be ascribed to a desire to imagine ourselves out of a world marred by environmental, social, economic and geo-political crisis?

But there is a third set of consequences that I have sought to tease out of Jameson's short but incisive intervention in theories of feeling. For more than simply forcing us to rethink the established wisdom on "affect" and "emotion," Jameson's euphoric intensities demand that we push past the binary logic that pits an interpretative model of emotion against a non-subjective, impersonal and unqualified affect in the first place. In the euphoric intensity, that is, we encounter a feeling whose interpretative response to a social Jameson repeatedly defines in the idiom of "deteriorat[ion]," "disintegrat[ion]" and "alienation" consists precisely in its effort to break with interpretation—a feeling, that is, that cannot be readily identified either as a mobile, free-floating Massumian affect on the one hand or as a fixed, rigid "emotion" on the other.

*Euphoria, Ecstasy, Sublimity* 51

In suggesting that we pay attention to the implications of this model, I do not by any means wish to devalue the important work that has taken place under the auspices of "affect theory" in the past two decades. Rather, I seek to challenge the assumption, animating a great deal of this work, that its objects and methodologies mark a radical critical break with the past—an assumption that "flattens out" older methods and forms of inquiry, at once blinding us to what they have to say about feeling and overstating the extent to which "'the new' [is] untouched by whatever we find ourselves currently transcending" in equal measure.[49] Seeking to apply to the interrogation of affect the same keen critical intelligence that has consistently been marshaled in affect's name, this section has shown that the work of a theorist routinely dismissed for his irrelevance or even hostility to current thinking about feeling may, in fact, yield a wealth of insights into the phenomenon.

## III

Though consistently celebrated and anthologized as a major postmodern thinker, Baudrillard sits in an ambivalent relation to the term *postmodernism* itself. Mike Gane, for one, has expended considerable theoretical energy in arguing not only that Baudrillard can be understood outside postmodernism, but that he stands in a position of "coherent rejection" of the field—and this argument is not without critical weight.[50] After an iconoclastic early engagement with semiotics, Freudianism, structuralism and Marxism, Baudrillard went on to build a rich and complex theoretical world that demands to be read "in [its] own terms," an arcane intellectual bestiary populated by concepts like "seduction," "transparency," and "obscenity" and overrun by "vengeful objects," "fatal strategies" and "banal seductions."[51] Yet if, despite his quirks, Baudrillard has become one of postmodernism's most influential icons and thinkers, the handful of tonal, thematic and conceptual qualities that his work shares with the proponents of postmodernism makes it easy to grasp why. The most immediate point of congruence here is stylistic or tonal, since the apocalyptic attitude struck throughout Baudrillard's oeuvre is strongly reminiscent of a popular strain of postmodern discourse characterized by its pronouncements about the end of history.[52] Second, despite Baudrillard's efforts to kick away the disciplinary scaffolding that sociology afforded his earlier work, his thought remains focused almost obsessively around the temporal and social referential of what Jameson calls "our own present of history"—a "present of history" whose parameters have, up until quite recently, been coterminus with the parameters of the postmodern.[53] Third, and perhaps most importantly, Baudrillard's foundational concepts of "simulation" and "the obscene" strike a powerful chord with postmodern engagements with media culture and postmodern critiques of positivistic thought and referentiality. Intention aside, then, Baudrillard remains a thinker "of" postmodernism, where the genitive retains its original sense of possession rather than the secondary sense of "about-ness."

## 52  *Euphoria, Ecstasy, Sublimity*

Indeed, regardless of whether he can properly be placed among postmodernism's exponents, Baudrillard has inarguably suffered a fate similar to those who can. Relegating Baudrillard's work to a chilly, anaesthetized realm beyond the reach of emotion, Steven Shaviro, for example, maintains that

> Jean Baudrillard's work is all about how 'the cool universe of digitality' has eclipsed the real, 'the "cool" cybernetic phase supplanting the "hot" and phantasmatic.' The argument goes something like this: Thanks to the new electronic technologies, the world has become a single global marketplace. Universal commodity fetishism has colonized lived experience. The real has been murdered by its representations. Every object has been absorbed into its own image. There is no longer (if there ever was) any such thing as a single, stable self ... The death of emotion is concomitant with all these other losses.[54]

For Cynthia Willet, meanwhile, Baudrillard's thinking traces the contours of a "global information net" in which "not emotion-laden language games but emotionless computer chips store memory and determine subjectivity."[55] And Vivian Sobchack's excoriation of Baudrillard's insistent "alienation from his own lived body," a body ostensibly both "repressed [and] disavowed" by the arguments advanced in his work, has become the stuff of critical legend.[56] As this sample of critical responses suggests, Baudrillard's theoretical universe is widely perceived as hostile to the very possibility of embodied emotional experience.

A cursory scan of Baudrillard's work, in fact, only corroborates this conventional view, since the quasi-descriptive concepts on which his work is built seem consciously calculated to erode the binary oppositions that sustain our established cognitive-appraisal models of emotion. In this respect, the concept of "simulation" is a useful case in point. Defined by Baudrillard as the "generation by models of a real without origin or reality," a simulation is an object or discourse that, as Mark Poster puts it, has "no firm origin, no referent, no ground or foundation."[57] A function of the procedure that Baudrillard dubs "intensification"—a procedure aimed at artificially re-energizing or revivifying a term through reference to its binary opposite, so that, in simulation's case, a weakening "true" is shored up and at least ostensibly secured by "absorb[ing] all the energy of" the "false"—the simulation is testament to the fact that, as Baudrillard warns, "the more [an entity] seeks to fulfill itself ... the more hyperreal it becomes and the more it transcends itself toward its own empty essence."[58] For whatever its "aims," simulation's ultimate *effect* is the collapse of reality and of the binary opposition that sustain it, namely the opposition reality/illusion. Neither true nor false, "bear[ing] no relation to any reality whatever," the emergence of the simulation entails the total extinction of "the referentials of production, signification, affect, substance, history and the whole equation of real contents that gave the sign weight by anchoring it with a kind of burden of utility."[59] Clearly, simulation's dissolution of the real/unreal binary has a number of

# Euphoria, Ecstasy, Sublimity 53

urgent implications for emotion, whose ties to subjective authenticity and expression give it a chronically over-determined relationship with notions of truth. The collapse of the true/false binary in an inflated culture of simulation thus calls the possibility of emotion into serious question.

Yet while the concept of simulation has acquired a certain cachet in critical accounts of Baudrillard's work, a number of his other concepts have equally far-reaching consequences for emotion. Exemplary here is what Baudrillard calls the "obscene," which names a contemporary technological and cultural state defined by a "pornography of information and communication," in which everything is rendered "immediately transparent, visible, exposed in the raw and inexorable light of information and communication."[60] Once again, the aim of obscenity is not to collapse the oppositions between subject and object, inside and outside, but to realize each term more fully through a strategy of intensification intended to raise objects "to the superlative power."[61] And, once again, instead of stabilizing the difference between subject and object, the process of intensification merely sends each term spiraling into a state of even greater confusion and collapse, effectively dissolving the stable poles of subject and object, inside and outside, within which communication—and thus the expression or projection of emotion—is meant to take place. At play here is what Baudrillard evocatively calls a "forced extraversion of all interiority, … [a] forced introjection of all exteriority," in which the subject becomes "a pure screen, a pure absorption and resorption surface of the influent networks."[62] For emotion, this corrosion of the modern paradigm that sets "the subject at odds with his objects and with his image" is disastrous in its consequences, ensuring that, as Baudrillard himself observes, "we no longer invest our objects with the same emotions, the same dreams of possession, loss, mourning, jealousy."[63] If what is inside is already outside, what need for the inside-outside trajectory underwriting the "expressive hypothesis" to which our cognitive-appraisal models of emotion still routinely pledge allegiance?[64] Conversely, if what is outside is already inside, what need for the judgments or appraisals that form cognitive-appraisal theory's conceptual cornerstones?

Together with simulation, then, obscenity ultimately points to a wider state of terminological and ontological collapse that Baudrillard dubs "reversibility," a state that, displacing "any content or quality" with a "spiral of redoubling" in which true and false, inside and outside, circle around each other without end, prompts Grace to remark rather ominously that "the reversion annuls."[65] To the extent that our dominant models of emotion rest on the rigid binary logic of "intentional states … directed at something," reversibility's strange ontological burlesque seems thoroughly incompatible with emotion, and Baudrillard's contention that "Desire, passion, seduction … are the games of the [old] hot universe" indicates that no one is more sensitive to this fact than Baudrillard himself.[66] The fate of emotion in the age of the simulacra and the obscene, then, seems all too clear. Yet we would be foolish to settle too quickly on any conclusions about work as mercurial and slippery as Baudrillard's, especially in light

## 54 *Euphoria, Ecstasy, Sublimity*

of the dizzying frequency with which borderline emotions like "ecstasy," "fascination," "giddiness" and "vertigo" arise in its pages. For while few would dispute the contention that the displacement of the "hot" universe by the "cold" bodes poorly for conventional emotional formations like "desire, passion [and] seduction," Baudrillard goes on to defy familiar thermal tropologies of emotion that equate "cold[ness]" with complete emotional lack by conferring on this "cool and cold universe" an idiosyncratic emotional climate of its own: "ecstasy, fascination, obscenity ... are games of the cold and cool universe."[67] This section will zero in on the term "ecstasy," a term that crops up for the first time in the transitional essay "Fatal Strategies" and is developed more fully in the later monograph *The Ecstasy of Communication*.[68] As "ecstasy" emerges across his later work as one of Baudrillard's major figures, it becomes clear that, for Baudrillard, the advent of "reversibility" marks less the expiry of emotion than a shift in its structure, as strongly object-directed, intentional and expressive emotions give way to a coterie of more "extreme" emotions.[69] Yet I will go further than this, suggesting that, more than simply withstanding reversibility's vertiginous regime, ecstasy comes to actually characterize that regime. In the process, it acquires a terminological and conceptual primacy in Baudrillard's work that has important consequences for how we conceive the origins and future of feeling theory as a critical practice.

It's easy enough to isolate the cluster of structural idiosyncrasies that enable ecstasy to ride out the "delirium of attributes" that, according to Meaghan Morris, marks the state of reversibility.[70] Whereas our customary cognitive-appraisal models of emotion hang on a strict subject-object binary, the model of "ecstasy" that surfaces across Baudrillard's engagement with the term involves a ceaseless shuttling between subject and object, between inside and outside, between animal and mechanical. Describing the conspicuously *un*playful "games" of the "cold universe," for example, Baudrillard announces that "These [games] no longer imply any game of the scene, the mirror, challenge or otherness duality; they are, rather, ecstatic, solitary and narcissistic. Pleasure is no longer that of the scenic or aesthetic manifestation but that of pure fascination, aleatory and psychotropic."[71] While the "scenic" logic of inside and outside has long organized our understanding of emotions like anger, fear and grief—emotions dependent on what Martha Nussbaum calls a "mind project[ed] outward like a mountain range"—for Baudrillard, to be "ecstatic" is to abandon the dualistic spatial chronotope of "the scene, the mirror."[72] In place of this "scenic" logic, he posits the logic of the *ob*scene, a logic characterized by the "forced extraversion of all interiority ... a forced introjection of all exteriority," and his account of the emotional force of this obscenity is striking in its vividness.

> If hysteria was the pathology of the exacerbated staging of the subject ... and if paranoia was the pathology of organization of the structuring of a rigid and jealous world—then today we have entered

Euphoria, Ecstasy, Sublimity   55

into a new form of ecstasy ... An over-proximity of all things, a foul promiscuity of all things which beleaguer and penetrate him, meeting with no resistance, and no halo, no aura. ... stripped of a stage and crossed over without the least obstacle.[73]

The collapse of boundaries between subject and object at stake here shows ecstasy breaking ranks with the cognitive-appraisal model's well-defined division between a judging, evaluating and emoting subject and a passive, receptive object. Yet this collapse is felt not as a disintegration of the opposition between subject and object, but as a perpetual frenzied *passage* between subject and object, in which we are "crossed over without the least obstacle," "beleaguer[ed] and penetrat[ed]." In staging the relentless, painful violation of the division between subject and object so close to the heart of cognitive-appraisal theory, then, ecstasy retains a definite relation to these terms, a relation that, in turn, ratifies its status as an emotion rather than, say, an affect.

It might, of course, be objected that in calling on "ecstasy" to function as a terminological stand-in for "reversibility," Baudrillard effectively divests the term of its usual emotional weight. Yet what is most striking about Baudrillard's model of ecstasy is the facts that it maps so cleanly onto the emotion's vernacular constructions. While ecstasy's chief contemporary usage identifies it with extreme happiness or joy, the term's etymological origins lie in the Greek *ekstasis,* which, drawing on *ek-* "out" and *histanai* "to place," means to "stand outside oneself."[74] This etymological history leaves its mark not just on ecstasy's secondary meaning—"an emotional or religious frenzy or trance-like state, originally one involving an experience of mystic self-transcendence"—but on ecstasy's more idiomatic incarnations.[75] For whereas the Oxford English Dictionary's entry for euphoria describes a "feeling or state of intense excitement and happiness," the same dictionary's definition of ecstasy sketches "an *overwhelming* feeling of great happiness or joyful excitement," where the term "overwhelming" implies a less than stable boundary between self and other.[76] Critical accounts of the emotion, of course, routinely seek to iron out the instability implied by the adjective "overwhelming" by charging ecstasy to the care either of subjectivity on the one hand or of objectivity on the other, so that the emotion registers either as an epistemically suspect or even pharmaceutically induced retreat into the recesses of the subject's private sensorium, or as a blissful absorption into the object. The value of these arguments, however, lies less in what they say than in what they add up to—namely, to a kind of echo, in the critical register, of the ceaseless equivocation between subject and object, inside and outside, that characterizes ecstasy in the experiential register. In taking the measure of ecstasy's duality, Gretchen M. Reevey's observation that ecstasy is *both* "associated with a dissolution of the self" and predicated on "a complete focus on one's own inner life ... leav[ing] little room for awareness of the external world" is a useful reminder of the extent to which this endless

## 56   Euphoria, Ecstasy, Sublimity

toggling between subjective and objective at the level of critical perception symptomatizes an equally endless toggling between subject and object at the heart of ecstasy itself.[77]

Baudrillard's model of ecstasy as a ceaseless crossing of terms, then, lines up neatly with colloquial constructions of the emotion. Yet in limning Baudrillard's suggestion that ecstasy marks a seesawing passage between subject and object, we have only begun to take the measure of ecstasy's definitional elasticity. For among the binary oppositions that ecstasy so capriciously flaunts is the opposition of the emotional to the non-emotional: in calling ecstasy a "fragile and total passion that excludes all sentiment," Baudrillard casts it at once as a "passion" and as entirely "exclu[sive of] all sentiment," while in dubbing ecstasy a "disembodied passion," Baudrillard's oxymoronic turn of phrase identifies the emotion both with subjective self-realization and with self-transcendence.[78] Indeed, if these sections describe ecstasy's ambivalence directly, later sections index that ambivalence indirectly, in offering widely conflicting blanket statements about the nature of the emotion. While there are a number of instances throughout Baudrillard's work where he aligns ecstasy very specifically with "passion"—as in the description of the "vertiginous effect" that has become our "only passion" cited above—he elsewhere identifies ecstasy bluntly as "the opposite of passion."[79] If, for many critics, this kind of inconsistency occasions questions about Baudrillard's methodological soundness, in this particular instance it serves a definite methodological purpose in tapping into the instability of the emotion at issue. And, given this instability, it scarcely comes as a surprise that, in another feat of elasticity, ecstasy is also capable of absorbing and containing boredom. Less an emotional excess than an affective registration of emotional lack, characterized not by self-loss but by an intensified self-consciousness, boredom constitutes ecstasy's would-be opposite number; yet as Baudrillard puts it, "Boredom is not the problem—the essential point is the increase of boredom; increase is salvation and ecstasy."[80] In an ample demonstration of ecstasy's capacious ambivalence, ecstasy, here, becomes boredom amplified.[81]

Yet the argument that ecstasy's transcendence of the boundaries between subject and object makes it a uniquely capacious emotion capable of *surviving* reversibility's vertiginous regime does not, I believe, quite go far enough. For more than merely suggesting that ecstasy withstands reversibility's ontological vaudeville, Baudrillard deploys the emotion adjectivally to describe the quality of this reversibility—the tone or condition that certain "bod[ies]" achieve when reversibility has evacuated them of all positive substance:

> Ecstasy is the quality proper to any body that spins until all sense is lost, and then shines forth in its pure and empty form. Fashion is the ecstasy of the beautiful: pure and empty form of an aesthetic spinning about itself. Simulation is the ecstasy of the real ...[82]

*Euphoria, Ecstasy, Sublimity* 57

More than simply enduring reversibility's ceaseless terminological evacuations, its senseless "spin[ning] until all sense is lost," ecstasy actually describes the state of reversibility. Far from extinguished, then, emotion is one of the only phenomena afforded anything like presence in the face of what Victoria Grace describes as Baudrillard's efforts to "unravel, sometimes quite brutally and uncompromisingly, every illusory ontological notion, every moralistic premise."[83]

But my aim in driving this point so insistently home is not simply to strengthen this book's claim for the importance of emotion to theoretical articulations of postmodernism. For alongside its implications for the emotional profile of postmodern theory, this argument has important implications for the genealogical profile of feeling theory. As we have already seen, the gesture that Meaghan Morris describes as a kind of conceptual "clearing out" or "demolition" is so endemic to Baudrillard's work that enumerating all the social and material phenomena he variously identifies as "having disappeared," currently "disappearing," or "being about to disappear" would warrant a chapter of its own.[84] It should come as no surprise, then, that the scholarly turn to affect and emotion—phenomena long identified with the solidly, even fleshily material world—is widely represented as a turn away from the heuristic habits and positing procedures associated both with Baudrillard in particular and with postmodern critical practice in general. Yet in tracking the critical career of ecstasy through Baudrillard's work, I hope to have foiled the all-too-easy claims of this logic. For Baudrillard, after all, the turn to emotion is not a turn away from this distinctively postmodern "demolition" work, but rather the direct and inevitable consequence of his commitment to it. It is precisely at the point that he has successfully "demoli[shed]" familiar conceptual scaffolds that Baudrillard has recourse to a phenomenon whose elasticity and flexibility affords it an unusual resilience in the face of reversibility's vertiginous ontological regime. If we accept an analogy between Baudrillard's individual theoretical evolution, and the evolution of the critical humanities as a whole, this reading of Baudrillard should prompt a radical reassessment of our existing understanding of feeling theory's genealogy and origins. For it suggests that, far from entailing a radical break with postmodernism, the recent turn to affect and emotion in the critical humanities and social sciences may not only be consistent with postmodernism's skeptical and interminable probing into the categories of experience, biology, selfhood and embodiment, but may be its one of its most enduring consequences. Rather than pegging recent work on affect and emotion as incompatible with postmodernism, that is, we may come to see this turn as a kind of realization of the postmodern enterprise.[85]

Tracing the (supposedly) cozy disciplinary embrace of feeling theory back to the (supposedly) icy climes of postmodern theory, this counter-history allows us to recast some of feeling theory's key terms in ways that foreground the affinities rather than the antagonisms between feeling theory and postmodernism. Consider Rachel Greenwald Smith's account of affect

## 58 Euphoria, Ecstasy, Sublimity

as "neither biologically deterministic nor humanistic" and both "culturally instigated and biologically registered"; or Melissa Gregg and Gregory Seigworth's description of affect as "aris[ing] in the midst of in-between-ness: in the capacities to act and be acted upon" and as "an impingement or extrusion of a momentary or something more sustained state of relation as well as the passage (and the duration of passage) of forces and intensities"; or Brian Massumi's reading of affect as a movement that is "not exactly passivity, because it is filled with motion, vibratory motion, resonation. And it is not yet activity, because the motion is not of the kind that can be directed."[86] In light of our analysis of Baudrillard's ecstasy, it becomes possible to see that without the postmodern critique of identity, of truth and of subjectivity—a critique epitomized by Baudrillard's own work—these meditative musings on an affect conceived not as a stable, ontological entity, but as "movement," as "potential," and as "relation," would be unthinkable.[87] While never the subject or focus of these accounts of "affect," that is, the postmodern critique of binary thinking forms the theoretical foundation on which they are built. Indeed, these models of affect not only depend on some of Baudrillard's signature critical gestures, but seem strikingly homologous with the model of emotion that Baudrillard himself extrapolated from these gestures—the relentless shuttling between action and reaction, activity and passivity, biology and culture that they inscribe an explicit echo of the shuttling between inside and outside that Baudrillard repeatedly rehearsed under the sign of "ecstasy." To argue that feeling theory would do well to acknowledge this debt to and ongoing resonance with postmodern thinking is not to say that no such acknowledgement has been offered. From Massumi's insistence that his project "was undertaken not in a spirit of opposition to 'Theory or 'cultural studies' but in the hope of building on their accomplishments," to Patricia Clough's contention that "the turn to affect and emotion extended discussions about culture, subjectivity, identity and bodies begun in critical theory and cultural criticism under the influence of poststructuralism and deconstruction," a range of comments, asides and disclaimers scattered throughout feeling theory, as commonplace as they are overlooked, explicitly trace work on feeling to the cradle of postmodern.[88] As Massumi and Clough already knew, then, but as many of us often seem to have forgotten, while casually dismissed as outdated where it is not completely condemned as wrong-headed, the work of critics like Baudrillard sets out many of the conceptual and theoretical co-ordinates within which the body of work we now know as "affect theory" has come to establish itself.

## IV

The preceding analyses have sought to show that while routinely cast as prophets of an inhuman, frigidly emotionless universe, both Jameson and Baudrillard have made the question of emotion foundational to their critical endeavors. Yet if Baudrillard and Jameson have been widely misread as

## Euphoria, Ecstasy, Sublimity 59

apostles of an emotionless postmodernism, Lyotard suffers under a slightly different misreading. While acknowledging that feeling has a significant place in Lyotard's vision, critics have tended to assimilate his arguments about feeling to the models of desubjectivized, noninterpretative "affect" currently in vogue across feeling-oriented work in both the critical humanities and social sciences. Admittedly, Lyotard does deliver a powerful and comprehensive theory of affect. From his early monograph *Libidinal Economy*, which sets up against an imprisoning "emotional theater" the free-flowing arousal of the "libidinal band," to the stream of later work that appeared after his more classically philosophical *The Differend*, Lyotard repeatedly sought to confront philosophy with what Claire Nouvet calls affect's "radical heterogeneity to articulation."[89] Yet as this section will argue, Lyotard's account of a presubjective, inarticulate affect is matched by an equally cogent account of emotion, namely in his important and influential analyses of the postmodern sublime. From his landmark 1982 essay, "An Answer to the Question: What is the Postmodern?" to the exhaustively detailed lectures collected in *Lessons on the Analytic of the Sublime*, Lyotard's work on the "sublime sentiment" not only attests to emotion's significant structural role in his work, but prompts us to reassess our understanding of the role of emotion in feeling theory.[90]

In order to fully fathom the implications of Lyotard's reading of the sublime for our orthodox accounts of emotion, however, we need to grasp the context in which Lyotard's turn to the aesthetics of the sublime takes place. Perhaps the initial impetus for this turn was a 1980 essay by the German philosopher Jürgen Habermas, which mounted a caustic critique of the theoretical and aesthetic practices associated with postmodernism for what he alleged was a "neo-conservative" commitment to furthering the fractures in contemporary social life.[91] Insisting, instead, that aesthetic practice should strive to "*bridge* the gap between cognitive, ethical and political discourses," Habermas argued that it was art's duty to anticipate in aesthetic form the social possibility of a "communicative rationality," in which the spheres of art, politics and ethics could be fully reconciled.[92] For Lyotard, however, not only is this kind of totality an unachievable "transcendental illusion" but the *desire* to achieve it is and has been profoundly dangerous.[93] Indeed, the proper "task" of art is not to reconcile artistic, political and ethical discourse but precisely to "activate the differences" between them, foregrounding the fractures and instabilities in the "unity ... identity ... [and] security" of our vision of social and ethical reality.[94] It is against this backdrop, then, that Lyotard has recourse to the sublime, an emotional or aesthetic phenomenon that, first profiled in classical Greek and Roman philosophy, before gaining prominence as a popular topos of philosophical debate in the eighteenth century, acquired its fullest, most realized working-through in the work of Immanuel Kant. Understood not only as a feeling (the "sublime sentiment"), but also as the name of the aesthetic practice designed to elicit the feeling (the "aesthetics of the sublime"), "the sublime," for Lyotard, has been

## 60  *Euphoria, Ecstasy, Sublimity*

the primary aesthetic instrument through which postmodern artists have sought to accomplish the task he has assigned art in general.[95] Configuring the postmodern—somewhat idiosyncratically—as the avant-garde or radical tendency within modernism itself, Lyotard contends that "postmodern" artists from Picasso, to Joyce, to Newman have consistently drawn on the sublime in their effort to "wage a war on totality."[96] Resonating powerfully with a range of other poststructuralist and postmodern critiques of unity, identity and totality, this argument acquired a broad conceptual currency in the 1980s and 1990s, especially as it bore on then-current questions of postmodern politics and aesthetics.

What is significant for our purposes, however, is that while many critics have offered balanced accounts of Lyotard's work on the sublime, those critics explicitly invested both in setting the sublime in the frame of feeling and in tapping into the sublime's radical political potential, have tended to turn up a thoroughly organic, depersonalized and nonsubjective model of the phenomenon that bears striking similarities to currently dominant models of affect. Placing Lyotard's sublime feeling beyond the reaches of "cognition," Andrew Slade, for example, makes a case for the sublime as a thoroughly organic, affect-like phenomenon:

> the stakes of … Lyotard's thought of the sublime lie precisely in the intractable difference between cognition and sensibility. The feeling of pleasure or displeasure, or of pleasure and displeasure, that is central to the sublime feeling, cannot come under the legislation of the rules of cognition.[97]

James Williams seconds this position, locating the sublime beyond the reaches not just of cognition but of language: "in the event as sublime feeling lies the limit of the claims of reason," since the sublime is "a feeling that cannot be preserved in forms of discourse that seeks [sic] to represent it"; for Peter Milne, similarly, in "introducing the affect into aesthetics … [Lyotard] attends to the interruption of something absolute in its singularity, something that resists forms, economies, prohibitions"; while Simon O'Sullivan trawls Lyotard's key texts on the sublime, most notably the essay "Critical Reflections," for claims that support his argument about the importance to art history of a theoretically impoverished model of affect as "moments of intensity, a reaction in/on the body at the level of matter," arguing that it is only through recourse to these "moments of intensity" that art is able to "work against the what Lyotard once called the 'fantasies of realism.'"[98] What is striking about these readings, however, is not just that the sublime is parsed in the idiom of affect, but that it is only *as* an affect that these critics are able to identify the sublime as a function of Lyotard's wider critical program, namely his "war on totality"; only *as* an affect that the sublime is able to escape what Slade calls "legislation of cognition"; only *as* an affect that it can be seen to work, as O'Sullivan puts it, "against

*Euphoria, Ecstasy, Sublimity* 61

the fantasies of realism"; only *as* an affect that it "resists forms, economies, prohibitions."

Even outside the purview of Lyotard's engagement with the phenomenon, of course, this reading of the sublime is far from unusual in contemporary theory. The reactive poststructuralist and postmodernist tendency to privilege non-rationality and embodiment over rationality or transcendence has seen Vanessa L. Ryan, for example, anachronistically recast philosopher Edmund Burke's eighteenth-century theory of the sublime as a prescient critique of reason, in which Burke supposedly "minimize[d] the role of the mind in the experience of the sublime and ... characterize[d] the sublime as a natural force that is by its very definition beyond man's ability to control."[99] Yet more than just critically predictable, the dominant reading of Lyotard's sublime does seem, on first blush, to offer a critical purchase on Lyotard's work. For like many postmodern theorists, Lyotard has "continually sought ways to destabilize and disrupt those systematic theories that attempt to provide totalizing or universal explanations," an enterprise that typically involves championing an object, practice or idea located outside of, other than or beyond what Brian Massumi calls "the grid itself"—something very like affect.[100] And if we restrict our focus to the 1984 essay "The Sublime and the Avant-Garde," an essay that came to exert an enormous influence on critical thinking about postmodern art, Lyotard's analysis of the sublime can be readily placed within this remit. In elaborating the aesthetics of the sublime, or what he calls the "focus of the sublime experience," for example, Lyotard has repeated recourse to the language of the ineffable, limning "an absolutely immense object ... or one that is absolutely powerful—a storm at sea, an erupting volcano" as an entity that "consciousness cannot formulate and even what consciousness forgets in order to compose itself."[101] And if the object of sublime experience is distinguished by its inaccessibility to "consciousness," the sublime emotion itself is distinguished by a corresponding and complementary inaccessibility to language and cognition. As Lyotard puts it, with typically ostentatious oratorical flourish, "Here then is a breakdown of the sublime sensation: A very big, very powerful object threatens to deprive the soul of any and all 'happenings,' stuns it ... the soul is dumb, immobilized, as good as dead."[102] Terms like "stun[ned] ... [struck] dumb ... immobilized" locate the initial effect of the sublime object on the same noninterpretative and organic plane that recent critical work on feeling has annexed for affect.

Yet if the great majority of readers of "The Sublime and the Avant-Garde" seem to have been as "immobilized" at this point in the article as the hypothetical spectator herself before "a storm at sea, an erupting volcano," to read *past* this sentence is to note how quickly this moment of paralysis and panic is caught up in a complex set of cognitive procedures that thwart the effort to elide the "sublime sentiment" with "affect." For Lyotard's announcement that "This frustration of expression [ie. meaning/interpretation] kindles a kind of pain" is soon succeeded by the claim that "this pain

## 62  *Euphoria, Ecstasy, Sublimity*

in turn engenders a pleasure, in fact a double pleasure: the recognition of the impotence of the imagination contrarily attests to an imagination striving to illuminate even that which cannot be illuminated ... and furthermore the inadequacy of images, as negative signs, attests to the immense power of ideas."[103] In other words, while the first stage of the sublime involves a feeling of incomprehension and inadequacy before something that one cannot begin to grasp through the faculty of imagination, this affective response is only the first stage in a three-part program. In the second stage, our painful imaginative impotence is rapidly coded at the level of cognition as "the *recognition* of the impotence of the [faculty of] imagination," only to be just as rapidly *re*-coded, in a third stage, into a counter-recognition of "the immense power" of our faculty of reason in being able to posit or conceive of an entity so boundless that it could leave our faculty of imagination "impoten[t]" in the first place. In sum, as Lyotard puts in "An Answer to the Question: What is the Postmodern?" the *affect* of pain that results from an imagination that cannot "present" what is before it, ultimately becomes the basis for the *emotion* of "pleasure that reason should exceed all presentation."[104] As Lyotard puts it bluntly "This feeling consists of two contradictory sensations, pleasure and displeasure, 'attraction' and 'repulsion'."[105] While this second, pleasurable moment of the sublime is indubitably marked by what O'Sullivan, citing Lyotard, dubs a certain "'excess,'" this "excess" names not the visceral throbs that O'Sullivan (wrongly) clusters under the rubric of "affect," but the cerebral, speculative positings of a supposedly transcendent faculty of reason; while the inaugurating moment of the sublime involves a certain failure of cognition, the culminating moment of the sublime is not just cognitive, but a positive, triumphal glorying in cognition's power.[106] And thus, as Steven Shaviro has argued, while many critics wish "to affirm the first moment, but defer or avoid the second," the logic of the sublime is incontestably that of "a rupture *followed by* a recuperation."[107]

What is striking here, of course, is that while the sublime is clearly not an affect, its dual, binocular structure ensures that—like Jameson's euphoric intensities—it is also not quite an emotion, or at least not an emotion that fits comfortably within the definitional confines of familiar cognitive-appraisal models. Yes, the specifically pleasurable, recuperatory moment of the sublime, with its gloating delight in reason's ability to conceive of something that the imagination cannot grasp, is in many ways just an emotion, predicated on a simple evaluative judgment. Yet as what Lyotard aptly calls a "contradictory feeling," the sublime also incorporates a far less cerebral and far more dysphoric moment, a moment in which we are "stun[ned]" and struck "dumb."[108] And the duality or oscillation between these two states affords the sublime an oddly meta- or reflexive relation to our understanding of feeling in general. As we have seen, feeling theory's stock understanding of the relation between affect and emotion casts "affect" as an organic, asignifying phenomenon whose "capture and closure" by a cognizing subject marks its transition into the domain of emotion, an emotion widely

*Euphoria, Ecstasy, Sublimity* 63

defined, in the wake of Massumi, as a "qualified intensity ... intensity owned and recognized."[109] And in its evolution from a painful affect into a pleasurable emotion, from "form" to "idea," from organic response to semiotically organized judgment, the sublime seems to dramatize or play out this transformation.[110] Rather than either an emotion or an affect, then, the sublime is better understood as a kind of meta-feeling that internalizes the relationship *between* "affect" and "emotion" as it is currently articulated across feeling theory. For Massumi, of course, this "capture" or "closure" of affect is never quite complete: If "emotion is the most intense (most contracted) expression of that capture" it is also a sign "of the fact that something has always and again escaped."[111] We should not be surprised to notice, then, that the pleasurable moment of the sublime can hardly be said to have the last word. Rather, as what Lyotard terms "an extreme *tension* (Kant's agitation)," a "pleasure mixed with pain, a pleasure that comes from pain," the sublime feeling involves a constant uneasy cycle back and forth between pain and pleasure, between the pain indexed to our imaginative and sensory failure before the sublime object, and the pleasure indexed to this failure's recoding as reason's ability to "exceed all presentation."[112]

Interestingly, if Lyotard's model of this sublime oscillation seems to dramatize or internalize the map of the relation between emotion and affect that holds sway in feeling theory, it equally seems to recapitulate the different ways in which "affect" and "emotion" have tended to be *affectively* codified across feeling theory. Perhaps unsurprisingly, given the chronically overdetermined relationship in Western philosophy between truth and dysphoric feeling, theorists in feeling theory have tended to frame affect—a phenomenon routinely celebrated, despite Massumi's strenuous proleptic protests, for its affinity with "a prereflexive, romatically raw domain of primitive experiential richness"—in relatively dysphoric terms; emotion, meanwhile, no less routinely dismissed as a kind of distorting or specious "capture" of an originary affect, tends to be equated with positive or euphoric feeling.[113] Close attention to the specific feelings that Massumi draws on to exemplify "emotion" and "affect" provide rich evidence of this tendency. On the one hand, Massumi appoints "confidence" as the emotion *par excellence*, contending, in his analyses of Ronald Reagan's presidential style, that "confidence is the emotional translation of affect as capturable life potential" and that "confidence is the apotheosis of affective capture."[114] On the other, as Rei Terada has noted, Massumi "all but identifies fear with affect," contending that "fear is the direct perception of the contemporary condition of possibility of being-human ... fear is the inherence in the body of the ungraspable multicausal matrix of the syndrome recognizable as late capitalist human existence (its affect)."[115] For Massumi, then, the movement from affect to emotion is a movement from a "real" but painful phenomenon to a false yet nevertheless euphoric one. In this sense, in chasing a painful affect with a pleasurable emotion, the "sublime sentiment" seems to recapitulate within the compass of a single emotional unit feeling theory's own broad

## 64  *Euphoria, Ecstasy, Sublimity*

theoretical postulates about the specifically euphoric or dysphoric burdens of "affect" and "emotion" respectively.

Lyotard's reading of the sublime, however, turns up the dial somewhat on this now-standard pair of equations between pain and affect on the one hand and pleasure and emotion on the other. For in the sublime, the progression from the moment of initial painful affect to the moment of pleasurable emotion is not simply a matter of one state smoothly and seamlessly incorporating another. Why is this? Recall that the object of the sublime's "delight" is the idea of reason's capacity to conceive of things "of which no presentation is possible," and thus that, more than just an emotion generated by an idea, the euphoric moment of the sublime is an emotion generated *by the idea of the power of ideas*.[116] For as feeling theory's tendency to pit "reason" and "affect" in opposition suggests, to attribute this supreme, transcendent power to ideas is, implicitly, to attest to the *lack* of power of affect.[117] The pleasurable moment of the sublime, then, is, in effect, a pleasurable emotion that takes the vanquishing of painful affect through a transcendent "faculty of reason" *as its object*. The pleasurable emotion in which the sublime culminates, in other words, is an emotion that rests on the idea that the painful, immobilizing affect that underpins it has been overcome or transcended.

It should be immediately clear here that, like Jameson's euphoric intensity—an emotional state that also reflexively pivots on or revolve around the figure of affect—this relation between the pleasurable moment of the sublime and the painful affect that is its object is riven with performative contradiction. As we have seen, this pleasurable moment of the sublime pivots on the idea of the absolute "power of ideas," that is to say, on the possibility of the complete "capture and closure of affect."[118] Yet the fact that this "idea" exerts such powerful and overwhelming affective impact—its wash of feelings of "relief," "delight" and "jubilation" clearly taxing Lyotard's linguistic proficiency in its demand for ever further synonyms for "pleasure"—suggests that the "idea" has not, or perhaps cannot, triumph at all.[119] It is not just that the pleasurable moment of the sublime, like all emotions, possesses a powerful affective substratum. Rather, it is that this moment of pleasurable recognition both emerges from—and will ultimately fall back into—the exclusively affective moment that predicates it, the dumbfounding, overwhelming "pain that imagination or sensibility should not be equal to the concept."[120] Resting on a belief in the complete "capture" of affect, the pleasurable moment of the sublime, then, effectively rests on a misrecognition or disavowal of its origin in, and ongoing relation to, affect. Just as the euphoric intensity's prototypically emotional structure flies in the face of the supposed triumph of affect that is its object, so the sublime's powerful affective ballast flies in the face of the supposed triumph of emotion that is *its* object.

Yet if the ways in which the structure of Lyotard's sublime mirrors Jameson's model of the euphoric intensity harbors a critical interest of its

Euphoria, Ecstasy, Sublimity   65

own, what is perhaps more interesting is the way in which the sublime diverges from the euphoric intensity—a divergence that foregrounds the differences not just between the two theorists' understandings of affect, but between their critical targets. Recall that, according to Jameson, affect is merely the chimerical bauble of a "hallucinatory" euphoria, and the misrecognition dramatized through the "euphoric intensity" is the notion of affect's *triumph* in a "world ... become a glossy skin."[121] At stake in Jameson's "euphoric intensity," then, is a disavowal of its own status as emotion. In Lyotard's view, by contrast, affect is very real, and the misrecognition dramatized in the "sublime sentiment" is the notion that emotion can entirely sever, through the mere "power of ideas," its ties to its affective underpinning.[122] The disavowal at stake in the pleasurable moment of the sublime, then, is a disavowal of its own affective infrastructure. If Jameson's euphoric intensities, then, invite feeling theory to interrogate its orthodox conception of affect, Lyotard's sublime euphoria, conversely, invites feeling theory to interrogate its orthodox conception of emotion. For as a "sentiment" in which emotion and affect are caught up in an ongoing, dynamic interplay, the sublime feeling reminds us how often dominant cognitive-appraisal models of emotion elide the fundamental affective foundation upon which emotion is predicated, with Martha Nussbaum, for example, not only casting emotions as "intelligent responses to the perception of value," but actively repudiating the idea that emotion might be bound up in *any* way with "energies or impulses that have no connection with our thoughts, imaginings and appraisals."[123]

It is not immediately clear, of course, what bearing this implicit critique of certain instantiations of the cognitive-appraisal theory of emotion might have on feeling theory, the body of scholarship that remains this book's primary interlocutor. Feeling theory, after all, has tended to appoint "affect" as its primary terminological vehicle, relegating "emotion" to a relatively marginal and subsidiary role. Yet while rarely playing a starring role in feeling theory, a Nussbaum-esque vision of emotion nevertheless makes frequent cameos—and not just as a widespread critical misconception that it is feeling theory's duty to correct, but as a genuine claim about emotion's contours and composition. Underwriting Deborah Gould's defense of an affect-oriented rather than emotion-oriented approach to the analysis of political protest, for example, is the contention that the former, emotion-oriented approach, in which "feelings are a necessary component of, rather than a barrier to rational thought," necessarily "evacuate[s] political emotion of its affective dimensions"—as if an emotion underpinned, as emotions often are, by "rational thought," were entirely incompatible with "affect."[124] Indeed, this oddly affectless model of emotion arguably underpins the tendency, more prominent among some theorists in feeling theory than others, to cast the relationship between "affect" and "emotion" in a binary, antagonistic, either/or register. What Lyotard's sublime reminds us, however, is that emotion, as Massumi has long insisted, cannot be understood outside the remit

## 66   *Euphoria, Ecstasy, Sublimity*

of affect—an affect that, in the case of sublime pleasure, supplies not only the emotion's initial catalyst, but its cognitive object *and* its material underpinnings.[125] Yet this is only one facet of the challenge that the sublime poses to the opposition between "affect" and "emotion," an opposition that in many respects recapitulates the Cartesian dualism of body and mind. If the sublime foregrounds the affective moment nestled at the heart of emotion, it equally traces the emotional horizon within which affect takes place. For Lyotard can only describe the "pain" of the initial affective moment of the sublime by evoking the "pleasure" of the specific brand of emotion from which it falls away. As Lyotard puts it, the feeling of "the beautiful"

> testifies that between the capacity to conceive and the capacity to present an object corresponding to the concept, an undetermined agreement ... may be experience as pleasure. The sublime is a different sentiment. It takes place, on the contrary, when the imagination fails to present an object which might, if only in principle, come to match a concept. We have the Idea of the world (the totality of what is), but we do not have the capacity to show an example of it. We have the Idea of the simple ... but we cannot illustrate it with a sensible object which would be a case of it.[126]

The pleasurable emotion of the beautiful depends an idealized "agreement" between imagination and reason, between "object" and "concept."[127] And as Lyotard's dialectical phrasing suggests, the painful, immobilizing affect that inaugurates the sublime and registers our *failure* to "present an object which might ... match a concept" materializes only through contrast with the idealized "agreement" of object and concept from which we have temporarily fallen so radically short.[128] To use Massumi's terms, without emotion's cognitive "capture," there could be no affective "escape."[129] As the sublime reminds us, then, the relationship between affect and emotion is less one of opposition and mutual exclusion than of cyclical interdependence.

It should be clear by now, then, that unlike Jameson's account of the misrecognition at the heart of the euphoric intensity, Lyotard's account of the misrecognition at the heart of the sublime does not ultimately come down on the "side" of either affect or of emotion.[130] And this refusal to endow either pain or pleasure, either affect or emotion, with a more significant role in the "sublime feeling" is not simply a function of his commentary on feeling. For Lyotard, after all, the stakes of the sublime extend far beyond its bearing on our understanding of feeling to its role in the effort to "wage a war on totality," a role that depends precisely on its ability to keep both terms in play.[131] As we have already seen, for many of the theorists who have broached Lyotard's work on the sublime, the sublime can only be conceived as a valuable instrument in Lyotard's much-vaunted "war on totality" to the extent that it is conceived as an affect—an equation of affect and political or social rupture that is echoed in feeling theory, which tends to assume that affect's radical or

*Euphoria, Ecstasy, Sublimity* 67

liberatory potential is negated by its "insertion ... into [the] semantically and semiotically formed progressions" of emotion.[132] Yet for Lyotard, the disruptive, productive force of the sublimes does not lie in its affective component, that is to say, in its "non-conscious and unformed" aspect.[133] Rather, it lies in the fact that, neither an emotion nor an affect, this "intrinsic combination of pleasure and pain" dramatizes the ceaseless movement *between* the spheres of affect and emotion, *between* "imagination" and "reason," *between* an immediate affective "pain that imagination should not be equal to the concept" and "the pleasure that reason should exceed all presentation."[134] This relentless movement works to open up and expose the chasm between what Lyotard calls the "concept and the sensible ... [and] the transparent and communicable," attesting to the irreconcilable gulf separating an epistemology predicated on what we can see, feel and know, and an ethics that can only ever function at the level of the Idea.[135] In other words, it is in its ability to stage the gap between affect and emotion, between the faculty of experience and the faculty of reason, that the sublime works to foreground the fractures and instabilities in the "unity ... identity" of our vision of social and ethical reality, and thus resist what Lyotard calls the "terror" of totality.[136]

Whereas many critics associated with feeling theory assume that affect alone can authorize the kinds of "shatter[ing]" that Lyotard calls for, for Lyotard himself, it is the complex, meta-feeling of the sublime, with its signature oscillation between affect and emotion, that becomes the most powerful instrument in the project of disrupting social totality.[137] For Lyotard, that is, radical feeling, thought or action does not depend on rallying triumphantly around a figure like affect that has been marginalized by a hegemonic order. Rather, it depends on tracing or as Lyotard puts it "activat[ing]" the difference *between* the hegemonic order and its marginalized other.[138] And what is striking is that versions of this same insistence can be tracked across Lyotard's *oeuvre*, perhaps most famously in his theory of the *différend*. There, across the course of a complex series of analyses of questions of speech, justice, politics and philosophy, Lyotard comes to the conclusion that the incommensurability between different "genres of discourse"—the incommensurability on which he confers the neologism *la différend*—is such that the task of philosophers, politicians and judges cannot be to resolve or reconcile these differences.[139] Rather, as he puts it, "One's responsibility before thought consists in detecting *différends* and in finding the (impossible) idiom for phrasing them."[140] As Simon Malpas paraphrases, "this is not simply a question of settling *différends* by resorting to a universal genre with rules applicable to all the parties ... Rather, it is a case of affirming or attesting to the existence of the *différend* and searching for new modes and idioms in which to phrase the dispute."[141] As an exemplary means of "phras[ing] the dispute" between what we can perceive and what we can imagine, the sublime can clearly be numbered among these "idioms."

While accounts of Lyotard's contribution to thinking about feeling are often proscribed to his work on affect, then, this section has argued that Lyotard

## 68 *Euphoria, Ecstasy, Sublimity*

also offers a cogent and consequential intervention in our understanding of emotion. In its flexible, capacious and meta-emotional structure, the theatre of the "sublime sentiment" delivers critical counsel to recent thinking about feeling by staging a drama in which far from opposed or mutually exclusive, "affect" and "emotion" can be shown to circle relentlessly around each other. Yet the implications of this argument extend beyond our conception of feeling *per se* to our conception of the relation between feeling and radical aesthetic practice, and between feeling and postmodernism. While feeling theory has long cast affect as the proper instrument of an aesthetic or critical practice devoted to political and social change, for Lyotard, both the despairing, organically-based, affective moment of the sublime and the pleasurable, reason-based emotional moment of the sublime must be in play when it comes to the aesthetic project of "shattering" totality, which rests on this peculiarly sublime movement between regret and assay, between "imagination" and "reason," between affect and emotion. [142] And the fact that, for Lyotard, this radical aesthetic project simply *is* the postmodern, is a measure of the extent to which—like Jameson and Baudrillard—Lyotard is committed to granting emotion a significant place in his vision of the postmodern programme.

Across the course of its analyses of Jameson's euphoria, Baudrillard's ecstasy and Lyotard's sublime, then, this chapter has provided a forceful answer to feeling theory's conviction that postmodernism has little or nothing to say to contemporary work on affect and emotion. More than just compatible with feeling theory, in fact, postmodern theory delivers a crucial challenge to some of feeling theory's structuring assumptions about emotion. Resisting cognitive-appraisal theory's familiar emotional script, the coterie of outlandish, borderline emotions that emerge in the postmodern throw up questions about the relation between feeling theory and affect, between emotion and affect, and between feeling theory and postmodernism. Yet in its reliance upon extreme, limit-case emotions like ecstasy, euphoria and sublimity, the work of Jameson, Baudrillard and Lyotard provides only a partial glimpse of the phenomenological geography of postmodern aesthetics, leaving open the question of the milder or more mundane emotions that coalesce in and around postmodern texts. Though not continually overcome with ecstasy or euphoria, we remain responsive and susceptible to postmodern texts in ways we take for granted. In the chapters that follow, then, I will examine some of the more routine emotions encrusting postmodern aesthetic and theoretical life—emotions of fear, bewilderment, boredom, fascination and knowingness.

## Notes

1. Jean-Francois Lyotard, "An Answer to the Question: What is the Postmodern?" In *The Postmodern Condition*, trans. Geoff Bennington and Brian Massumi (Minneapolis: Minnesota University Press, 1984), 77.
2. Ibid.

*Euphoria, Ecstasy, Sublimity* 69

3. Fredric Jameson, "Postmodernism, or, The Cultural Logic of Late Capitalism," *New Left Review* 146 (1984); Perry Anderson, *The Origins of Postmodernity* (London: Verso, 1998), 54.

4. Jameson, *Postmodernism, or, The Cultural Logic of Late Capitalism* (Durham, NC: Duke University Press, 1990), 8, 11.

5. Ibid., 8.

6. Ibid., 9.

7. Martha Nussbaum, *Upheavals of Thought: The Intelligence of Emotions* (Cambridge: Cambridge University Press, 2000), 2.

8. Jameson, *Postmodernism*, 15.

9. Massumi, *Parables for the Virtual*, 41, 28, 28.

10. Ibid., 27.

11. Jean-Francois Lyotard, *Libidinal Economy*, trans. Iain Hamilton Grant (London, 2004), p. xiv; Gilles Deleuze, *Difference and Repetition* (London, 2004); Jameson, *Postmodernism*, p. 15–6.

12. Jameson, *Postmodernism*, 15–16.

13. Ibid., 6.

14. Ibid.

15. Massumi, *Parables for the Virtual*, 27; Lawrence Grossberg, *We Gotta Get out of this Place: Popular Conservatism and Postmodern Culture* (New York, 1992), 22; Lauren Berlant, "Thinking about Feeling Historical," *Emotion, Space and Society* 1 (2008), 7.

16. Affect's enshrinement in the title of Melissa Gregg and Gregory Seigworth's field-defining 2010 collection *The Affect Theory Reader* seems the best evidence of this. (Melissa Gregg and Gregory J. Seigworth, *The Affect Theory Reader* [Durham, N.C., 2010].) Exceptions to this rule, as we have seen, include the work of Rei Terada, who offers a radically non-subjective model of emotion, and the work of Sianne Ngai, who troubles the absoluteness of the distinction between emotion and affect. (Rei Terada, *Feeling in Theory: Emotion after the Death of the Subject* [Cambridge, MA, 2002]; Sianne Ngai, *Ugly Feelings* [Cambridge, MA, 2005], 25–9.).

17. Hemmings, "Invoking Affect": 550.

18. Jameson, *Postmodernism*, 11, 15.

19. Buchanan, *Fredric Jameson*, 93.

20. Jameson, *Postmodernism*, 15–6.

21. Steven Shaviro, *Post-Cinematic Affect* (Hants: Zero Books, 2010), 5.

22. From Hemmings' interrogation of affect's reification as "'the answer' to the problems of cultural theory," and Eugenie Brinkema's critique of affect theory's repudiation of formalism, to Diedre Reber's genealogical account of affect's relation to free-market capitalism and Ruth Leys' important critique of affect theory's mobilization of scientific studies, the recent upsurge in the critical stocks of "affect" has been met with skepticism from some quarters (Hemmings, 548; Brinkema; Leys; Reber).

23. Jameson, *Postmodernism*, 34.

24. Ibid.

25. Ibid., 34.

26. Ibid., 27.

27. Ibid., 27.

28. Ibid., 34.

70 *Euphoria, Ecstasy, Sublimity*

29. Gregg and Seigworth, introduction to *The Affect Theory Reader*, 1.
30. Jameson, *Postmodernism*, 34.
31. Ibid., 15, 34.
32. The phrase "structure of feeling" is borrowed from Raymond Williams, "Structures of Feeling" in idem, *Marxism and Literature* (Oxford: Oxford University Press, 1977), 128–135.
33. Jameson, *Postmodernism*, 9.
34. Ibid., 10.
35. Massumi, "Autonomy of Affect," 86; Seigworth and Gregg, *The Affect Theory Reader*, 1.
36. Gerald L. Clore and Andrew Ortony, "Cognition in Emotion: Always, Sometimes, or Never?" in *Cognitive Neuroscience of Emotion* (Oxford: Oxford University Press, 2000), 25.
37. Philip Fisher, *The Vehement Passions* (Princeton, NJ: Princeton University Press) 115; Massumi, "Autonomy of Affect," 550.
38. Massumi, "Autonomy of Affect," 85, 96, 96.
39. Don M. Tucker, Kathryn Vannatta and Johannes Rothlind, "Arousal and Activation Systems and Primitive Adaptive Controls on Cognitive Priming," in *Psychological and Biological Approaches To Emotion*, ed. Nancy L. Stein, Bennett Leventhal and Thomas R. Trabasso (Hillside, NJ: Laurence Erlbaum Associates, 1990), 151; Gretchen M. Reevy, *Encyclopedia of Emotions* (Santa Barbara, CA: Greenwood, 2010), 245.
40. Jameson, *Postmodernism*, 6.
41. Ibid., 34.
42. Immanuel Kant, *Critique of the Power of Judgment* (Cambridge: Cambridge University Press, 2000), 257.
43. Jameson, *Postmodernism*, 16.
44. Ibid., 33–34.
45. Massumi, *Parables for the Virtual*, 24.
46. Lauren Berlant, *Cruel Optimism* (Durham, N.C., 2011), Kindle Edition: "Introduction: Affect in the Present."
47. Hemmings, "Invoking Affect," 565; Massumi, *Parables for the Virtual*, 36.
48. Massumi, *Parables for the Virtual*, 90.
49. Hemmings, "Invoking Affect," 550.
50. Mike Gane, *Baudrillard: Critical and Fatal Theory* (London: Routledge, 1991), 55.
51. Rex Butler, *Jean Baudrillard: The Defence of the Real* (London: Sage, 1999), 5. Victoria Grace, for example, maintains that rather than impose a preconceived conceptual framework on Baudrillard's thinking, it is more important to read his work in a way that "continually modifies and refines one's understanding of his concepts and use of language and rhetorics in light of their repeated appearance in his work." (Victoria Grace, *Baudrillard's Challenge: A Feminist Reading* [London: Routledge, 2000], 1.)
52. Kellner, for one, has made this connection, arguing that to the extent that we see postmodernity primarily as "a radical break and rupture from modernity," Baudrillard is a postmodernist, for his discourse extensively deploys "the discourse of 'no more' and 'no longer'," "describ[ing] the rupture between his former analysis of modern objects and the new postmodern condition." (Douglas Kellner, *Baudrillard: A Critical Reader* [Oxford: Basil Blackwell, 1994], 11, 13, 13.)

## Euphoria, Ecstasy, Sublimity   71

53. Fredric Jameson, *Archaeologies of the Future: The Desire Called Utopia and Other Science Fictions* (New York: Verso, 2005), 187.
54. Steven Shaviro, "The Life, After Death, of Postmodern Emotions," *Criticism* 46.1 (Winter, 2004): 126.
55. Cynthia Willet, "Baudrillard, 'After Hours,' and the Postmodern Suppression of Socio-Sexual Conflict," *Cultural Critique* 34 (1996): 148.
56. Vivian Sobchack, "Beating the Meat/Surviving the Text," in Sobchack, *Carnal Thoughts: Embodiment and Moving Image Culture* (Berkeley: University of California Press, 2004), 166, 167. In a similar vein, Ackbar Abbas has suggested that "Baudrillard's advocacy of fascination ... snubs affectivity," interpreting Baudrillard's investment in fascination as the signature posture of the third order of simulacra as a sign of his refusal of feeling (Ackbar Abbas, "On Fascination: Walter Benjamin's Images," *New German Critique* 48.9 [1989]: 61.).
57. Jean Baudrillard, "Simulacra and Simulation," in Baudrillard, *Jean Baudrillard: Selected Writings*, ed. Mark Poster [Palo Alto: Stanford University Press], 169; Mark Poster, introduction to Jean Baudrillard, *Jean Baudrillard: Selected Writings*, ed. Mark Poster [Palo Alto: Stanford University Press], 1.
58. Baudrillard, *Fatal Strategies* (London: Pluto Press, 1999), 27, 28. The passage is worth quoting in full here: "A passion for intensifying ... any quality at all, provided that, ceasing to be relative to its opposite (the true to the false, the beautiful to the ugly, the real to the imaginary) it becomes superlative, positively sublime, as if it has absorbed all the energy of its opposite. Imagine a thing of beauty that has absorbed all the energy of the ugly: that's fashion. Imagine the true that has absorbed all the energy of the false: there you have simulation." (Ibid.).
59. Jean Baudrillard, "Simulacra and Simulation," in *Jean Baudrillard: Selected Writings*, ed. Mark Poster (Palo Alto: Stanford University Press), 173; Jean Baudrillard, "Symbolic Exchange and Death," in *Jean Baudrillard: Selected Writings*, ed. Mark Poster (Palo Alto: Stanford University Press), 128.
60. Baudrillard, *Ecstasy of Communication* (New York: Semiotexte/Foreign Agents, 1988), 21–22.
61. Jean Baudrillard, *Fatal Strategies* (London: Pluto Press, 1999), 9.
62. Baudrillard, *The Ecstasy of Communication*, 26, 27.
63. Ibid., 16, 12.
64. Terada, *Feeling in Theory*, 11.
65. Baudrillard, *Fatal Strategies*, 27; Grace, *Baudrillard's Challenge*, 43. Initially elaborated in the early *Symbolic Exchange and Death* (1972) and underpinning many of his later writings, reversibility describes the operating principle of what Baudrillard calls the system of symbolic exchange. According to Baudrillard, "symbolic exchange" structures social relations in a number of ancient societies, in which it functions to forestall the production of positive, essentialized identities. Whereas in our current system of economic exchange an object is assumed to possess a fixed, innate being, in a system of symbolic exchange, the object is without positive attributes or value, but is itself constituted in and through the act of exchange. Similarly, whereas in a system of economic exchange objects work to "seal the subject as an individual unit within the consumer system," symbolic exchange annuls or erases the individual subject and their ownership or self-definition in what William Pawlett calls "a convulsive moment, an experience of sacredness or ritual festivity." (William Pawlett, *Jean*

## 72  *Euphoria, Ecstasy, Sublimity*

*Baudrillard: Against Banality* [London: Routledge, 2007], 21.) At stake here is what Baudrillard calls a kind of "constant reversibility" where "the animal form, the human form, the divine form are exchanged according to a rule of metamorphosis in which each ceases to be confined to its definition," and which ensures the ceaseless dissolution of the boundaries and oppositions that sustain identity. (Jean Baudrillard, *Passwords*, trans. Chris Turner [London: Verso, 2003], 16.) Yet if this early work frames reversibility as an actual feature of particular ancient societies, later work, from "Fatal Strategies" onward, broadens the reach of the term to render it a kind of abstract mechanism, the key agent of the state of ontological collapse marked by the terms simulation and obscenity. While modes of symbolic exchange are officially less relevant than ever, reversibility's disappearance on a practical or ritual level heralds its reappearance in systemic form, as the maleficent reversal of the system itself.

66. John Deigh, "Primitive Emotions," 9; Baudrillard, *The Ecstasy of Communication*, 26.

67. Ibid.

68. The essay "Fatal Strategies" has recently been republished in monograph form and it is on this monograph version that I rely.

69. Baudrillard himself says, "In applying our old criteria and the reflexes of a scenic sensibility, we run the risk of misconstruing the irruption of this new ecstatic and obscene form in our sensorial sphere." (Baudrillard, *The Ecstasy of Communication*, 25–6.).

70. Morris, *The Pirate's Fiancee*, 188.

71. Baudrillard, *The Ecstasy of Communication*, 25.

72. Nussbaum, *Upheavals of Thought*, 1.

73. Baudrillard, *The Ecstasy of Communication*, 26–7.

74. *Oxford English Dictionary*, s.v. "ecstasy"

75. Ibid.

76. *Oxford English Dictionary*, s.v. "euphoria"; *Oxford English Dictionary*, s.v. "ecstasy."

77. Gretchen M. Reevy, *Encyclopedia of Emotions* (Santa Barbara, 2010), 215.

78. Baudrillard, *Fatal Strategies*, 26; Baudrillard, *The Ecstasy of Communication*, 33.

79. Baudrillard, *Fatal Strategies*, 27; Baudrillard, *The Ecstasy of Communication*, 26.

80. Baudrillard, *Fatal Strategies*, 223.

81. The argument that reversibility's semiotic order is characterized not by the end of emotion but by the rise of a certain brand of "extreme" emotion is best exemplified not in Baudrillard's texts, but by them. For the euphoria and outrage that surrounds Baudrillard's work seems in direct proportion to its refusal to "represent the direction the world is moving in." (Pawlett, *Jean Baudrillard*, 107.) It can be no accident that the moment in his theoretical career when Baudrillard began matching his piercing critique of reference with an ostentatious refusal of reference is coterminus with the escalating critical excitement surrounding his work—an excitement that prompts Meaghan Morris, for one, to observe that hers is "a delight in a Baudrillard who declares the real no longer exists." (Morris, *The Pirate's Fiancee*, 191.) This observed congruence between Baudrillard's refusal of reference and his capacity to excite of intense emotion is borne out in Kim Toffoletti's contention, in relation to Baudrillard, that, in the absence of reference, emotion takes over: "It is in the process of our encounters with Baudrillard that the possibilities of his writings emerge—their power to challenge, incite, infuriate,

Euphoria, Ecstasy, Sublimity   73

provoke and seduce." (Kim Tofoletti, *Baudrillard Reframed: Interpreting Key Thinkers for the Arts* [London: I. B. Tauris, 2011], 3).

82. Baudrillard, *Fatal Strategies*, 28.
83. Grace, *Baudrillard's Challenge*, 1.
84. Morris, *Pirate's Fianceé*, 196.
85. Yet if we are willing to accept this account of feeling theory's origins and genealogy, we can't help but note that, from some critical perspectives, it might be cause for caution rather than for celebration. Baudrillard's work has been widely criticized for being "confusing, unempirical, unsettling, whimsical and sensationalist" or as Michael Hays puts it, "vague" and "abstract"—a vagueness that is part and parcel of his commitment to postmodern precepts. In its promiscuous availability to "mean" both feeling and its absence, Baudrillard's model of ecstasy is a case in point here. Tofoletti, *Baudrillard Reframed*, 3; Michael Hays, "A Response to Mark Poster on Jean Baudrillard," *Boundary 2* 8.1 (1979): 292.) Whether or not one believes that this vagueness and abstraction serves a purpose within the context of Baudrillard's particular *oeuvre*—and many theorists have passionately insisted that it does—it is hard to shake the sense that it provides a poor methodological example for contemporary feeling theory. Critics affiliated with feeling theory have consistently sought to stake out the political value of the study of feeling, for example, by mapping the relation between affective formations and institutional and legislative developments, as in Lauren Berlant's efforts to trace the connection between "political depression" and "cruel optimism" and "the state's withdrawal from the uneven expansion of economic opportunity, social norms and legal rights." (Berlant, *Cruel Optimism*, Kindle Edition: Introduction.) If it's easy enough to see that this much-vaunted political agenda is inconsistent with the vagueness and instability that necessarily marks Baudrillard's construction of emotion, it's equally easy to see that the models of feeling circulating through feeling theory are often touched by just such vagueness and instability.
86. Rachel Greenwald Smith, "Postmodernism and the Affective Turn," *Twentieth Century Literature* 57.3–4 (2011): 423; Melissa Gregg and Gregory Seigworth, introduction to *The Affect Theory Reader*, ed. Gregg and Seigworth (Durham, NC: Duke University Press, 2010), 1; Massumi, *Parables for the Virtual*, 4.
87. Massumi, *Parables*, 4–5.
88. Massumi, *Parables for the Virtual*, 27; Patricia T. Clough, "The Affective Turn: Political Economy, Biomedia, and Bodies," in *The Affect Theory Reader*, ed. Melissa Gregg and Gregory Seigworth (Durham, NC: Duke University Press, 2010), Kindle Edition.
89. Jean-Francois Lyotard, *Libidinal Economy*, trans. Iain Hamilton Grant (Bloomingtogn, IN: Indiana University Press, 1993), 3; Jean-Francois Lyotard, *The Différend: Phrases in Dispute*, trans. Georges Van Den Abbeele (Minneapolis: Minnesota University Press, 1988); Claire Nouvet, "The Inarticulate Affect: Lyotard and Psychoanalytic Testimony," in *Minima Memoria: In the Wake of Jean-Francois Lyotard* (Stanford, CA: Stanford University Press, 2007), 107.
90. Lyotard, "An Answer to the Question"; Jean-Francois Lyotard, *Lessons on the Analytic of the Sublime* (Stanford: Stanford University Press, 1994).
91. Jürgen Habermas, "Modernity: An Unfinished Project" in *Habermas and the Unfinished Project of Modernity: Critical Essays on The Philosophical Discourse of Modernity*, ed. Maurizio Passerin d'Entreves and Seyla Benhabib (Cambridge, MA: MIT Press, 1997), 53.

74  *Euphoria, Ecstasy, Sublimity*

92. Jean-Francois Lyotard, "An Answer to the Question: What is the Postmodern?" in *The Postmodern Condition*, trans. Geoff Bennington and Brian Massumi (Minneapolis: Minnesota University Press, 1984), 72; Jürgen Habermas, *Theory of Communicative Action* (Boston, MA: Beacon Press, 1985), 75. "Modernity: An Unfinished Project" was originally delivered by Habermas in his acceptance speech on receiving the Theodor W. Adorno Prize awarded by the City of Frankfurt in September 1980. In it, Habermas warned of the danger that lay in "the definitive segregation of science, morality and art into autonomous spheres split off from the lifeworld and administered by specialists" (Habermas, "Modernity," 54).

93. Lyotard, "An Answer to the Question," 81. Describing what he calls the "terror" of totality, he argues that the massive human costs of modernity's political and military machinery show that "we have [already] paid a high enough price for the nostalgia of the whole and the one, for the reconciliation of the concept and the sensible, of the transparent and the communicable experience." (Ibid., 81–82.)

94. Ibid., 81, 82, 73.

95. Ibid., 77; Lyotard, "Sublime and Avant-Garde," 36.

96. Lyotard, "An Answer to the Question," 82.

97. Andrew Slade, *Lyotard, Beckett, Duras and the Postmodern Sublime* (New York: Peter Lang Publishing, 2007), 20.

98. James Williams, *Lyotard and the Political* (London: Routledge, 2000), 131; Peter Milne, "Lyotard's Critical Aesthetics," in *Rereading Jean-Francois Lyotard: Essays on his Later Work*, ed. Heidi Blickis and Rob Shields (Farnham: Ashgate Publishing limited, 2013), 254; Simon O'Sullivan, "The Aesthetics of Affect: Thinking Art Beyond Representation," *Angelaki* 6.3 (2001): 126, 126, 125. The problem with O'Sullivan's model of affect is that it identifies affect with bodily materiality. Yet as Massumi has expressly contended, affect names the *in*corporeal dimension of the body. It is "Of [the body], but not it. Real, material, but incorporeal." (Massumi, *Parables*, 5.)

99. Vanessa L. Ryan, "The Physiological Sublime: Burke's Critique of Reason," *Journal of the History of Ideas* 62.2 (2001): 267.

100. Simon Malpas, *Jean-Francois Lyotard* (London: Routledge, 2003), 103; Massumi, *Parables*, 3.

101. Jean-Francois Lyotard, "Sublime and the Avant-Garde," *ArtForum Intenational* (April, 1984): 36, 40, 37.

102. Lyotard, "Sublime and the Avant-Garde," 40.

103. Ibid., 40.

104. Lyotard, "An Answer to the Question," 78.

105. Lyotard, *Lessons*, 109. My italics.

106. Indeed, just how far Lyotard's actual argument departs from its representation in Simon O'Sullivan's work on affect can be measured by the fact that O'Sullivan's engagement with Lyotard's work on the sublime takes place in the service of a call for a mode of art historical practice that "attend[s] to the specificity of an art work." (O'Sullivan, "Aesthetics of Affect," 130.) Yet, in keeping with the sublime's rapid evolution from a moment of visceral, immediate feeling to a moment of cerebral ratiocination *about* feeling, Lyotard actually seems uninterested in anything to do with the specificity or materiality of the object that provides the sublime's catalyst. If, in "An Answer to the Question," "it [was] not [his] intention to analyze in detail" the specificities of the artworks in

*Euphoria, Ecstasy, Sublimity* 75

question, it was clearly not his "intention" to compensate for this omission in any later work, since both the essays collected in *The Inhuman*, and the influential essay "The Sublime and the Avant-Garde" are, as art theory, conspicuously bereft of any artistic specificity (Lyotard, "An Answer to the Question," 78). And this was not just a matter of inclination, but of principle, since, as he put it, "the Avant-gardes are perpetually flushing out artifices of presentation which make it possible to subordinate thought to the gaze and to turn it away from the unpresentable." (Ibid.) The only point in "An Answer to the Question: What is the Postmodern?" that he affords these texts any identifiable positive attribute is when, quoting Kant, he names "'formlessness, the absence of form' as a possible index to the unpresentable" (Ibid.).

107. Steven Shaviro, "Beauty Lies in the Eye," *Symploke* 6.1 (1998): 96.
108. Lyotard, "The Sublime and the Avant-Garde," 37, 40, 40.
109. Massumi, *Parables*, 35, 28.
110. Lyotard, *Lessons*, 180.
111. Massumi, *Parables*, 35.
112. Lyotard, "The Sublime and the Avant-Garde," 40, 42; Lyotard, "An Answer to the Question," 81. It is for this reason, I suggest, that Lyotard is able to stress, on different occasions, different aspects of the sublime feeling, arguing on one page that "The sublime ... takes place ... [when] we can conceive the infinitely great, the infinitely powerful, but every presentation of an object destined to make visible this absolute greatness or power appears to us painfully inadequate" (so that the emotion is identified with the subject's euphoric belief in the power of their reason to compensate for their failure of imagination); and on the other that the sublime "indicates that there is something beyond the limits of experience that we can conceive of even if we can't represent or imagine it" (so that the emotion identified with the moment in which that failure of imagination once more engulfs the power of reason). (Lyotard, "An Answer to the Question," 79, 78.)
113. Massumi, *Parables*, 29.
114. Ibid., 41.
115. Rei Terada, *Feeling in Theory*, 174, n. 23; Brian Massumi, "Everywhere You Want to Be: Introduction to Fear," in *The Politics of Everyday Fear*, ed. Brian Massumi (Minneapolis: University of Minnesota Press, 1993), 12.
116. Lyotard, "Sublime and the Avant-Garde" 40, 40; Lyotard, "An Answer to the Question," 78.
117. Brian Massumi, for example, treats "reason" as affect's other, representing affect as the "interruption of the operative principles of reason." (Massumi, *Parables*, 130).
118. Lyotard, "Sublime and the Avant-Garde," 40; Massumi, *Parables*, 35.
119. Lyotard, "Sublime and the Avant-Garde," 40, 40; Lyotard, "An Answer to the Question," 77, 80.
120. Ibid., 81.
121. Jameson, *Postmodernism*, 34.
122. Lyotard, "An Answer to the Question," 77; Lyotard, "Sublime and the Avant-Garde," 40.
123. Martha Nussbaum, *Upheavals of Thought: The Intelligence of Emotions* (Cambridge: Cambridge University Press, 2002), 1. Indeed, Nussbaum contends flatly that no case has been made for the argument "that we need to include [affect] as a distinctive item in the definition of emotions, over and

## 76  *Euphoria, Ecstasy, Sublimity*

above the elements" that she has set out as essential to it. (Nussbaum, *Upheavals of Thought*, 61.)

124. Deborah Gould, "Affect and Protest," in *Political Emotions*, ed. Janet Staiger, Ann Cvetkovich and Anne Reynolds (Routledge: New York, 2009), 35. For Gould, in other words, to link a feeling to "rational thought," as most models of emotion do, is to expel the "affect" from the emotion altogether. Reading of "affect" and "emotion" as mutually exclusive, Gould ignores the extent to which critics such as Massumi tended to represent affect as a force that underlies and catalyses our emotional life.

125. For Massumi, the "capture and closure of affect" by emotion does not amount to a cancelling out of affect, which, after all, supplies emotion's basic "force." Indeed, in Massumi's framework, the idea that emotion could possibly negate affect makes no sense, since as he puts it grandly, "affect *is* the whole world." (Massumi, *Parables*, 43. Italics Massumi's own).

126. Lyotard, "An Answer to the Question," 78.

127. Ibid.

128. Ibid.

129. Massumi actually takes up a position on the matter that is very similar to the position I am here ascribing to Lyotard. In the context of an analysis of the affective economy of sport, Massumi suggests not only that is affect central to emotion, but emotion is central to affect: "this capture and containment [of affect by emotion] is not simply negative. Its very transcendence becomes a productive element in the mix whose effect is the field of immanence ... if the game were not repeated, variation would never have a chance to restart." (Massumi, *Parables*, 79.).

130. Indeed, Lyotard goes to some lengths to insist that, while every postmodern text will end up leaning more heavily on either the affective or the emotional moment of the sublime—with the German expressionists, Malevich, Chirico and so on placing greater "emphasis ... on the powerlessness of the faculty of presentation," and artists like Picasso, Lissitzky, Duchamp, in turn, placing greater "emphasis ... on the increase of being and the jubilation which result from the invention of new rules of the game, be it pictorial, artistic or any other"—neither tendency affords an advantage in the promotion of the "sublime situation." (Lyotard, "An Answer to the Question," 80.)

131. Lyotard, "An Answer to the Question," 82.

132. Massumi, *Parables*, 28. Massumi repeatedly equates affect with the "potential for change," a term that recurs with almost hypnotic regularity across the course of *Parables for the Virtual* (Massumi, *Parables*, 3.)

133. Eric Shouse, "Feeling, Emotion, Affect," *M/C Journal* 8.6 (2005): 6.

134. Lyotard, "An Answer to the Question," 81.

135. Ibid., 82.

136. Ibid., 77, 80, 81.

137. Ibid., 77.

138. Ibid., 82.

139. Lyotard, *The Différend*, 138.

140. Ibid., 142. As he puts it elsewhere, "What is at stake in a literature, in a philosophy, in a politics perhaps is to bear witness to différends by finding idioms for them." (Ibid., 13.)

141. Malpas, *Lyotard*, 67.

142. Massumi, *Parables*, 1.

# 2 Fascination
## Between the Rough and the Glossy

## I

A celebrated crystallization of canonical critical models of postmodernism, David Cronenberg's *Crash* (1996) is also uniquely if unexpectedly useful to the effort to reappraise them. The film's final scene, for example, finds protagonists James Ballard (James Spader) and his wife, Catherine (Deborah Kara Unger), in a carefully contrived car chase that culminates—predictably, for a viewer by now cued to the perverse narrative and spectacular predilections of this controversial screen adaptation of J. G. Ballard's no less controversial 1977 novella—in James's deliberately driving his wife's silver coupe off the freeway and down a grassy embankment. Yet like many another ripple in what Jesse Fox Mayshark has christened the "cultural tide of pop postmodernism," the scene's dramatically and morally inflammatory content is matched by a certain formal flatness, the same "flatness or depthlessness" that Fredric Jameson, writing in 1990, traced to postmodern aesthetics' renunciation of hermeneutic depth.[1] The formal strategies through which the film sustains this flatness are readily identified. Cinematographically, the scene favors the aloof, aerial detachment of the extreme long shot over the facial close-ups through which film texts conventionally secure meaning and identification.[2] Whether descending toward the grassy median strip to disclose Catherine's bloodied body and mangled car, or re-ascending into the end credits, the mobile, crane-mounted camera maintains a crisp, unimpeachable distance from its subjects that invites us to consider the image as an aesthetic surface rather than as a representation of a spatially and psychologically rounded world. Musically, the relentless, one-note repetitiveness of Howard Shore's spare synthetic strings muffles the tonal cues through which we're customarily asked to apprehend symbolic and psychological significance. Characterologically, meanwhile, Spader's stiff, unhurried gait exudes none of the emotional "urgency" one might expect of a man who has just witnessed his wife tumble down a freeway embankment.[3] Any effort to infer motive or meaning in Spader's gestures is blocked by the "bored, abstracted, trancelike emptiness of expression" with which, possessed of all the time in the world and none of the animation, James surveys the battered interior of the car before finally turning his gaze to the prostrate Unger.[4] While quite literally "trafficking" in emotionally

78    *Fascination*

and morally incendiary subject matter—from wound-sex, to car-crash fetishism to plain dangerous driving—the film is nevertheless marked by what Jameson calls "a new kind of superficiality" that resists restoration to any "larger context."[5]

For Jameson, of course, as for the legion of critics who followed in his wake, the hermeneutic flatness of the postmodern image was the all-too-natural bedfellow of emotional flatness.[6] This critical conjugation of flatness and emotionlessness has left a predictable mark on the reception of *Crash*, informing scholarly consensus not only on the film's tone and effect, which is routinely figured in the register of "affectless alienation," "emotional vacuity," "cool, detached anality," and "boredom," but on its narrative, which has congealed across repeated critical retellings into a sociological fable in which the Ballards' drive to reinvigorate an emotional and sexual life impoverished by postmodernity's flat, depthless surfaces compels the couple into the cult-like force-field of the charismatic crash-fetishist, Vaughan (Elias Koteas).[7] Admittedly, the formal decisions to which critics ascribe the film's "shrinking of three-dimensional space" are far from uniform.[8] Parveen Adams points to Cronenberg's penchant for attaching the camera to a moving car's running board, so that the image's putative dynamism is undercut by its compositional uniformity; Mark Dery taps the film's relentless switch-ups of the participants, objects and modes of sexual excitement; while Alan Jones blames the mannequin-like, two-dimensional characters.[9] That its flatness and depthlessness leaves *Crash* stubbornly impervious to identification and emotional engagement, however, is now a matter of critical accord—an accord, moreover, whose consequences extend far beyond the reception and interpretation of *Crash*. To the extent that affect and emotion have emerged as star terms in the diverse, interdisciplinary constellation of work perhaps best clustered under the rubric of "feeling theory," the postmodern image's presumed resistance to emotion has helped hasten postmodernism's recent fall from critical favor.

Yet closer attention to *Crash*'s arresting final scene—and to the many like it in the film—invites a reconsideration of the critical consensus regarding the film's literal, hermeneutic and emotional "flatness." This is not to deny that the film's parting image, the eerie triumvirate of husband, wife and car, is bereft of the hermeneutic depth that Jameson ascribes to the modernist text. Rather, it is to suggest that this lack of depth is so richly embellished by texture that both "flatness," with its connotations of matteness, evenness and dullness, and "depthlessness," with its purely negative specification of the surface as absence of depth, seem spectacularly inadequate to convey the unusual character of the film. The final low-angle shot that sets the lacquered metal of the overturned car's hood against the grisly, tenderized flesh of Catherine's bloodied body is exemplary here. While resistant to an interpretation that would promise to plumb its symbolic or psychological depths, its riot of texture equally precludes an interpretation that would reduce it to mere surface lack.

Fascination 79

*Figure 2.1* The rough and the glossy.

Hardly isolated to *Crash*'s final, climactic scene, this kind of textural play becomes almost routine in a film in which narrative and character development are less subordinate to than strategically confounded with the loving delineation of bruises, scars and gleaming metal. It is the film's glossy luster, of course, that first makes a claim on the viewer's attention, as the opening titles' glistening chrome font emerges out of a vanishing point into the glare of a light-beam simulating oncoming headlights. Quickly established as the salient feature of the film's set design, this slickly airbrushed aesthetic soon stamps everything from the sleek bent steel of the Ballards' Marcel Breuer dining set to the waxy buff of the hospital linoleum, and where actual chromatic surfaces are absent, their effect is simulated through the use of lighting or even water, the saturation of blue lighting throughout, for example, affording even conventionally soft, matte surfaces such as human flesh a dull, metallic glow.[10] Yet if *Crash* is a film captivated by the high polish of the glossy surface, it is at least as fascinated by its opposite: the rough, the broken, the bruised and the fractured. The film's preoccupation with the spiderwebbed glass of a shattered windscreen, for example, or the vulva-like scar worming its way down the back of Gabrielle's (Roseanna Arquette) thigh, makes the question of texture in assessing the film as seemingly pressing as it has been, so far, critically elided. Indeed, above and beyond its spectacular value, the rough surface acquires substantial narrative traction in the film, whose plot is centrally animated by the characters' efforts to shatter, pierce or puncture various technological or corporeal surfaces, in a quest for Vaughan's much-vaunted but perennially elusive "intensity of experience." Admittedly, texture's profile in modernist aesthetics and philosophy precludes its identification as an exclusively postmodern phenomenon. Yet postmodernism's own glossy and rough surfaces seem phenomenologically

80  *Fascination*

distinct from their modernist counterparts. In its second-hand, reflected gleam, postmodern gloss finds its most fitting embodiment not in the live body of a charismatic celebrity—as in the modernist "shine" or "incandescen[ce]" that Anne Anlin Cheng attributes to the fetishized bodily surfaces of the iconic modern "race beauties" Josephine Baker and Anna May Wong—but in the inhuman, sterile and mass-produced objects of what Sonya Shannon has called postmodernity's "Chrome Age," an "age" that finds its metonymical acme in the lustrous, mirrory magnetism of the car.[11] And *Crash*'s ragged flesh wounds and planes of pulverized metal have no more in common with their modernist analogues than its glossier surfaces do with theirs. Whereas the creased and tattered peasant shoes that Martin Heidegger celebrates in "The Origin of the Work of Art" remain untouched by the gleamingly industrial dystopia they are set up rhetorically against, a tear in the steely polish of a car's side panel is inseparable from the brilliant glossy finish that it disrupts.[12]

Subtleties aside, the point to be telegraphed here is that if postmodern aesthetics is conventionally coded as "flat" or "depthless," in *Crash* this flatness is crosshatched by an almost entirely untheorized textural rubric, which counters a dominant model of surface as lack—lack of depth, lack of meaning and lack of emotion—with a model of surface as variegated, complex plane. But what are the consequences of this peculiar profusion of texture for postmodernism and emotion? From Nigel Thrift's celebration of "the little, the messy and the jerry rigged," to Ann Cvetkovich's paean to "the textures of everyday experience," recent work in feeling theory has afforded "texture" an unmistakable, if also largely untheorized, critical pedigree that is best accounted for by Eve Kosofsky Sedgwick's contention that "a peculiar intimacy seems to subsist between textures and

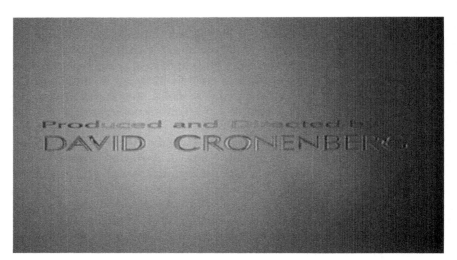

*Figure 2.2* The gleaming bent steel of the opening credits.

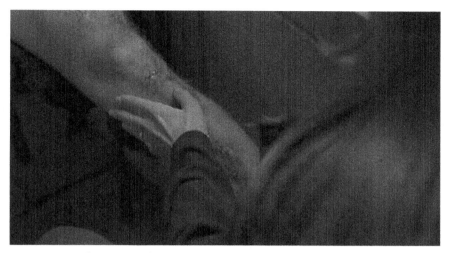

*Figure 2.3* Catherine runs her hand over James's scars.

emotions."[13] As feeling theory's methodological watchword, specifying both the critical scale (close and detailed) and the critical mode (tactile and embodied) most congenial to grasping the affective specificity of a text, texture has come to index feeling theory's transcendence of older forms of postmodern analysis that ostensibly disregard affect and emotion.[14] Yet the prominence of textural tropes in a paradigmatically postmodern text like *Crash* tends to problematize texture's designation as the definitive switch point between a postmodern past and a feeling-oriented present, opening up the possibility that the postmodern surface may possess its own distinctive emotional valence. Given the tight critical fit between texture and emotion, in fact, it should come as no surprise that the film's texture-laden denouement is no more emotionally flat than it is physically flat. *Crash*'s critical reception records the fascination the film exerted over its viewers, from Mark Browning's "mesmeriz[ed] fascination," to Janet Maslin's "grim fascination," and Robin Dougherty's account of the film as "pleasantly hypnotic"—and fascination's strange synthesis of fixity and animation, stasis and excitement, is anticipated in James's own behavior.[15] While wholly surface-oriented—to the extent that he seems to observe little distinction between the body of the smashed car and the body of his wounded wife—James's connoisseur-like absorption in the wreckage is quite at odds with the principle of postmodern emotionlessness. As he runs his fingers over the car's jagged doorframe and dabs at the florid bruises on his wife's leg, it is clear that if he cannot "feel" in any traditional sense, he is also unable to look away. Looked at as "flat," postmodernism's depthless, metallic landscapes seem wholly impervious to emotion; looked at as "textured," however, these same depthless, metallic landscapes turn up a wealth of emotional possibility.

82    *Fascination*

As this suggests—and as this chapter will argue—*Crash*'s eclectic patchwork of rough and glossy surfaces demands a reassessment of our understanding of both postmodernism and emotion. Yet while this chapter will pursue this argument primarily through a close reading of *Crash*, Cronenberg's cinematic tribute to the tickle and titillation of postmodern texture cannot be interpreted in isolation. Rather, the film's engagement with texture must be understood as a rejoinder to the strategic *dis*engagement from texture that marks postmodern theory, whose frequent if unsystematic recourse to textural tropes is matched only by its efforts to quash texture's unsettling hermeneutic and emotional implications. In what follows, then, this chapter will briefly chronicle texture's equivocal critical career in postmodern theory before returning to *Crash* in order to stake out two key lines of argument. First, it will argue that the film's preoccupation with scarred flesh and high-gloss metal confounds orthodox understandings of postmodernism's emotional life that cross-implicate hermeneutic and emotional flatness. Recoding postmodern "flatness or depthlessness" as a visual banquet of etched and gilded surfaces, *Crash* brokers a distinctively postmodern emotional logic in which an hostility to cognitive-appraisal forms of emotion goes hand in glove with a receptivity to a more idiosyncratic emotional mode. Far from frostily emotion-free, then, postmodern aesthetics is ripe with emotional promise. Yet as this chapter will also argue, if the analysis of postmodern texture shakes up sedimented critical models of postmodernism, it may equally enrich and extend our understanding of emotion. The unique, triangulated emotions yielded by an analysis of *Crash*'s rough and glossy surfaces, in fact, may enable us to salvage emotion from its syndication to the cognitive-appraisal paradigm—and thus from its status as the dreary, pedestrian cousin of a mobile, non-interpretative and non-subjective "affect."

## II

If *Crash*'s textural logic seems striking in its reinscription of the familiar binary surface/depth, even more striking is how readily this same logic can also be shown to be at work in postmodern theory. For postmodern theory's reappraisal of the hermeneutic opposition surface/depth is encoded in a vividly textural vocabulary that—running a reckless gamut from glossiness, shininess, gleam, on the one hand, to the fractured, the broken and the punctured, on the other—is as untheorized in postmodern theory itself as it is unremarked in retrospective critical discussions of the field. While the most heavily cited section of Jameson's analysis of Andy Warhol's *Diamond Dust Shoes,* for example, proclaims the picture's "new flatness or depthlessness," a subsidiary section invokes "the glitter of gold dust, the spangling of gilt sand" that attends that flatness, a "glitter" or "spangling" that shimmers with unexplicated significance.[16] Jean Baudrillard, likewise, represents the rise of the simulacra through the trope of encroaching gloss, "the very last traces of marginality excised as if by plastic surgery: new faces, new

*Fascination*  83

fingernails, glossy brain-cells"; Andreas Huyssen refers to postmodernism's "gleaming facades"; and Ziaudden Sardar describes both its "high-tech gloss" and its "glitzy yuppie euphoria."[17] While neither explicit nor fully elaborated, the insistence of this vocabulary throughout postmodern theory makes it clear that—as Renu Bora's reference to "postmodernism's predominant The Emotional Life of Postmodern Film" already implies—there is something inherently glossy about what we might call the phenomenological texture of postmodernism.[18] The question of just what kind of critical weight we should assign this "The Emotional Life of Postmodern Film," of course, is formidable enough.[19] Yet postmodern theory's recurrent reliance on the figure of the glossy, gleaming surface is matched by its repeated recourse to a series of variants on the "rough" surface—from the "moment of rupture" that, for Joseph P. Natoli and Linda Hutcheon, "mark[s] the birth of postmodernity," to Jameson's "fragmentation" of subjectivity and cultural forms, and from Roland Barthes' "*punctum*" to Baudrillard's "contusions, scars, mutilations and wounds."[20] Wounds, ruptures, breaks and fragments: while varying in function and in kind, these figures are united by their status as points at which a uniform plane is shattered or disturbed.

As my reading of *Crash* will show, the makeshift opposition glossy/rough that runs through postmodern theory is rich with phenomenological and conceptual possibilities. What needs to be noted here, however is that postmodern theory has not only failed to tap into these possibilities, it has tended to restore this opposition to the conceptual embrace of the more conventional opposition surface/depth, by asking the glossy to *figure* depthlessness, and the rough to *figure* depth. It is this former gesture, for example, that catalyzes the glossy surface's longstanding lamination to the commodity—a figure that functions bilaterally as both source and symbol of postmodern superficiality. For Jameson, "the cult of the glossy image" constitutes "the ultimate form of the consumption of streamlined commodities"; Angela McRobbie speaks of "the glossy objects provided ... by consumer capitalism"; while Laura Mulvey refers to "the shiny, glossy surface fascination of the screen ... [which masks] the process of production concealed behind it."[21] Though Baudrillard's reference to the way commodity culture caters to our "craving for the antique ... the rustic, the artisanal, the handmade" reminds us that the actual commodity is quite as often rough as it is glossy, the commodity's readiest metonym remains the "seductive sheen" of a burnished metal, a lacquered wood or a high-gloss plastic.[22] Consistently correlating the glossy surface with the superficiality of the commodity, postmodern theory has quite as consistently correlated the rough surface with hermeneutic depth. From Jacques Derrida's "wound," to Baudrillard's "fragment" and Jameson's professed yearning for "something both more ugly and less proficient or expert, more home-made and awkward," the rough surface seems the recognized conceptual currency for transacting claims about deep social or linguistic structures—whether *différance*, simulation, or social relations.[23] Phenomenologically, of course, there is an intuitive sense to this differential

84    *Fascination*

coding of the glossy and the rough. Where the rough surface accentuates the stubborn materiality of the object in a way that seems to promise untapped depths, the glossy surface spotlights its visual qualities in a way that seems to transfigure it into a medium, a reflective device, a mirror, a mirage or, as Judith Brown puts it, "into a sparkling play of light."[24] Yet we needn't be, as Sedgwick might put it, very "long out of theory-kindergarten" to pick up on the fact that, despite these opposing phenomenological effects and semiotic framings, both the rough and the smooth *are simply kinds of surface*.[25] Nor would it tax any scholar's critical faculties too far to observe that those critics seeking to resurrect, in the figure of the rough, a kind of quasi- or substitute depth are the same critics who have elsewhere expended considerable theoretical energy in problematizing depth hermeneutics. Rather than concede the extent to which texture's glossy, grainy particularity imperils conventional conceptions of hermeneutics and emotion, postmodern theorists prefer to run directly against the grain of their hermeneutic convictions by configuring the "rough" surface as the site of hermeneutic depth, while dismissing the "glossy" surface as the site of an hermeneutic deficiency.[26]

Of greatest significance for our argument here, however, is the extent to which this consensus on the relation between texture and hermeneutics mandates a corresponding consensus on the relation between texture and emotion. Fully licensed by the snug cultural fit between emotion and depth, postmodern theorists routinely, even reflexively, marry the rough surface to genuine emotion, and the glossy surface to emotional inauthenticity. It is this schema, for example, that informs Barthes' panegyric to the photographic *punctum*, which, in a miracle of metaphorical efficiency, places the rough, "punctured" surface of the photograph, and the state of being moved by that photograph, under the semiotic umbrella of one word.[27] This same schema subtends Baudrillard's fetishization of the "gash mark, [the] bruise, [the] scar" as a "vehement answer" to emotion's disappearance from postmodern life.[28] In both cases, the rough, wounded or punctured surface is yoked to the kind of emotional directness and dynamism that Philip Fisher ascribes to Western literature's "vehement passions," the classic emotions of grief, rage, fear and disgust whose form has provided the blueprint for a long-dominant cognitive-appraisal model of emotion.[29]

Indeed, if this schema has seen some postmodern critics claim the rough surface for intense, direct and dynamic emotion, it has equally seen critics like Jameson and David Harvey stake out the glossy surface for a certain dubious anti-emotion: fascination. Long condemned as a "zombie emotion", fascination diverges on a number of counts from the norms of cognitive-appraisal theory.[30] Whereas the cognitive-appraisal paradigm takes "the state of being, in one way or another, moved" as one of emotion's necessary conditions, *Collins English Dictionary* defines the verb to fascinate as "to render motionless, as with a fixed stare or by arousing terror or awe"; whereas the cognitive-appraisal paradigm represents emotion as an effect of hermeneutic judgment, fascination connotes a certain suspension of judgment, as its origin

Fascination  85

in "from the Latin *fascinare*, meaning to bewitch or enchant" suggests.[31] And it is fascination's consequent status as a byword for fake, inauthentic or "zombie emotion" that Jameson exploits in his dystopian evocation of postmodernism's "mesmerizing new aesthetic mode."[32] "Endow[ing] present reality and the openness of present history with the spell and distance of a glossy mirage," nostalgia's capacity to "mesmerize" or fascinate is predicated, in Jameson's postmodern imaginary, on the twin deceptions—both natural and supernatural—of "distance" and a "spell," deceptions whose tropological insignia is the figure of the "glossy mirage."[33] Harvey draws on a similar tradition in his argument that postmodernism's "evident fascination with ... reflecting glass surfaces" effectively "draw[s] a veil over real geography through [the] construction of images and reconstructions, costume dramas, staged ethnic festivals, etc."[34] Like Jameson before him, Harvey condemns fascination as a fake or apparitional emotion whose genesis lies in the glossy obfuscation of a "real geography." In postmodern theory, it seems, whereas the rough surface delivers genuine emotion, the glossy surface promotes only fascination's misleading—and ultimately deadening—emotional special effects.

Somewhat ironically, then, given its self-proclaimed theoretical radicalism, postmodern theory has given short conceptual shift to texture's implicit injunction that we reassess our assumptions about postmodernism and emotion. From Baudrillard to Barthes to Jameson, postmodern critics have repeatedly sought to press the rough and the glossy into the service of more traditional hermeneutic and emotional paradigms—condemning the emotional deficits of a glossy surface dismissed as depthless while celebrating the emotional bounty of a rough surface masquerading as modernist depth. In the effort, however, to enfold the rough/glossy binary into a more familiar depth/surface=emotion/emotionless framework, the term "fascination" sticks out—its protean semiotic possibilities resonating beyond its ambit as an emblem of emotional lack. Its mesmerized origins at odds with the interpretative judgments so central to cognitive-appraisal models of emotion, and its deadening, spellbinding effects at odds with the physical changes that are meant to accompany cognitive-appraisal, fascination will nevertheless become a mainstay of this chapter's efforts to reconcile emotion with postmodernism's signature superficiality. Returning to the film text with which this chapter opened, I will argue that while fascination clearly diverges from conventional cognitive-appraisal models of emotion, *Crash* not only provides persuasive evidence for fascination's status as an emotion but limns its paradoxical affinity with the same glossy surface that boilerplate models of postmodern aesthetics suggest should rule out emotion altogether.

Fascination's credentials as an emotion in *Crash* are not, at first sight, very promising. Consider, for example, the film's opening scene, a thematic and visual set piece in which the crane-mounted camera makes a clinical inventory of the contents of an airplane hangar—the glossy, phallic noses, gleaming floats and streamlined fuselages of a series of light aircraft—before fastening at last on the fascinated face of its female protagonist, Catherine.

86  Fascination

From a conventional cognitive-appraisal perspective, this cut should inaugurate the film's shift in focus from the spectacular protocols of the establishing shot to the narrative protocols of character development, from inanimate backdrop to the "animation" or "movement" that is the most legible physical signature of this model of emotion. Yet far from exemplifying the dynamism often attributed to emotion, Catherine's fascination with the glossy veneer of the aircraft over which she leans seems to freeze and immobilize her. In keeping with the dictionary definition that frames the verb *to fascinate* as "to render motionless, with a fixed stare or by arousing terror or awe," Catherine's eyes are glazed and her face an "expressionless static countenance" as, confronted with the "willed erasure of ... history" that marks the planes' uniform, mass-manufactured finish, she leans robotically over the cigar-shaped nose of the plane and places her breast against the cold, metallic surface.[35] Indeed, the stultifying power of fascination quickly finds dramatic and narrative expression with the arrival of a male figure, whose entry into the frame, and then into Catherine, is greeted with indifference not only by his lover, whose attention remains riveted by the plane's glossy, pearlescent surface, but also by the film itself. Restricting the lover's portrayal to a pair of polished business shoes and a grasping, seemingly disembodied hand, the camera maintains an exclusive focus on the real liaison taking place between Catherine and the nose of the plane, resulting in an idiosyncratic two-shot that conflates the strangely dehumanizing state of fascination with the literally inhuman prop that is its object. So compelling is this conflation, in fact, that critics of the film have tended to attribute the plane's textural properties to Catherine herself, extolling her "mirror-smooth surface," her "lacquered insentient beauty," and even her "glossy features."[36]

*Figure 2.4* Catherine's fascination with the gleaming surface.

Fascination    87

Yet Catherine's peculiar paralysis does not necessarily push fascination outside the purview of emotion. While the physical effects of emotion are typically tagged as vigorous and dynamic, there's nothing to say these physical effects can't operate in an exclusively narcotic, negative register. Indeed, if submitting to a seeming stranger's groping and fingering could be expected to prompt any sentient subject to some kind of reaction, erotic or otherwise, Catherine's silent stupefaction may be read as a token not of a lack of responsiveness to her partner but of the strength of her responsiveness to the glossy surface—prefiguring both Vaughan's paralysis before the heavily lacquered and period-perfect Porsche he will use to recreate James Dean's fatal collision, and James's fugue before the glossy silver coupe at the center of a celebrated set piece at a Mercedes-Benz showroom. Fascination, that is, may be an emotion in which we are moved, paradoxically, to *stop* moving. This near-narcoleptic model of fascination is corroborated in the work of psychologist Silvan S. Tomkins, who correlates the way we are "passively caught" by fascination to "a cessation of breathing." [37] While substituting a "cessation" of breath for the quickening of breath we traditionally associate with emotion, fascination's physiological effects are no less physiologically consequential—which is to say, no less emotional—for that.

Yet *Crash*'s opening scene proposes an answer to the taxonomical problems opened up not only by fascination's frosty immobility, but by its oddly depthless object. "Defiantly or even invisibly block[ing] or refus[ing]" all "information about how, substantively, historically, materially, it came into being," the plane's silken, mass-produced surface is smugly resistant to the hermeneutic judgment that sustains conventional cognitive-appraisal models of emotion—meaning that while fascination's physical paradoxes might be intelligible, its cognitive operation remains opaque.[38] Closer scrutiny of the scene, however, reminds us that this tactile and hermeneutic lack co-exists with a certain glistening visual exuberance. Granting little besides its glacial cool to Catherine' touch, the glossy surface is far more generous in its affordances to her gaze, and the forensic intensity with which she traces the surface's subtle, shifting glow rivals the "predatory glide" with which cinematographer Peter Suchitsky's steadicam close-up ogles Unger herself.[39] Cycling endlessly between hand and eye, between a lack of tactile stimulation and an excess of visual stimulation, Catherine may be unable to move, but she also cannot stop looking, caught in an visio-tactile game-loop that Jameson encapsulates in his evocation of the "gilt" postmodern surface's dual power at once to "seal[] the surface ... and yet continue[] to glint at us."[40]

A clue as to the cognitive machinery powering this strange amalgam of motor diminution and ocular animation is unexpectedly furnished by the famous passage in *Postmodernism* that Jameson devotes to an analysis of Philip Johnson's Bonaventure Hotel in downtown Los Angeles—a passage

88    *Fascination*

preoccupied, like *Crash* itself, by the luster of the glossy surface. According to Jameson, the building's mirror-glass exterior

> repels the city outside, a repulsion for which we have analogies in those reflector sunglasses which make it impossible for your interlocutor to see your own eyes and thereby achieve a certain aggressivity and power over the Other. In a similar way, the glass skin achieves a peculiar and placeless dissociation of the Bonaventure from its neighbourhood; it is not even an exterior, inasmuch as when you seek to look at the hotel's outer walls you cannot see the hotel itself but only the distorted images of everything that surrounds it.[41]

What is most immediately apparent about the passage is a certain contradiction between what it says and what it does. For where at the constative level of the utterance Jameson bemoans the surface's obstinate resistance to any kind of epistemic or emotional investment, these claims are belied at the performative level by the utterance's sheer duration, which bespeaks a persistent, affectively charged diagnostic effort spurred on, rather than put off, by the surface's mirrory gloss. Yet if Jameson's own manifest fascination with the building's "great glass skin" appears, initially, as a moment of odd, untheorized excess, closer attention allows us to reconceive the passage as a whole as a coherent bid to position this tension between enchantment and disengagement as the very essence of fascination itself. The opening sentence of the extract is exemplary here. While its first half seems intent on delivering us to the purely negative opinion that the glossy surface resists both understanding and engagement, describing the way the glass "repels the city outside" and "makes it impossible to see" what is going on within, the tail end of the sentence takes an unexpected turn, with the contention that, "repulsion" aside, the glossy surface nevertheless "achieve[s] certain ... *power over the Other*."[42] Inherent in this shift is not just a modification but a wholesale transfiguration of the character of the glossy surface being described. For the characteristics that give one "power over" something or someone seem incompatible with the characteristics that "repel" something or someone: in many dictionary definitions, to have "power over" something is to enthrall or to captivate. While the first part of the sentence, then, frames the glossy surface as a mechanism of repulsion, the second frames it as an object of attraction and allure.

The critical stakes of this shift become clearer when we observe that the repelled subject and the magnetized subject are actually semantically distinct. Insisting that while "reflector sunglasses ... make it impossible for *your interlocutor* to see your own eyes," they nevertheless "achieve a certain ... power over *the Other*," Jameson fastidiously adjudicates between an "interlocutor" whose gaze is short-circuited by the sheen of "reflector sunglasses," and an "Other" whose gaze is enthralled.[43] And the passage goes on to reinforce this differential distribution of feeling between subject

Fascination   89

and other through its binary characterization of the nature of the surface. While initially shown "repel[ling] the city outside," the "glass skin" is later shown absorbing and even digesting its surroundings, "inasmuch as when you seek to look at the hotel's outer walls, you cannot see the hotel itself but only the distorted images of everything that surrounds it." Sizing up these observations, it would appear that while the glossy surface yields nothing to the subject directly, its mirrory enshrinement of the "distorted images of everything that surrounds it" evokes the gleaming specter of an "Other" whose gaze is less repelled than entranced by what it sees, less confused than enlightened. And it is on this specter, I suggest, that fascination depends. Just as, for Slavoj Zizek, "the real object of [our postmodern] fascination [with film-*noir*] is not the displayed scene but the gaze of the naïve other, absorbed, enchanted by it," so, what fascinates us in the glossy surface is less the surface itself than its scintillating promise that for some other, somewhere, it yields real meaning and emotion.[44] Calling to mind both Jacques Lacan's theory of the desire of the other, and René Girard's theory of mimetic desire, fascination is a triangulated emotion that recuperates the emotion foreclosed by the failure of hermeneutic depth as an infinitely deferred and constantly beckoning possibility.[45] Indeed, in keeping with Cheng's insistence that "Shine mobilizes the interstitiality between sight and feeling, visuality and textuality," fascination's triangulations are played out across a dialectic of sight and touch: the glossy surface's *visual* sheen captivates the viewer with the possibility that, for some other, it offers an emotion more immediate and more intense than the glossy surface's *tactile and hermeneutic* lack might suggest.[46] At stake in this account of fascination is not simply the claim that the judgment animating the emotion is embedded in existing social-cultural regimes, a claim readily reconcilable with recent iterations of the cognitive-appraisal paradigm eager to acknowledge the cultural and linguistic embeddedness of individual judgments. What is at stake, rather, is the sense that the emotion emerges in the *absence* of any individual judgment of its ostensible object, as the encounter with the initial opacity and repellant chilliness of reflective surfaces is synthesized into fascination through the projection of a knowing, fascinated other. Perfectly calibrated to the glossy surface, this triangulated model of the emotion is reflected in the ease with which the definition of *fascination* moves from denoting a generalized intransitive condition ("the state of being fascinated") to indexing a particular transitive power ("the state of being fascinating"). What fascinates, it seems, is always fascination itself.[47]

The significance of this shimmering, spectral other in sustaining fascination is efficiently borne out in the final tableau of *Crash*'s opening sexual triptych—a scene that, in transporting Catherine from the ceaseless solicitations of public space to the supposed sanctuary of her and James's private dwelling, only *appears* to close down fascination's triangulated logic. Beginning with a prolonged close-up shot of James's eyes that casts him as the source of a presiding gaze, the scene deftly transfigures marital dyad

## 90 Fascination

into perverse triad by depicting his disquisition into the details of his wife's earlier sexual encounter:

> JAMES: Where were you?
> CATHERINE: In the airplane hangar.
> JAMES: Did you come?
> CATHERINE: No.

Retrofitting the sexual scenario in the aircraft hangar as a performance stage-directed by and aimed at James, the scene casts James himself as an other whose putative power to take direct sexual pleasure in the shellacked forepart of a light aircraft mediates Catherine's own indirect fascination with that surface. Yet this mediation cuts both ways. While the camera keeps its gaze trained steadily on James, the inquiry shifts its focus from wife to husband, with Catherine's own questioning—"what about your camera girl?"—eliciting James's confession that, in his own extra-marital encounter, he too had failed to "come." As Catherine's cryptic consolation "maybe the next one, darling, maybe the next one" echoes on the sound track, a long-awaited reverse shot reveals Catherine from James's point of view—a polished, skirt-suited centerfold whose semblance of obliviousness to her husband, as she leans seductively, her back to him, against the balcony of their apartment, is suspended only when she lifts her skirt to expose the cleft of one perfectly toned, satiny buttock. Endowing her with precisely the "mirror-smooth surface" necessary to cast her as an object of fascination for James, her peculiar posture prompts him to approach Catherine and enter her from behind, as the camera drifts tactfully over her shoulder and into a twilit vista of the asphalt flyover below.[48] If James mediates Catherine's fascination, then, Catherine, in turn, mediates James's. In a series of emotional favors that Iain Sinclair limns as performances "enacted by one partner and directed by the other," each member of the couple contrives to spur the other's ability to invest affectively in the chrome-plated world around them by occupying the position of an other who truly, intensely feels.[49] In this sense, Catherine's rather cheerless promise, "maybe the next one, darling, maybe the next one," sounds throughout the film's glistening urban interiors as a pledge peculiarly apposite not just to fascination's status as an eerily triangulated emotion, but also to the film's no less triangulated narrative trajectory, which seems to multiple continuously into new couplings and new permutations of mimetic desire. If, superficially, this is a film about characters obsessed with car crashes, fascination's pivotal role in the text ensures that, structurally, it is a film actuated by the logic of influence, insistently testing the limits of its characters' fanatical submission to the sway of the other.

While often dismissed as frigidly emotion-free, then, postmodernism's signature glossy surfaces are graced by a complex textural grammar that is curiously congenial to emotion. The object of repeated and futile bids on the part of prominent postmodern theorists to claim its grain and gloss for more conventional depth-oriented models of emotion and hermeneutics, texture's unique emotional landscape confounds the cartological limits of the cognitive-appraisal program. Whereas cognitive-appraisal theory traces emotion to hermeneutic interpretation, fascination entails an hermeneutic failure that is only latterly transfigured into feeling through the intercession of a profoundly insightful, intensely feeling "other"; whereas cognitive-appraisal theory identifies emotion with some form of physiological "animation" or arousal, fascination traffics in the physiological suspension of stilled breath and interrupted movement.[50] The implications of these observations for my larger argument about emotion's value to feeling theory lie in their ability to broker a model of emotion that shares many of the traits often ascribed exclusively to affect. In large part, affect's prominence in feeling theory rests on the insights affect yields into the ways we cathect to social and political regimes at levels below conscious awareness, such that our political attachments "frequently diverge from our reasoning selves."[51] Emotion, meanwhile, is dismissed as an all-too-knowable and stodgily subjective phenomenon: as affect "reduced" through its links to the subject, and as affect "tamed" through its association with forms of ratiocination, it is routinely assumed to have less value for understanding what Lauren Berlant calls the non-rationality "at the heart of the political."[52] What *Crash* offers to feeling theory, however, is the spectacle of an emotion that is itself marked by a certain non-rationality. While felt and registered by a subject, fascination is never owned or mastered by her; while involving judgment, this judgment pivots not around its ostensible object, but around the purely hypothetical phantom of a glimmering, absent other.

In what follows, I seek to widen the reach of this texture-oriented, triangulated model of emotion in postmodern aesthetics by deconstructing our stock account of the "vehement passions" that are ordinarily opposed to fascination. For the majority of the film's critics, *Crash* tells story of a couple whose emotional exhaustion in the face of a gleamingly commodified postmodern world sees them seek out the alternative forms of emotion proffered and embodied by the charismatic Vaughan, and its narrative charts a shift from an emotional lack exemplified by the stiff, triangulated fascination of the glossy surface, avatar of postmodernism superficiality, to an emotional fullness exemplified by the highly animated, ostensibly untriangulated emotions of the rough or broken surface, emblem of modernist depth. Seamlessly recapitulating postmodern theory, this reading contrasts a triangulated, "zombie" fascination, on the one hand, to a direct, "vehement" emotion on the other. Yet doubling down in our attention to *Crash*'s formal economy discloses the subtle but insistent pressure the film puts on this opposition. As I will demonstrate, while clearly idiosyncratic in both its cognitive structure and its bodily effects, fascination provides a paradigm for all the emotions in *Crash*, which can be shown to share its spectral, triangulated quality. In this sense, *Crash* becomes less a case study in the emotional

## 92 *Fascination*

atrophy of the postmodern surface, than a meditation on the singular, idiosyncratic emotional formations that cluster around both the surface's gloss and its grain. Whereas Massumi's celebration of affect dismisses emotion as an "old surprise to which we have become more or less accustomed," then, *Crash*'s peculiarly postmodern textural universe yields an eccentric and surprisingly social model of emotion that may prove invaluable to those of us working on feeling.[53]

## III

Superficially, of course, *Crash*'s visual economy seems only to heighten the opposition between a zombie-like, triangulated fascination and the vigorous, supposedly more direct emotions attaching to the jagged, coarse or craggy surface. If the film's extended opening sequence is dominated by the hypnotic fascination of the glossy surface, it is the repudiation of this strangely ossified emotion that propels the narrative, as the Ballards seek to locate in crushed metal, shattered glass, and scarred human flesh the kind of emotional immediacy and animation that fascination famously lacks. The Ballards' investment in this "battered and broken body" finds clearest expression in a scene that locates James on the sunny balcony of the apartment after the previous scene's midnight rendezvous with Vaughan.[54] James's afternoon reverie is interrupted by his wife's slightly narcotized whisper in his ear: "my car." A cut to the garage shows Catherine crouching next to her silver convertible, a visible dent blighting the otherwise perfectly streamlined panels of its right side. Her question to James—"Could it have been deliberate?"—is immediately answered by the audience, who can draw on its memory of Vaughan's repeated ramming of the side of James's car in the previous scene to infer that this, too, was Vaughan's doing. James, however, chooses to bypass the workings of psychological deduction, and to rely, instead, on direct textural experience: pitting the personalized signature of the dent against the depersonalized anonymity of the mass-produced vehicle, he gets his own answer—"it was Vaughan"—by running his hand directly over its uneven surface (fig. 2.5). What follows, in fact, implies that in addition to its hermeneutic bounty, the simulacral depth of the crumpled surface provides a certain emotional premium: a cut to a close-up of James's face seems to radiate just the kind of vigorous, direct, untriangulated emotion that the glossy surfaces of the opening scenes militate so strongly against, bearing out Botting and Wilson's suggestion that *Crash* locates in "the battered and broken body ... the last remnant of a human erotic imaginary in the face of a fully automated form of desire."[55]

Indeed, the connection implied here between rough texture and strong emotion is consolidated during James and Vaughan's first one-on-one sexual encounter, the dramatic and sexual climax of which takes place not in Koteas and Spader's rather self-conscious back-seat make-out session but in the moment of vehicular collision that caps it off. In a spatial and temporal

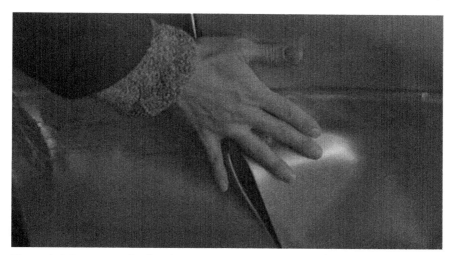

*Figure 2.5* James runs his hand over his wife's dented side panel.

hiatus clearly contrived to circumvent the representation of the homosexual sex act, the film's unusually explicit homosexual action suddenly gives way to a discreet cutaway pan along a wall, before cutting once more to the image of James emerging from Vaughan's Lincoln (the owner of the car is nowhere to be seen). After wandering a short distance to a conveniently placed scrap metal yard, James gets into a waiting totalled car; as if on cue, the Lincoln, now occupied by a maniacally grimacing Vaughan, appears from around the corner and rams into James's car repeatedly, as James collapses orgasmically against the dashboard, eyes closed. Two things become apparent here. First, that whereas the glossy surface transforms direct contact into distance and mediation, the rough surface of the outside of the car seems magically to transform distance—James is not, after all, being directly touched—into a kind of deep-bodied, visceral contact. Second, with James's closed eyes we are led to believe that whereas fascination is mediated by the visual, a sense dependent on distance, the emotion generated by the rough surface bypasses the visual, heralding a more direct knowledge of the object and a more intense, more "real" emotional experience predicated on the more primal moment embodied by sensation.[56] As William Beard describes it, *Crash* shows the body being directly "*imprinted* with the hard edges and shapes of the car in the form of wounds," where the notion of imprinting manages to collapse the rough surface, a depth model of signification and the emotional overtones of psychological "imprinting," into one highly efficient figure.[57]

Given the film's apparent allegiance to postmodern theory's reactionary hermeneutic and emotional grammar, then, it seems only logical that both scholarly and journalistic responses to *Crash* should read like (differently inflected) facsimiles of postmodern orthodoxy. Among the film's journalistic

## 94  *Fascination*

detractors, of course, the emphasis falls on the "glossy and neutralized" commodities that furnish *Crash*'s bravura opening sequences, and sees them second Jameson in condemning the glossy surface's impoverished hermeneutic lexicon as a betrayal of emotional depth.[58] Deeming the film "annoyingly superficial," Gary Johnson, for example, argues that while

> Cronenberg has created a fascinating world in *Crash* ... he never gets beyond the surface allure, the glisten of chrome and the oily glow of human bodies desperately fucking ... Cronenberg doesn't let us inside the characters' pain so that we can understand their obsessions.[59]

Here, Johnson attributes the director's failure to "let us inside the characters" to the distracting "surface allure" of "glistening chrome" and the "oily glow of human bodies"—a "surface allure" that diverts the director's gaze from the deep emotional "pain" that should be his object.[60] Among *Crash*'s mostly academic advocates, by contrast, the emphasis falls on the coarse, fractured surfaces that rise to prominence later in the film. Ventriloquizing Barthes and Baudrillard's visionary odes to the hermeneutic and emotional profundity of the "punctum" and the "gash," this critical chorus ranges from Botting and Wilson's suggestion that, "from being a mechanical failure of diminishing returns, sex is transformed by the crash and becomes, again, a liberating experience," to Beard's contention that "the revitalization of the James-Catherine relationship" is "founded ... on the abjection of crashes and crash-like injuries."[61] Yet while opposite in their judgment of the film and divergent in their professional agendas, the film's journalistic and academic scholars are nevertheless identical in their capitulation to postmodern theory's hermeneutic and emotional credo.

But there are fractures in this seemingly immaculate critical carapace. For if the critical calculus that cinches the textural opposition glossy/rough to the hermeneutic opposition surface/depth effectively echoes postmodern edict, it also seems to do little more than transcribe into scholarly or journalistic terminology the sentiments of *Crash*'s characters. When Botting and Wilson observe that *Crash* locates in "the battered and broken body ... the last remnant of a human erotic imaginary in the face of a fully automated form of desire," the reader is immediately reminded of Vaughan's proclamation—to Ballard, as the two men speed through the night in the derelict, open-topped Lincoln—that "the car crash is a fertilizing rather than a destructive event, mediating the sexuality of those who have died with an intensity that's impossible in any other form."[62] In fully identifying the film's rhetoric with that of its characters, however, Botting and Wilson leave no space for narrational irony, internal self-difference or simple performative contradiction—no space, that is, for the formal "wounds," "*puncta*" or "fragments" that complement the literal rough surfaces that they reify. As this suggests, the widely sanctioned scholarly reading of the film's textural, hermeneutic and emotional logic may be rent by internal contradictions.

Fascination   95

The analysis of these contradictions, in turn, may help us deconstruct the textural, hermeneutic and emotional logic of the postmodern theoretical doctrine to which *Crash*'s scholarly commentators appear to subscribe. To exploit these points of contradiction, however, it is necessary to refocus our critical attention from narrative and character, the level at which texture is described and portrayed, to formal rhetoric, the level at which texture is experienced.

On first blush, *Crash*'s unique cinematic labor seems to corroborate critical dogma on the relation between texture and hermeneutics through a meticulously coordinated series of alignments between the formal and representational registers. Perhaps the most telling example of this tendency is the film's insistent cross-implication of the glossy surface and the tracking shot—a formal device which, within the oft-maligned yet abidingly powerful explanatory paradigm of classic film theories of suture, impedes emotional engagement with the story-world by converting the camera from a neutral, transparent observer of the scene into an ostentatious "accomplice" or "intruder," effectively arresting the spectator's gaze on the surface of the image.[63] In relying on the "precise silent smoothness" of cinematographer Peter Suschitzky's virtuoso tracking shots as the vehicle for its satin-smooth veneers, then, *Crash* bears out and authenticates our received ideas about the glossy surface at the level of form, transforming critical axioms about the glossy surface's superficiality or depthlessness into formal truths.[64] As the camera dollies slowly into the Ballards' bedroom to disclose the couple copulating quietly against the backdrop of their gleaming bedroom set, for example, the different alienation effects we associate with the extended, unattributed tracking shot on the one hand and the subtle glimmer of the postmodern consumer fetish on the other are consubstantialized. The implication is that the glossy surface, like the "glossy" shot, is somehow resistant to deep emotional investment.

Insistently identifying the glossy surface with a formal gambit that holds the spectator hostage on the surface of the image, *Crash* no less insistently associates the roughened, fractured surface to a formal device celebrated for its capacity to suture the viewer into a spatially and psychologically rounded world: the "cut" of filmic montage. In keeping with the cool, clinical visual style of the film up to this point, the film's first collision sequence opens with a prolonged pan along the rain-slicked hood of James's car before cutting to an equally sustained shot of James inside it. Yet as James's loss of control of the car propels him inexorably toward the scene's closing tableau of cut glass stalactites, wounded flesh and tarnished metal, we transition suddenly to a series of cross-cuts between exterior action shots of the car sliding over the wet road, and interior over-the-shoulder shots of James attempting to regain control of the wheel. Indeed, this fusion of the "cut" of filmic montage to the rough, broken surface is further secured at a figurative level, in an unusual car-interior view of the crash that captures the exact moment at which the body from the car opposite penetrates James's windscreen. For

96   *Fascination*

the propulsive, plummeting blur of flesh and fabric so completely obscures the view from the camera that the subsequent cut to a view outside the car reads as a sign that the body had pierced not just the glass of the windshield but the surface of the lens. The implication here is that the car crash had licensed so raw and indexical a connection to the object that the camera had been forced to seek relief in the inviolable distance of an exterior shot. In supposed synch with the provisions of postmodern theory, then, *Crash* not only endows its glossy surfaces with the patina of superficiality that conventionally attaches to the tracking shot, but bestows upon its rough, broken surfaces the semblance of depth and immediacy that conventionally attaches to the cut. If the glossy surface ostentatiously remains just that—a surface—the rough surface is imagined as affording a range of immediate emotional experiences that are not just unmediated by the other, but unmediated by (cinematic) language itself.

Yet unsurprisingly, perhaps, for a director identified not with cinematic and theoretical orthodoxy but with "censorial apprehension and retribution," Cronenberg ultimately uses *Crash*'s fastidious formal and thematic eco-system to promote a subtle critique of postmodern theory's proclamations on texture, emotion and hermeneutics.[65] As Marc Jancovich has shown in his careful re-reading of New Critical rhetoric, New Critical paeans to the perfect confluence of form and content tend to rely on a rubric of "integrity" and "wholeness" whose capacity to connote a certain glossy luster holds even where both the form and the content at issue are, to quote Vaughan, as "ragged and dirty" as it they are in *Crash*'s many collision scenes.[66] In all too faithfully synchronizing its representational and formal registers—that is, in trying to validate through a series of complementary cuts the hermeneutic and emotional profundity of, say, Vaughan's trademark facial scarring—*Crash* not only effectively forecloses the "fragments," "puncta" and "wounds" associated with direct or animated emotion, but transfigures itself into a flawless, shimmering object of fascination. Even as its characters extol the epistemic and emotional value of broken skin, torn metal and shattered glass, then, *Crash* itself invites critical reflection on its glamorous celluloid polish. Almost invariably yielding some version of the observation that "for all of its macabre content, Cronenberg's film is a glossy affair, his car crashes varnished in celluloid," or that "Cronenberg's *Crash* aspires to a kind of fleshy, abject raggedness, but never quite makes it," reviews of the film were characterized less by the intense, quasi-Deleuzian excitement anticipated by the film's radical scholarly critics, than by a certain "grim fascination."[67] As a text, then, *Crash* seems to constitute the same glossy, seamless postmodern commodity that its characters devote their screen-time to fracturing, shattering or generally roughing up.

But while the film's perverse predilection for New Critical form precludes the vigorous, "direct" emotions fetishized by Vaughan and his associates, not every moment in the film displays so decisive a mating of form and content—and nor, for that matter, is every review so deficient in animated, vehement emotion. The scene in the hospital immediately after James's first accident is exemplary here. While the scene's *mise-en-scene* presents a plethora of rough, abrasive surfaces, from torn flesh, to florid bruising and ladder-like stitching, its cinematography is characterized by the smooth, uniform movement of the panning shot, as the camera glides slowly up the length of James's mutilated body. For many critics, of course, this hyphenation of "rough" surface and "glossy" form significantly compromises the raw, bloody force of its characters' injuries. According to Beard, for example, as

> Cronenberg's camera tracks over and cuts among these injuries with utter serenity ... it requires every ounce of abjection emanating from James's wounds to prevent these massive bruises and contusions from being assimilated into the overpoweringly calm grey and violet design scheme.[68]

Yet if, for Beard, the scene's formal "serenity" substantially weakens the emotional clout of the rough surface, it is, oddly enough, precisely this scene and scenes like it that provoked the most intense emotion from critics—a fact nowhere more evident than in Beard's own testimony. At the constative level, the passage is a scathing jeremiad against the way the glossy "serenity" of Cronenberg's tracking shots attenuates the emotional impact of its rough content. At the performative level, however, Beard's vivid inventory of "injuries ... wounds ... massive bruises and contusions" actually manifests the emotional impact whose absence it bemoans. An analogous performative contradiction underlies an influential article on the film by Barbara Creed, whose passionate parataxis of "sheaths of metal, shards of glass, ripped leather upholstery, blood glistening on a steering wheel, two crash survivors copulating in a car, a man fucking a wound in the leg of a female crash victim, repeated episodes of anal sex" segues irrationally into the reproof that "*Crash* is oddly and unexpectedly detached." [69] While both Beard and Creed condemn the gap between rough content and glossy form on the basis that it undercuts animated, dynamic emotion, then, the vehemence of their responses to this gap speaks in the unmistakable tongue of the emotion whose foreclosure they deplore.

Yet if Beard and Creed's reviews seem to exemplify the kind of dynamic, direct response forecast by critics like Botting and Wilson, the peculiar provenance of that response forces us to reassess its structural and cognitive coordinates. For in both cases, the catalyst is not the rough surface itself, but the suspicion that the putative emotional power of that rough surface is being blunted by the putative emotional deficiency of the film's glossy form. Beard's response to "the abjection emanating from James's wounds," for example, is triangulated through his conviction that the "utter serenity" of Suschitzky's camerawork threatens to absorb them into "the overpoweringly calm grey and violet design scheme," while Creed's response to the film's "sheaths of metal, shards of glass, ripped leather upholstery" depends on what she reads as the cinematography's incongruous "detach[ment]." In both cases, the critic's emotionally exorbitant response to the film's jagged and torn surfaces rests on his or her belief that Crash's glossy formal strategies are emotionally inadequate to a mise-en-scene littered with "shards of glass" and "ripped leather upholstery." This juxtaposition of rough image and glossy form, that is, produces a second-level filmic gap or fracture that is actually capable of communicating the rough to the audience, but only in and through the mediation of the glossy, recalling Stanley Corngold's insistence that literary feeling arises precisely from "the conflict between what sentences say and what they do, between the propositional meaning and the rhetorical effects … such tensions are concentrated to elicit new forms of feeling."[70] Indeed, this logic is just as apparent at the level of the individual image itself as it is in the dialectic between image and form. The vulva-like scar that runs along the back of Gabrielle's thigh, for example, acquires its aura of abjection through its proximity to the sheen of her patent leather and chrome accessories; James's leg wounds seem all the messier for their juxtaposition with the gleaming metallic leg brace in which they are enclosed. Numerous critics have championed the film's rough, broken or punctured surfaces as incitements to direct, unmediated emotion. Yet to the extent that our response to James's grisly flesh wounds depends on their delivery through a series of cool, polished tracking shots that are ostensibly unable to do them justice, that response is patently no less mediated than the fascination fomented by, say, the dull metallic glow of Crash's fluorescent-blue lighting on a rain-slicked street.

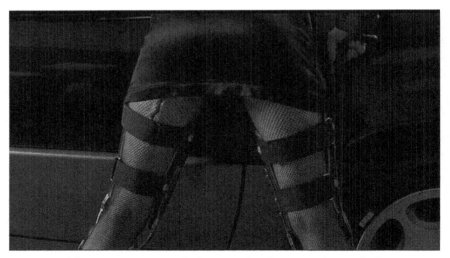

*Figure 2.6* The scar comes into relief against the gleaming side panel of a car.

*Fascination* 99

If fascination and the more recognizably "vehement" passions are homologous in their structure, however, they clearly carry very different semiotic burdens. Whereas the fascination of the glossy surface is actuated by the feeling that someone is experiencing the emotion that I lack, the more vehement emotions of the rough surface are fueled by the feeling that someone is lacking the real, direct emotion that I experience. While both the rough and the glossy, then, participate in emotion's triangulated structure, fascination conceives the other as the hidden repository of real emotion, whereas the vehement passions conceive the other as the graveyard of emotional lack. This opposition is best exemplified by the different conceptualizations of "traffic" with which the two emotional categories are subliminally associated. In their tentative early forays into Vaughan's ghoulish "nexus of car crashes and sex," the protagonists' fascination with cars prompts them to attribute a mysterious purpose to automobiles everywhere.[71] As Helen Remington (Holly Hunter) puts it, much to James's excited recognition, "When I left the hospital I had the strange feeling that all these cars were gathering for some reason I didn't understand ... there seemed to be ten times as much traffic." Yet by the final few minutes of the film, James is moved to remark to Catherine as the couple coast down an empty stretch of freeway, "The traffic! Where is everyone? They've all gone away ..." If the fascination that animated the first section of the film depended on an other charged with a vigorous, empowered sensuality, an other "gathering for some reason I didn't understand," the characters' taste of the raw, animated emotion yielded by the rough surface evokes a deflated, empty other, an other who is, in James's words, "gone away." One of the benefits of this argument, I would suggest, is its capacity to account for the outraged reception of the film by British and U.S. conservative groups, whose efforts to have *Crash* banned otherwise seem oddly anachronistic in light of the relative ubiquity that "perverted acts" and "sexual deviance" enjoyed in mainstream cinema by the mid-1990s.[72] In view of my analysis, however, these censorship campaigns can be traced not to the film's content but to the unsettling disparity between the film's content and its form, between the rough surface and its glossy packaging. After all, this disparity projects a specter that stirs the anxieties of late twentieth century Western conservative movements far more deeply than mere sex perversion itself—namely, the specter of the evacuated, dehumanized, affectless subject who fails to fully register sex perversion's horror.

For many in feeling theory, of course, postmodernism was a panoply of supine, depthless surfaces, resistant, even hostile, to the emotional formations that currently captivate critical and cultural scholarship. Yet as this essay as has shown, the aesthetic and theoretical language that limns postmodernism's flat, depthless surfaces is laden with a vividly textural vocabulary that troubles the stark binary logic through which these surfaces are often read. Many critics—both postmodern and otherwise—have worked to reclaim this idiom of warp and weave for a more familiar conceptual

100    *Fascination*

lexicon by wedding the glossy surface to a model of icy, emotionless superficiality and the rough to a model of emotionally charged depth. Yet as I have shown, neither of these alignments do justice to the specificity of postmodern texture's emotional structure or effect. Attention to the particularities of texture in *Crash*, in fact, makes it clear that rather than merely retreading the emotional logic of the surface/depth opposition, the rough and the glossy have a unique—and uniquely postmodern—emotional syntax of their own. This is not to say that *Crash* is *not* hostile to emotions like fear, grief or pleasure that fall readily into the descriptive ambit of cognitive-appraisal theory. Rather, it is to suggest that *Crash* plays host to a distinctive, borderline species of emotion that should prompt us to reconsider our prevailing paradigms for understanding both emotion as a category of feeling and postmodernism as a now-historical critical and aesthetic apparatus. As Sedgwick has suggested,

> To perceive texture is never only to ask or to know What is it like? nor even just How does *it* impinge on *me*? Textural perception always explores two other questions as well: How did it get that way? and What could I do with it?[73]

Texture, in other words, projects a series of social, discursive and material worlds, and it is through these worlds that texture facilitates feeling. I experience fascination when the glossy surface's hermeneutic and thus emotional bounty magnetizes me with the promise of an other ostensibly possessed of the emotional immediacy I conceive myself as lacking. I feel more direct emotions, conversely, when the coarse, craggy surface's imagined hermeneutic and emotional wealth evokes an other ostensibly lacking the emotional immediacy I conceive myself as possessing.

Revealing the fascinatingly glistening and grainy consistency of a surface often dismissed as an empty, emotionless plane, then, this chapter has advanced this book's effort to elucidate the emotional dimension of the postmodern aesthetic universe. Yet it has also, I hope, contributed to the book's concurrent project, namely its effort to expand the envelope of our thinking about emotion. Recent scholarship on feeling is marked by a strikingly binary view of affect and emotion. Affect is reified as a set of mobile, pre-conscious, organic forces whose analysis can afford us insight not only into how we cathect to political and ideological regimes, but also, conversely, into how we might escape or resist such regimes; emotion, meanwhile, is dismissed as an all-too-knowable and all-too-conservative phenomenon whose reliance on cognitive appraisal means that not only can it not tell us anything about what Berlant calls "political desire" that we don't already know, it also can't possibly help reroute normative forms of this desire. The strange, ghostly emotions that circulate around postmodern texture, however, pose a challenge to this reading of emotion. If their minimally interpretative and personal quality puts them outside the definitional limits of

*Fascination* 101

a non-interpretative "affect," they seem equally inaccessible to definitional capture by familiar, cognitive-appraisal models of "emotion." Indeed, in their slavish subjection to the epistemic and emotional specter of a shadowy, invested "other," whether an other charged with the intense feeling I lack, or an other deprived of what I possess, they seem completely lacking in the kind of subjective mastery and cognitive self-sufficiency that feeling theory has long associated with—and impugned in—our models of emotion. In relation to fascination, perhaps, this argument seems only too easy to make. An emotion that Oliver Harris dubs "an obscure attraction, an experience we can capture only in the process of being captivated," fascination is stamped by very obvious physiological and cognitive idiosyncrasies that have made it something of a bugbear for dominant models of emotion—where it has been admitted to the canon of emotion at all.[74] Yet if this chapter has sought to show that, despite its eerily triangulated quality, fascination *is* an emotion, it has equally sought to show how a range of seemingly more straightforward and conventional emotions might *not* fall within emotion's familiar remit. For the strange, triangulated structure that fascination so vividly and troublingly foregrounds also governs the strong, vehement emotions that *Crash*'s critics have tended to set up in opposition to fascination. Whereas fascination posits an intensely emotive other in order to compensate for its own emotional lack, the vehement emotions posit an emotionally impoverished other in order to bolster their own emotional endowment; both groups of feelings, however, openly surrender the kind of subjective and cognitive autonomy that cognitive-appraisal models conventionally ascribe to emotion. Less entities to be owned or mastered than gleamingly impossible promises, and less "old surprises to which we have become more or less accustomed" than seemingly familiar forms we never fully grasped in the first place, then, the emotions this chapter has examined offer feeling theory a way of understanding our inarticulable, obscure feeling for cultural objects—without reverting to the depersonalized, non-conscious "affect" that has for some time now taken center stage.[75]

## Notes

1. Jesse Fox Mayshark, *Post-Pop Cinema: The Search for Meaning in New American Films* (Westport, CT: Praeger Publishers, 2007), 1. Fredric Jameson, *Postmodernism, or, The Cultural Logic of Late Capitalism* (Durham, NC: Duke University Press, 1990), 9.
2. For the assumption that the close up of the face constitutes the primary currency of cinematic emotion, see Bela Belazs, "Visible Man, or the Culture of Film," trans. Rodney Livingstone, *Screen* 48.1 (2007): 100.
3. Philip Fisher, *The Vehement Passions* (Princeton, NJ: Princeton University Press, 2002), 76.
4. William Beard, *The Artist as Monster: The Cinema of David Cronenberg* (Toronto: University of Toronto, 2006), 384.
5. Jameson, *Postmodernism*, 9, 8.

102    *Fascination*

6. It was his perception of this relationship that prompted Jameson's formulation of a phrase now recited with almost slogan-like regularity in connection with postmodern thinking: "the waning of affect" (Jameson, *Postmodernism*, 15).

7. William Beard, *The Artist as Monster: The Cinema of David Cronenberg* (Toronto: University of Toronto, 2006), 384; Terry Harpold, "Dry Leatherette," *Postmodern Culture* 7.3 (May 1997), 3; Fred Botting and Scott Wilson, "Sex-Crash," *Crash Cultures: Modernity, Mediation and the Material* (Bristol: Intellect Books, 2003), 83. "Boring," of course, seems a feeble approximation of the emotional atmosphere of a film that opens with a triptych of sex scenes structured around the fetishistic deployment of industrial technology. Yet, as Botting and Wilson elaborate, for the central characters of *Crash*, "sex becomes the same dull daily grind as work: a banal, repetitive, mundane event," evacuated of feeling and charged with what Harpold calls a "cerebrality, disconnectedness, and abstraction" that is likely to "disappoint" viewers whose expectations of the film are coloured by its sexual content. (Botting and Wilson, "SexCrash," 83; Harpold, "Dry Leatherette," 3.)

8. Parveen Adams, "Death Drive," *The Modern Fantastic: The Films of David Cronenberg*, ed. Michael Grant (Wiltshire: Flicks Books, 2000), 114.

9. Adams, "Death Drive," 102–22; Mark Dery, "An Interview about Sex and Death in the Posthuman Age," *Rage Magazine* (September 1997): 44; Alan Jones, "*Crash*: David Cronenberg Turns S&M Injury to S.F. Metaphor," *Cinefantastique* 28.3 (October 1996): 8.

10. Critics attest to *Crash*'s status as a "chrome-plated construct" in virtually every review and essay on the film. (Roberta Jill Craven, "Ironic Empathy in Cronenberg's *Crash*: the Psychodynamics of Postmodern Displacement from a Tenuous Reality," *Quarterly Review of Film and Video* 17.3 [2000], 187.)

11. Anne Anlin Cheng, "Shine: On Race, Glamour and the Modern," *PMLA* 126.4 (October, 2011): 1022, 1024, 1024; Sonya Shannon, "The Chrome Age: Dawn of Virtual Reality," *Leonardo* 28.5 (1995): 369–380. Nor, for that matter, is the glossy like the "shine" that Martin Heidegger attributes to moments of "revealing" in his discussion of the work of art. (Martin Heidegger, "The Origin of the Work of Art," *The Continental Aesthetics Reader*, ed. Clive Cazeaux [London: Routledge, 2000], 91). Heidegger deploys shine in his analysis of the work of art as an entity capable of revealing "earth" as the fundamental substrate upon which all "world" is formed. (Heidegger, *The Origin of the work of art*, 91.) Arguing that the earth resists efforts at direct penetration, Heidegger argues that "Color shines and wants only to shine. When we analyze it in rational terms by measuring its wave-lengths, it is gone. It shows itself only when it remains undisclosed and unexplained ... earth appears openly cleared as itself only when it is perceived and preserved as that which is by nature undisclosable." (Heidegger, *The Origin of the Work of Art*, 91.) Whereas "shine" is unidirectional, the radiance of pure inwardness, the glossy is duplicitous and mirrory, both reflected and, in turn, reflecting the gaze of the onlooker.

12. Martin Heidegger, as cited in Stuart Elden, *Mapping the Present: Heidegger, Foucault, and the Project of a Spatial History* (New York: Continuum, 2001), 65.

13. Nigel J. Thrift, *Non-Representational Theory: Space, Politics, Affect*, (Oxon: Routledge, 2008), 197; Ann Cvetkovich, *An Archive of Feelings: Trauma, Sexuality and Lesbian Public Cultures* (Durham, NC: Duke University Press, 2003), 3–4; Sedgwick, *Touching Feeling*, 17.

## Fascination    103

14. Thrift, *Non-Representational Theory*, 197; Cvetkovich, 17; Sedgwick, *Touching Feeling*, 13–17.
15. Mark Browning, *David Cronenberg: Author or Film-maker?* (Bristol: Intellect Books, 2007), 145; Janet Maslin, "*Crash*: An Orgy of Bent Fenders and Bent Love," *New York Times*, March 21, 1997, http://movies.nytimes.com/movie/review?_r=1&res=9402EFDD163BF932A15750C0A961958260, accessed, June 12, 2010; Robin Dougherty, "Sleek Chrome and Bruised Thighs," *Salon*, March 21, 1997, accessed June 13, 2010, http://www.salon.com/march97/crash970321.html.
16. Jameson, *Postmodernism*, 10.
17. Baudrillard, *America* (London: Verso, 1999), 110; Andreas Huyssen, "Mapping the Postmodern," in *A Postmodern Reader*, ed. Linda Hutcheon and Joseph P. Natoli (Albany, NY: State University of New York Press, 1993), 128; Ziaudden Sardar, *Postmodernism and the Other: The New Imperialism of Western Culture* (London: Pluto Press, 1998), 146.
18. Renu Bora's excellent survey discussion of texture and fetishism, "Outing Texture," can be found in *Novel Gazing: Queer Readings in Fictions*, ed. Eve Kosofsky Sedgwick (Durham, NC: Duke University Press, 1997), 103. For more on the varied cultural deployment of the glossy surface, see Judith Brown, *Glamour in Six Dimensions: Modernism and the Radiance of Form* (Ithaca: Cornell University Press, 2009); Cheng, "Shine"; Krista Thompson, "The Sound of Light: Reflections on Art History in the Visual Culture of Hip-Hop," *Art Bulletin* 91.4 (2009): 481–505.
19. Bora, "Outing Texture," 103.
20. Joseph P. Natoli and Linda Hutcheon, "Representing the Postmodern," in *A Postmodern Reader*, ed. Natoli and Hutcheon (Albany, NY: State University of New York Press, 1993), 194; Jameson, *Postmodernism*, 22, 19; Roland Barthes, *Camera Lucida: Reflections on Photography*, trans. Richard Howard (New York: Hill and Wang, 1981), 26; Jean Baudrillard, "Simulacra and Science Fiction," *Science Fiction Studies* 18.3 (November 1991): 314. While Roland Barthes' postmodern credentials are far from indisputable, a number of critics have earmarked *Camera Obscura* as part of what they read as the critic's late-career "postmodernist turn."
21. Fredric Jameson, *Signatures of the Visible* (New York: Routledge, 1992), 85; Angela McRobbie, *Postmodernism and Popular Culture* (London: Routledge, 1994), 40; Laura Mulvey, *Fetishism and Curiosity* (London: British Film Institute, 1996), 180.
22. Jean Baudrillard, *Revenge of the Crystal: Selected Writings on the Modern Object and its Destiny, 1968–1983* (London: Pluto Classics, 1999), 36; Laura Mulvey, *Fetishism and Curiosity* (London: British Film Institute, 1996), 4. Subtending this equation, I suggest, is the glossy's capacity to theatricalize the effacement of the process of production that is at the heart of the Marxist view of the commodity: indexically, gloss signifies the labour that went into polishing and perfecting the object, even as, iconically, it implies that the object has never been touched at all, its gleaming patina, as Sedgwick puts it, "defiantly or even invisibly block[ing] or refus[ing]" all "information about how, substantively, historically, materially, it came into being." (Sedgwick, *Touching Feeling*, 14.) It is no wonder, then, that the glossy surface seems to have assumed the figurative burden of signifying the loss of depth that the commodity traditionally marks.

104   *Fascination*

23. Derrida, *Writing and Difference*, 121–2; Baudrillard, *The Intelligence of Evil or the Lucidity Pact*, trans. Chris Turner (New York: Berg, 2005), 209; Jameson, *Signatures of the Visible*, 85.
24. Brown, *Glamour in Six Dimensions*, 151.
25. Sedgwick, *Touching Feeling*, 94.
26. No wonder, then, that Jameson, faced with the image of the glossy filmic surface, admits that he "long[s] from time to time for something both more ugly and less proficient or expert, more home-made and awkward": where gloss is the stock in trade of the depthless and the false, these sites of brokenness and irregularity, conversely, hold out the promise of truth and revelation. (Jameson, *Signatures of the Visible*, 85.) Indeed, where the text fails to yield fault-lines of its own, it is the role of the critic to engender them. Slavoj Zizek contrasts modern and postmodern interpretative strategies on exactly this basis, arguing that where modernist interpretation aims to transfigure trauma's open wound through the coherent gloss of critical interpretation, postmodern criticism is to be defined, conversely, by its attempt to make the glossy surface rough by "estranging" the commodified popular culture text, effectively exfoliating a superficial gloss to disclose the rough surface underneath. (Slavoj Zizek, "Introduction: Alfred Hitchcock, or, The Form and its Historical Mediation," *Everything You Always Wanted to Know about Lacan, But Were Afraid to Ask Hitchcock*, ed. Slavoj Zizek (London: Verso, 1992), 1, 2, 1.
27. Barthes, *Camera Lucida*, 42.
28. Baudrillard, "Ballard's *Crash*," 315–6.
29. Fisher, *The Vehement Passions*, 35.
30. Steven Shaviro, "The Life, After Death, of Postmodern Emotions," *Criticism* 46.1 (2004): 139.
31. Ngai, *Ugly Feelings*, 91; *Collins English Dictionary*, 10th ed., s.v. "fascinate"; Steven Connor, "Fascination, Skin and the Screen," *Critical Quarterly* 40.1 (1998): 9. David Hume's treatise "On the Rise and Progress of the Arts and Sciences" conceives fascination as a tool in government's subjugation of the populace: "as large states can afford great expense, in order to support the pomp of majesty, this is a kind of fascination on mankind, and naturally contributes to the enslaving of them." (David Hume, "On the Rise and Progress of the Arts and Sciences," *Essays and Treatises on Several Subjects* [London: A. Millar, 1809], 74–5.) Maurice Blanchot's description of fascination provides a somewhat more existential version of this model, formulating the emotion as an effect of a specifically visual encounter in which "what is seen imposes itself upon the gaze, as if the gaze were seized" in a way that "is not an active contact, not the initiative and action which there still is in real touching. Rather, the gaze gets taken in, absorbed … ." (Maurice Blanchot, *The Space of Literature*, trans. Ann Smock [Lincoln: University of Nebraska, 1982], 32.) Theodor Adorno's description of the modern subject's "will-less fascination" with the new frames fascination as an intellectual paralysis that blinds its victims to "the fact that there is no longer anything new" in a society increasingly dominated by mass production. (Theodor Adorno, *Minima Moralia: Reflections on a Damaged Life* [London: Verso, 2005], 238, 235.)
32. Jameson, *Postmodernism*, 21.
33. Ibid. The connotations that Jameson here attaches to the fascination of the glossy postmodern image prefigure his later, more explicitly pejorative—and

Fascination    105

more famous—descriptions of fascination in *Signatures of the Visible*. There, what he calls the "essentially pornographic" quality of the visual—what he will later call the "cult of the glossy image"—derives from its taking "mindless, rapt fascination" as its aim and telos. (Jameson, *Signatures of the Visible*, 1, 85, 1.) Again, fascination is framed as an index of cognitive and subjective atrophy, less a genuine emotion than a delusory effect of the kinds of "cult" attachments that form around the glossy image. The full quotation is: "The visual is essentially pornographic, which is to say that it has its end in rapt, mindless fascination." (Jameson, *Signatures of the Visible*, 1.)

34. David Harvey, *The Conditions of Postmodernity: An Enquiry into the Origins of Cultural Change* (Malden, MA: Blackwell Publishing, 1990), 88, 88, 87.
35. *Collins English Dictionary*, 10th ed., s.v. "fascinate"; Beard, *Artist as Monster*, 397; Sedgwick, *Touching Feeling*, 15.
36. Beard, *The Artist as Monster*, 403, 397, 397.
37. Silvan S. Tomkins, *Affect, Imagery, Consciousness, Volume 1: The Positive Affects* (New York: Springer Publishing Company, 2008), 187.
38. Sedgwick, *Touching Feeling*, 14.
39. Sinclair, *Crash*, 46.
40. Jameson, *Postmodernism*, 10.
41. Ibid., 42.
42. My italics.
43. My italics.
44. Slavoj Zizek, *Looking Awry: An Introduction to Jacques Lacan Through Popular Culture* (Cambridge, MA: MIT Press, 1992), 114.
45. Rene Girard, *Deceit, Desire and the Novel* (New York: Continuum International Publishers, 1988); Jacques Lacan, *Ecrits: A Selection*, trans. Bruce Fink (New York: W.W. Norton, 2002), 7.
46. Cheng, "Shine," 1034.
47. On one level, this triangulated model of the emotion seems inadequate to account for the critical hostility fascination has inspired within postmodern circles. For in many respects, this model maps almost too neatly onto a post-structuralist hermeneutics in which meaning is not located in the object itself as a positive essence, but is infinitely deferred through a linguistic and social network within which the object is embedded. Yet as Teresa Brennan puts it, "If we accept with comparatively ready acquiescence that our thoughts are not entirely independent, we are, nonetheless, peculiarly resistant to the idea that our emotions are not altogether our own." (Teresa Brennan, *The Transmission of Affect* [Ithaca: Cornell University Press, 2004], 2.) While postmodern and poststructuralist theory's critical labor over the past forty years has predominantly revolved around securing, for the social and linguistic, territory once held to be the exclusive domain of the sovereign subject, it seems less hospitable to incursion of the social and linguistic into the domain of the emotions.
48. Beard, *Artist as Monster*, 403.
49. Iain Sinclair, *Crash* (London: British Film Institute, 1999), 47.
50. John Deigh, "Primitive Emotions," *Thinking about Feeling: Contemporary Philosophers on Emotion*, ed. Robert Solomon (Oxford: Oxford University Press, 2004), 9.
51. Deborah Gould, "Affect and Protest," in *Political Emotions*, ed. Janet Staiger, Ann Cvetkovich and Ann Reynolds (New York: Routledge, 2009), 24.

## 106   *Fascination*

52. Steven Shaviro, *Post-Cinematic Affect* (Hants: O-Books, 2010), 3, 3; Lauren Berlant, "The Epistemology of State Emotion," in *Dissent in Dangerous Times*, ed. Austin Sarat (Ann Arbor, MI: University of Michigan Press, 2005), 46–78.
53. Massumi, *Parables for the Virtual*, 220–1.
54. Botting and Wilson, "SexCrash," 84.
55. Botting and Wilson, "SexCrash," 84.
56. James and Catherine's association of the rough surface and a kind of "raw" or direct emotion is most clearly condensed in the figure of the wound. The scene immediately following Catherine's would-be rape at the hands of Vaughan, which shows Catherine lying naked on her bed with a number of dark bruises, depicts James's careful inventory of his wife's injuries. The camera slowly tracks in as Ballard leans over her, placing his fingers gently on the blossoming imprints of Vaughan's hand, its raw surface facilitating a direct, frontal intimacy between the couple that is in clear contrast to their earlier refusal to "face" each other. Simultaneously tender and disturbing, the scene frames the bruise as a site of unique self-expressive vulnerability.
57. Beard, *The Artist As Monster*, 88.
58. For more on this see Bellamy; Barker, Arthurs and Harindranath 45; Johnson.
59. Gary Johnson, "David Cronenberg Examines Sex and Smashed Fenders in *Crash*," *Images* 2 (2008), accessed November 3, 2011, http://www.imagesjournal. com/issue02/reviews/crash.htm.
60. The language in which Johnson frames his attack on the glossy surface for diverting the director from the task of penetrating his characters' "obsessions" inadvertently reveals a knowledge that the glossy surface may be itself the object of those obsessions. For Johnson's equation between the glossy surface of the "chrome" and the "oily" surface of the "bodies desperately fucking"—of metallic gloss and the sweat of intercourse—tends to accord to the glossy surface a kind of sexual allure, drawing an analogy between the supposed depths of human character, sexuality, and the glossy surface of a plane. Thus, while Johnson's critical presupposition is that the emotional truth of character basks in a kind of crevasse-like invagination beyond the glossy surface which the film has failed to penetrate, the form in which the attack is framed suggests a latent awareness of the glossy surface's emotional power, and, as a corollary, an awareness of the possibility that Cronenberg's refusal to penetrate the glossy surface of his characters' lives *is* his critical insight into their character—as characters whose emotional lives are focused around that glossy surface.

   Importantly, even for those critics who do acknowledge fascination as an emotion, there remains something disturbing about its odd, triangulated structure, especially in the context of the Ballards' marriage, where its divergence from the more "direct" emotions that conventionally sustain romantic and sexual attachments reads to many critics as cold and sordid. This critical distaste for the key role played by fascination in James and Catherine's relationship is rouintely articulated in terms of the characters' refusal to "face" each other. As Barker, Arthurs and Harindranath observe, many of the interviewees questioned about their responses to *Crash* read the sex scenes "as lacking intimacy, as being cold and emotionless, because there is no eye contact and the angle of their heads often accentuated the degree to which the characters were looking out and away from the other person." (Martin Barker, Jane Arthurs and Ramaswami Haindranath, *The Crash Controversy: Censorship Campaigns and*

*Fascination* 107

*Film Reception* [London: Wallflower Press, 2001], 45.) James Bellamy, likewise, complains that though "James and Catherine have a passionate looking sex scene near the middle of the film ... even in that scene they are essentially fucking someone else," in a triangulation that is implicitly incompatible with true feeling. (James Bellamy, "The Conversations: Crash," *Slant Magazine,* January 7, 2010, accessed July 29, 2011, http://www.slantmagazine.com/house/2010/01/the-conversations-crash.)

61. Wilson and Botting, "SexCrash," 87; Beard, *The Artist as Monster*, 405.
62. Wilson and Botting, "SexCrash," 84.
63. Sinclair, *Crash*, 47; Stephen Heath, "Notes on Suture," *Screen* 18.4 (1977): 57.
64. Beard, *Artist As Monster,* 395.
65. Harpold, "Dry Leatherette," 6.
66. Mark Jancovich, *The Cultural Politics of the New Criticism* (Cambridge: Cambridge University Press, 1993), 84. The quote "ragged and dirty" belongs to the character Vaughan.
67. Unattributed, "The Car Wreck in Rich, Silent Colour," *The Melbourne Age*, February 21, 2004; Harpold, "Dry Leatherette," 22.
68. Beard, *The Artist as Monster*, 398.
69. Barbara Creed, "Anal Wounds, Metallic Kisses," *Screen* 39.2 (Summer 1998): 175.
70. Stanley Corngold, *Complex Pleasure: Forms of Feeling in German Literature* (Stanford, CA: Stanford University Press, 1998), xii–iii.
71. Beard, *Artist as Monster*, 380.
72. Martin Barker, Jane Arthurs and Ramaswami Harindranath, *The Crash Controversy: Censorship Campaigns and Film Reception* (London: Wallflower Press, 2001).
73. Sedgwick, *Touching Feeling*, 13.
74. Oliver Harris, "Film Noir Fascination: Outside History, but Historically So," *Cinema Journal* 43.1 (Fall, 2003): 6.
75. Massumi, *Parables for the Virtual*, 220–1.

# 3 Fear
## Dead Subjects and Living Dolls

### I

Flanked from above by two terrified, frostily blue eyes, and from below by the hand reaching up to cover it, what Gilles Deleuze vividly dubs "the shadowy abyss" of the screaming mouth forms a kind of visual fissure at the center of the publicity poster for Wes Craven's 1996 neo-slasher sleeper-hit, *Scream*—an eerie chasm that relegates everything around it, from the title of the film to the names of the cast, to the status of insignificant fine print.[1] Minimal and monochromatic, the image would be striking in any context. Yet its force is only heightened when it is set against what had become, around the time of *Scream*'s release, a rising note of critical panic about the horror genre's failure to move a newly jaded and "affectless" audience.[2] As the preeminent sign and expression of fear, the scream possesses a powerful cachet in the horror genre's physical grammar that far supersedes that of rival responses like "tension, cringing, shuddering, recoiling, tingling, frozenness, momentary arrests, paralysis [and] trembling."[3] For while its oral source yokes it to speech, the vehicle of language and meaning, its baggy, amorphous form, by contrast, ties it to pure noise—a noise, moreover, that, as what Mladen Dolar dubs "the most salient inarticulate presymbolic manifestation of the voice," appears to issue not from the throat but from the deepest psychic recesses of the subject.[4] Indeed, for Deleuze, the scream threatens not just to disclose our psychic contents, but to turn us inside out, "to escape, to flow out of itself ... to disgorge itself through a tip or hole" in a violent discharge that the poster's deployment of the figure of the hand *over* the mouth only amplifies, by standing in for the conventional social and cultural mechanisms ostensibly operating to suppress or contain it.[5] Foregrounding the scream, then, this key piece of promotional material makes a promise at once entirely implicit and screamingly explicit: to restore the emotional power of a generic tradition now routinely figured in the rubric of "crisis," "fatigue" and "dissatisfaction."[6]

It does not tax our critical acuity very far, of course, to see that the semiotic status of the poster's scream is far from stable. In lowering our gaze from the scream of the image to the scream of the title, we transition from the ostensible immediacy of the visual to the manifest slipperiness of the linguistic. This slipperiness is not only semantic (a "scream," after all, is just

*Fear* 109

*Figure 3.1* *Scream*'s publicity poster.

as commonly used to refer to a text, object or person capable of inducing laughter as it is to a cry of pain or fear), but syntactic, since the howl in question oscillates grammatically between noun and imperative, between a pure emotional release and a disciplinary instruction—"Scream!"—that recalls a Foucauldian analytics of the confessional body. This instability in the status of the film's titular expression is hardly surprising, of course, for as scholars and critics never tire of reminding us, *Scream* is an ostentatiously "postmodern" horror film.[7] A slickly produced and cleverly written installment in the popular "slasher" sub-genre, its account of a group of friends in the fictional town of Woodsboro, who become the target of a masked killer known as "Ghostface," is laden with the "knowing pastiche" and "consistently arch references to previous work in the genre" that have become the calling cards of postmodern aesthetics' relentless appeal to spectatorial self-consciousness.[8] By contrast, as what Tom Gunning describes as a kind of visceral convulsion in which "credulity overwhelms all else, the physical reflex signaling a visual trauma," the scream seems to epitomize a guileless spectatorial naïveté.[9] Within the fixed horizon of this opposition, the kind of immediacy and naïveté often ascribed to the scream, and the kind of

## 110  *Fear*

savvy reflexivity associated with postmodern aesthetics, are fundamentally incompatible. And while Gunning's insistence that the identification of the scream with spectatorial naïveté is an insidious *mis*reading reminds us that the opposition between the scream, on the one hand, and postmodern aesthetics, on the other, is an unstable one, the models of emotion that prevail in film theoretical readings of horror today tend to perpetuate and reinforce it. Importing a basic cognitive-appraisal model of emotion into the domain of horror criticism, for example, Carroll's influential take on "art horror" argues that the "abnormal physical agitation (shuddering, tingling, screaming, etc.)" elicited by horror has been "caused by … my thought: that [the monster] is a possible being, and my evaluative beliefs that (b) said [monster] has the property of being threatening in the ways portrayed in the fiction."[10] For Carroll, then, and for the many other film critics who draw, explicitly or otherwise, upon cognitive-appraisal models of emotion, the fearful response to a horror film depends on an "evaluative belief" that the monster poses some kind of immediate or possible threat to the spectator—and thus on an uncomplicatedly referential reading of and relation to the image that the reflexive postmodern text forecloses.[11] While the other emotions this book examines are characterized by an idiosyncrasy and recursivity that makes them more accommodating of the basic tenets of postmodern film aesthetics, the scream of fear, read in this rigidly cognitive way, seems obdurately resistant to postmodern credo.

Given the scream's longstanding status as postmodern aesthetics' other, then, it comes as no surprise that Fredric Jameson's account of the postmodern "waning of affect" should take Edward Munch's 1893 expressionist painting *The Scream* as its foil, pointing to the "vanish[ing]" of the scream depicted therein as "a dramatic shorthand parable" of the gulf between modernism and postmodernism.[12] Nor does it come as a surprise that, despite the burgeoning of interest among film scholars in the emotional and sensational capacities of cinema, the extensive critical work on the so-called "postmodern" slasher film has almost entirely passed over the question of the genre's capacity to scare us. A genre that encompasses not just *Scream* itself, but a raft of films that followed in *Scream*'s wake, from 1997's *I Know What You Did Last Summer* (Jim Gillespie) to the seemingly inexhaustible *Scary Movie* franchise (Keenan Ivory Wayans, 2000; Keenan Ivory Wayans, 2001; David Zucker, 2003; David Zucker, 2006; Malcolm D. Lee, 2013), the postmodern neo-slasher has tended to register critically as a cerebral or not-so-cerebral exercise in "spot-the-allusion," interesting not for its capacity to tap into the kind of intense feeling we associate with the horror genre, but for its capacity to engage reflexively with horror tradition. In fact, far from functioning as an appropriate critical resource for exploring fear, and its most privileged bodily confession, the scream, postmodern horror has become a critical magnet for anxieties about the *demise* of emotion in postmodernism. Writing of the "contemporary teen horror film," Pamela Craig and Martin Fradley bemoan the "numbing of the sub-genre's affective

*Fear* 111

content" and the "apathetic political sensibilities of [horror flm's] youthful consumers"; following sociologist George Ritzer, Paul Wells analyzes what he calls a "McDonaldisation of horror" in the "postmodern text," lamenting the way that these "knowing deconstructions of the sub-genre speak only limitedly about the culture that produces them"; in a vitriolic review of Marcus Nispel's 2003 remake of horror classic *Texas Chainsaw Massacre* (Tobe Hooper, 1974) Mark Kermode refers to the "cynical modern sensibility" of the horror remake's "jaded 21st century audience"; while Aviva Briefel and Sam J. Miller pit the "darker, more disturbing and increasingly apocalyptic" tone of horror cinema after 2001 against the self-consciously postmodern horror of the 1990s, suggesting that it was only after the events of 9/11 made "critique and reflexivity ... suddenly unacceptable" that the genre relinquished "national apathy ... disengagement [and] retreading the fundamental tropes of the genre" in order to offer "narratives that are frighteningly timely."[13] In part through the evocation of the specter of a "jaded," "cynical" and "apath[etic]" postmodern spectator, these critics cast the signature gestures of postmodern horror aesthetics—"knowing deconstruction," "critique and reflexivity"—in the register of emotional exhaustion and ennui, a register in which the kind of guttural, full-bodied fear augured by the film's billboard campaign has no place. As Matt Hills's survey of the critical literature on postmodern horror concludes, "po-mo horror ... apparently no longer works to code [or, it would appear, elicit] social/cultural fears, but instead reflects only on previous genre texts."[14]

On first blush, this conclusion finds ample ratification in *Scream* itself. While the poster proffers the reassuringly human spectacle of a woman screaming, the film's narrative delivers up a far less consoling figure—the open-mouthed, elongated latex "scream" mask that, along with a black, full-length cloak, becomes Ghostface's trademark garb. At once recalling Jameson's figure for an anxiety-ridden modernism (the shape and expression of the mask is clearly modeled on Munch's original painting) and confirming Jameson's hunch about the figure's redundancy in a commodified, depthless "postmodern" world, the mask becomes a measure of the scream's transformation, in postmodernism, from an expression and source of anxiety to a mass-produced Halloween toy. This is a point Woodsburo's Sheriff (Joseph Whipp) rams home when he notes, upon finding a mask abandoned at the scene of one murder, that the floppy latex bauble has no value as evidence: "you can buy these at every five and dime store in the country." Stripped both of the promise of an anguished inwardness, and of the empathic swirls of cloud and landscape that bespoke, in Munch's original scream-landscape, a sympathetic world, the mask's silent emotional histrionics are unmoored from the subject and from the social in equal measure. Indeed, the toy is deprived even of that scene of origin that enables many classic slashers to magically invest a mass-produced object like, say, Jason's hockey mask (*Halloween*, John Carpenter, 1977) with a certain "aura" of distinctive psychic significance. So conspicuously free of aura is the scream-mask, in fact,

## 112   *Fear*

that many of the film's plot-points pivot on the question of whether the masked figure is the real killer or a prankster posing *as* him. In its relentless circulation throughout the film, then, the scream mask tends to bear out Vera Dika's claim that "The stalker film ... is made up of dead things ... from parts of old films," embodying precisely the logic of seriality, mechanical repetition and exhaustion that has led critics to proclaim the horror genre's emotional demise in postmodernism.[15]

Yet if the gaping latex "scream" mask is itself a telling emblem of the failure of the emotion it simulates, this failure finds even stronger substantiation at the level of *Scream*'s form. For in a strategy typical of postmodern cinema's penchant for generic hybridity, but rarely, until *Scream*, so clearly realized in horror cinema, the film's violent slasher scenarios not only fail to evoke the screams promised by its poster, but are uneasily matched by comic affective cues. Certainly, the film's narrative is familiar enough, with the opening set piece placing us in an antiseptically well lit, suburban ranch-style home with a home-alone teenager, Casey (Drew Barrymore), whose blonde hair, creamy complexion and white-on-white outfit make her ideal slasher-film fodder. And it's not long before the film delivers on its generic promise, with Casey receiving a series of phone calls from a dusky, Jack-Nicholson-esque voice, whose light banter suddenly turns sinister when Casey's interlocutor reveals that he can see her: "I want to know who I'm looking at." Shattering at once the fantasy of physical distance established by the device of the telephone, and the fantasy of meta-filmic distance established by the self-aware horror film chit-chat, the revelation is striking in its equation of voyeurism and physical threat—an equation secured when Ghostface actually bursts through the glass sliding doors, knife at the ready. The extended chase sequence that ensues culminates in Casey's slaughter, and, in a final spectacle that consolidates the episode's status as the film's "primal scene," she is left to hang, "gutted," from a tree. Yet while the narrative and characterization of this scene traffic in familiar horror-genre cliché, complete with screaming, pleading and tears, the film's tonal and emotional plane diverges from tradition by inviting us to assume a position of amused, self-reflexive distance from the very real violence *Scream* depicts. On the one hand, this invitation is built into the very structure of the scene, as Ghostface proposes what he calls "a little game," a snap "horror film history" quiz in which failure to answer correctly spells instant death. On the other hand, it's apparent in the visual allusions with which the scene is loaded, from the Jiffy Pop Casey is heating up on the stove, a clear reference to years of teen-horror direct-marketing ploys, to the homage to Dario Argento's *Suspiria* (1977) offered up in the image of Barrymore hanging from the garden tree. *Scream*'s taste for yoking scenes of slasher-style violence to humorous reflexive commentary is only consolidated as the film proceeds and we are introduced to our protagonist, the beautiful, virginal Sidney Prescott (Neve Campbell), whose mother was killed one year before in identical slasher-style, and whose own life now appears to be at risk. For even as the killer begins knocking off the core cast, the film provides dramatic and emotional space for an amused, knowing response. Throughout, its characters relay narrative events through their knowledge of a range of slasher texts, noting connections between 'real' events and those in classic slasher film, speculating as to who will play them in a movie version, and arguing about the "rules" for "surviving" a slasher.[16] The kind of knowing, detached spectatorial posture these strategies invite seems to give credence to the widespread critical anxiety that postmodern horror breeds numb, desensitized spectators.

If *Scream*'s tonal register is marked by an effort to turn "slasher flicks into slapstick," moreover, the primary characters' emotional deviance both matches and feeds into the film's own.[17] Vernacular incarnations of postmodernism's favorite monster, the numb, affectless subject, the characters seem more concerned with exploiting the film's various horrific scenarios for wise-cracks than with registering the full horror befalling their butchered peers. When Randy receives a phone call informing him that the school principal has been murdered and "found hanging from the goalpost on the football field," his friends' jubilant response is to drive over to the school to have a look "before they pry him down"; likewise, when Sidney notes that Casey Becker, the film's first victim, "sits beside [her] in English," her best friend Tatum (Rose McGowan) is quick to quip: "not anymore." If, as Carroll has suggested, "the responses of characters [in horror film] often seem to cue the emotional responses of the audience," the "callousness" of *Scream*'s teenage cast would seem to mark out a position not for a horrified spectator, but for a knowing, amused and distanced one, an audience who—to borrow John Kenneth Muir's description of *Scream*'s characters—care only about their "own entertainment, not the feelings of other people" and whose "exposure to sanitized movie violence has left them with no concept of real pain and suffering."[18] As the title's playful collapse of laughter and fear suggests, then, *Scream*'s comic tone and characterization turn the pained, anguished screams of its victims into "a scream," conjuring all too starkly the glacially emotionless postmodern horror spectators projected by panicky cultural commentators.

With this in mind, it is hardly surprising that the film should have achieved such critical currency in the argument about the waning of emotion in, and as an effect of, postmodern horror spectatorship. As Steffen Hantke has shown in a thorough analysis of the film's hostile academic reception, according to many popular and scholarly commentators, "*Scream* was ... the worst thing to happen to horror film," its "recycling of 'classic' precursors transform[ing] the more politically attuned horror film of the previous generation into self-indulgent postmodern play."[19] Thomas S. Sipos, for example, deploys the familiar opposition between self-referentiality and genuine emotion in order to argue that "*Scream*'s self-referential and smart-alecky, tongue in-cheek attitude ... diluted its own horror, and that of the cycle it spawned."[20] *Scream* emerges here as both underproductive

114  *Fear*

and monstrously over-productive, at once "dilut[ing]" real horror and "spawn[ing]" a cycle of equally affectless commercial film product. Likewise, pegging *Scream*'s satirical, self-reflexive bent as an index of its failure to grapple with the "general sense of hysteria, fear and paranoia" that "grip[s] the country," Kendall Phillips holds the film responsible for the fact that "the American horror film has fallen back into one of its periods of slumber."[21] Yoking genuine spectatorial fear to the realistic, serious depiction of substantial politically or socially charged threats, then, Sipos and Phillips take *Scream*'s affectively compromised, thematically evacuated and self-reflexive comic horror as a sign that the slasher is losing both emotional efficacy and popular ground.[22]

Yet there are a number of conspicuous instabilities in the argument that *Scream*'s evocation of the numb, affectless subject expresses a culture-wide waning of responsiveness to horror film, and that this, in turn, heralds the demise of the genre. First of all, while foregrounded with an unusual clarity in *Scream*'s idiosyncratic juxtaposition of violence and humor, the figure of the numb, desensitized subject was hardly a new figure in the reception of the slasher film. In fact, this figure had begun circulating in response to much earlier examples of the genre, where relentless repetition and sequelization within the horizon of a fixed formula had, according to many critics, already resulted in a conspicuous emotional gap between the screaming victims on screen, and amused, detached and "desensitized" spectators—a gap, then, that *Scream* would appear to underscore rather than originate. Robin Wood's description of watching *The Texas Chainsaw Massacre* (Tobe Hooper, 1974) alongside what he delineates as "a large, half-stoned youth audience who cheered and applauded every one of Leatherface's outrages against their representatives on the screen" is typical here, both in its disapproving juxtaposition of "cheer[ing] and applaud[ing]" audience with the "outrages ... on the screen," and in its determined recoding of a moralized *im*proper feeling ("cheer[ing] and applaud[ing]") as a sign of a pseudo-scientific *lack* of feeling.[23] Along similar lines, Tania Modleski tellingly structures her 1986 argument about perversions of subjectivity in postmodernism around a discussion of unfeeling slasher film spectatorship. Describing "the audience's great glee" as "an unseen nameless presence" "annihilates one by one their screen-surrogates," Modleski aligns this cinematic scenario with a broader sociological one, a "kind of joyful self-destructiveness on the part of the masses" in the culture at large.[24] The rhetorical force and value of both descriptions depends on the putative discrepancy between emotion and act, between "glee" and annihilation, between "joyful[ness and] self-destructiveness." While *Scream*'s explicit disparity between comic affective cues and on-screen violence is notable for bringing the figure of the numb, desensitized spectator into sharp cultural focus, analysis of passages from Wood and Modleski suggests that the history of this figure is at least as long as the history of the slasher genre itself. The sheer longevity and durability of the figure's hold on the critical imagination calls the figure's

*Fear* 115

status as a harbinger of the slasher's demise into serious question. If Wood's "cheer[ing] and aplaud[ding]" spectator of 1974 was really a portent of a new post-emotional age, in which teenagers would be wholly inaccessible to emotional appeal, it remains to be seen why were people still attending slasher films—and attending in such numbers—in 1996.[25]

At least as striking as the observation that the figure of the numb subject has a lengthy critical history, however, is the converse observation that the fear that that figure is said to have displaced has a powerful critical present. For the anxious fretfulness with which critics write of the "waning of affect" in postmodern horror seems to *constitute* the fearful response they insistently claim has fallen away. According to Kim Newman, for example, *Scream*'s comic approach to horror signals a degeneration of its capacity to depict "the horrors and neuroses of the age," a function that, once essential to horror, has now been "passed on to other types of movies."[26] Yet the performative register of Newman's argument sits uneasily alongside its constative claims. Arguing that *Scream*-like "comic horror has all but driven the real stuff out of the marketplace," rendering the "non-camp horror movie ... an endangered species," Newman projects the emotionally effete "comic horror" in conspicuously non-comic—and even horrific terms—terms: as a raging, monstrous entity capable of driving the feeble, non-camp "real stuff out of the marketplace."[27] In doing so, Newman's work seems both to exude and to evoke the fear he insists is precluded by postmodern horror's excessive levity. Jonathan Lake Crane's reading of *Scream* is also suffused with a pervasive disquiet, and again, that disquiet seems, paradoxically, to revolve around the spectacle of fear's demise. After a breathless account of the film's opening sequence, which sees Casey Becker executed for poor recall of *Friday the 13th*, Crane observes that in a film

> defined by knowing pastiche, death is a matter of trivia [and] a trivial matter ... [T]he generic representation of gory death becomes a playful game for initiates only. The trivialisation of death through the consistently arch reference to previous work in the genre, a monstrous version of cinematic homage, reaches an even more enfeebling point near the conclusion of the film ... Climactic scenes from *Halloween* (1978) play on the television as the casualties mount. Within the knowing constraints of the postmodern horror film ... film feeds upon film as the genre embraces the acquisitive logic of cannibalism.[28]

What is notable about this passage is less Crane's insistence that *Scream*'s substitution of "cinematic homage" and intertextual "reference to previous work" functions to "enfeebl[e]" or "trivial[ize]" our emotional experience, than his tendency to encode the process of emotional enfeeblement or trivialization in sensationalized and "monstrous" terms, so that, in a tropological slippage that confers on the film's emotional deficiencies all the "monstrous" and "gory" power of the violent events to which they so conspicuously fail

116   *Fear*

to respond appropriately, the *figurative* incorporation inscribed in the practice of "cinematic homage" becomes the brutally *literal* incorporation of "cannibalism." As with Newman, these monstrous projections manifest a persistent critical fear that recursively takes the film's ostensible deficit of fear as its object, ensuring that whatever emotion Crane contends is lacking in the spectatorial response to the postmodern horror is recuperated at the level of critical response. This is, of course, a fear displaced and ectopic, less a response to the film's gory violence than a meta-response to a spectre seemingly even more horrible—namely the spectre of the numb, emotionless subject over whom cinematic violence has no sway. Yet as both Adam Rockoff's description of the journalistic hoopla around slasher-spectator numbness as a "scare" and Wood's description of watching *Texas Chainsaw Massacre* with numb, affectless teens as a "terrifying experience" suggest, a displaced or secondary critical response cannot be differentiated in any final way from the "immediate" spectatorial response to the film.[29]

But how do we account for these anxieties in light of claims about the desensitized, affectless spectator? For feeling-oriented theorists like Massumi, as we have seen, the anxiety that coalesces around the postmodern slasher should be construed as a sign that postmodern speculations about the numb, emotionless spectator are just plain wrong. In Massumi's terms, the figure of the numb subject is a critical misconception oblivious to the intensity of feeling that encrusts contemporary cultural and social forms, and whereas Jameson heralds "the waning of affect," Massumi counters that "belief has waned for many, but not affect. If anything, our condition is characterized by a surfeit of it."[30] Yet rather than subscribe either to the notion that fear has expired in postmodernism, or to the idea that it is in simple, uncomplicated "surfeit," this chapter will suggest that in postmodern aesthetics the emotion of fear is importantly *bound up with* the spectacle of fear's demise.[31] To the extent, that is, that the spectre of the numb, desensitized spectator has recurred again and again across the history of slasher reception, without appearing to compromise the genre's spectatorial cachet, we should assume that this figure is, in some way, essential to the slasher's continuing emotional appeal. Arguing this, of course, involves complicating the model of fear that has become the template both for our understanding of cinematic fear, and for our sense that fear is incompatible with postmodern aesthetics. Yet as I will show through a re-reading of Sigmund Freud's classic essay "The Uncanny"—a somewhat idiosyncratic, yet nonetheless important instance of this model of fear—this paradigm is by no means the only optic available for understanding the emotion.[32] While the key through-line of "The Uncanny" is an argument for a quintessentially modern model of fear as a response to the threat that the other poses to the subject's bodily and psychic integrity, the essay's suppressed dialogue with another text, Ernst Jentsch's "On the Feeling of the Uncanny," offers us glimpses of a very different, and quintessentially postmodern model of fear—a model of fear that may help us theorize a link between the scream

*Fear* 117

and the kind of numb subjects that populate *Scream*.[33] When read through the lens of this revisionist analysis of "The Uncanny," then, *Scream*'s poster's promise to restore the emotional power of the horror genre may have more currency than one might initially suppose.

## II

Freud's investigation of the "specific affective nucleus" of the uncanny draws initially, and perhaps most famously, on the term's complex etymological relation to home or the "Heimlich."[34] Yet this etymological discussion is followed and reinforced by an extended reading of a literary example, that of E.T.A. Hoffman's dream-like, gothic little tale "The Sandman." It's not hard to see what drew Freud to the story, whose reliance on characterological doubling and shifting identities provides rich affordances for analytic exploration. A twisted, proto-surrealist coming of age story, the narrative centers less on its protagonist, Nathaneal himself, than on his endlessly displaced and metonymical anxiety, which fastens, first, on the nightmarish fairy-tale figure the "Sandman," then, on the malicious Coppelius, a family friend, and later, in his student days, on the barometer and eye-glass dealer Coppola, whose construction of a wooden automaton named Olimpia precipitates both Nathaneal's figurative descent into madness and his final quite literal descent into a convenient nearby abyss when he discovers her true, mechanical status.[35] What is important for our purposes, however, is that while marked by an investment in processes of psychic symbolization and displacement peculiar to psychoanalytic theory, the model of fear that emerges from Freud's reading of "The Sandman" bears striking structural similarities to the basic cognitive appraisal model of emotion that organizes our orthodox understanding of what it is to scream before, to shudder at and to fear a film. According to Freud, the fear the story generates in its readers can be traced, "beyond doubt," to the triplicate figure of Coppola/Coppelius/the Sandman.[36] As Freud observes, "psychoanalytic experience reminds us that some children have a terrible fear of damaging or losing their eyes," an anxiety whose persistence into adult life seems substantiated by a multitude of "dreams, fantasies and myths."[37] For Freud, then, it is significant that in each of its three instantiations, the Coppola/Coppelius/the Sandman complex poses a threat to the eyes, whether through the Sandman's legendary status as a thief of little children's eyes, Coppelius's sinister doubling of the Sandman, or Coppola's literal production of ocular prosthetics. In keeping, then, with Carroll's emphasis on the perceived danger posed by the monstrous other to one's physical or mental well-being, for Freud, the fear that crystallizes around the triad pivots on the threat each figure poses to bodily integrity. This model is profoundly complicated, of course, by Freud's insistence that the anxiety aroused in a reader by the Sandman's threat to vision exists in a substitutive relation to an ancient, formative anxiety about castration.[38] Yet while Freud's psychoanalytic

## 118 Fear

reading of fear remains idiosyncratic in its insistence on the emotion's tie to deeper, infantile emotion, the basic emotional paradigm on which this reading depends—in which fear is a physiological response to the judgment that one is imperiled from outside by a menacing other—is reminiscent of more familiar cognitive appraisal paradigms.

This might, of course, be the end of the story, were it not for the fact that the model of fear Freud establishes here is so closely bound up with an earlier, far less stable model of the emotion. This is the model established by Jentsch in 1906 in a paper "On the Psychology of the Uncanny," which Freud cites as the sole discussion of the uncanny preceding his own and which also, significantly enough, deploys the Hoffman story. Jentsch's argument, however, is quite different to Freud's. For whereas Freud ascribes the uncanny effect of the Hoffman story to Coppelius/Coppola/The Sandman, for Jentsch, these fears coalesce around the mechanical doll Olimpia. As Jentsch points out, Olimpia's claim to human status is shaky: while seeming the height of feminine perfection, possessed of "beautifully molded features," a "shapely figure" and a voice like a "glass bell," she also seems peculiarly *in*human, with a "peculiar rhythmic regularity" in her dancing and a "stiff and measured" gait.[39] And for Jentsch, it is precisely Hoffman's strategy of "leav[ing] the reader in uncertainty as to whether he has a human person or rather an automaton before him" that is the key to the story's diffuse anxiety.[40] As Jentsch puts it more generally, "among all the psychical uncertainties that can become a cause for the uncanny to arise, there is one in particular that is able to develop a fairly regular, powerful and general effect: namely, doubt as to whether an apparently living being really is animate, and, conversely, doubt as to whether a [seemingly] lifeless object may not in fact be animate."[41] In the latter case, our uncertainty revolves around a sense that a lifeless object might, in fact, be animate, as in Jentsch's examples of dolls, wax figures and tree-trunks that unexpectedly turn out to be snakes; in the former, conversely, our uncertainty turns on a sense that an apparently living being might, rather, be *in*animate.[42] Despite the different directionality of the imagined transformation, however, both examples elicit in the reader an anxiety that turns on our failure to determine with any certainty the provenance of the object before us, which thus undulates unsettlingly between human and inhuman, animate and inanimate, animal and mechanical. Yet as Jentsch goes on to make clear, the emotion's true object is less the ambiguously animate status of the other *per se* than the implications of this ambiguously animate status for our own subjective and emotional life. As Jentsch puts it, our observation of these figures suggests "that not everything in the psyche is of transcendental origin," and that "mechanical processes are taking place in that which [we were] previously used to regarding as a unified psyche."[43] Caught between the mechanical and the human, the ambiguously animate other awakens in us through a process of identification latent doubts about our *own* claim to be energized by natural, spontaneous pulses of feeling.

*Fear* 119

As this comparative reading suggests, Freud and Jentsch's models of the workings of the uncanny can be opposed almost point for point. Where for Freud, the uncanny rests on a certainty that the other is threatening or dangerous, likely to take out our eyes or even "castrate" us altogether, for Jentsch, the uncanny derives from *un*certainty about the animate or inanimate, human or inhuman, mechanical or organic status of the other. Where for Freud, our fears echo an originary anxiety about the threat posed by symbolic castration, and are thus independent of dramas of imaginary identification, for Jentsch, our fears turn on a dreaded identification with the (in) human other, an other whose ambiguous emotional credentials call into question our own. Where for Freud, the "uncanny" is merely a variation on the familiar and homely, and thus leads us back into the circle of the intimately subjective, for Jentsch, the uncanny is wholly other, provoking us to doubt the stability of our familiar categories of self and other, inside and outside, animate and inanimate.[44] Where for Freud, then, the figure of the numb, affectless other has little or no relation to the subject's feeling of fear, for Jentsch, the spectacle of the ambiguously animate other has been installed in a pivotal position, the intellectual uncertainty it engenders about its status in turn sparking fears for our own status as feeling subjects. Importantly, Freud does not let this marked divergence between his own position on fear and that of Jentsch pass unchallenged. While the question of the uncanny might seem like an inconsequential one in relation to Freud's broader theses—and while, in fact, Freud is quick to devalue "emotional impulses" as secondary phenomena unusually "restrained, inhibited" in their aims in comparison to the drives that are his more general preoccupation—for Freud, as for many psychoanalytic film scholars after him, the screams, cries and shivers documented in and elicited by the horror text fulfill an important supplementary function, their powerful evidential value capable of authenticating claims about the significance of castration anxiety in the genesis of the subject.[45] It is hardly surprising, then, that in his own essay on the aesthetics of the uncanny, Freud sought to discredit Jentsch's argument, repeatedly insisting, in no uncertain terms, that "uncertainty as to whether an object is animate or inanimate" is "quite irrelevant" to the story's "uncanny effect." [46]

Yet there are a number of moments in the Hoffman story itself that seem to quietly bear out Jentsch's argument that it is Olimpia rather than the Sandman who exerts the story's most potent uncanny effect—perhaps the most memorable of which can be found, paradoxically, in a scene that Freud enlists to support his own argument. This is the scene in which the young Nathanael is caught spying on the nocturnal activities of his father and Coppelius, and in doing so, glimpses

> human faces ... visible on all sides, but without eyes, and with ghastly, deep, black cavities instead ... 'Bring the eyes! Bring the eyes!' cried Coppelius in a hollow rumbling voice. Gripped by uncontrollable terror, I *screamed* and dived from my hiding place on to the floor.[47]

120   *Fear*

Alerted by Nathaneal's cries to the presence of the spying boy, Coppelius—like the fairytale figure with which the boy has equated him—threatens to take out his eyes, announcing, "Now we've got eyes—eyes—a fine pair of child's eyes."[48] In response, continues the narrator, "My father raised his hands imploringly and cried: 'Master! Master! Let my Nathaneal keep his eyes! Let him keep them!'"[49] As both Nathaneal's scream and his father's cry of protest attest, the scene is awash with an unspeakable dread that Freud predictably traces to the threat of castration, a threat figured first in the sight of the "human faces ... without eyes" and subsequently in Coppelius's announcement that he intends to extract the boy's eyes. Yet this distinctively psychoanalytic reading of the scene's mounting horror depends on an elision of the context in which the threat to the eyes takes place, a context in which the "eyes" seem less yoked metaphorically to the testicles than yoked metonymically to the "hands and feet" as just one of a number of "parts" of the body that Coppelius has commandeered for some kind of obscure epistemological enterprise. It is worth noting, for example, that after relenting and allowing the boy to "'keep his eyes,'" Coppelius proclaims his intention of "examin[ing] the mechanism of his hands and feet." As the narrator recalls, "he seized me so hard that my joints made a cracking noise, dislocated my hands and feet, and put them back in various sockets."[50] Far more uncanny here than the specific threat to Nathaneal's eyes, then, is the diffuse threat indexed in his wholesale conversion into a veritable collection of spare parts, an inert, insensible object whose bodily members have become fair scientific game. While Freud seeks to suspend the metonymical slide between "eyes" and "limbs" by belatedly coding the unscrewing of the limbs as yet another "castration equivalent," the language of "examin[ation]" in which Hoffman casts Coppelius's actions bears closer resemblance to the rubric of scientific investigation than to the rubric of punishment. In this sense, it seems clear that the unease that suffuses the scene derives not from the tropological link between the eyes/legs and the penis, but from the symbolic oscillation between animate and inanimate generated by Coppelius' scientific inquiries into the production of life out of inert matter, inquiries that inevitably throw up the converse operation: the treatment of living beings as insentient objects.

Yet while the Hoffman story itself seems to reinforce Jentsch's model of fear, it is Freud's own tireless effort to discredit Jenstch that finally ratifies the latter's contention that fear derives from "doubt as to whether an apparently living being really is animate." For the rhetorical twists and torsions that structure Freud's argument function ultimately testify to the value of Jentsch's. Consider, for example, the fact that Freud takes Jentsch's quite antithetical understanding of fear as a starting point for "[his] own investigation," to the point of re-deploying as his central text a literary example initially offered by his theoretical antagonist—ensuring that Freud's theory of fear as a phenomenon independent of the question of numb, affectless other paradoxically originates in and as a reflexive recoil from a notion of a

*Fear* 121

fearful subject whose emotions are bound up with a numb, affectless other. Even as Freud refutes Jentsch's theory, that is, he exemplifies the kinds of anxieties that attend instabilities in the other's occupation of the categories human/inhuman, animate/inanimate. Consider also Freud's concluding statements to what he sees as a thorough refutation of Jentsch:

> This brief summary will probably make it clear beyond doubt that in Hoffman's tale the sense of the uncanny attaches directly to the figure of the Sandman—and therefore to being robbed of one's eyes, and that intellectual uncertainty, as Jentsch understands it, has nothing to do with this effect.[51]

Here, Freud deploys the rhetorical device of contrast to pit his own fearful subject, shaken by the very concrete fears of "being robbed of [his] eyes," against the dry, abstract "intellectual uncertainty" of Jentsch's fearful subject. In doing so, he invokes a binary schema that identifies the concrete with the living, and the intellectual or conceptual with the non-living. Yet to the extent that it is precisely our nervous shrinking from this latter term in the binary (Jentsch's coldly "intellectual" subject) that persuades us to accept the former (Freud's figure of a subject wracked with fears of castration), the rhetorical force that compels us to acquiesce to Freud's thesis effectively confirms Jenstch's thesis. However insistently we seek to break the connection, the scream remains stubbornly shackled to the figure of the ambiguously animate other.

How does this re-reading of Freud's "The Uncanny" inflect our understanding of a form of physical and emotional expression that seems everywhere problematized across the field of the postmodern neo-slasher? As we have seen, while famous for triangulating our anxieties through deeply entrenched psychic paradigms, Freud predicates these anxieties on an assessment of an external or physical threat in a manner that is structurally homologous with basic cognitive-appraisal models of emotion. Yet while the cognitive-appraisal paradigm may very well qualify us to understand fear in modern instantiations of the horror genre, it entirely *ill*-qualifies us to understand the emotional organization of the postmodern slasher, not least because it fails to account for the tension between the persistent currency of the figure of the numb spectator in slasher discourse on the one hand, and the continued popularity of the slasher genre on the other. It thus becomes significant that while on a surface level "The Uncanny" endorses an orthodox cognitive-appraisal model of fear as a response to an external threat, it also sustains a kind of proto-postmodern counter-theory of fear that binds the emotion, paradoxically, to the spectacle of its own demise. In this model of fear, the emotion is routed not through a belief in the psychic or physical threat posed by a dangerous other but through the belief that fear itself is under threat, whether in the other or in the subject herself. This ghostly, recursive model of fear marks the emotion's displacement from the

## 122  *Fear*

immediate level of a reaction to an external peril to the reflexive level of what Sally Markovitz calls "meta-responses," in which we respond to and "aestheticize our reactions" (or, in this case, our lack thereof.)[52] In mobilizing this idiosyncratic, alternative topology of fear, it is possible not only to reconcile the ubiquitous critical figure of the numb, indifferent slasher spectator with the continued popular fascination of the slasher genre, but to argue that it is precisely this coupling of fear and the numb subject that propels *Scream*'s immensely successful narrative and filmic project.[53] And as I will show, this coupling of fear and its other takes place on multiple levels: at the level of character identification, in which our fear operates on behalf of the numb, affectless other; at the level of dreaded identification, in which our fear is of the numb affectless other; and at the level of a kind of anxious subjective split, in which the film's comic affective cues threaten to transfigure us *into* the numb, affectless other.

## III

The memorable set-piece in which Tatum is trapped in the garage with Ghostface offers a particularly precise illustration of the first dynamic. So given to making light of the events in Woodsboro that she decides to descend alone into the basement while a killer is on the loose, the heroine's wise-cracking, gum-chewing best friend epitomizes the figure of the numb, jaded teen that circulates through *Scream*'s critical and cultural reception. Even when Ghostface makes his long-awaited appearance on the scene, Tatum is impassive and imperturbable, and the dialogue that follows is a patchwork of movie references: "Is that you, Randy?" she asks. "What movie is this from?" she inquires drolly as she walks toward him: "*I Spit On Your Garage?*" When Ghostface blocks her exit, Tatum is still skeptical: "O, you want to play psycho killer?" Indeed, it is only when her attacker reaches for his knife and cuts her forearm that Tatum shows real fear. Yet whereas the film's critics have been united in assuming that *Scream*'s characters' relentless reflexivity and allusion forecloses a fearful spectatorial response, in fact, Tatum's amused knowingness only compounds the tension of the scene and the fear of spectator. Far from inviting a spectatorial amusement that matches hers, Tatum's unshakeable impassivity has us shouting at the screen, in a way that anticipates horror-buff Randy's (Jamie Kennedy) insistent exclamations to Jamie Lee Curtis's oblivious, entirely un-affected Laurie, at the very point that she is just about to be attacked: "*look behind you!*" This twinning of desensitized character and animated audience, of course, marks an exact reversal of the traditional logic of character identification, a logic spelled out in Carroll's insistence that in the horror context the responses of the characters in the text tend to bolster and even "*cue* the emotional responses of the audience."[54] Drawing on the work of David Hume, however, Philip Fisher has offered a useful explanation of this reversal. For Fisher, where a text's characters fail to model the expected audience response directly,

*Fear* 123

they may invite what he calls a volunteered passion, "where we feel something exactly because the other does not."[55] And in many respects, this rings doubly true of *Scream*, where our desire to "supply the missing fear" is amplified by the film's tendency to single out its most jaded, affectless characters very particularly for punishment.[56] Indeed, in staging its key scenes of slaughter as ripostes to the characters' verbal and behavioural displays of cultural erudition, *Scream* can be said to give a self-conscious twist to the classic slasher's identification of sexual experience and violent death, by substituting cultural knowledge in place of sexual knowledge. Whereas in *Halloween*, for example, it's the sexually voracious Lynda (P. J. Soles) who is first in line for the slaughter, in *Scream*, it's the wise-cracking Tatum, her pop-culture references running a promiscuous gamut from *All the Right Moves* (Michael Chapman, 1983) to *Friday the 13th*, who's earmarked for the film's bloodiest death. It is in keeping with this same logic that Sidney Prescott, the only member of the core teenage cast who survives *Scream*'s bloody mise-en-scene, is also the only character who, while not actually virginal, is nevertheless the postmodern equivalent: inexperienced in the rules and conventions of horror, quite open about her refusal to watch horror film, and thus the ideal (because so easily-horrified) horror-film viewer. Carefully coding its most jaded and knowing characters as those most at risk for their lives, then, *Scream* works to shackle our screams to the film's numb, desensitized subjects.

Yet if *Scream* invites us to feel fear *on behalf of* the numb, disaffected subject, it equally invites us to take these subjects as fear's *object*, transfiguring it into the genre's newest monster. Replete with dead eyes, flat stares and monotone drawls, Billy and Stu, the two young men finally exposed as the masterminds behind Ghostface, are self-conscious embodiments of a millennial nightmare of teenagers "turn[ed] psychotic" by horror: "watch a few movies, take a few notes ... It was fun!" Indeed, the film's marriage of monstrosity to media-saturated emotionlessness achieves a kind of narrative apotheosis when the pair's disclosure that they are the killers is brokered through the disclosure that they possess an unexpected knowledge of horror film. As Billy divests himself of the pretense that he is an anguished stabbing victim and reveals himself, instead, as a cold-blooded killer, the transition is marked and even defined by his quotation of Anthony Perkins in *Psycho*: "we all go a little mad sometimes." If Carol Clover's classic analysis of the 1970s slasher film could ascribe to the killer a certain psychosexual "fury," by the 1990s, it appears, the slasher was less furious than blank, affectless, or amused. Indeed, the tension sustained by Billy's cold, affectless demeanor is, if anything, defused by a momentary humanizing glimpse of the genuine rage and hurt that underpins it.[57] When Sidney's interrogation of his motives prompts him to recall how "[Sidney's] slutbag mother was fucking my father ... and she's the reason my mother moved out and abandoned me," Billy's air of impervious, affectless cool is displaced by a rage that, while initially more intense, is also less scary. The tension is restored, however, when

124   *Fear*

the cut back to Billy—after a long shot reveling in Sidney's awed absorption of the information—shows him turn away from Sidney to address Stu with a flippancy that undercuts his earlier display of vulnerable humanity: "How's that for a motive? Abandonment causes serious deviant behaviour." Fear, it would seem, is alive and kicking in postmodern aesthetics, with the qualification that it now crystallizes not around an external threat but around the question of its own continued existence—that is, around the anxious speculation that in someone, somewhere, emotion is in dire paucity. Recruiting as its villains precisely those numb, desensitized young people "turn[ed] psychotic" by horror that—for most critics—augur the exhaustion of the genre, *Scream* transforms the figure of the numb, affectless spectator into the engine rather than the expiry of the slasher form.

Beyond both our fear both for and of this throng of jaded, disaffected characters, however, lies a fear for ourselves, as the tantalizing emotional lure of *Scream*'s comedy threatens to transmute us into precisely the knowing, affectless spectators it depicts. Again, the scene with Tatum exemplifies this dynamic. While on a narrative level the scene punishes Tatum's knowing disbelief with death, on an emotional level the scene repeatedly tempts us into occupying an analogous position of amused skepticism. This is especially evident in relation to the masked killer, whom the film encourages us not to fear but to ridicule. Not only is his costume a degraded, commercialized, trick-or-treat version of Munch's high-modernist seriousness, but his farcical tumbles—skidding on beer, sent flying by an opening fridge door, the victim of Tatum's flying beer cans—continually threaten to tip his air of menace into slapstick. Even when he has irrevocably established his serious intent by murdering Tatum, the ludicrously comic physical details of the murder, which sees her severed mid-torso in the garage-door cat-flap, accompanied by exaggerated foley noises to indicate squashed internal organs, make it hard to resist assuming the posture of knowing amusement that got her there in the first place. The orthodox critical line on the relationship between comedy and horror in slasher cinema casts comedy as a formal technique for relieving the tension built up by the spectacle of violence. As Noel Carroll has it, "Horror, in a sense, oppresses; comedy liberates. Horror turns the screw; comedy releases it."[58] In *Scream*, however, the film's humour actually serves to escalate the tension, in dangling, tauntingly, before the viewer precisely the position of knowing, satirical amusement that gets the characters in so much trouble.

It should be clear by now, of course, that this scream is as much an effort to define ourselves as those who would not be caught dead laughing as it is an spontaneous, visceral cry of horror; as much a function of the definition as of the expression of the fearful subject. And the weight that this places on the scream—as the ultimate evidential foundation for the distinction between feeling and unfeeling subjects—is immense. Yet as a hybrid text whose allegiance to the spectacular mandates of the slasher is matched by its allegiance to the narrative mandates of the "whodunnit,"

*Fear* 125

*Scream* is especially well equipped to dramatize the evidentiary significance of the scream. Indeed, the film everywhere presses this most guttural of utterances into narrative service in the effort to distinguish between killer and potential victim. An illustrative incident here sees Sidney, having extricated herself from Ghostface's vicious embrace, flee up the path toward the seeming sanctuary of Tatum's family home. Rather than pursue her, however, her attacker seems suddenly to disappear; we see Sidney's point-of-view shot of the road, note that it is empty and then cut back to her terrified face, before a deliberately skewed and unsteady tracking shot follows her up to the porch, where she frisks the deputy sheriff's prostrate body for a gun. At this point, we hear voice-off cries, and the reverse shot shows Randy dragging himself up the path, pleading for help and clasping his apparently wounded thigh. While the audience knows that he is innocent, and that his sudden appearance on the scene bears no relation to the equally abrupt *dis*appearance of Ghostface, Sidney's first intuition is that he is the killer, trickily divested of his costume and feigning injury, and as we cut back to the house, we see her cocking the gun, prepared to defend herself. Now, however, her point-of-view shot discloses yet another figure arriving at the house; this time it's Stu, also clasping his thigh. Here, the boys' terrified screams—"Sidney!" "Help me!" "It's him! He's a killer!"— are as much pleas for Sidney to recognize them as fearful subjects as they are expressions of their very real fear of the killer, as much attempts to differentiate themselves from what they have rightly intuited to be the distinctive emotionlessness of the killer as they are vocalizations of their own emotion. Our spectatorial horror at *Scream*'s numb, affectless killers is analogous in its collapse of the performative and the expressive. Screaming at the sight of postmodern horror's assembly of numb, affectless subjects, we not only express our fear of them, but seek desperately to distinguish ourselves from them.

Whether materialized through the idiom of character, monstrous other, or formal cue, then, the figure of the desensitized subject becomes the paradoxical condition for the preservation of the feeling spectator. Thanks to what Tarja Laine calls an "affective nonsynchronicity between the emotion embodied in the film and the emotion with which the spectator responds," the fearful subject is resurrected within the postmodern slasher as a subject fearful for the future of emotion itself. [59] While film critics wedded to the cognitive-appraisal paradigm assume that spectatorial fear depends on an "evaluative belief" about an immediate physical threat to the subject, then, *Scream* gives credence to Jentsch's suggestion that fear can recursively take as its object the question of feeling itself—and in doing so, it bears out Cosimo Urbano's contention that "both monsters and the manner in which they are depicted change precisely so that their effects can stay the same."[60] Yet while this argument would seem to project a rosy picture of emotive subjects issuing miraculously from the corpses of dead ones, *Scream* makes it clear that the movement is far from unidirectional. If Tatum's emotional deficiencies

126  *Fear*

procure spectatorial fear, moments of character terror seem to foreclose spectatorial response. While, as Carroll puts it, the shuddering "recoil" of Dracula's Jonathan Harker from the sight of the vampire is meant to "structure [the reader's] emotional response," in *Scream*, on the contrary, Casey Becker's show of emotion actually obviates ours.[61] As the camera tracks in on Casey's tearful, terrified face, her display of horror leaves this scene entirely devoid of the compelling tension that characterizes the rest of the film. Where the object of fear has shifted from the violence itself, to the emotional deficiencies of its victims, violence accompanied by healthy, robust response leaves us cold, actually relieving the spectator of the anxiety about insufficient response that attends the scene of Tatum's death. Slavoj Zizek's notion of "interpassivity" provides a useful resource for understanding this kind of emotional economy, in which one subject's emotion seems to deter rather than prompt another's.[62] Observing, of canned laughter, that "where laughter is included in the sound track ... the TV laughs for me—that is, it realizes, takes over" the spectator's emotional function, Zizek suggests that at stake in emotional display is not so much an expression of a deep-seated internal urge, as an exhibition for the benefit of what he calls in psychoanalytic terms the Other, in which what is significant is not that *I* in particular respond but that *someone does*.[63] It is within the orbit of this logic that both our failure to respond to Casey's cries, and our eagerness to respond to Tatum's impassivity, take place.

In this light, *Scream* is less a reassuring fable about our endlessly renewable emotional resources, in which even the spectacle of the end of feeling works to engender emotion, than a disturbing warning that in postmodern culture, it may be *only* the spectacle of the end of feeling that is capable of animating us—and that, as a consequence, the scream and its opposite may be bound together in what Massumi might call a "mass production line of fear."[64] The film's final sequence bodies this principle forth in the form of a frenzy of reversals and unmaskings, in which numbness and fear continually switch places, and in which a continually migrating human scream leaves a throng of numb, affectless subjects in its wake. While Billy's charade of gasping and crying falls rapidly away when he discloses himself as the killer, his scream finds an avid displacement in Sidney; after an extended scene in which Billy and Stu stand off against a terrified Sidney, Gail Weathers returns from the dead ("I thought she was dead"; "She looks dead"), transferring the burden of the scream to the two young men; foiling her plan and regaining the knowing, amused upper hand, the two men temporarily reduce their victims to cowering, pathetic terror, until Sidney—having escaped with the gun—assumes the posture of cool-headed, ironic knowingness that made the killer so unsettling in the first place (to the point of actually calling Billy and Stu on the phone using the voice-encoder). Mimicking the relentless displacement of the latex scream mask itself, the scream's circulation through the sequence operates according to a kind of hydraulic model of emotion, in which a scream is incapable of occupying two characters at once: every scream is bound to numb affectlessness, every cry has its silent partner. If, for Samuel Beckett, "the tears of the world are a constant quantity. For each one who begins to weep, somewhere else another stops," the same seems to be true of screams.[65] Rather than fully sublating the mechanical and the emotionless, the film's coupling of the numb subject and the scream together merely displaces emotionlessness to the systemic level of a cinematic programme that produces both feeling subjects and numb subjects in equal measure.

*Figure 3.2* Casey's screaming face is mapped onto Ghostface's latex "scream" mask.

In arguing this, it is worth returning full circle to what Humphries calls the film's "brilliantly orchestrated opening" scene.[66] Having temporarily evaded Ghostface by escaping outside, Casey attempts to ascertain his position on the property in order to determine her own next move. As she ducks under the window and then undertakes a quick reconnaissance of the interior, a point of view shot shows the kitchen filling quietly with smoke from the burning Jiffy-Pop, and, at the window, a dark, ambiguous shape whose sudden movement across the room quickly reveals it as the killer's. At this point, however, something odd happens. Cutting suddenly to a reverse shot that has us briefly occupying the slasher's point of view, we are shown not only Casey's screaming face, on the other side of the glass, but—superimposed upon it in a shadowy reflection—the killer's own latex scream mask, the instantly recognizable grimace reflected in the glass of the brilliantly illuminated interior. The shot appears for no more than a second before we cut back to an action shot of the killer breaking through the window, yet its message is clear. Here, the mask whose palpable inauthenticity has made it a cultural cipher for the loss of emotion, and the very real horror of a girl in fear for her life, are bound together in a kind of double-helix structure; Casey's cries at once a defiance of, and inextricable from, a culture everywhere marked by the "waning of affect."

128   *Fear*

## IV

Whereas the other chapters of this book analyze postmodern aesthetics' affiliation with borderline, marginal emotions, this chapter has argued for the persistence of a familiar emotion—fear—in a new, dialectical form. In its unsettling alignment of old-school slasher violence and comic tonal cues, *Scream* committed the emotional heresy of encouraging us to respond to suffering with knowing amusement, if not outright laughter. Throughout the 1990s, the film became a kind of byword for the notion, then flourishing across both popular and scholarly cultures, that postmodern aesthetics are marked by a waning of feeling, provoking both panicky speculations about desensitized young people and turgid requiems for a supposedly exhausted slasher genre in equal measure. Yet as my close analysis of the film has shown, while formally and thematically preoccupied with the figure of the numb, affectless spectator, *Scream* can hardly be called bereft of emotional power. On the contrary, the film's engagement with this figure provokes a displaced, self-reflexive form of fear that revolves precisely around the creeping conviction that fear is on the wane, whether in the subject or in the other. Drawing on Jentsch's reading of Hoffman's "The Sandman," that is, I have argued that while cognitive appraisal theories of spectatorial fear tend to ascribe the emotion to the subject's belief in an immediate physical threat, *Scream* provides the aesthetic co-ordinates for a more recursive, supplementary form of fear in which the emotion converges on a belief about the possible demise of fear itself. While a conventional cognitive-appraisal reading has ruled out of the possibility of fear's survival in postmodern aesthetics, then, fear's vampiric capacity to fortify itself through the very spectacle of its own demise gives it a persistent, recursive quality that defuses postmodern reflexivity's supposed threat. Certainly, it is only by figuring fear as supplementary to, rather than expressive of, a suddenly problematized feeling that we can account for the contradictions within a postmodern moment in which endless proclamations of fear's disappearance are matched by an equally endless stream of commercial horror product. This argument allows us to resist the opposition between "comic horror" and what Newman calls the "real stuff" of the "non-camp horror movie"—and the related notion that the descent into ineffectual "comic horror" "through repetition and spoof to ridiculousness" is, according to some divine law of diminishing emotional returns, the manifest destiny of every horror cycle.[67] As the example of *Scream* clearly demonstrates, repetition, spoof and ridiculousness are less a sign of the genre's flagging capacity to scare us, than the lifeblood of a fear that thrives on the spectacle of its own expiry.

## Notes

1. Gilles Deleuze, *Francis Bacon: The Logic of Sensation* (London: Continuum, 2003), 61.

*Fear* 129

2. Christopher Sharrett, introduction to *Mythologies of Violence in Postmodern Cinema*, ed. Christopher Sharrett (Detroit, MI: Wayne State University Press, 1999), 14.
3. This morbid parataxis of possible physical indexes of fear comes from Noel Carroll, "The Nature of Horror," *The Journal of Aesthetics and Art Criticism* 46.1 (1997): 54.
4. Mladen Dolar, *The Voice and Nothing More* (Cambridge: MIT Press, 2006), 27.
5. Deleuze, *Francis Bacon*, xiii.
6. Steffen Hantke, "They Don't Make 'Em Like They Used To: On the Rhetoric of Crisis and the Current State of American Horror Cinema," in *American Horror Film: The Genre at the Turn of the Millenium*, ed. Steffen Hantke (Oxford, MS: University of Mississippi Press, 2010), viii.
7. See, for example, Todd F. Tietchen, "Samplers and Copycats: The Cultural Implications of the Postmodern Slasher in American Film," *Journal of Popular Culture* 26.3 (1998): 98–107, esp. 99; Valerie Wee, "The Scream Trilogy, Hyper-postmodernism, and the Late Nineties Teen Slasher Film," *Journal of Film and Video* 57.3 (Fall, 2005): 44–61.
8. Jonathan Lake Crane, quoted in Matt Hills, *The Pleasures of Horror* (London: Continuum, 2005), 191.
9. Tom Gunning, "An Aesthetic of Astonishment," *Viewing Positions: Ways of Seeing Film*, ed. Linda Williams (New Jersey: Rutgers University Press, 1995), 115.
10. Noel Carroll, "The Nature of Horror," 54.
11. As Rei Terada's comment that "fear makes a good exemplary emotion (a nice, clear emotion)" suggests, there's something about fear that offers itself very readily to this model of emotion. (Rei Terada, *Feeling in Theory: Emotion after the Death of the Subject* [Cambridge, Mass.: Harvard University Press, 2002], 152.).
12. Fredric Jameson, *Postmodernism, or The Cultural Logic of Late Capitalism* (Durham, NC: Duke University Press, 1991), 11.
13. Pamela Craig and Martin Fradley, "Teenage Traumata: Youth, Affective Politics, and the Contemporary American Horror Film," *American Horror Film: The Genre at the Turn of the Millennium*, ed. Steffen Hantke (Oxford, MS: University of Mississippi Press, 2010), 78 and 82; Paul Wells, *The Horror Genre: From Beelzebub to Blair Witch* (London: Wallflower Press, 2004), 94, 97, 97; Mark Kermode, "What a carve up!" *Sight and Sound* 13.12 (December 2003): 16 and 13; Aviva Briefel and Sam Miller, *Horror After 9/11: World of Fear, Cinema of Terror* (Austin, TX: University of Texas Press, 2011), 1, 2, 2, 3.
14. Matt Hills, *The Pleasures of Horror* (London: Continuum, 2005), 190.
15. Vera Dika, *Recycled Culture in Contemporary Art and Film: The Uses of Nostalgia* (Cambridge: Cambridge University Press, 2003), 207.
16. The characters' cinematic references run the gamut from *Psycho* (Alfred Hitchcock, 1960) to *Halloween* (John Carpenter, 1977), to *Friday the Thirteenth* (Sean S. Cunningham, 1980). It is worth noting that the film's reflections on genre are complemented by a series of meditations on media voyeurism: the callous professional investment of TV journalist Gale Weathers (Courtney Cox) in extracting Sidney's "story" at all costs, for example, functions self-reflexively as a figure for the film's own "exploitative" relationship to human suffering.
17. Liam Lacey, "Review," *Globe and Mail*, April 12, 2002, accessed August 16, 2011, http://www.rottentomatoes.com/m/1074316-scream/.

## 130 *Fear*

18. Carroll, "The Nature of Horror," 52; John Kenneth Muir, *Wes Craven: the Art of Horror* (Jefferson, NC: McFarland and Company, 2004), 205. Carroll's contention here, that spectatorial emotional response involves an empathic imitation of character response, is at odds with his subscription elsewhere to the cognitive-appraisal reading in which spectatorial emotion is predicated on an evaluation of the monster's dangerousness. This tension between empathic and evaluative readings of spectatorial emotion runs through a great deal of work on cinematic feeling. For examples of the "empathic" model of spectatorial emotion, see Linda Williams, who argues that "the spectator is caught up in an involuntary mimicry of the emotion or sensation of the body on screen" (Linda Williams, "Film Bodies: Gender, Genre and Excess," *Film Quarterly* 44.4 [Summer, 1991]: 44), and Berys Gaut, "Emotion and Identification," in idem, *A Philosophy of Cinematic Art* (Cambridge: Cambridge University Press).
19. Steffen Hantke, "Academic Film Criticism, The Rhetoric of Crisis and the Current State of American Horror Cinema," *College Literature*, 34.4 (Fall 2007): 191, 191–2.
20. Thomas M. Sipos, *Horror Film Aesthetics: Creating the Visual Language of Fear* (Jefferson, NC: McFarland and Company, 2010), 23.
21. Kendall Phillips, *Projected Fears: Horror Films and American Culture* (Westport, CT: Praeger Publishers, 2005), 195, 196.
22. I am limiting my citational canvas to the domain of film theory, but *Scream* has also emerged as the go-to text for grounding arguments about "desensitization" across a body of work in the social sciences. Victor C. Strasburger and Barbara J. Wilson, for example, contend that "The popularity in recent years of graphically violent serial killer movies such as *Hannibal* and *Scream* suggest to some that we are experiencing a shift in our tolerance for violence ... and the danger is that such an effect will spill over into real life resulting in a society that is increasingly indifferent to real life violence." (Victor C. Strasburger and Barbara J. Wilson, Children, Adolescents and the Media [Thousand Oaks, CA: Sage, 2002], 102). Similarly, after a summary of *Scream* as a text in which "seven grisly murders take place"—a summary woefully inadequate to the film's generic and cultural specificity—social scientist Steven J. Kirsch describes how, "in the past few decades, concern has been raised over the fact that repeated exposure to increasing levels of violence in television and movies may make children callous and indifferent to violence." (Steven J. Kirsch, *Children, Adolescents and Media Violence* [Thousand Oaks, CA: Sage, 2012], 218, 219.)
23. Robin Wood, "An Introduction to the American Horror Film" in *The American Nightmare*, ed. Andrew Britton, Richard Lippe and Robin Wood (Toronto: Festival of Festivals, 1979), 22.
24. Tania Modleski, "The Terror of Pleasure: The Contemporary Horror Film and Postmodern Theory" in *Film Theory and Criticism: Introductory Readings*, eds. Leo Braudy and Marshall Cohen, (Oxford: Oxford University Press, 2004), 770.
25. To say that people were "still attending" slasher films in 1996 is an understatement, for far from dying out, what Roger Ebert has called the "dead teenager" genre enjoyed an unprecedented spike in popularity in the wake of *Scream*. (Roger Ebert, *Roger Ebert's Movie Yearbook, 2009* [Kansas City: Andrew McMeel Publishing, 2009], 860.) Not only did *Scream* gross $173 million worldwide on a slim $15 million production budget, but it spawned a series of copycats, from the *I Know What You Did Last Summer* franchise to the *Scary Movie* franchise, which mimicked both its basic comedy-horror paradigm and

*Fear* 131

its popular success. ("Box Office History For Scream Movies," The Numbers, http://www.the-numbers.com/movies/series/Scream.php, accessed July 6, 2009.) Hantke concedes as much when, despite his argument that the horror film is "in a slump," he notes that "as far as popularity and profitability go, the horror film seems near the top of its game." (Hantke, "Academic Film Criticism," 191.) Yet in insisting that to the extent that they have lost the capacity to scare "the vast majority of these films just aren't any good," the explanation Hantke implicitly offers for this discrepancy between putative aesthetic failure and continued popular appeal is that the fans simply lack the nous to measure their actual numbness against the film's intended fright-effect. (Hantke, "Academic Film Criticism," 191.) In Hantke's model, horror film is "actually" dead; its audience—possibly because they're dead too—just doesn't know it yet.

26. Kim Newman, *Nightmare Movies: Horror on Screen Since the 1960s* (London: Bloomsbury, 2011), 289, 288.

27. Newman, *Nightmare Movies*, 288.

28. Crane, quoted in Matt Hills, *The Pleasures of Horror* (London: Continuum, 2005), 191.

29. Adam Rockoff, *Going to Pieces: The Rise and Fall of the Slasher Film, 1978–1986* (Jefferson, NC: McFarland and Company, 2002), 17; Wood, "An Introduction to the American Horror Film," 22. Newman and Crane were not the only critics to express anxiety about the gap *Scream* stages between (horrific) narrative content and (comic) affective cues. Roger Ebert was aghast at the extent to which the moral implications of the violence were "defused by the ironic way the film uses it and comments on it." (Roger Ebert, "Scream," *Chicago Sun-Times*, December 20, 1996, accessed July 6, 2012, http://rogerebert.suntimes.com/apps/pbcs.dll/article?AID=/19961220/REVIEWS/612200306/1023).

Janet Maslin of the *New York Times*, meanwhile, chided Craven for "want[ing] things both ways, capitalizing on lurid material while undermining it with mocking humour. Not even horror fans may be comfortable with such an exploitative mix." (Janet Maslin, "Scream: Tricks of the Gory Trade," *New York Times*, December 20, 1996, accessed July 6, 2012, http://movies.nytimes.com/movie/review?res=9F0CEEDE1431F933A15751C1A960958260&partner=Rotten%20Tomatoes). Here, Maslin figures the film's juxtaposition of satirical humour and graphic violence as a kind of hypocrisy, a means of having it "both ways," enabling the viewer to enjoy (and thus the director to "capitaliz[e] on,") the violence, while simultaneously allowing them to escape the moral implications of that violence by "undermining it with mocking humour." Bob Stevens of the *San Francisco Examiner* also framed his critique of the film's constitution of graphic violence as an object of amusement in terms of hypocrisy: "Wes Craven makes an artificial and hypocritical attempt to escape the artistic limitations of teenage slasher flicks ... hypocritical because he relies on the very cliches he pretends to satirize for shock value." (Bob Stephens, "Stifled Scream: Wes Craven's Over-the-top Efforts Sink Teen Slasher Flick to Rock Bottom," *San Francisco Examiner*, December 20, 1996, accessed July 12, 2012, http://www.sfgate.com/cgibin/article.cgi?f=/e/a/1996/12/20/WEEKEND8125.dtl.)

30. Massumi, *Parables for the Virtual: Movement, Affect, Sensation* (Durham, NC: Duke University Press, 2002), 27.

31. Massumi, *Parables for the Virtual*, 27.

## 132  *Fear*

32. Sigmund Freud, *The Uncanny*, trans. David McLintock (London: Penguin Classics, 2003), Kindle edition, "The Uncanny." While there are important distinctions to be made between anxiety, fear, terror and the feeling of the "uncanny," this chapter will tend to conflate these four terms as different species of fear.
33. Ernst Jentsch, "On the Psychology of the Uncanny," trans. Roy Sellars, accessed June 3, 2010, http://art3idea.psu.edu/locus/Jentsch_uncanny.pdf.
34. Freud, *The Uncanny*, "The Uncanny." In an analysis of an extended dictionary excerpt, Freud demonstrates that the term "uncanny" yields two distinct sets of meanings, one of which relates to the familiar and comfortable and the other of which relates to the strange and foreign. Indeed, "among the various shades of meaning that are recorded for the word 'heimlich' there is one in which it merges with its formal antonym, 'unheimlich,' so that what is called heimlich becomes unheimlich" in a kind of semantic impaction whose effect, Freud concludes, is felt in the uncanny's inherently ambivalent status as "that species of frightening that goes back to what was once well known and had been long familiar." (Ibid.).
35. E.T.A Hoffman, "The Sandman," in *The Golden Pot and Other Stories*, trans. Ritchie Robertson (Oxford: Oxford University Press, 1992).
36. Freud, *The Uncanny*, "The Uncanny."
37. Ibid.
38. Ibid. In line with Freud's earlier-elaborated notion that "the uncanny is something familiar that has been repressed and then reappears," then, the threat of the loss of one's eyes only acquires its intense emotional charge because of its ability to reawaken a repressed oedipal anxiety about another threat: the threat of the loss of the penis. (Ibid.)
39. Hoffman, "The Sandman," 108, 108, 108, 109, 108.
40. Jentsch, "On the Psychology of the Uncanny," 11.
41. Ibid., 8.
42. Ibid., 14.
43. Ibid.
44. Where Coppelius is merely a regular fellow with a memorably irregular appetite for little children's eyes, Olimpia's unstable occupation of the category human prompts unsettling questions about the status, orientation and nature of emotion.
45. Freud, *The Uncanny*, "The Uncanny."
46. Ibid.
47. Hoffman, "The Sandman," 90.
48. Ibid.
49. Ibid.
50. Ibid., 90–91.
51. Freud, *The Uncanny*, "The Uncanny."
52. Sally Markowitz, "Guilty Pleasures: Aesthetic Meta-Response and Fiction," *Journal of Aesthetics and Art Criticism* 50 (1992): 307.
53. In this sense, it can be no accident that though reviewers extrapolating directly from the disparity between the film's comic affective cues and its violent narrative content unquestioningly assume that the primary emotion provoked in *Scream*'s audience was amusement, acquaintance with the user responses on the IMDB forum makes it clear that the primary response of its audience, despite the affective cues, was one of terror. Recurring terms in the mostly ecstatic reviews are words like "terrifying" and "chilling"; one respondent titles his review "One of the scariest slasher movies ever made—one of the year's best films"; while

*Fear*   133

another claims that "th[e] film would have to be the scariest movie I have ever seen."

54. Carroll, "The Nature of Horror," 52. Italics mine.
55. Fisher, *The Vehement Passions* (Princeton, NJ: Princeton University Press, 2002), 142. Structurally, this dynamic recalls that of dramatic irony. Yet as Fisher notes, whereas "traditional literary thinking about ... gaps between the frame of the central person and that of the reader or spectator has concentrated on epistemological questions, on what is known or not known," the emotional effects of these gaps are equally worthy of comment (Fisher, *The Vehement Passions* 144).
56. Fisher, *The Vehement Passions*, 142.
57. Carol Clover, *Men, Women and Chainsaws: Gender in the Modern Horror Film* (Princeton, NJ: Princeton University Press, 1993), 27.
58. Noel Carroll, *Beyond Aesthetics: Philosophical Essays* (Cambridge: Cambridge University Press, 2001), 238.
59. Tarja Laine, Feeling Cinema: Emotional Dynamics in Film Studies (London: Bloomsbury, 2013), 6.
60. Noel Carroll, "The Nature of Horror," 54; Cosimo Urbano, "What's the Matter with Melanie? Reflections on the Merits of Psychoanalytic Approaches to Modern Horror Cinema," *Horror Film and Psychoanalysis: Freud's Worst Nightmare*, ed. Steven J. Schneider (Cambridge: Cambridge University Press, 2004), 27.
61. Carroll, "The Nature of Horror," 52.
62. Slavoj Zizek, *The Zizek Reader*, ed. Elizabeth Wright and Edmond Leo Wright (Oxford: Blackwell, 1999), 104.
63. Zizek, *The Zizek Reader*, 104–5.
64. Brian Massumi, preface to *The Politics of Everyday Fear*, ed. Brian Massumi (Minneapolis: University of Minnesota Press, 1993), viii.
65. Samuel Beckett, *Waiting For Godot: A Tragicomedy in 2 Acts* (New York: Grove Press, 1982), 32.
66. Reynold Humphries, *The American Horror Film: An Introduction* (Edinburgh: Edinburgh University Press, 2002), 189.
67. Newman, *Nightmare Movies*, 288.

# 4 Bewilderment
## The Ravaged Face of Postmodern Theory and Aesthetics

## I

In David Lynch's *Mulholland Drive* (2001), the broken, fragmented or troubled face acquires a symbolic and thematic significance that finds its acme in an isolated yet indelible set-piece midway through the film. Thoroughly detached from the film's primary narrative and characterological co-ordinates, the scene sets us face to face with two unnamed men who—like many another character in the film's nightmarish reshuffling of the L.A.-*noir* archive—possess little obvious relation either to each other or to the detective story we thought we'd signed up for. Seemingly motivated as much by the audience's confusion as by his companion's, one of the men—a nervous, bushy-eyebrowed man identified in the end credits as "Dan" (Patrick Fischler)—offers a tenuous explanation for the set-up, announcing that he "just wanted to come here" after having had "a dream about this place." And in response to the slightly skeptical prompting of his companion, Herb (Michael Cooke), Dan discloses the dream's content:

> DAN: It's the second one I've had, but they're both the same. They start out that I'm in here, but it's not day, or night. It's kind of half-night, you know? But it looks just like this. Except for the light. And I'm scared, like I can't tell ya. Of all people, you're standing right over there, by that counter. You're in both dreams, and you're scared. I get even more frightened when I see how afraid you are ... and then I realize what it is. There's a man ... in back of this place—he's the one who's doing it. I can see him through the wall. I can see his face. I hope that I never see that face, ever, outside of a dream.
> HERB: So ... you came to see if he's out there.
> DAN: [*nodding*] To get rid of this godawful feeling.

A figure in which visibility and invisibility, human and inhuman, natural and supernatural, uneasily converge, the figure of the face that can be seen "through the wall" only ratchets up the mounting dread that a battery of other suspense cues—from Angelo Badalamenti's haunting score to Peter Deming's floating camerawork—have already afforded the scene. And despite Dan's subscription to the uplifting therapeutic premise that to confront what is "out there" will be to dispel or "get rid of" the fear that attaches to it, what follows fully realizes this dread. As we move from the restaurant's interior to the brightly painted exterior, the intercutting between a series of tense, unsteady shoulder-mounted shots of the wall floating up toward us from restaurant's backlot, and a series of equally tense, unsteady reverse shots of Dan descending the steps into the lot, engenders an escalating unease that very quickly proves prescient. From behind the drab concrete block wall, a dirt-coated face appears, occupying the frame for one single, horrifying close-up. Neither male nor female, neither young nor old, neither quite alive nor quite dead, the face remains on screen just long enough for us to register that it is a face, but not long enough for us to ground that face in a body, let alone in any kind of narrative or characterological context. Encrusted by a thick membrane of dirt and filth, the face has undergone a passage from the status of an expressive, animated vehicle of the subject to the status of an object barely differentiated from the wall from behind which it appears. The credits' identification of this quasi-character as a "Terrifying Bum" (Bonnie Aarons) only corroborates this passage, indexing the "front" of the subject to its "behind," the cosy familiarity of the face to the abominable abjection of a backside that—as Lee Edelman observes—has come to embody "what's left behind, what doesn't count … [what's] emptied of meaning except for its residual meaning as waste."[1] And the bewildering effect of the insertion of this waste-like and waste-covered face into a familiar shot/reverse-shot structure is at once indexed in and heightened by a cut back to Dan himself. As he collapses limply into the arms of his baffled friend, Dan's face assumes a blankness that echoes not only the blankness of the face that excited his response, but the "blank[ness]" that Silvan Tomkins attributes to the emotion of bewilderment itself.[2] The traumatic effect of this double

*Figure 4.1* The face of the "Terrifying Bum."

## 136  Bewilderment

facial collapse is underscored in post-production, by a series of very visible shudders that compromise the boundaries of the filmic image.

In place of the anticipated therapeutic or narrative resolution, then, the scene's climax ushers in a flurry of bewildered questions: who or what is the "Terrifying Bum"? Is he real or a projection? Why does his face instill such horror in Dan? And how is the scene connected to the wider thematic and narrative mandates of the film as a whole?[3] In the context of a film that Jonathan Romney calls "a bewildering, labyrinthine construction," that George Toles dubs a series of "bewildering, pathless, teasingly thorny episodes," and that Stephen Holden characterizes as a "little like peering into the semidarkness from the front car of a runaway subway train," there's nothing particularly unusual about the scene's bewildering, stupefying effect. What is unusual, however, is that whereas the majority of *Mulholland Drive*'s critics chalk up the film's bewildering emotional force to its complex, multi-layered narrative, this scene tethers bewilderment very tightly to the figure of the troubled or occulted face—that is, to the transformation, centred around the Terrifying Bum, of subject into object, of conscious being into stupefied heap, of human face into mud-caked monstrosity. It would not do, of course, to automatically extrapolate the relation between bewilderment and troubled faciality that holds in this particular scene across the film as a whole. Yet, once noticed, it is hard to *un*-notice *Mulholland Drive*'s traffic in collapsing and metamorphosing faces, faces that—from the dirt-encrusted face of the Terrifying Bum to the rotting visage of Diane Selwyn's putrescent corpse—emerge as some of the film's most consistent and powerful leitmotifs. It is hardly insignificant, for example, that the enigma that animates the film's narrative is a face without a name, a face belonging to a bewildered amnesiac beauty, "Rita" (Laura Harring), whose effort to establish her true identity forms the core of the detective plot that develops when she is taken into the care of a blonde ingénue named Betty (Naomi Watts), fresh off the plane from Deep River, Ontario. And if the figure of failed faciality is key to the film's bewilderment at the level of character and narrative, it is no less central at the level of form. From the explosive narrative drive of the film's opening sequence to the stagnant tapering-off of its final scene, *Mulholland Drive* institutes an escalating assault on the lineaments of the face that culminates three quarters of the way through the film when the diegesis that contains our putative protagonists, Betty and Rita, vanishes, and the lead actresses are capriciously recast as players in a second story-world that is at once "troublingly continuous" with, and impossibly remote from, the first.[4] If, as Jacques Lacan suggests, the human subject's "permanent appearance over time" is "strictly only recognizable through the intermediary of the name," the contours of a face to which no name will "stick" cannot ever be fully finalized.[5]

But what is so bewildering about these troubled instantiations of the face? To recall the face's role as a keystone figure in the theory of suture—a theory that, despite years of sustained critique, retains a powerful grip on our understanding of basic structures of identification—is to gain a certain critical

*Bewilderment*   137

leverage on the bewildering power of failed or troubled faciality. According to Jean-Pierre Oudart, whose arguments in the 1977 essay "Cinema and Suture" have been elaborated by numerous theorists since, the spectator's engagement with the image inside the frame is threatened by the persistent possibility that he or she will become cognizant of the frame itself, a telltale indicator of the visual field's subjection to an unpredictable, unknowable other—literally, the industrial and authorial machinery of cinema, but figuratively felt, according to Oudart, as a shadowy "Absent One."[6] In classical cinema, then, a cut from the initial image to its reverse shot—the image of a character to whose gaze that initial image can be ascribed—ensures that the determining agency that the spectator is in danger of disruptively attributing to forces *outside* the film is instead attributed to a character *within* it. And as what Mary Ann Doane calls "the very locus of subjectivity," this face's reassuring humanism dissimulates the infinite, unknowable workings of cinematic agencies as the effect of character point of view.[7] Taking up this line of thinking in his classic reading of the face in Otto Preminger's *Laura* (1944), Lee Edelman contends that "narrative cinema's obsessive preoccupation with faces ... figures (or gives face to) and thus disfigures (or effaces) the apparatus of cinematic inscription—an apparatus that, by means of these processes, attempts, as Jacqueline Rose puts it, 'to close itself off as a system of representation.'"[8] Indeed, suture theory's own "obsessive preoccupation" with the face as the pivot and predicate of spectatorial emotion is a function of a much longer philosophical tradition that Eugenie Brinkema has dubbed "a humanism organized around faciality as the site of subjectivity."[9] Despite the fundamental structural differences between, say, Guillaume Duchenne's expressive paradigm of emotion as a divine "spirit" that is then "paint[ed] ... on the face of man," and William James's insistence that physical, observable bodily or facial changes *precede* the internal, psychological emotion, such that "we feel sorry because we cry, angry because we strike, afraid because we tremble," theories of emotion have been remarkably uniform in their assumption that the face is the physiological aspect of a privileged psychological phenomenon, its twitches, grimaces and spasms the "pathway to the soul," inextricably coupled to something "within" the subject.[10]

Yet if the face's status as the emblem and expression of a presiding subjectivity has seen it pressed into a long service across both the philosophical and the cinematic archive, postmodern aesthetics seems committed to ending the face's critical and cultural reign. Arthur Kroker and Davis Cook's observation that the postmodern body is "an infinitely permeable and spatialized field whose boundaries are freely pierced" speaks for a much larger corpus of postmodern aesthetic and theoretical scholarship that represents the body not as the expression of an internal reality, but as "a certain effect of [an external] power"—a model of the body that conspicuously fails to deliver the fixed and unitary faces foundational to theories of suture.[11] To the extent, then, that the blank, fragmented, blurred, doubled or wholly dilapidated faces that people *Mulholland Drive* instantiate this distinctively

138  *Bewilderment*

"postmodern" model of the body, it should come as no surprise that, far from eliding the social and cinematic machinery that animates them, these faces are far more often vivid insignia of that machinery, unsettling signs of the visual field's thrall to the whims and caprices of a chimerical "Absent One." The face's disruptive potential, of course, long predates the postmodern turn in film aesthetics. As Doane has argued in her suggestive counter-history of the cinematic facial close-up, the face's historical deployment as an instrument of suture has been repeatedly confounded by its "lurking danger, [its] potential semiotic threat to the unity and coherency of the filmic discourse."[12] *Mulholland Drive*'s implicit contention, however, is that in postmodern aesthetics, this problem becomes more pressing. Projecting its dizzying catalogue of collapsing and metamorphosing faces against the backdrop of a Hollywood whose endless "role-playing and self-invention" has, for many critics, come to emblematize the postmodern, *Muholland Drive* suggests that, in postmodern aesthetics, the face has been fully de-coupled from subjectivity, and consequently from its capacity to guarantee spectatorial suture.[13]

But why is it bewilderment, in particular, that these moments of failed faciality magnetize? Why, conversely, is the figure of the troubled, inverted or occulted face the emotion's privileged rubric in *Mulholland Drive*? And what, for that matter, *is* bewilderment? Mortgaging spectatorial emotion to the viewer's "suturing" into the fabric of the film, film theorists have typically assumed that the failure of suture rules out the possibility of spectatorial emotion altogether. And while critics remain reluctant to show their theoretical hand by insisting on suture's centrality to spectatorial emotion, the *suspension* of suture is nevertheless routinely construed as deleterious to spectatorial emotion, as "interrupt[ing] the emotional spell of the narrative."[14] In this sense, the fact that bewilderment is so thoroughly at home with the suture-disrupting figure of troubled or subverted faciality speaks to its status as an emotion that falls outside the cognitive-appraisal co-ordinates through which emotion's presence and possibility is conventionally assessed. This chapter, then, will trace the remarkably equivocal aesthetic and theoretical consequences of bewilderment's "falling outside." On the one hand, as I will show, the emotion's uniquely chiastic structure resonates closely with some of the characteristics commonly ascribed to postmodernism, and, as a result, bewilderment has achieved a peculiar currency in postmodern theory and aesthetics as a sign of postmodern social and aesthetic phenomena. On the other, the emotion's corrosive subjective and bodily effects pose a powerful challenge to a postmodern critical and aesthetic apparatus that, notwithstanding its investment in fragmentation and self-loss at the level of theory, continues to prize autonomy and agency at the level of practice. In light of this ambivalence, it should come as no surprise the critical and aesthetic reification of bewilderment is matched by critical and aesthetic efforts to contain, to project and to displace it. And by tracking the formal career of the "face" of bewilderment through a range of canonical postmodern texts, this chapter will demonstrate that these efforts of containment, projection and displacement offer a glimpse into some of the postmodern field's more disconcerting proclivities.

## II

While the term bewilderment pops up repeatedly, even promiscuously, in accounts of postmodern aesthetics, it is seldom afforded a more than superficial definition. An important exception to this rule, however, is Fredric Jameson's extended analysis of John Portman's Westin Bonaventure hotel, a bold theoretical set-piece that not only forms the rhetorical apotheosis of the opening chapter of his *Postmodernism, or, The Cultural Logic of Late Capitalism*, but that has become "one of the most famous (indeed, most fetishized) scenes in the theoretical archive of postmodernity."[15] Installing bewilderment as the postmodern emotion *par excellence*, Jameson's quasi-diaristic description of this "complacent if bewildering leisure time space" draws repeatedly on the term to convey the specifically emotional effects of the cognitive and social problematics the space allegorizes.[16] Yet what is most striking about Jameson's oddly confessional chronicle of his "bewildering immersion" in the pastel-green dystopia of the hotel lobby is the way in which it unsettles the cognitive-appraisal codes through which emotion has conventionally been understood.[17] Where the intentionality criterion of emotion demands that emotion be, as John Deigh puts it, "directed at something," Jameson's bewilderment rests on the disorientating failure of a stable subject-object relation, in which the object is "impossible to seize" due to the failure of "that distance that formerly enabled the perception of perspective or volume."[18] Similarly, where the cognitive criterion of emotion grounds feeling in a belief or judgment, bewilderment turns precisely on the failure of our capacity to formulate a belief or judgment: with "hanging streamers ... suffus[ing] this empty space [of the Bonaventure hotel] in such a way as to distract systematically from whatever form it might be supposed to have," judgment is compromised if not impossible.[19] Finally, where the physiological criterion of emotion demands that emotion correlate to some kind of identifiable physiological change, bewilderment expresses itself only in a kind of ocular "scanning," a ceaseless shifting from one object to another that sees Jameson's verbal dilation on the Bonaventure devolve into a kind of breathless parataxis.[20]

In fact, more than just falling short of cognitive theory's projection of a neat representational correspondence between a bewildered subject and bewildering object, the model of bewilderment the passage limns depends on a kind of felt chiastic inversion of the customary relation between the terms "subject" and "object." On the one hand, Jameson's record of his experience at the Bonaventure hotel sees the object acquire many of the properties conventionally accorded to a subject. Not only do the building's plethora of technological conveniences "plummet[] ... down," "shoot up"

## 140 Bewilderment

and "splash down" again, as if in a constant state of independent movement, but these movements are granted actual agency and intelligence: the "milling confusion" that the lobby produces in guests at the hotel is figured as the "vengeance this space takes on those who still seek to walk through it," while the lobby's decorative elements are said to "distract systematically and *deliberately* from whatever form it might be supposed to have," as if the building were consciously contriving to baffle and bewilder its guests.[21] Indeed, the inverted view of the object registered here at the level of description is matched by the similarly inverted view of the object traced at the level of theory, in Jameson's contention that the Bonaventure embodies a kind of "mutation in the object" that "we ourselves, the human subjects who happen into this new space, have not kept pace with," as if the hotel were an uncanny agent capable of mutating and evolving of its own accord.[22] And in repeatedly confounding the customary grammatical relationship between a building and the person moving through it by granting the building itself the privileges of the grammatical subject, Jameson builds this same inversion into the passage's peculiar syntactical structures:

> The gardens in the back admit you ... the front entry admits you ... the elevator lifts you to one of those revolving cocktail lounges in which, seated, you are again passively rotated about.[23]

While perhaps logical in the case of the elevator, this attribution of grammatical agency to an insentient object seems noticeably less so in the case of a garden or an entrance way.

Yet if bewilderment affords the object the imprimatur of a subject, it equally reduces the subject to the status of an object, divesting him of his cognitive and perceptual faculties and plunging him into a state of helpless, paralyzed embodiment. It is not just that, unable to perceive "perspective or volume," Jameson's bewildered hotel visitor is "in this hyperspace up to [his] eyes and [his] body," an image that replaces the Cartesian fantasy of the subject moving triumphantly *through* space with the figure of the insentient object immersed *in* space.[24] It is also that—and more importantly for my argument that bewilderment finds its most fitting embodiment in the troubled or occulted face—the subject's demotion here from a masterful, presiding consciousness to a sluggish, material body is encoded in the register of facial fragmentation, as the face, stripped of its credentials as the "locus of subjectivity," is shattered into series of discrete, fragmented entities ("body" and "eyes"). The immediate spatial catalyst for this bewildering chiastic exchange, Jameson suggests, is postmodern architecture's "dialectical heightening" of the narrative models that have begun to infiltrate architectural theory:

> We know, in any case, that recent architectural theory has begun to borrow from narrative analysis in other fields and to attempt to see

Bewilderment 141

our physical trajectories through such buildings as virtual narratives or stories, as dynamic paths and narrative paradigms which we as visitors are asked to fulfill and to complete with our own bodies and movements. In the Bonaventure, however, we find a dialectical heightening of this process: it seems to me that the escalators and elevators here henceforth replace movement but also, and above all, designate themselves as new reflexive signs and emblems of movement proper …[25]

Promoting its escalators and elevators to the office of "signs and emblems of movement proper," the building effectively demotes its actual visitors to the status of superfluous corporeal residue—and once again this instability is registered grammatically, this time in a series of slippages in the passage's use of the first person pronoun.[26] Brown has suggested that in the context of a book notable for its apparent aspiration to critical omniscience, the Bonaventure sketch stands out as a moment in which one "feels fully in thrall of the autobiographical"; yet what is more remarkable about the passage than its adherence to the constraints of confessional first-person narrative is its continual divergence from these constraints: [27]

What one is still tempted to think of as the front entry, on Figueroa, admits you, baggage and all, onto the second story shopping balcony from which you must take an escalator down to the main registration desk. What I first want to suggest about these curiously unmarked ways in is that they seem to have been imposed by some new category of closure governing the inner space of the hotel itself …[28]

Manifest in an instability in the relation between speaker and addressee that sees the impersonal "one" become the second person "you" only to return full circle into the embrace of the first person "I," the bewilderment that Jameson claims to feel seems to institute a profound tremor in the subject's status *as* subject.

More than just failing to conform to a cognitive-appraisal model of emotion, then, bewilderment actually turns the cognitive-appraisal model on its head, conferring on the object the agency and intelligence conventionally ascribed to the subject, and on the subject the stolid impassivity conventionally ascribed to the object. Indeed, both these dimensions of the emotion are enshrined in its etymology, which, tracing the term to the late seventeenth-century verb *wilder*, meaning "to lead or go astray," allies bewilderment with a sense not only of lost orientation ("led *astray*") but of lost agency ("*led* astray"). In this light, it seems unsurprising that bewilderment should find its most compelling form in the problematization of the face, a bodily trope historically close to cognitive-appraisal theory's heart. Nor is it surprising that the emotion's signature phenomenological effects should come to coalesce around the disruption of cinematic suture. In both Jameson's account of his experience at the Bonaventure hotel, and Oudart's

## 142   *Bewilderment*

account of failed suture, the guest/viewer is made aware of the operation of a pervasive, unknowable agency whose interventions at the margins of the visible effectively regulate what we see. And in both cases, the guest/viewer experiences themselves as an object, a defenseless target for the work of what Oudart evocatively calls "phantom" forces.[29]

Yet bewilderment's phenomenological and taxonomical unruliness is not the whole story. For, more than just a disruptive or troublesome emotion, bewilderment also seems to have acquired a certain critical distinction as an emotional cipher of postmodern aesthetic and social co-ordinates. Jameson's dalliance with bewilderment, after all, is no mere authorial indulgence or expressive flight of fancy. Rather, his engagement with bewilderment is a function of his effort to appoint an emotional emblem for what is, to Jameson's mind, one of postmodernism's most prominent features, namely the failure of the project of charting social totality that Jameson calls "cognitive mapping."[30] At the heart of this failure is the sudden "incapacity of our minds, at least at present, to map the great global multinational and decentred network in which we find ourselves caught," as a result of the gulf between local subjective experience and the global political and economic matrix.[31] And until we can, as Jameson puts it ironically, "grow new organs ... expand our sensorium and our body to some new, yet unimaginable, perhaps ultimately impossible, dimensions," bewilderment's epistemic and ontological impasses will remain the most trenchant "analogon" of that totality.[32] To the precise extent that it so clearly materializes our *failure* to grasp "the various forces and flows that shape and constitute our world situation," that is, bewilderment becomes the social totality's provisional—if not exactly ideal—emotional hieroglyph, a "ghostly profile" of something we can neither conceptualize nor imagine.[33]

Yet Jameson is far from alone in his sense that bewilderment offers an unusually powerful purchase on postmodernism, for while rarely afforded the kind of loving theoretical attention that Jameson lavishes on the emotion, bewilderment recurs with surprising frequency in accounts of postmodern aesthetic and social phenomena.[34] Barry Lewis, for example, refers to the "bare, bewildering landscapes of the original [literary] postmodernists"; Norman K. Denzin to "this bewildering, frightening, terrifying, exhilarating historical moment"; while Stephen Bonnycastle notes that "many people feel ... disoriented and dismayed by postmodern works of literature: they contain such a mixture of styles, genres, and language that they can seem bewildering."[35] And while bewilderment has an ontological and emotional weight missing from Jacques Derrida's "aporia"—that "tired word of philosophy and of logic" that acquired a new lease of life within Derridean deconstruction as the name for a logical impasse or paradox in which the condition of something's being is also the "condition of [its] impossibility"—the similar critical prestige that has come to adhere to the latter term provides further evidence of postmodern criticism's high valuation of disorientation as a mode, however different its various instantiations.[36] Indeed, that bewilderment should have acquired this kind of currency in theoretical accounts of post-modernism should be less than surprising, since more than just an emotional cognate for the failure of cognitive mapping, bewilderment maps neatly onto the two primary poles around which most accounts of social, economic and political postmodernism tend to coalesce. On the one hand, critics from Jean Baudrillard to Douglas Kellner have pegged postmodernism as a moment in which "human beings are transformed into things," whether this process is understood as an effect of reification and exploitation, as a function of systems of governmentality, as part and parcel of the commodification of the self, or simply as a result of her enmeshment in a global totality she can neither control nor fully understand; within the horizon of this model, even one's emotions become, as Rey Chow puts it in her classic essay "Postmodern Automatons," "eruption[s] of the machine," effects of "the automatizing of the human body," and thus less subjective expressions than signs of that subject's subjugation and administration.[37] On the other—though this gesture is perhaps less explicit—theorists have just as routinely identified postmodernism with the promotion of the object to the status of subject. From Jacques Lacan's lyrical evocations of the object as the vehicle of the Gaze, to Michel Foucault's reading of Bentham's panopticon, which models a paranoid universe whose saturation by a "visible and unverifiable" surveillant gaze turns all objects into a potential proxy for a watching subject, postmodern theories advance a vision of the world in which the object has become suffused with the agency and intelligence more conventionally ascribed to a subject.[38] To the extent that bewilderment, then, is defined as a feeling of subject-object inversion, it seems to have a special affinity with a "postmodern condition" marked both by the death of the subject and by the failure of epistemic certainty, both by the reduction of subject to an object, and by the saturation of the object by social, political and ideological forces. Where other emotions are merely symptoms of the system that shapes and regulates us, bewilderment takes that system as its object. And where other emotions are merely effects of coercion, bewilderment provides an emotional distillation of coercion's operation. Leaving aside the question of whether these aesthetic and social co-ordinates "really" describe postmodernism—or whether postmodernism is a "thing" at all—it is clear that bewilderment has earned its critical place as an important emotional cipher of the postmodern condition.

Despite its ubiquity as a critical gesture, however, bewilderment's appointment as the corporeal hallmark of postmodern social condition is far from straightforward. For if bewilderment is a valuable synecdoche of postmodern social conditions, it nevertheless squares poorly with postmodern critical practice, compromising the forms of lucid, autonomous critical subjectivity that remain a normative requirement of any scholarly discourse—the lip-service paid in postmodernism to fragmentation and self-loss notwithstanding. This impasse becomes starkly manifest in the ambivalence that plagues Jameson's relation to bewilderment in the Bonaventure passage. At the level of content, Jameson celebrates bewilderment's vertiginous inversions of

144    *Bewilderment*

subject and object as an experiential "analogon" of the failure of cognitive mapping in postmodernism. At the level of form, however, he maintains a posture of studied autonomy and control, effectively quarantining to the past tense the destabilizing—and implicitly feminizing—experience he so enthusiastically champions.[39] These efforts to maintain authorial mastery through form culminate in the passage's final paragraph, which reasserts the theorist's ascendancy over the visual field by invoking an implicitly feminized "Los Angeles itself [that is] spread out ... before us."[40] Indeed, the lucidity and control of Jameson's tone is so pronounced that Brown is moved to comment on Jameson's "perceptual *activity*" or even "aggressivity in fixing phenomena," and to suggest that "Jameson posits himself as the epic or novelistic hero."[41] In these terms, it is difficult not to register a certain disingenuousness in the one moment in the text where Jameson does gesture toward the possibility that bewilderment's effects might infiltrate the scene of writing itself, in claiming to be "at a loss when it comes to conveying the experience of the thing itself, the experience of space you undergo when you step ... into the lobby or atrium"—especially when this claim is immediately undermined by the authority with which he goes on to "convey" just that.[42]

But if bewilderment's shattering, devastating force is unwelcome in the postmodern critical program, who is petitioned to feel it in our place? Whose bodies, that is, are asked to disintegrate under the heuristic force of bewilderment's destabilizing impact, and at what cost? In what follows, I wish to think through the implications of bewilderment's equivocal status in postmodern theory and aesthetics by exploring the emotion's narrativization in *Mulholland Drive*. On the one hand, in insistently destabilizing the human face that has conventionally served as the linchpin of both cinematic suture and theories of human subjectivity, the film shows its commitment to promoting bewilderment's symbolic and allegorical credentials as a sign of the "postmodern condition." On the other, bewilderment remains incompatible with the normative models of aesthetic coherence that—despite Lynch's reputation as a "wizard of odd"—prove central to his own and others' cinematic enterprise.[43] The value of the film as a critical object, however, lies in the starkness with which it dramatizes some of the bodily costs of bewilderment's unique combination of emotional unruliness and aesthetic prestige. For it is no accident, I will suggest, that *Mulholland Drive* tends to body bewilderment forth in the form of certain social and sexual others, nor that its narrativization and thematization of bewilderment finds its crowning inscription in the figure of the female corpse.

## III

While *Mulholland Drive*'s opening sequence ultimately delivers an arresting example of the troubled or fragmented face's threat to the protocols of cinematic suture, the more immediate threat it poses involves the *absence* of a face. The sequence in question sees the camera trailing a slow-moving,

*Bewilderment* 145

hearse-like limousine along an isolated, unlit hillside road, which a brief shot of a street sign identifies as the labyrinthine highway of the film's title. It is night, and only the two gleaming backlights and the patch of dusty illumination cast on the road by the car's headlights break up the prevailing darkness. The pro-cinematic suspense cues are numerous: there's the sooty, insidious gloom that saturates much of the image; there's the mystery of the car's late night errand; there's composer Angelo Badalamenti's haunting synths. Yet the primary source of the scene's tension lies neither in the film's content nor in its soundtrack. Rather, where a single establishing shot of the car would suffice to set the scene, the series of long, lingering tracking shots, repeatedly re-framing what is essentially the same image by alternately veering in close and falling back, tend to instantiate the camera as a hovering, voyeuristic and somewhat sinister presence. On the one hand, the objects on screen are no longer entirely objects, available to be known and understood by the viewer, but engines of the unpredictable agency imaginatively personified by Oudart as an enigmatic "Absent One." On the other, we ourselves are no longer entirely subjects, but pawns whose free exercise of epistemic and worldly agency is limited by our restricted access to the real machinations of power, which clearly take place off-screen. What is particularly striking about this sequence for our purposes is the extent to which its bewildering failure of suture is articulated in the register of a kind of *anti*-face: whereas, for Deleuze, the quasi-universal "formula" for the face is "white wall/black holes," these extended shots of a limousine's gleaming backlights trailing through the darkness of a deserted street in the Hollywood Hills deliver a counterposing *black wall/white holes* configuration.[44] In laminating the failure of suture to the image of the anti-face, *Mulholland Drive* reminds us that what is at stake in our investment in the face is the need to humanize and therefore dissimulate the disturbingly *in*human mechanisms that regulate and define what we see.

Yet the face's status as both the "very locus of subjectivity" and the long-standing linchpin of theories of suture only makes what happens when *Mulholland Drive* finally does seek to institute "suture" all the more striking.[45] At first, all is well: cutting at last from the exterior shot of the car to a close-up reverse shot inside the car that purports to disclose the bearer of the look, we see the face of a beautiful, voluptuous brunette. A dead ringer for a classic *femme fatale*, Harring—soon to christen herself "Rita"—is just the kind of heroine guaranteed to assuage our anxieties about our mastery over the visual field, her perfectly made up visage the very essence of focused, goal-oriented fixity. Yet no sooner have we been established in identification with her than something happens to mock and undermine our investment in her face. Pulling the limousine abruptly to a halt, the driver turns in his seat, cocks a gun at our mysterious heroine and demands that she "get out of the car." A reverse shot shows the brunette seemingly evacuated of the combative impulse that just a few seconds before had prompted her to observe angrily, "We don't stop here"; her neck muscles stiffen, her eyes widen and her lip is aquiver. At stake in this transformation is bewilderment's capacity to transfigure subject into object, as Rita's subjective experience of herself as an object—helpless patsy to the gun-toting driver's caprice—is recapitulated in her physical assumption of two of the salient characteristics of an object: inertia and passivity. Importantly, however, just as fascination is also itself a source of fascination, so the bewildered face is always also, in turn, a bewildering face. Far from a vehicle of a focused subjectivity capable of *displacing* the bewilderment engendered in the spectator by an awareness of "the apparatus of cinematic inscription," Rita's face is a tremulous, unstable mechanism that *induces* bewilderment by actually advertising and theatricalizing the work of this apparatus.[46] Confronted with the bewildered face, then, the film's capacity to knit us into its imaginary fabric is proscribed if not entirely thwarted.

*Figure 4.2* Harring's face initially functions to secure the suture.

*Figure 4.3* The bewildered face seems to theatricalize the mechanisms of suture.

Yet the scene is not over: as if the peril embodied in the cocked handgun were not enough, it is immediately followed by a second menace, which becomes visible in a cutaway shot of a pair of cars careening at high speed down the same hillside road. The force of both these threats culminates in a reverse shot of the brunette's face—a quivering screen across which the threat not just of a gun about to be discharged, but of a dangerously out-of-control car, pass simultaneously. Importantly, while the combination of the pointed gun and the unruly joyriders *embody* some of the forces that might act upon our bodies, they also operate to *figure* one set of forces specifically: that of the camera (a "shot") and lighting ("headlights") that form the technological arm of a larger cinematic/industrial complex. Their total effect, however, is to underscore even more clearly her face's status as what Roland Barthes, in his famous paean to the face of Greta Garbo, calls a cinematic "face-*object*," whose contours he lovingly traces thus: the "make-up has the snowy thickness of a mask; it is not a painted face, but one set in plaster … Amid all this snow at once fragile and compact, the eyes alone, black like strange soft flesh, but not in the least expressive, are two faintly tremulous wounds."[47] Two things are notable about this congruence between Lynch's Harring and Barthes' Garbo. The first is how clearly Barthes's account of Garbo captures the strangely paradoxical quality of a face that, no less an "object" than Harring's own, seems both easily impressionable (far from vehicles of emotion or perceptual tools of vision, the eyes are "wounds"; far from expressive and mobile, the face is "set in plaster") and endlessly transformable (just as the brunette's face is subject to the pressure of "lights, camera [and] action," so Garbo's famous visage is susceptible to Barthes' compulsive authorial reinscriptions, which cast it, alternately, as "plaster," as "snow," and as "strange soft flesh.")[48] The second, however, is that the most celebrated images of Garbo's face belong to the silent era, and thus hail from a moment in cinematic history just *prior* to the modern face-making program that reduces the human visage to an instrument of suture. In this sense, the resonance between Harring's face and that of Barthes's Garbo rather strikingly suggests the return, in postmodern aesthetics, of the disruptive, spectacularized faces of early cinema, faces that proudly emblazoned rather than dissimulated their status as illusory projections of what Tom Gunning calls the "wonders of [early cinema's] magic theatre."[49] Indeed, it is as if to illustrate its capricious agency as the master behind these "wonders" that *Mulholland Drive* delivers its next move. A climactic series of shots show the oncoming vehicle plummeting directly into the limousine's side and precipitating it into a roadside ditch, in what initially seems to augur the end both of this line of narrative, and of the face that so conspicuously fails to carry it.[50]

At a physical level, of course, this death never takes place: through the proverbial puff of smoke that conventionally flags moments of cinematic transformation, we see the brunette emerging awkwardly from the smoking, upturned car and stumbling down the hill to the light-studded city below. Despite her obvious disorientation, her hair remains untousled, her black

148    *Bewilderment*

cocktail dress immaculate and her face pristinely made-up. Yet while physically intact, on a figurative level, her death is very real. Dazzled by the lights of passing cars, overwhelmed by glimpses of passersby, amnesiac and without real agency, she can barely be called a "subject." On the contrary, she seems to have assumed the "blankness" that unsettled her features as she stared into the headlights of the oncoming car as a permanent expression, her face a bewildered and bewildering visual map of the cinematic, industrial and social forces that have acted and continue to act upon her from without. And given the threat that this face poses to the imaginary fabric of the film itself, it seems only logical that it should come to pose a similar threat to the imaginary fabric of the world it depicts, in which her face acquires a troublesome, volatile status that demands its concealment, dissimulation or even disposal. When a laughing couple emerges from a house on Sunset, Rita crouches in the foliage nearby, as if terrified of discovery; when Louise Bonner (Lee Grant), who will become Rita and Betty's slightly deranged, psychic neighbour, appears at the door of the pair's apartment one night to announce that "there is trouble" within, Rita seems to embody a terrifying, diffuse potential for harm; when Coco (Ann Miller), the owner of the complex, gets wind of Rita, she barely warrants a humanizing pronoun, and must be disposed of: "if there is trouble in there," she warns Betty, "*get rid of it.*" A living symbol or beacon of postmodernity's doubly troubling failure of both subjectivity and objectivity, Rita's face's capacity to unsettle the binaries usually secured by the face bewilders not just the spectator but everyone who encounters her. It is the need to resolve or dispel this bewilderment that sets the narrative machinery of the film itself—as well as the ideological machinery it depicts—in motion.

But this is not the whole story. Just as, for Jameson, bewilderment is simultaneously a disruptive entity best quarantined to the past and the clearest emotional diagnosis of the present, so, for Lynch, the destabilizing effect of Rita's bewildered face is matched by its diagnostic and erotic power. It is no accident that the film has elected, in Harring, a former Miss Texas USA as the emotion's poster-girl. And, having done so, the film pays loving, fetishistic homage to her doe-eyed, lost-looking face as she makes her way through the broad, empty boulevards of West Hollywood in a series of tracking close-ups that are always just a little *closer*-up than those that attend the faces of the film's other characters—as if the cropping of a chin or the truncation of a hairline have been judged a worthwhile concession to proximity to that exquisitely sensile visage.[51] But what is the source of the bewildered face's manifest visual magnetism, beyond Lynch's characteristic sympathy for the repressed and the marginalized? For Jameson, of course, bewilderment's authority is primarily diagnostic, and, certainly, the diagnostic dimension of Rita's bewilderment has a great deal to do with its distinction in *Mulholland Drive*. The film's vision of Hollywood, after all, is a peculiarly postmodern vision of a world in which the actual locus of agency or authority seems, in a kind of hellish infinite regress, to retreat continually from

*Bewilderment* 149

view, so that the psychopathic studio backers we meet early on in the film (Angelo Badalamenti and Tom Morris) are quickly revealed as proxies for a higher-powered, under-sized mafia boss (Michael J. Anderson)—who himself appears to be in thrall to a different authority again. As a sign of her defeated and demoralized intuition of these "great global and multinational networks in which we find ourselves caught," Rita's bewilderment, then, paradoxically radiates with an arresting diagnostic authority, affording her a definite epistemic edge over characters like Betty who seem entirely oblivious to their role in such circuits.[52] In a cinematic context, however, the diagnostic power of the bewildered face is matched by its aesthetic and erotic power. If, as Laura Mulvey has notoriously argued, the appearance of the woman in the film is "coded for strong visual and erotic impact so that they can be said to connote *to-be-looked-at-ness*," Harring's stupefied, disorientated post-accident Rita (quite *un*like the self-possessed, pre-accident Rita), is the ideal erotic object, her tremulous, pliant face offering itself to the camera's gaze with an implicit promise of total visual revelation.[53] And if bewilderment's erotic appeal goes hand in hand with it ongoing threat to suture, this is in some sense only to the extent that it epitomizes the process by which, as Mulvey has also noted, "the presence of woman ... tends to work against the development of a story line, to freeze the flow of action in moments of erotic contemplation."[54]

Indeed, *Mulholland Drive*'s tendency to valorize the aesthetic and diagnostic affordances of Rita's bewilderment is only amplified by the appearance of the completely *un*bewildered Betty.[55] As closely identified with a kind of subjective autonomy as Rita is with subjective atrophy, Betty is quick, of course, to recode the profoundly ontological bewilderment of the amnesiac beauty she finds crouching in the shower of her aunt's apartment in terms more in keeping with the straightforwardly epistemological confusion of the detective plot. Confronted with Harring's disarmingly ingenuous, infinitely vulnerable "I don't know who I am! I don't know what my name is!" Betty sensibly recalls the black purse that Harring had with her on her arrival at the house, and demands, first, that her new housemate search the purse for clues about her identity, and second, when that strategy only turns up more questions, that the two do some sleuthing to establish Harring's personhood once and for all, deploying as their tools a range of detective methods scraped together from popular culture: the anonymous phone-call, the use of the "back entrance," and the thoroughly probed flashback. In keeping with the film's allegiance to the diagnostic and erotic value of bewilderment, however, the "merely" epistemic confusions thrown up by the detective narrative are continually undermined by a deeper, ontological bewilderment that registers as a series of disturbances in the status of the face. In what is perhaps the climax of the detective narrative, for example, Betty and Rita break into a rather dank, lightless apartment that they suspect may be the home of Diane Selwyn, one of "Rita's " possible identities, only to encounter a putrescent corpse rotting on the bed in the master bedroom. As the rise of harsh synthesizer notes on the soundtrack ushers in the complete evacuation

150  *Bewilderment*

of diegetic sound that marks the film's key moments of psychic intensity, the pair advance toward the bed, as if unable to fully verify the body's biological status until they have seen its face—a face which, finally revealed as a gaping, decaying mess, sees Rita, like Dan before her, collapsing silently into her friend's arms. Literalizing bewilderment's chiastic inversion of the characteristics of subject and object, the inanimate cadaver on the bed suddenly possesses an imperious power, while the living, breathing Rita is struck helplessly down. Yet if Rita is incapable of looking directly *at* the dilapidated face, she is equally incapable of looking away, remaining in Betty's arms at the bedside for a whole minute of barely interrupted screen time as we cut repeatedly between her stricken face and the rotting, collapsed non-face of the corpse. And the implicit alignment this repeated shot-reverse shot establishes between the subjectively evacuated face of the bewildered subject and the objectively evacuated face of the dead woman is only consolidated by Rita's behaviour when she does finally tear herself away. Cutting at last from the suffocating interior of the house to an exterior shot of the apartment from outside, we see Rita, closely followed by Betty, bursting through the front door and down the pathway toward the fixed camera, where she pauses and, significantly, *covers her face with her hands*. Where an unbearable sight conventionally prompts us to cover our eyes, here, as throughout the film, the bewildered subject's terrifying receptiveness to external control and administration is identified as a threat to the face—a threat that Rita can avert only by hopelessly gripping the sides of her face as if in an effort to clamp it down, to keep it in place, to prevent it from sliding away. This apparent instability in the boundary between face and environment is compounded by the unusual visual effects applied to the shot in post-production, in which the superimposition of several iterations of the same shot of Rita clasping her face effects a kind of smudging or melting of the facial contour.

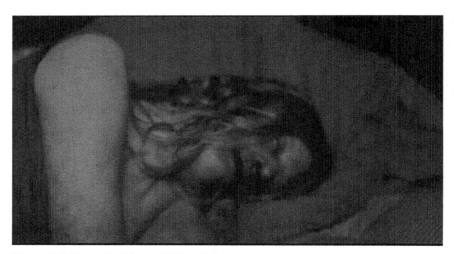

*Figure 4.4* The ruined face of Diane Selwyn.

*Figure 4.5* Harring grasps her face as if to keep it in place.

Yet if this post-production effect works as a powerful inscription of bewilderment as a felt experience, it is also a compelling reminder of the extent to which any threat to the on-screen face is also a threat to the consistency of the diegesis. And it is a measure of the film's ambivalence with respect to this threat that if this particular scene's mandate is to compromise the contours of Rita's face, the subsequent scene works strenuously to shore them up. Fading from the image of Rita's blurred face in the courtyard of the "Diane's" apartment to the image of Rita back at Havenhurst, feverishly cutting her hair into the bathroom sink, the film places us among the familiar paraphernalia of the makeover, a ritual whose paradoxical promise of stability through change, of identity through influence, of invulnerability through susceptibility, make it, as Brenda Weber puts it, "a potent cure for the postmodern condition, bringing coherence, solidity and empowerment to the fractured and schizophrenic state."[56] It should come as little surprise, however, that our protagonists' efforts to secure the difference between Rita's face and that of the corpse through the tools of feminine self-improvement only destabilizes that face further—though this time not through disintegration but through multiplication. Transported by the temporal ellipsis conventional to the makeover scenario from a labored, frenzied "before" to a lavish, spectacular "after," we pan across the array of hair and beauty products that sit open on the dresser and up to a mirror into which Betty draws Rita for her post-makeover "reveal." Yet in a gimmick reminiscent of the famous double-mirror scene in Ingmar Bergman's *Persona* (1966), not only are both women doubled by their mirror images, they are also shown to double each other, with Rita's blonde, bobbed wig and "natural" make up echoing the fresh-faced look of her younger companion. Far from restoring her to herself, the makeover merely turns her into a copy of another, underscoring the tension between the homogenized

## 152   *Bewilderment*

facial ideal installed by postmodern mechanisms of bodily transformation like cosmetics, dieting and plastic surgery, and the singularity and difference that has long been the cornerstone of modern mechanisms of cinematic suture.

Yet furthering our grasp of the bewildering effects of postmodern faciality is not the only narrative labor with which the makeover scene is tasked. For in embedding this bewilderment in the specific context of the makeover—a cultural scenario that, as Jackie Stacey puts it, has "an immediate association with femininity"—the scene also underscores the uncanny isomorphism that sees the cultural logic of bewilderment mirror, almost point for point, the cultural logic of femininity.[57] It is, as we have already hinted, not just any "body" that the film has mobilized as its vehicle for this most extreme and destabilizing of emotions. Rather, in a decision that immediately calls to mind Chow's wry observation that a woman's departure from male modernist norms becomes an occasion for "male romantic musings," it is that of a woman.[58] Indeed, the decision to quarter bewilderment in the body of a woman is all the more marked, and all the more clearly deliberate, because it relies on a striking inversion of the film *noir* conventions that *Mulholland Drive* otherwise seems content to draw relentlessly upon: whereas the sedate confusion of the classic film *noir* casts the *femme fatale* as the embodiment of what Doane calls "an epistemological trouble" for a male detective figure, the bewilderment of *Mulholland Drive*'s postmodern neo-*noir* casts Harring's *femme fatale* as herself epistemologically *troubled*.[59] It's easy enough, of course, to account for this coupling of "woman" and "bewilderment" by cataloguing the striking similarities between the two figures: the cultural semiotics of bewilderment, read as a sign of the subject's recognition of their status as a vulnerable and *scriptable* corporeal surface, map all too neatly onto the cultural semiotics of a "woman" who, having come to "overrepresent" the body in Western culture, is conventionally "more closely associated with the surface of the image than its illusory depths."[60] What is unsettling here, however, is the extent to which the film's reliance on this homology suggests an effort to protect a series of male gender and aesthetic norms from bewilderment's destabilizing effects. Quarantining bewilderment in a fetishized female figure allows *Mulholland Drive* simultaneously to reify bewilderment and to strategically distance itself—and its viewers—from the emotion's more deleterious epistemic and ontological implications.[61]

Indeed, if the woman provides a valuable vessel for this simultaneously valorized and unsettling emotion, the lesbian proves even more serviceable in the work of containing and exculpating the film's engagement with bewilderment. And this is a fact to which the film seems keenly alert, as the rubric of the makeover scene, in which one woman comes to resemble another, segues into the love scene rubric of one woman making love to another. The story, of course, is familiar enough. Intimacy deepened by the makeover episode, the two women opt to share the master bedroom, where a goodnight kiss metamorphoses into a passionate embrace, identification sliding

*Bewilderment* 153

all too seemingly seamlessly into desire. Yet what is most striking about what Heather Love sardonically calls Lynch's "very breasty, very kissy" idea of lesbian sex, is the extent to which Rita's sexual advances to her friend are cast not as a correlate of any kind of profound lesbian identity but as a correlate, rather, of opportunity and context, of responsive susceptibility to circumstance, or, as Lee Wallace puts it, "pre-eminently a matter of cinematic time and place."[62] After all, as Rita's comically ingenuous answer to Betty's hackneyed enquiry, "have you done this before?" reminds us, the amnesiac Rita can't possibly "know" either way. And if this responsive susceptibility recalls the tropes of failure and self-loss that congregate around bewilderment, it also, significantly, resonates with the "contagion," "hypnosis" and "mesmerism" tropes that, as Diana Fuss has shown, dominate a certain figuration of lesbian desire—tropes in which the notion of sexual proximity and exposure, sexual influence and infection, have priority over any notion of sexual "identity."[63] If woman is all surface, in this model, the lesbian is woman *plus*: her bodily boundaries ideally permeable and susceptible, ideally available to being "taken over and inhabited by an infectious agent."[64] One might almost suggest that whereas, as Lee Edelman has shown, the gay man is imagined as an essence without a face, and thus a fitting challenge for the face-making project of classical cinema, the lesbian is imagined as a face without an essence, and thus the perfect figure for a postmodern cinema committed to bodily destabilization.[65] Here, while inviting us to feel bewilderment as the emotional epitome of postmodern experience, the film seems strikingly eager to avoid bewilderment's potential threat to the boundaries of the autonomous masculine subject by containing it to the fetishized receptacle of the lesbian other.

With lesbianism installed as bewilderment's aesthetic and social alibi, *Mulholland Drive*'s assault on the coherence of the face hits its stride, as subsequent scenes work to ravage not just the face's capacity to guarantee suture, but the camera's capacity to imply the presence of the face. Again, we are set up with a hermeneutic project, embodied in the new lovers' discovery of the triangular blue key that is the exact match to the locked blue box discovered in Rita's bag earlier—and again that hermeneutic project unravels. Positioned in the bedroom as Betty and Rita enter with the key at the ready, the camera pans to the right to display Betty, in profile, place her bag on the bed. A pan back to left, showing Rita excitedly retrieving the blue box from the wardrobe, sees Betty disappear behind the camera. So far, so conventional. Yet while a character's disappearance behind the camera traditionally indicates a double transfer of properties—in which the camera's gaze is attributed to the character, while the character's face is fantasmatically conferred on the camera—the film quickly takes a turn that shatters this presumption. Having recovered the blue box and with the blue key at the ready, Rita looks toward the space occupied by the camera for reinforcement from her friend, only to find Betty missing. A series of unanswered exclamations reveal that Betty has entirely vanished from the

## 154  *Bewilderment*

diegetic space. Calling the bluff of the cinematic conventions that purport to personify and "give face" to the camera's mechanical gaze, thereby suturing us into the film, Betty's abdication of her "point of view" exposes the absence that lies at the heart of the cinematic machine, jolting us out of the fantasy that we are less addressees of a mechanical and industrial event than empathic observers of a poignant human scene. If the face itself has lost its capacity to conceal the maneuvers and strategems of the camera, now, too, the camera has lost the capacity to stand in for a face. Unsurprisingly, perhaps, it is Rita's sudden awareness that she is *alone* that prompts her long, nervous scan of the room around the room, her sudden sense of "being watched," her impossible awareness of the presence of the camera; for it is the "faceless" look of the camera—rather than an affectionate look from a friend—that fully warrants the sinister Lacanian term "gaze."

It is the film's central diegetic break, however, that most forcefully demonstrates the face's capacity to foreground the cinematic and industrial forces that play upon it. With Rita entering the blue key into the blue Pandora's box, the film is sucked into a kind of pre-cinematic darkness from which a series of brief, displaced fragments—the menacing cowboy appears at a bedroom door with the announcement "Hey pretty girl, time to wake up"; Betty's "Aunt Ruth" arrives home to find her apartment curiously evacuated—resolve finally into a story-world as narratively and formally different as a common location and an unchanged cast allow it to be: Watts's perky, upbeat Betty is transformed into the sallow, aging "Diane," embittered and frustrated by the recent departure of Harring, her lover, who is now inexplicably referred to as "Camilla." And while these newly christened faces are embedded in a *mise-en-scéne* that has as much or as little verisimilitude as the earlier one, now, far from securing suture, both Watts and Harring's faces become painfully obvious indexes of the cinematic agencies that can arbitrarily reassign them new names and identities.[66] Like Barthes' Garbo, who is "plaster," "snow" and "flesh" all at once, these infinitely malleable, impressionable faces remain clearly in thrall to what Judith Butler calls "the tenuousness of imaginary identification."[67] To a large extent, this central diegetic break is quite as aleatory as it seems, the stamp less of directorial calculation than of a fragmented, piecemeal production history marked by an array of conflicting financial, industrial and cultural pressures. Originally conceived as a television series, the two-hour pilot produced for ABC was rejected for broadcast, and it was only when *Mulholland Drive* was picked up by StudioCanal for release as a feature film that the second section was shot and appended to provide a resolution of sorts. The key point for our purposes, however, is that the film exploits the very literal intervention of industrial and cinematic forces in the naming and constitution of Watts and Harrings' faces as an occasion to extend its reification of the problematized or subjected face. For in deploying a number of narrative cues to suggest that section one has been a dream—most prominently by ushering in the new *mise-en-scéne* with the image of Diane

*Bewilderment* 155

waking from a mid-afternoon torpor—the film effectively promotes section two's bewilderment as a "real" from which the first, less bewildering diegesis falls short, whether as dream, fantasy or hallucination.

But how can a film committed to the production of bewilderment through the destabilization of the figure of the face reach any kind of resolution? If, as Linda Williams has argued, emotions can be lined up with corresponding generic forms, what is the characteristic "plot" of bewilderment?[68] The power of *Mulholland Drive* lies in the way in which its ending starkly dramatizes the price of bewilderment's theoretical and aesthetic reification. And this ending comes quickly, with the film's foreshortened second section plummeting headlong to its finale: Camilla has terminated her relationship with Diane after embarking on an affair with the male director of the film in which the two appear; a devastated and resentful Diane is persuaded by Camilla to attend a party at Adam's hilltop mansion; Camilla and Adam announce their engagement; Diane meets with a hit-man to discuss the murder of Camilla, and is promised that when the hit is completed she will find a "blue key." Energizing Diane's plans, of course, is the desire to restore her own agency by erasing Camilla's. Yet the act meant to liberate Diane from her hopeless attachment to Camilla only further consolidates her abjection, establishing Watts as the new avatar for the bewilderment that overtook Harring's Rita in section one. Immediately subsequent to the meeting with the assassin, we cut to black, the bottom dropping suddenly out of the film's briefly stable and reliable spatial co-ordinates. What follows—a blurry, grainy interior panning shot—suggests a text struggling to re-establish its relation to a presiding subjectivity: a jerky pan across a room digests the glass table-top, the carpet, the couch and finally the beige hem of Diane's dressing gown, before panning up to her face, a cinematic conflation of actor and setting that flattens out the distinction between animate and inanimate, subject and object, person and thing in a way that seems to recapitulate a postmodern logic of reification. Yet even when we do locate Diane's face, the face itself is inadequate to establish her as the locus of a presiding gaze, its transfixed, rigid expression suggesting a look that is less an instrument of vision than a function of her thingification. A reverse shot finally discloses the object of her look, in an extreme close-up of the blue key that signals Camilla's successful assassination. Yet the cutaway to the reverse shot of the key seems no more than a prelude to the film's next move, in which, cutting back again to Diane, we are delivered a low-angle shot of our heroine that is perversely established as *the key's point of view*—effectively granting the object subjective sovereignty, while reducing the subject to an inert thing, in a neat exemplification of bewilderment's chiastic structure. And once again, this bewilderment is articulated through a progressive disintegration of Diane's face, as a series of extreme close-ups fragment her visage into a cluster of disparate, disconnected part-objects: an eye, with a quivering eyelash; the curve of a nose and a shock of brittle hair; as she looks back at the key, an extreme close up on the eye again. Indeed, this series of fragmented

## 156   *Bewilderment*

extreme close-ups of the face seems to dramatize at a very literal level the fragmentation that Jean Epstein isolates as the facial close up's general figurative effect:

> A head suddenly appears on screen and drama, now face to face, seems to address me personally and swells with an extraordinary intensity. I am hypnotized. Now the tragedy is anatomical. The décor of the fifth act is this corner of a cheek torn by a smile. [...] The orography of the face vacillates. Seismic shocks begin. Capillary wrinkles try to split the fault. A wave carries them away. Crescendo. A muscle bridles. The lip is laced with tics like a theater curtain. Everything is movement, imbalance, crisis. Crack. The mouth gives way, like a ripe fruit splitting open. As if slit by a scalpel, a keyboard-like smile cuts laterally into the corner of the lips.[69]

If, for Epstein, the close up is always the occasion for a kind of dramatic semiotic and physical fragmentation, *Mulholland Drive* dramatizes that fragmentation on a cinematographic level in a gesture emblematic of postmodern aesthetics' elevation of early cinematic accident into post-cinematic imperative.

It is the sequence that immediately follows this one, however, that clearly spells out the stakes of our investment in an emotion yoked to facial fragmentation. An unsteady, hand-held close up shows Diane, apparently "driven mad by remorse," fleeing down the corridor, and—as if enacting a wholly ineluctable course—assuming the same position on the bed as the corpse encountered by Rita and Betty in section one, before blowing her face off with a gun.[70] As the scene fades out, the film consecrates the body with a puff of dry ice, retreating—this time—away from the face rather than lingering gormlessly at the bedside, as in the earlier scene that it now seems, uncannily, to chronologically precede. The effect of that face, however, is unchanged: here, as there, this dilapidated ruin or gaping abscess provides a chillingly literal mirror of the more figurative fragmentations and destabilizations undergone by Rita's face. Yet the particular horror of this, the face's second appearance, lies in the way it shifts the status of the ruined face from unhappy accident to ineluctable fate, from a singular instantiation of one woman's misery to a kind of filmic destiny, the painful apotheosis of any aesthetic or theoretical system that elects bewilderment as its emotional mascot. If bewilderment is our *modus operandi*, it would seem, no matter what genre we pick—whether the buoyant detective fantasy of section one, or the bleak social (sur)realism of section two—we end up in the same place. Indeed, the "impossibility" of bewilderment's face is driven home as we cut from the now smoke-filled bedroom to what appears to be a blurry recapitulation of images from Diane's dream, a series of blown-out close-ups of Rita and Betty's faces projected against a night-lit L.A. backdrop. Virtual transparencies, pockmarked and studded with the lights of the urban background against which they are projected, these faces are literally inseparable

Bewilderment 157

from what they are facing, crystallizing the bewildered subject's inability to quite "objectify" its object. Yet as such, they are also ghostly, substanceless, ectoplasmic projections, built entirely of light. As Hal Foster has argued, while "for many in contemporary culture truth resides in the traumatic or abject subject, in the diseased or damaged body," "there are dangers with this siting of truth," for "if there is a subject of history for the cult of abjection at all, it is not the Worker, the Woman, or the Person of Color, but the Corpse."[71] Foster's reminder of the embodied form taken by postmodern theory's tendency to reify some of the extremes of experience is timely, yet the strange non-equivalence of the categories he invokes, in which a list of identity positions are lined up alongside a biological state, allows him to overlook one thing: that no corpse is innocent of raced, gendered or classed categories, and that, in this case at least, the corpse is, not at all accidentally, the corpse of a (lesbian) woman.

As this chapter has shown, bewilderment is an emotion whose unique congealment of epistemic and ontological defeat has made it an ideal emotional emblem of a postmodern moment in which the impossibility of cognitive mapping is matched by the demise of the autonomous, agential subject. If Jameson's famous meditation on the Bonaventure hotel bestows on bewilderment the ambivalent distinction of postmodern emotion *par excellence*, his near-contemporary "Cognitive Mapping" only steps up these claims, dismissing alternative emotional responses to postmodern co-ordinates, such as paranoia, as "the poor person's cognitive mapping in the postmodern age ... the degraded figure of the total logic of late capital, a desperate attempt to represent the latter's system."[72] And *Mulholland Drive*'s glamorization of the troubled, desubjectivized or vacant face provides extensive aesthetic and narrative support for Jameson's position, valorizing Rita's bewildered and bewildering *femme fatale* as the emotional embodiment of the ontological and epistemic instability it locates in postmodern Hollywood. Against the epistemic optimism of Betty's fanciful, linear detection plot, the film pits the accelerating, vertiginous tug of Rita's bewildering, non-narrative neo-*noir*.

Yet as this chapter has also argued, the elevation of bewilderment to the status of a kind of emotional standard-bearer for the postmodern enterprise is a remarkably ambivalent gesture. An apt and accurate emotional metonym of postmodern social and economic conditions, bewilderment is also an emotion incompatible with our most basic theoretical and aesthetic mandates. This ambivalence leaves a powerful mark on the narrative and form of *Mulholland Drive*. As I have shown, the film's investment in this simultaneously critically valorized and subjectively confounding emotion not only entails the emotion's containment in the body of a lesbian, but ends in her quite literal defacement, epitomizing what feminist theorists have anatomized as a tendency for "male hegemony [to] rel[y] on the 'loose woman' ... for a projection of that which is subversive, improper, marginal, unspeakable, and so forth."[73] In light of bewilderment's narrative destiny in *Mulholland Drive*, it seems hardly surprising that—recanting many of the claims advanced in the

## 158   *Bewilderment*

Bonaventure passage—Jameson was later to contend that while epistemically problematic, the conspiracy narrative's desperate attempt to "figure out where we are and what landscapes and forces confront us in a late twentieth century" has value in and of itself as a "wild stab at the heart" of a global network whose true contours remain inaccessible.[74] Admittedly, Jameson qualifies this claim somewhat with the caveat that "nothing is gained by having been persuaded of the definitive verisimilitude of this or that conspiratorial hypothesis."[75] Yet as he puts it, it is "the intent and the gesture that counts" in assessing conspiracy narrative: however clearly these hypotheses displace the social totality's essential unrepresentability, they remain essential to our capacity to live and thrive in the world.[76] Conversely, as the recurring figure of the defaced woman in *Mulholland Drive* suggests, while bewilderment may rigorously reflect the conditions of postmodernity, it is also a state whose clearest cultural archetype is a defaced female corpse.

## Notes

1. Lee Edelman, "*Rear Window*'s Glasshole," in *Out Takes: Essays on Queer Theory and Film*, ed. Ellis Hanson (Durham, NC: Duke University Press, 1999), 75.
2. Silvan S Tomkins, *Affect, Imagery, Consciousness, Volume II: The Negative Affects* (New York: Springer Publishing Company, 2008), 297.
3. Jonathan Romney, "*Mulholland Drive*: Lynch Opens up his Box of Tricks," *The Independent*, January 6, 2002, accessed July 10, 2010, http://www.independent.co.uk/arts-entertainment/films/reviews/mulholland-drive-15–662448.html; George Toles, "Auditioning Betty in Mulholland Drive," *Film Quarterly* 58.1 (2004): 4; Stephen Holden, "Hollywood, A Funhouse of Fantasy," *The New York Times*, October 6, 2001.
4. Lee Wallace, *Lesbianism, Cinema, Space: The Sexual Life of Apartments* (London: Routledge, 2009), 100.
5. Jacques Lacan, quoted in Judith Butler, *Bodies that Matter: On the Discursive Limits of Sex* (New York, NY: Routledge, 1993), 153.
6. Jean-Pierre Oudart, "Cinema and Suture," *Screen* 18.4 (1977): 35–6. Published alongside Oudart's article in *Screen*'s aegis-defining dossier on suture was the psychoanalytic discussion on which Oudart's work was based, Jacques-Alain Miller's "Suture (Elements of the Logic of the Signifier)," and an excellent elaboration of Oudart's work by Stephen Heath. (Jacques-Alain Miller, "Suture [Elements of the Logic of the Signifier]," *Screen* 18.4 [1977]: 24–34; Stephen Heath, "Notes on Suture," *Screen* 18.4 [1977]: 48–76).
7. Mary Ann Doane, "The Close-Up: Scale and Detail in the Cinema," *differences: A Journal of Feminist Cultural Studies* 14.3 (2003): 90.
8. Lee Edelman, *Homographesis: Essays in Gay Literary and Cultural Theory* (New York: Routledge, 1994), 195.
9. Edelman, *Homographesis*, 195; Eugenie Brinkema, "Laura Dern's Vomit, or, Kant and Derrida in Oz," *Film-Philosophy* 15.2 (2011): 55.
10. Guillaume Benjamin Amand Duchenne De Boulogne, quoted in Joanna Bourke, *Fear: A Cultural History* (Washington, DC: Shoemaker and Hoard, 2007), 12; William James, *The Principles of Psychology* (New York: Cosimo Classics,

*Bewilderment*   159

2007), 450; Barbara Johnson, *Persons and Things* (Cambridge, MA: Harvard University Press, 2008), 180.

11. Arthur Kroker and David Cook, *The Postmodern Scene: Excremental Culture and Hyperaesthetics*, (Montreal: New World Perspectives, 1986), v. As Susan Bordo has put it, "Formerly, the body was dominantly conceptualized as a fixed, unitary, primarily biological reality. Today, more and more scholars have come to regard the body as a historical, plural, culturally mediated form." (Susan Bordo, "Postmodern Subjects, Postmodern Bodies," *Feminist Studies* 18.1 [Spring, 1992]: 166.) In postmodernism, that is, the body is seen not as the expression of an internal reality or identity, but as a fabric of corporeal gestures organized and animated by social and political discourse.

12. Doane, "The Close-Up," 90.

13. Holden, "Hollywood, a Funhouse of Fantasy."

14. Peter Wollen, "Godard and Counter-Cinema: Vent d'Est," in *Narrative, Apparatus, Ideology: A Film Theory Reader*, (New York: Columbia University Press, 1986), 121. See also Cynthia Baron's contention, in an account of Robert Altman's *The Player*, that the strategies through which the film "disrupt[s] classical-realist suture" work to create a "Brechtian distance" between the audience and the film. (Cynthia Baron, "The Player's Parody of Hollywood: A Different Kind of Suture," in *Postmodernism in the Cinema*, ed. Cristina Degli-Esposti [Kent: Berghahn Books, 1998], 35.) Given the critical and popular traction of this idea, it should come as no surprise that what Slavoj Zizek has claimed of David Lynch's earlier *Lost Highway*—that is, that it was read by critics as "a cold postmodern exercise ... emphasising the thoroughly artificial, inter-textual, ironically clichéd nature of Lynch's universe"—could equally be applied to *Mulholland Drive*, a film replete with disruptions of suture. (Zizek, *The Art of the Ridiculous Sublime: On David Lynch's Lost Highway* [Seattle, WA: Walter Chapin Simpson Center for the Humanities, 2000], 3). For *Variety*'s Todd McCarthy, for example, the central narrative break completely ruptures the spectator's connection to the film. As he argues, "the sudden switcheroo to head games is disappointing because, up to this point, Lynch had so wonderfully succeeded in creating genuine involvement": "After methodically building for an hour and three-quarters to a mesmerizing level of emotional intensity and narrative fascination pic makes a severe and unwelcome turn down a lost highway, never to return to the main drag." (Todd McCarthy, "*Mulholland Drive*," *Variety*, Wednesday, May 16, 2001, accessed July 10, 2010, http://www.variety.com/review/VE1117798101.html?categoryid=31&cs=1).

15. Bill Brown, "The Dark Wood of Postmodernity: Space, Faith, Allegory," *PMLA* 120.3 (2005): 735.

16. Fredric Jameson, *Postmodernism, or, The Cultural Logic of Late Capitalism* (Durham, NC: Duke University Press, 1991), 44.

17. Jameson, *Postmodernism*, 43.

18. John Deigh, "Primitive Emotions," in *Thinking about Feeling: Contemporary Philosophers on Emotion*, ed. Robert C. Solomon (Oxford: Oxford University Press, 2004), 9; Jameson, *Postmodernism*, 43.

19. Jameson, *Postmodernism*, 43.

20. Tomkins, *Affect, Imagery, Consciousness*, 297. Bewilderment's status as a kind of failed or aborted experience has interesting implications for some of the criticisms that have been directed at Jameson's reading of the Bonaventure, most prominent

## 160  *Bewilderment*

among which is the objection that the Bonaventure is "not really as bewildering as he says it is." (Ian Buchanan, *Deleuzism: A Meta-Commentary* [Edinburgh: Edinburgh University Press, 2002], 110.) For this insistence on the disjunction between theory and reality, between Jameson's reading and the concrete architectural space, actually plays into and supports his reading: it is precisely this non-coincidence with the object that, for Jameson, constitutes the experience of bewilderment in the first place. Paradoxically, then, the less objectively justified the experience of bewilderment is, the more truly it warrants its name.

21. Jameson, *Postmodernism*, 43. My italics.
22. Ibid., 38.
23. Ibid., 43.
24. Ibid.
25. Ibid., 42.
26. Ibid.
27. Brown, "Dark Wood of Postmodernity," 736.
28. Jameson, *Postmodernism*, 39.
29. Oudart, "Cinema and Suture," 43.
30. Jameson, *Postmodernism*, 44. Extrapolating geographer Kevin Lynch's analysis of spatial structure to the realm of global totality, Jameson's "cognitive map" is "an abstract concept whose effect is to render visible the various forces and flows that shape and constitute our world situation." (Ian Buchanan, *Fredric Jameson: Live Theory* [London: Continuum, 2006], 109).
31. Jameson, *Postmodernism*, 44.
32. Jameson, *Postmodernism*, 39; Buchanan, *Fredric Jameson*, 101.
33. Buchanan, *Fredric Jameson*, 109; Fredric Jameson, "Cognitive Mapping," in *Marxism and the Interpretation of Culture*, ed. Cary Nelson and Lawrence Grossberg (Urbana and Chicago: University Illinois Press, 1988), 352. As Brown has suggested, "Allegory comes to stand as a placeholder through much of Jameson's work—for successful cognitive mapping: Postmodern networks may not be mappable, but contemporary phenomena are allegorizable as the symptoms of postmodernism. Allegory appears as the productive sublimation of a cartographic drive; the allegorical operation substitutes hermeneutic certainty for cartographic clarity." (Brown, "Dark Wood of Postmodernity," 737.) Jameson's commitment to bewilderment's negative revelatory power is inscribed in his insistence that "if individual experience is authentic, then it cannot be true; and ... if a scientific or cognitive model of the same content is true, then it escapes individual experience." (Jameson, "Cognitive Mapping," 349.) Jameson further elaborates his concept of cognitive mapping in Fredric Jameson, *The Political Unconscious* (London: Routledge Classics, 2002), and Fredric Jameson, *The Geopolitical Aesthetic* (Bloomington: Indiana University Press, 1995).
34. Admittedly, critics such as Mike Davis have questioned the validity of the model of postmodernism limned in Jameson's reading of the Bonaventure, and thus, by extension, the validity of Jameson's recourse to bewilderment as postmodernism's best emotional proxy. According to Davis, Jameson's recruitment of the Bonaventure hotel as a representative postmodern experience buys wholesale into the illusion these buildings seek strategically to propogate—namely, that they have "recreated within the precious spaces of ... super-lobbies the genuine popular texture of city life." (Mike Davis, "Urban Renaissance and the Spirit of Postmodernism," *New Left Review* 151 [May-June, 1985]: 112). For Davis, that

Bewilderment    161

is, the experience of bewilderment precipitated by the Bonaventure is an experience that disavows "the real Zeitgeist of postmodernism," which is emblematized not by the Bonaventure itself, but by the relation between the Bonaventure and the poor Latino neightbourhoods that aurround it. This relation is one of "systematic segregation from the great Hispanic-Asian city outside," in which, in the face of the crisis of the inner city (as industry and middle classes fled to the suburbs and the downtown area became populated by poor people) the big civic amenities were no longer designed to interact with the public but became fortresses designed to defend against the public "skyscraper-fortress-enclaves" (Davis, "Urban Renaissance," 112, 111). The essence of postmodernism, that is, is not the polite disorientation of subject and object precipitated by what Davis calls the Bonaventure's "claustrophiobic space colony," but the "profoundly anti-urban impulse" that polarizes the city into "radically antagonistic spaces" organized around class and racial difference. Yet given this book's agnosticism with respect to the nature or even existence of postmodernism as a historical moment, what is more to the point for my purposes is the fact that, whatever our opinions of the accuracy of Jameson's diagnosis, that diagnosis has indispitably achieved a broad critical uptake.

35. Barry Lewis, "Postmodernism and Fiction," *The Routledge Companion to Postmodernism*, ed. Stuart Sim (New York: Routledge, 2005), 113; Norman K. Denzin, *Images of Postmodern Society: Social Theory and Contemporary Cinema* (London: Sage, 1991), 156; Stephen Bonnycastle, *In Search of Authority: An Introductory Guide to Literary Theory* (Ontario: Broadview Press, 2007), 258.

36. Jacques Derrida, *Aporias: Dying-Awaiting (One Another At) "The Limits of Truth"* (Palo Alto: Stanford University Press, 1993), 15. As Derrida indicates in the book *Aporias*, the figure of the "aporia" has recurred throughout his work to convey the internal contradictions that haunt the logic of the gift, hospitality, mourning, death and forgiveness. (Derrida, *Aporias*, 15–6.) Yet if aporia is a condition of an object to be known—or not known—it is also, and crucially for our argument here, a condition of the subject, a state that we "undergo" or "experience" as we would an emotion, and a state that Derrida glosses as "the not knowing where to go … the experience of the non-passage." (Derrida, *Aporias*, 33, 33, 12.) Indeed, Derrida is careful to distinguish the state of aporia from the logical or rhetorical tropes with which it is often identified. As he puts it, "aporia … is neither an 'apparent or illusory antinomy,' nor a dialecticizable contradiction in the Hegelian or Marxist sense, … but instead an interminable *experience*." (Derrida, *Aporias*, 16; italics mine.)

37. Steven Best and Douglas Kellner, *The Postmodern Turn* [New York: The Guilford Press, 1997], 76; Rey Chow, *Writing Diaspora: Tactics of Intervention in Contemporary Cultural Studies* (Bloomington: Indiana University Press, 1993), 60. For Jean Baudrillard, advanced, post-industrial capitalist society involves "the disappearance of the subject into the object"; Kathleen Woodward characterizes "the emotional style required by [a postmodern] society" as one in which "the self is conceived of as an object, a material object"; while according to David Harvey, postmodernity is marked by a sense of "the plasticity of the human personality through the malleability of appearances and surfaces." (David B. Clarke, Marcus A. Doel, William Merrin and Richard G. Smith, "Introduction: The Evil Genius of Jean Baudrillard," in *Jean Baudrillard: Fatal Theories*, eds. David B Clarke, Marcus A Doel, William Merrin and Richard

## 162 *Bewilderment*

G Smith [Oxon: Routledge, 2009] 6; Kathleen M. Woodward, *Statistical Panic: Cultural Politics and Poetics of the Emotions* [Durham, NC: Duke University Press, 2009], 17; David Harvey, *The Condition of Postmodernity* [Malden, MA: Blackwell Publishing, 1990], 7.)

38. Jacques Lacan, *The Seminar of Jacques Lacan Book XI: The Four Fundamental Concepts of Psychoanalysis* (New York: W.W. Norton and Company, 1998), 96; Michel Foucault, *Discipline and Punish* (London: Vintage Books, 1979), 201.

39. Jameson, *Postmodernism*, 44.

40. Ibid. 43.

41. Brown, "Dark Wood of Postmodernity," 739. Italics in original.

42. Jameson, *Postmodernism*, 42–43.

43. Unattributed, "David Lynch Interview," *EmpireOnline*, undated, accessed May 3, 2014, http://www.empireonline.com/interviews/interview.asp?IID=641.

44. Gilles Deleuze and Felix Guattari, *A Thousand Plateaus: Capitalism and Schizophrenia* (London: Continuum, 2004), 189.

45. Mary Ann Doane, "The Close-Up: Scale and Detail in the Cinema," *differences: A Journal of Feminist Cultural Studies* 14.3 (2003): 90.

46. Edelman, *Homographesis*, 195.

47. Roland Barthes, *Mythologies* (Frogmore: Paladin, 1973), 56.

48. Ibid.

49. Tom Gunning, "An Aesthetic of Astonishment: Early Film and the (In)Credulous Spectator," in *Viewing Positions: Ways of Seeing Film,* ed. Linda Williams (New Jersey, NJ: Rutgers University Press, 1995), 119.

50. Importantly, just as Rita's face induces bewilderment, so Barthes links Garbo's face to a certain self-loss or bewilderment: not just to a question of "losing one's way" (as Barthes puts it, "Garbo still belongs to that moment when … one literally *lost oneself* in a human image as one would in a philtre"), but, perhaps more disturbingly, to death (the face of Valentino, Barthes claims, "caus[es] suicides") (Ibid.).

51. Indeed, in keeping with its glorification of the bewildered Harring, *Mulholland Drive* works strenuously to endow its darker, more bewildering second diegesis with an epistemic and narrative priority over the sanguine optimism of the first. And the film's own tendency in this respect is echoed in its criticism, with most scholars earmarking the much longer section one as a dream, hallucination or "retrospective fantasy sequence" that serves to dissimulate the "real" enshrined in section two. (Wallace, *Lesbianism, Cinema, Space*, 101.) While criticism of *Mulholland Drive* has varied in specific content, it almost invariably fetishizes the film's central diegetic break as the pivot around which to substantiate or process a version of this highly hierarchicalized opposition. For McGowan, for example, the film provides a perfect stage for articulating a familiar psychoanalytic argument about the way fantasy displaces the painful, contradictory reality of desire; for Jay R. Lentzer and Donald R. Ross, the film stages a dream that "represents [Diane's] deeply conflicted wishes" in relation to a painful reality; for Jennifer A. Hudson, the film is an allegory of the triumph of "non-logical sense" over "traditional sense." (Todd McGowan, "Lost on *Mulholland Drive*: David Lynch's Panegyric to Hollywood," *Cinema Journal* 43.2 [2004]: 67–89; Jay R. Lentzer and Donald R. Ross, "The Dreams that Blister Sleep: Latent Content and Cinematic Form in *Mulholland Drive*," *American Imago* 62.1 [2005]: 103; Jennifer A. Hudson, "'No Hay Banda, and Yet We Hear a Band':

Bewilderment 163

David Lynch's Reversal of Coherence in *Mulholland Drive*," *Journal of Film and Video* 56.1 [Spring, 2004]: 23.) Such is the magnetic power of the film's invitation to this kind of reading that performing an analogous reading here—pitting bewilderment and some other term against each other in a kind of diagnostic stand-off in which section two's bewilderment somehow "trumps" section one's more conventional narrative mode—remains difficult to resist.

52. Jameson, *Postmodernism*, 44.

53. Laura Mulvey, "Visual Pleasure and Narrative Cinema," in *Film Theory and Criticism: Introductory Readings*, ed. Leo Braudy and Marshall Cohen (New York: Oxford University Press, 1999), 837.

54. Mulvey, "Visual Pleasure," 837.

55. Betty's inaugural appearance in the film, which shows her arrival at LAX accompanied by an elderly couple that she appears to have befriended on the plane, is distinguished by a series of extended tracking shots that capture her beaming face. If, as Benedict de Spinoza has argued, our affective states can be divided into the categories of those that "increase[] or aid[] man's power of acting," and those that mark a decrease of power, Betty's insistent optimism tends to fall into the former category, her "Bett-ific" smiles suggesting a robust sense of autonomy and "increase" that is entirely lacking in a bewilderment most clearly marked by its sense of stark subjection to external control. Benedict de Spinoza, *Ethics*, trans. Edwin Curley (London: Penguin Books, 1996), 90. Yet within *Mulholland Drive*'s filmic world, this distinction between empowered and disempowered emotions is only apparent: the empowering, uplifting emotions consistently modeled by Betty throughout the film are merely emotions that elide the machinery of their own solicitation. As Betty and the elderly couple go their separate ways, we cut, quite unexpectedly, not to the interior of Betty's cab, but to that of "Irene" and her unnamed husband. A long, narratively redundant shot of the couple, clearly still thrilled by their encounter with the young acting hopeful, shows them grinning "moronically," their faces contorted into tormented masks of joy. (Wallace, *Lesbianism, Cinema, Space*, 102). If Betty's smile had seemed to exude agency and control, these jarringly toothy, mechanical, anguished grins register less as organic expressions of an inner emotion than as robotic agitations painfully extracted from or imprinted on their faces. In its insistence, then, that even the most active, enabling, empowering and agential of emotions, like happiness, are mortgaged to our status as what Chow calls "postmodern automatons," the logic of the scene clearly echoes the logic of postmodern theory.

56. Brenda Weber, *Makeover TV: Self-hood, Citizenship and Celebrity* (Durham, NC: Duke University Press), 14.

57. Jackie Stacey, *The Cinematic Life of the Gene* (Durham, NC: Duke University Press, 2010), 119.

58. Chow, *Writing Diaspora*, 64.

59. Mary Ann Doane, "Gilda: Epistemology as Striptease," *Camera Obscura* 4 (1983): 10.

60. Mary Ann Doane, *Femme Fatales: Feminism, Film Theory, Psychoanalysis* (New York: Routledge, 1991), 2, 20.

61. With this in mind it becomes significant that of the many "bewildering" films released in 2001, only *Mulholland Drive*—a film about bewildered women—received universal critical acclaim, and that Cameron Crowe's *Vanilla*

## 164  *Bewilderment*

*Sky*, which traces the figure of postmodern bewilderment through the figure of an emasculated male character, was dismissed as an incoherent jumble by the same critics who praised *Mulholland Drive* for its pleasurable perplexity.

62. Heather Love, "Spectacular Failure: The Figure of the Lesbian in Mulholland Drive," *New Literary History* 35.1 (Winter, 2004): 127. Wallace, *Lesbianism, Cinema, Space*, 102.

63. Diana Fuss, *Identification Papers: Readings on Psychoanalysis, Sexuality and Culture* (New York: Routledge, 1995), 111, 128, 139.

64. Fuss, *Identification Papers*, 123.

65. Edelman, *Homographesis*, 219.

66. The generally warm colour tones that dominated the initial chronotope give way to dull taupes, blues and sages, while the rich, mysterious space of Aunt Ruth's apartment, a space whose conformity to the hermeneutic norms of the detective story lies in the extent to which its promise of depth is matched by its guarantee of spatial stability, gives way to the more properly "noir" space of Diane's apartment, whose flat, depthless emptiness is matched by a constantly shifting spatial co-ordinates.

67. Judith Butler, *Bodies That Matter: On the Discursive Limits of "Sex"* (New York: Routledge, 1993), 109.

68. Linda Williams, "Film Bodies: Gender, Genre and Excess," *Film Quarterly* 44.4 (Summer, 1991): 2–13.

69. Jean Epstein, "Magnification and Other Writings," *October* 3 (Spring, 1977): 9; Doane, "The Close-Up," 89.

70. Love, "Spectacular Failure," 123.

71. Hal Foster, *The Return of the Real* (Cambridge: MIT Press, 1996), 166.

72. Jameson, "Cognitive Mapping," 356.

73. Chow, *Writing Diaspora*, 64.

74. Jameson, *The Geopolitical Aesthetic*, 3.

75. Ibid.

76. Ibid.

# 5 Boredom
## Avant-Garde and Trash

I

*Figure 5.1* Gummo's frames are filled with junk.

An emotion we might provisionally characterize as the painful, recursive feeling of feeling nothing at all, boredom seems to leak through the pores of what one reviewer called the "poverty-stricken, numbingly boring" town of Xenia, Ohio, to saturate every aspect of the film—Harmony Korine's *Gummo* (1997)—that takes Xenia as its setting.[1] The dominant mood of the slackers, loners and misfits that make up *Gummo*'s motley cast of characters, boredom also permeates the film's narrative, which replaces the worthy, dramatic endeavors in which anger or fear might find expression with the trivial, inconsequential mini-projects more appropriate to apathy and ennui: a tawdry trio of sisters (Darby Dougherty, Clarisa Glucksman and Chloe Sevigny) bathe their house-cat in the bathroom sink; the feeble-minded Ellen (Ellen M. Smith) shaves her eyebrows; delinquent teens Solomon and Tummler (Jacob Reynolds and Nick Sutton) break into a rival's home and riffle through his photographs. In fact, as much a critical metonym for artistic failure as it is a dysphoric emotion, boredom is as omnipresent in *Gummo*'s critical reception as it is in the lives of its characters and the turn of its plot.

166   *Boredom*

For Walter V. Addiego, in a curiously mixed metaphor that combines the "off" and the "overcooked," "Korine's trying to offer a radical vision of rotten America, but the whole thing seems warmed over"; for David Denby, the film is "boring and redundant"; for Dennis Schwarz, "I found myself becoming bored and tuning the film out"; while for Ed Scheid, "the film loses interest because Korine never gets beneath the surface of his troubled characters."[2] While the intensity of the emotion varies considerably in these reviews, from Addiego's resentful frustration to Schwarz's mild ennui, the structure of the emotion seems remarkably consistent, in doggedly gauging the gap between an urgent desire to feel and the lack of occasion for feeling, between the promise of cultural "rot" and the reality of culture "warmed over."

In itself, of course, a boring film is far from unusual in a mainstream cinematic landscape dominated by practices of recycling, sequelization and pastiche. What affords *Gummo*'s tedium its profound if paradoxical critical interest, however, is the fact that a series of cues both external and internal to the film invited us to situate it in the tradition of the realist avant-garde—a tradition long identified, of course, with shock. On the one hand, advance endorsements by directorial luminaries Bernado Bertolucci and Gus van Sant drew heavily on an avant-garde rubric notorious for conflating artistic with political progress, "experimental art" with "historical change," in dubbing the film "a revolution in cinema" (Bertolucci) and "a completely original creation" (van Sant).[3] On the other, *Gummo* bears all the classic formal stamps associated with the avant-garde's resistance to "the bourgeois principles of an autonomous art and an expressive artist," from its use of everyday, found or industrial materials, to its practice of collage or fragmentation, and its aggressive assault on beauty—a triad that Michael O'Pray's three-pronged model of avant-garde film, meanwhile, adapts for a cinematic context, where the resistance to "bourgeois [aesthetic] principles" manifests as the use of "different distribution and exhibition circuits," the rejection of the formal protocols of "mainstream cinema," and the engagement with "radical social and political ideas."[4] The use of alternative production and distribution channels is clearly in evidence, for while financed and backed by FineLine features, *Gummo* was made on a modest $1.3 million budget by a director whose vision pervades every aspect of the film. The formal resistance to "mainstream cinema" is there, too. Not only does *Gummo*'s mixture of film-stocks, formats and media privilege the strategy of "collage" or "fragmentation" that Bürger dubs "the fundamental principle of *avant-gardiste* art" over the coherence of Hollywood continuity editing, but its use of found and stock footage calls to mind the trademark avant-garde "embrace [of] everyday objects."[5] Indeed, *Gummo*'s apparent allegiance to the filmic avant-garde is rounded off by its "radical social and political ideas," namely an investment in the depiction of dispossessed and marginalized populations that resonates powerfully with Brazilian avant-garde director Glauber Rocha's commitment to "draw[ing] the audience's attention to ... poverty in order that it should be capable of

*Boredom* 167

revolutionary action."[6] Reminiscent of the impoverished thugs of Pier Paolo Pasolini's *Porcile* (1969) and the cruel street-children of Luis Bunuel's *Los Olvidados* (1950)—both realist avant-garde classics—the film's menagerie of wasters, outcasts and delinquents seems handpicked to fulfill the aesthetic and political mandates of the filmic avant-garde.

The rub here, however, is that despite all the claims of its production and publicity, a film almost universally decried as boring seems a remarkably weak example of an aesthetic mode so long identified with shock. Shock's significance to the avant-garde is well established. While decidedly at odds in their accounts of the avant-garde's status and destiny, critics in the field, from Peter Bürger, Clement Greenberg and Renato Poggioli to Fredric Jameson, Marjorie Perloff and Hal Foster are almost indistinguishable in their accounts of the mode's animating affect, the emotional "stimulus" through which its vaunted social and political aspirations are actualized.[7] At the heart of this argument are two assumptions: first, that in propagating the illusion that "the institution of art [is] autonomous," "bourgeois" art short-circuits art's ability to effect social transformation; second, that avant-garde shock can work to rupture this illusion, "break[ing] through the aesthetic immanence and ... usher[ing] in (initiate[ing]) a change in the recipient's life practice."[8] To insist on shock's centrality to avant-garde practice and criticism is not, of course, to discount the prominent role that boredom has played in the historical avant-garde enterprise. From cinematic experiments such as *Sleep* (1963), Andy Warhol's five-hour, single-shot document of his slumbering friend John Giorno, and *Jeanne Dielman, 23 Quai du Commerce, 1080 Bruxelles* (1975), Chantal Akerman's unrelenting record of domestic tedium, to what Sianne Ngai calls the "systematically recursive" art of "Robert Ryman, Jasper Johns, John Cage and Philip Glass," boredom has been an ingredient in a host of avant-garde exercises in serialization and repetition.[9] Yet as Ngai's own distinction between these works' "shocking, innovative and transformative" critical status and their "tedious" spectatorial effect suggests, the drudgery they demanded of their readers and viewers was offset by the symbolic "shock" they administered to the artistic and critical norms of the day.[10] Whether manifest at the level of form, as a tactical utilization of non-normative representational strategies, or at the level of content, as a representation of dispossessed populations resisting the social structures that oppress them, shock remains the dominant emotional idiom in which the avant-garde's artistic and political agenda has been articulated.

Yet if *Gummo*'s reliance on a battery of avant-garde strategies is indisputable, in *Gummo*, these strategies seem to fall, as if inevitably, under the lackluster sign of boredom. Though the film's fragmented, episodic format and use of found footage is an avant-garde signature, for example, it can hardly be called radical, for not only have avant-garde filmmakers been exploring the possibilities yielded by anti-narrative, mixed media filmmaking for several decades, the techniques have migrated into advertising, television and mainstream cinema. Far from inspiring shock, then, they seem old-hat, even cliché.

168   *Boredom*

Likewise, although a degraded, impoverished setting is a realist avant-garde mainstay, *Gummo*'s scenes of poverty seem divested of both urgency and extremity. A montage of grainy stock footage of Xenia locals, the film's opening sequence clearly telegraphs the social and emotional climate of these lives: a skinny, bare-chested boy shows off his puny pectoral muscles; an obese woman reclines on the steps of a cheap, clapboard house, petting a cat; a man with a goatee and a death metal t-shirt grins toothlessly from the front seat of a wrecked car; an adolescent boy races by on a bike. Pettily cruel rather than brutally violent, poor rather than dying, structurally disenfranchised rather than violently downtrodden, these are, as Thomas Carl Wall puts it, "the *ordinary* poor: the vulgar, the vernacular, the most innocuously impoverished of the socially overlooked."[11] The signature emotion of this "poverty-stricken, numbingly boring place," then, is less anger, shock or suffering than yawning ennui.[12]

In light of *Gummo*'s conspicuous tedium, then, what are we to make of Bertolucci and van Sant's efforts to elect the film to the ranks of the avant-garde? Dismissed by psychologist Haskell Bernstein as "a trivial and unworthy feeling" and by the *Situationiste Internationale* as "always counter-revolutionary," boredom, after all, is more than just *not* shock. Despite the energetic revisionist efforts of critics such as Siegfried Kracauer, Walter Benjamin and Martin Heidegger, boredom has emerged as shock's would-be obverse, a prime contender for the emotion "least likely to play a role in any kind of oppositional praxis."[13] Indeed, whereas shock is a strong, vehement emotion that has played an important role in anchoring cognitive-appraisal theories of emotion, boredom is a weak, recursive emotion that the sway of the cognitive-appraisal paradigm over our grasp of feeling ensures is all too often excluded from the definitional domain of emotion altogether, and identified, instead, with indifferent, apathy and neutrality.[14] Some critics, of course, have begun to float the idea that a newer avant-garde programme might peddle in more muted, deferred or complex emotions, with John Richardson, for example, arguing that a "neo- or even post-avant-garde practice" might deploy "wonder" in place of shock. Yet boredom is not readily rehabilitated as an accessory to radical artistic practices.[15] Indeed, this chapter will avoid the temptation to try its hand at such this kind of recuperatory labour, triumphantly revealing as profound, weighty and socially minded an emotion that has long been denounced, as Patricia Spacks puts it, as "superficial, frivolous and atomistic."[16] Should we, then, conclude that Bertolucci, Herzog and van Sant are simply mistaken in celebrating *Gummo* as a belated entry in the history of the avant-garde? Or does their enthusiasm for *Gummo* suggest that the avant-garde has learned to harness this most "superficial, frivolous and atomistic" of marginal emotions to avant-garde ends?

In beginning to answer these questions, it is necessary to establish just what it is about boredom that, even beyond the fact that it is conspicuously *not* shock, seems to cast it so far outside the ken of avant-garde practice. Boredom's antagonism to the classical avant-garde agenda is elucidated only too clearly by *Gummo* itself, in which a thematic and visual set-piece shows a group of Xenia locals gather for a drinking session in a typically derelict kitchen, only to find themselves palpably, manifestly bored. One character leans against a fridge; another sits slumped at the table; a third watches lazily from the doorway. What is striking here, however, is that whereas, as Philip Fisher has argued, "strong" or "vehement" passions like shock and anger "fill up awareness" and possess an "outward-streaming energy" that expresses itself in powerful and potentially revolutionary action, boredom seems to empty out—and consequently immobilize—its sufferers. On the one hand, the figures are marked by an internal emptiness that finds external expression both at the level of *mise-en-scene*, in the barren, formica-clad kitchen that is the scene's setting, and at the level of characterization, in the film's failure to afford them the depth or backstory usually granted filmic character. On the other, they are living embodiments of boredom's colloquially attested power to immobilize and fatigue: not only are their postures stultified and their dialogue atrophied, but their lack of the "desire" that customarily propels a narrative's "move forward" results in *Gummo*'s air of narrative exhaustion and repetition.[17] Unsurprisingly, perhaps, boredom's lack of subjective force—and its consequent inhibition of powerful action—is key to its critical theorization. Bernstein, for example, identifies a kind of "hollowness" or "emptiness" at the heart of the bored subject, while the psychoanalyst Otto Fenichel attests to its "lack of instinctual impulses" that makes powerful action impossible.[18] Given this notoriously "empty" emotion's vexed relation to action, then, boredom's deployment in an aesthetic endeavour inextricably bound up with action seems incongruous to say the least.

To say that the bored subject's internal emptiness forecloses vigorous or militant action is not, of course, to say that the bored subject doesn't act at all. Indeed, if inert stupor is boredom's minor key, a restless, giddy search for distraction is its major one, and the scene's episodes of lassitude alternate with garrulous sing-alongs and arm-wrestling matches. As if mirroring a subject restlessly scanning the visual field for interest, the hand-held camera that records their exploits sees the camera shift erratically from face to face, opportunistically dolly in on movement and whip-pan to capture a speaker in action. Finally, one man—egged on by encouraging cries from his pals to "Kill it!" and "Get that motherfucker!"—resorts to wrestling a chair, an absurd simulacrum of conflict that underscores the pathos of boredom's indiscriminate investment in feeling something rather than nothing. Recalling Fenichel's suggestion that "instead of manifesting itself in the form of instinctual impulses, [boredom] require[s] incitements from the outside world," and Bernstein's observation, that, lacking any internal emotional spur, the bored subject will "create external situations calculated to evoke feelings of so much intensity that those feelings will break through their internal insulating barriers to awareness," the bored subject seems forced to seek out external objects to supply the emotional arousal with which other, better-resourced subjects appear to come fully equipped.[19] Yet this idiosyncratic inversion of the conventional relation between emotion and action

## 170   Boredom

brings us to the second snag in boredom's conscription to the avant-garde. This is that if boredom is not subjective *enough* to animate the avant-garde project, it also seems somehow *too* subjective, reducing action in the world to distractions for the self. Whereas the angry or shocked subject has feelings that are expressed in action, the bored subject acts in order to feel, seeking "incitement[s]" or "creat[ing] external situation[s]." Whereas the angry or shocked subject's feelings are orientated around an object in the world, the bored subject merely uses objects to create vibrations within the recesses of her private sensorium.

Simultaneously inadequately and excessively subjective, then, boredom's capacity for mobilization within avant-garde praxis already seems strikingly tenuous. Yet as if boredom's distinctive composite of subjective atrophy and subjective indulgence were not damning enough, this morphology of the bored subject seems to map all too readily onto models of the *consumer* subject—icon and cipher of the commodity culture that the avant-garde has traditionally pitted itself against.[20] Like the bored subject, the consumer subject is routinely distinguished by a singular combination of self-absorption and vacancy. For Mike Featherstone, for example, the consumer subject is marked by a "new Narcissism, where individuals seek to maximize and experience the range of sensations available," while for Stephen Miles, conversely, postmodern consumer practices are indexed to "a spiritually empty and immoral society where money is all and where the soul is degraded."[21] In this respect, it should come as no surprise that scholars like Jean Baudrillard, Fredric Jameson and Gianni Vattimo have enlisted boredom as the emblematic emotion of a critically devalued postmodern consumer culture, the characteristic condition of hyper-consuming and hypo-affective subjects whom the commodity has lost its power to move.[22] An undeniably negative emotion, then, boredom is not, however, an oppositional one. Far from resistant to the mainstream consumer culture that is the avant-garde's traditional target, boredom's querulous protests are merely a plaintive, irritable cry of inadequate immersion in it. Far from delivering up an affective critique of capitalist consumer culture, boredom simply registers a frustrated desire to be more satisfactorily or more completely a part of it.

Yet there are still further anomalies associated with *Gummo*'s reliance on an emotion so long conceived as the signature malady of a financially overstretched and mentally anaesthetized consumer. For more than just *in*appropriate to its clear avant-garde oppositional agenda, boredom is all *too* appropriate to a widespread and demeaning stereotype of the uneducated rural white populations the film depicts, in which that population is routinely cast, as Gail Sweeney puts it, as a group of "total consumer[s] and non-producer[s]."[23] Best condensed in the vicious pejorative label "white trash," which metonymically identifies as their very essence the "trash" that these groups supposedly produce through their voracious, uninhibited habits of consumption, this stereotype is a function of a wider tropological procedure by which, as Daniel Miller has it, "materialism, understood as

Boredom   171

a concern for increasing one's possession of goods often at the expense of a concern for other people, tend[s] to be strongly associated with poverty rather than wealth."[24] Unsurprisingly, perhaps, this imaginary alliance of poverty and consumerism has been a key rhetorical projectile in the effort to explain and justify the social dispossession of poor white populations through reference to their supposed moral and spiritual inadequacy. In these terms, *Gummo*'s identification of Xenia's residents as bored—a term burdened with its own hyper-consumerist overtones—serves merely to reinforce the stigmatizing moral and social discourse that already circulates around these marginalized populations.

What, then, is at stake in *Gummo*'s engagement with the emotion that Reinhard Kuhn, opposing boredom to ennui, dismissed as a "superficial and vague disquiet"?[25] Why would a film with clear avant-garde aspirations establish as its dominant emotion climate an emotion not only hand in glove with the late-capitalist consumer culture that the classical avant-garde strives to resist, but defamatory to the very groups the classical avant-garde strives to defend? Quick to register its craving for avant-garde status, and equally quick to observe its apparent falling short, most critics diagnosed a simple case of directorial deficiency, a study in shock aesthetics falling flat. For Walter V. Addiego, "Korine's trying to offer a radical vision of rotten America, but the whole thing seems warmed over."[26] Russell Smith dismissed those who, apparently mistakenly, believe "they're seeing something original or groundbreaking in *Gummo*."[27] For Paul Tatara of CNN, meanwhile, whereas the true avant-garde was "railing against social and economic oppression" through "instantaneous, disposable outbursts," *Gummo* is merely "making fun of people" to no apparent political purpose; whereas the true avant-garde was doing something new, *Gummo* is "not telling us anything we don't already know."[28] Indeed, just as the film itself was roundly condemned as an aesthetic failure, so its characters were denounced as failed dissidents. Janet Maslin's description of one character's conspicuously weak effort at public dissent—"spitting and urinating on the highway below [a bridge] in silent protest"—is exemplary here in its unbridled contempt for what she construes as the characters' futile attempts at provocation and incitement, attempts that are measured unfavourably against a persistent cultural fantasy of a spontaneously animated, angered proletarian subject.[29]

Given boredom's manifest antagonism to traditional avant-garde aspirations, however, what is most curious about *Gummo* is its sheer *insistence* on the emotion, an insistence that invites us to read the film's boring tone not as mere directorial failure, but as deliberate, calculated policy. While an uneventful evening at a friend's might seem a relatively appropriate object for boredom, *Gummo* routinely articulates boredom not just to everyday tedium, but to the more disastrous and destructive implications of poverty, occasions on which a much stronger, more radical emotion might seem called for. Exemplary here is the opening sequence of the film, in which

## 172  Boredom

a series of grainy, poorly shot stock images of disaster (a dog is caught on a television antenna; a boy lies injured on the road) are synched to a voice-over narration's litany of horror:

> A few years ago. A tornado hit this town. It killed the people. Dogs died, cats died, houses were split open and you could see necklaces hanging from the branches of trees. People's legs and neck bones were stickin' out. Oliver found a leg on his roof. A lot of people's fathers died or were killed ...

Despite the sensational informational content of both sound and image track, however, the voice itself, constantly on the point of expiring into a feeble whisper, is torpid to the point of being catatonic. The palpable boredom the voice both communicates and elicits is all the more marked in that, judging by the speaker's strenuous efforts to transfigure a scene of violent death into visual spectacle ("people's legs and neck bones were stickin' out"), the narrative's purpose is precisely to evoke intense emotion of some kind—an intuition corroborated by the speaker's last-ditch effort to endow the panorama of violent death with the additional titillation of the semi-pornographic, in the story's brief post-script ("I saw a girl fly through the sky and I looked up her skirt").

*Gummo* ratchets up its commitment to boredom even further in repeatedly encouraging us to expect the revelation that a stronger, more profound emotion underpins the prevailing boredom—only to just as frequently dismiss these expectations. In one brief, transitional scene whose simultaneous sweetness and inconsequence exemplifies what Wall has identified as the film's "incongruously gentle placidity," Tummler plies Solomon with a string of poignant questions about his mother, who will appear repeatedly in film's second half.[30] "Does your mother ever make you food?" Tummler asks, picking up his bike. "Has she ever made you crêpe suzette?" In their wistful conflation of emotional and physical nourishment, the questions can't help but drive home the absence of Tummler's own mother from the film's narrative and diegesis. Appealing to the popular assumption that, as Patricia Meyer Spacks puts it, the politically and artistically anemic emotion of boredom usually "masks another condition," the now-conspicuous absence of Tummler's mother holds out the tantalizing promise of an elaboration of fuller, more profound motives for the boy's delinquency than the peculiarly hollow, etiolated figure of boredom has thus far been able to provide.[31] Yet immediately after introducing the charged motif of the mother, the film abruptly shifts from the realist register associated with fuller emotions to the direct-address format characteristic of vaudeville or stand-up comedy, cutting to a long shot of the two boys on their bikes accompanied by Tummler's voice-over singing a frivolous popular song: "This man I know ... had gravy on his vest, gravy on his tie, gravy on his shirt, gravy all over him ... that dirty old man." At the very point that we are expecting Tummler to reveal the roots of his boredom in, say, maternal loss, the film effectively recodes the character's gesture

*Boredom* 173

toward deeper issues as yet another attempt to distract himself from tedium. In this light, the tedium that reads on first sight as aesthetic failure or misstep might be more accurately read as deliberate, calculated strategy.

But why would a film so committed to staking out its avant-garde credentials install the weak, trivializing emotion of boredom as its dominant mood and effect? One gloss on the film's methodical, even systematic engagement with boredom, of course, is that it constitutes a kind of commentary on a broader historic crisis in the function and efficacy of the avant-garde—a "crisis" whose co-ordinates have been mapped by numerous critics in the past three decades. Arguing that avant-garde devices like shock have been assimilated into the cycle of commodity production, Krysztof Ziarek maintains that "the shock characteristic of avant-garde art has been subsumed and neutralized by the shock-like aesthetics of popular culture"; for Andreas Huyssen, "the exploitation of shock in Hollywood productions [demonstrates] that shock can be exploited to reaffirm perception rather than change it"; while according to Jameson, "our clothing, furniture, buildings and other artefacts are now intimately tied in with styling changes which derive from artistic experimentation."[32] These arguments about the emotional vagaries of the avant-garde are bolstered by a set of broader arguments about a new emotional or "immaterial" economy, an economy whose contours have been traced exhaustively in recent work by critics such as Michael Hardt, Antonio Negri and Zygmunt Bauman, among many others. Arguing that emotion as a category has been converted into an object of productive labor and commodity consumption, Michael Hardt and Antonio Negri's concept of "immaterial labour," for example, stitches "ease, well-being, satisfaction, excitement or passion" into the fabric of late capitalism's "ensemble of intellectual, communicative, relational and affective" commodities, while Zygmunt Bauman limns the shift from a producer to a consumer society as a passage from the ethics of work to an aesthetics of consumerism that "puts a premium on the sublime experience."[33] Set against the backdrop of these theories, *Gummo*'s engagement with boredom might be read as a reflective rumination on the crisis of avant-garde shock in the context of the immaterial economy's co-optation and commercialization of "the new and unprecedented sensation."[34]

But while the above account of the film's trademark tedium is not without explanatory power, this chapter's gambit is that, far from a symptom of or engagement with the avant-garde's demise, *Gummo*'s calculated ennui marks an effort to remodel and repurpose the avant-garde for changed aesthetic conditions. Both defenders of the avant-garde's continuing relevance, like Jean-Francois Lyotard, and eulogists of the avant-garde's failure, like Jameson, tend to champion or elegize the *same* avant-garde. This is an avant-garde that struggles for formal innovation, that orientates itself around strong emotion, and that culminates in revolutionary political action. As Hal Foster argues, however, in his impassioned 1994 defense of the avant-garde, "What's Neo about the Neo-Avant-Garde?" embracing an avant-garde that persists beyond the modern moment depends on acknowledging the

174   *Boredom*

avant-garde's capacity to change. Subscribing, then, to Sianne Ngai's contention that "the nature of the sociopolitical itself has changed in a manner that both calls forth and calls upon a new set of feelings," this chapter will contend that *Gummo* exemplifies an avant-garde practice whose emotional ethos—and whose relation to formal and political change—is specifically tailored to the economic and social co-ordinates of affluent Western societies in the late twentieth and early twenty-first centuries.[35] Importantly, this argument that *Gummo*'s engagement with boredom marks the transformation rather than the expiry of the avant-garde will be advanced through an overhaul of our orthodox conceptions of boredom itself. While often dismissed as an emotional accessory of consumer culture, boredom is, I will show, more properly understood as consumer culture's ultimate trash—an abjected status that affords it a certain unexpected utility to an avant-garde project intent on resisting consumer culture's siren-like call.

But what underpins this transformation in boredom's cultural standing? The key to this shift, I suggest, lies in the above-remarked and now widely accepted claim that *shock*'s status has shifted in postmodern aesthetics from a powerfully oppositional emotion, to a highly invested aesthetic commodity.[36] If shock once possessed a disruptive and antagonistic power, runs this argument, shock now constitutes a kind of emotional merchandise, bought and sold within the very aesthetic and cultural formations that it was once represented as resisting. Yet while critics have been quick to pick up on shock's sublimation into the status of commodity, the knock-on implications for shock's opposite number, boredom, haven't attracted the same sustained scrutiny. Boredom, as we've seen, is shock's direct obverse: where shock is a powerful, overwhelming emotion long identified with oppositional or radical action, boredom is a frustrating, irritable feeling of feeling nothing at all long identified with consumer culture. In this respect, it seems relatively obvious that boredom's purchase on the culture should have undergone an about-face mirroring shock's own. If shock is now a hot emotional commodity in an aesthetic economy that prizes strong feeling, a weak, etiolated emotion like boredom can only amount to a kind of emotional discard or waste-product, a kind of emotional trash; if "the excitement of the new and unprecedented sensation is now the name of the consumer game," the emotion of boredom must be the lot of those Bauman identifies as "shut off or excluded from the social feast."[37]

A quick survey of *Gummo* bears out this sense that in the new affective and emotional economy, boredom is less an emotion morally reprehensible for its complicity in mainstream commodity culture than an emotion socially forsaken for its position on the squalid margins of economic life. For *Gummo* embeds its tonal and characterological tedium in a series of conspicuously trash-strewn bedrooms, hallways, and kitchens—from the junk-lined hallways and corridors of Solomon's mother's house, to the kitschy mess of the girls' upstairs bedroom, to the literal rubbish-dumps in which a coterie of neighbourhood boys play. Critics everywhere commented

*Boredom* 175

on the film's clutter: Maslin, for example, noted of the production design that "directorial instruction d[id] not apparently extend beyond asking the cast to conserve about a year's worth of laundry and litter"; the *Chicago Reader* critic observed, of the scene between Solomon and his mother, that it transpired in "a basement piled high with junk"; while Nathan Adams of FilmSchoolRejects mentions "the crap-packed, filthy houses that much of the movie takes place in."[38] Yet while the objects that furnish *Gummo*'s frames are clearly junk, these frames are not, in fact, any more "piled high" or "packed" than those of another film. The persistent critical preoccupation with the sheer abundance of *Gummo*'s trash, however, effectively confirms its status *as* trash in its resonance with the classic Marxist opposition between the "commodity" and the "thing"—an opposition which, in conferring exchange value on the commodity and stripping it from what Peter Stallybrass calls a "mere thing," effectively affords the former a kind of ethereal abstraction, while confirming the latter in its stubborn materiality.[39] As Stallybrass's concise gloss of Marx's analysis suggests, "the commodity becomes a commodity not as a thing but as an exchange value. It achieves its purest form, in fact, when most emptied of particularity and thingness."[40] In their incorrigible "particularity and thingness," *Gummo*'s mountains of old clothes, bits of broken furniture and stacks of newspapers clearly fall into the category of things, and thus visually "fill up" the frame in a way that the commodity—abstracted into a moment of pure, transparent exchange value—does not. If *Gummo*'s characters are bored, then, their boredom must be traced not to their immersion in commodity culture but to their immersion in the graveyards of its refuse.

For the majority of the film's critics, of course, the boredom that saturates the film's narrative and *mise-en-scene* invites criticism not for its biologically dubious position on the fetid periphery of consumer culture, but for its morally dubious over-implication in consumer culture. What is striking however, is that even as they reassert the critical equation of boredom and consumerism, critical attacks on the film's tedium repeatedly register the more recent cultural coupling of boredom and trash. Maslin's disgusted denunciation of the film is exemplary here in its mobilization of an account of the film's rubbish-filled *mise-en-scene*—the "trash-strewn" bridge on which bunny-boy walks, the "tawdry" clothes worn by the three sisters—to stand in for assessment of its aesthetic failure as an avant-garde text. In making it near-impossible to distinguish between her revulsion at the film's failure as an oppositional text, and her revulsion at its abundance of trash, she dramatizes a crucial slippage between two divergent reasons for repudiating its tedium: because it is not sufficiently opposed to consumer culture or because it doesn't sufficiently embody its norms. Ken Fox's review in the *TV Guide* is marked by a similar ambivalence. Arguing that "Korine's loose, improvisatory script is all over the place, picking up the garbage-strewn lives of Xenia's other inhabitants in fragments," he effectively elides the difference between inadequately radical film form and junk-laden *mise-en-scene*, using

## 176  Boredom

terms with strong associations with the vernacular rubric of trash ("loose", for example, tends to echo "garbage strewn") to condemn the film's formal failure.[41] The same slippage afflicts Edward Guffman's review in the *San Francisco Chronicle*. For Guffman, the film's tedium can be traced to its immature grasp on the mechanisms of shock, as Korine "takes the festering rot that hid beneath the surface of David Lynch's *Blue Velvet*, brings it completely into the open and then congratulates himself for having the artistic courage to show us the raw, grotesque truth."[42] Yet in Guffman's evocation of the film's "festering rot" and "raw, grotesque truth," it is hard not to hear echoes of his earlier description of the film's Ohio setting, "a filthy place that got hit by a tornado 20 years ago but has yet to sweep up its literal and emotional debris." These figurative oscillations between attacks on the film's overly consumerist form and attacks on its inadequately consumerist content register in real time the shift that historically marks boredom itself—from an emotion tainted by the moral stigma of consumerism to an emotion tainted by its association with literal waste.

Indeed, this critical tendency to trace boredom causally, if only implicitly, *to* trash, culminates in a no less noticeable tendency to cast boredom itself *as* trash. In the regular critical variations on the claim that the film was "pointless garbage," "the vilest waste of two hours of my life," or "wasting 88 minutes of my time," boredom and trash are very precisely conflated.[43] Yet perhaps the strongest evidence of this historically novel identification of boredom and trash lies in the fact that, hot on the heels of the boredom that dominates the film's reviews is what Wall calls, with minimal exaggeration, "a nearly universal spasm of revulsion."[44] If boredom is itself a kind of meta-emotion, an emotion about emotion's absence or failure, it seemed to trigger in critics, in a second level of emotional supplementarity, a disgust *at the fact of boredom* itself. Out of all proportion to an emotional target whose ostensible crime was merely its implication in consumer culture—a "crime" to which moral censure or disapproval might be a more appropriate negative response—the shudder of disgust that runs through much of the commentary on the film's tedium indexes a sea-change in boredom's status, from an emotion morally reprehensible for its complicity in mainstream commodity culture, to an emotion socially forsaken for its position on the squalid margins of economic life.

Yet if, as this widespread critical disgust confirms, boredom is our emotional trash, it is also, *Gummo* reminds us, an emotion that makes trash of those it afflicts. Having degenerated irreversibly from commodity to thing, from abstract value to material object, the debris scattered throughout *Gummo*'s interior spaces becomes the marker of its owners' failure to make the inverse transition: from worthless objects for a panoptic-cinematic gaze to autonomous, emotive consuming subjects. This failure is registered in the film's repeated refusal to observe the cinematic conventions conventionally enlisted to distinguish between people and things, foreground and background, subject and object. One scene opens with a shot of a small boy lifting a framed picture from his living room wall. Disclosing and upsetting—in a gruesome *cinema-verité* touch—a swarm of cockroaches hiding beneath it, he instigates an unsettled relation between animate and inanimate that is only intensified as the mobile camera pulls away from him and begins to scan the room. Taking in broken toys, stacked newspapers, chipped crockery and heaped clothes before lighting at last on the figures of Solomon and Tummler, who are seated on the couch huffing glue from a plastic bag, the camera's patient, paratactic inventory effectively conflates our protagonists with the detritus that surrounds them in a kind of cinematographic enjambment of barely human person and literally inhuman thing. This cinematographic effect is subtly augmented by the audio track, which delivers up a diegetically-anchored string concerto that seems to exist solely to point up the yawning social and cultural distance between the scene's dehumanized characters and the sublimely emotional products of elite high culture. If strong feeling, the emotional effect of achieved possession, certifies our status as commodifiable subjects, boredom, the emotional index of dispossession, appears to reduce us to a worthless, lifeless thing. In light of this sense that boredom demotes those who feel it to the status of human waste, we are able to develop an alternative genealogy of the appellation "white trash," in which the term denominates not a category of person—a person who creates trash—but a person who, lacking in the feeling conferred by the commodity, falls into the forlorn category of trash.

But if boredom is less postmodern aesthetics' emotional apotheosis than its emotional waste-product, why has boredom so long served as consumerism's moral and spiritual patsy? In a sequence that has Solomon's characteristically croaky voice-over guide us through the lives of two middle-class brothers, *Gummo* establishes a powerful and complex relation between boredom and consumerism that goes some way toward accounting for the strange chiastic exchange that sees boredom, sign of consumer failure, assume consumer culture's moral taint—even as shock, consumer emotion *par excellence*, remains pristinely untouched by the stigma of the commodity. So disconnected from the narrative and social co-ordinates of the rest of the film as to leave us in doubt as to whether it should be read as objective representation or as Solomon's subjective projection, the sequence is structured as a kind of idyllic home-video montage reel. Cast against the backdrop of a well-heeled suburban home that boasts a boat, a lavish-looking car and a luxuriously fitted-out kitchen, the two sturdy adolescent boys play with a dog, work out on their expensive exercise equipment, and engage in a faux-fist fight. Yet while their inane grins register their obliviousness to the commodities that buttress their experience, Solomon's voice-over narration contrastingly foregrounds his acute awareness of and rapacious desire for the commodities that fail to buttress his own. His commentary alternates between envious catalogue of the boys' possessions and the slack boredom of his own dispossession: "There were these two kids I know, two brothers ... They came to school in really nice shorts and polished tennis

## 178 Boredom

sneakers and their shirts were always collared with buttons and their hair was always slicked back ..." Barred from participation in "the social feast," a bored and frustrated Solomon thinks only of the gleaming commodities that festoon it. Just as, according to Gay Hawkins, trash's hyper-visibility as a "thing" sees it recruited as the disgraced symbol of the dissolute consumer culture from which it is in fact the abjected waste product, so boredom's all too visible zeal for the commodity ensures it will forever be identified with the very consumer culture whose infinite distance it indexes.

Yet if Solomon's bored, frustrated exclusion from consumer culture paradoxically brands him with the stigma of consumerism, the opposite is also true: the brothers' material affluence affords them a semblance of lofty detachment from material considerations. This chiasmus finds its clearest crystallization in the series of weightlifting exercises that form part of the sequence's visual chronicle of the brothers' daily routine. Expressing just the kind of emotional and moral qualities that consumer culture ostensibly militates against, these purposive, goal-oriented activities serve at once to distinguish the two brothers from our callow, drifting protagonists, Solomon and Tummler, and to mark off this episode from the purposeless, unfocussed activity that seems to saturate the other sections of the film. In its painstaking ocular record of the boys' possessions—a measured pan absorbs the textures of their clothes, the sheen of their car and the opulent appurtenances of their home gym—the film works hard to establish a correlation between the industry and perseverance the boys exhibit and the exercise equipment through which these emotional and moral qualities are, as it were, exercised. So readily do these qualities dissociate themselves from the commodities on which they depend, however, that, irrespective of the film's careful visual auditing, the boys' diligent, focused expressions register not as emotional states contingent on a set of material objects but as emotional traits that index an essential, inherent disposition.[45] In a chiastic face-off that sees shock and boredom swap their moral and ethical physiognomies, then, if those who can't buy their way into consumer culture financially are equally unable to buy their way out morally, those with access to the commodity can equally purchase a moral and emotional distance from the worldly goods that anchor their experience.

But how does this re-reading of shock and boredom bear on our wider argument about *Gummo*'s deployment of boredom to renew avant-garde praxis? If shock's relatively novel status as an emotional commodity voids its claim to the ranks of the avant-garde, it should not be assumed, conversely, that boredom's status as trash automatically primes it for the avant-garde. Yet I would contend that our emotional trash does possess a certain unique utility as an instrument of postmodern oppositional praxis. If—as anthropologist Mary Douglas has famously argued—dirt is less "a residual category, rejected from our normal scheme of classifications," than a term that can make that "normal scheme of classifications" starkly manifest, the same, I suggest, is true of boredom, which, as our emotional "trash," can bring the emotional economy in which we live into powerful relief.[46] Indeed, Korine

*Boredom* 179

is careful to exploit boredom's diagnostic power by ensuring that even as the film diverges emotionally from conventional avant-garde methods, it remains scrupulously faithful to conventional avant-garde ends. In the classic literature on the avant-garde, the reification of shock rides on its capacity to institute a feedback loop between spectatorial and character emotion that facilitates political identifications across class boundaries, "draw[ing] the audience's attention to ... poverty in order that it should be capable of revolutionary action."[47] This is a moment of recognition that, despite its emotional idiosyncracy, *Gummo* forcefully delivers, matching the affective deprivation embodied in spectatorial boredom to the mundane material deprivation of poverty: as video and performance artist Mike Kelley, himself a practitioner of a latter-day avant-gardism, put it, "I was in a half-nod watching people in a half-nod."[48] Yet though *Gummo*'s boredom effectively honours the traditional aims of avant-garde praxis, critics of *Gummo* almost unanimously condemned the emotion's deployment in place of more time-honored avant-garde emotional rubrics. In doing so, these critics effectively draw on the figure of shock (or rather, its absence) as a pretext for warding off the moment of identification that shock has been so celebrated for its capacity to secure—making it painfully clear that their investment lies not in the avant-garde's avowed political objectives but in its bracing emotional strategems. In re-circulating our emotional trash in a cinematic context usually equipped with far more appealing emotional fixtures, then, *Gummo* is able to highlight very starkly not only the fact that emotion is a commodity, but the fact that spectators remain invested in these emotional commodities over and above the political effects they supposedly guarantee.

This paradoxical deployment of the figure of shock to elude the ethical and political claims that underpin shock's lionization is scathingly satirized in a sequence that—shot through with mathematically precise ironies that give the lie to the film's apparent haphazardness—sees a leathery-skinned old man approach our three female protagonists, claiming to have sighted their missing house cat. Predictably enough, his offer to drive them to the place "just out of town" at which he'd spotted the cat is a scam: having reached a suitably isolated suburban carpark with the three girls bundled in his backseat, he allows one of his hands to find its way between thighs of the middle sister, Helen, while ostensibly searching the car for a map. Rebuked by the girls' triplicate outrage as they pile out of the car, he drives rapidly away, but not before offering a contemptful parting shot calculated both to excuse his attempted molestation and to dismiss their fury: "*nothing new to trash like you*." Neatly yoking emotional trash ("nothing new") to the social trash ("trash like you") of the poor white population to which the girls belong, this self-serving maxim resonates with the aesthetics of shock in its assumption that whereas the "new" might warrant resistance and protest, the structural, familiar and ongoing status of an event nullifies its claim on our revolutionary impulses. In couching this appeal to shock in the context of, and as an excuse for, an attempted abuse of power, *Gummo* slyly

180   *Boredom*

and pointedly underscores its absurdity. Once again, the apathy and ennui implied by the old man's disdainful "nothing new" effectively foregrounds the emotional economy of which it is the abjected waste-product.

As the preceding analyses have made clear, *Gummo*'s substitution of boredom for shock is a mark neither of a local aesthetic failure, nor of the historical expiry of the avant-garde. Yet nor should the film's appointment of boredom as its emotional *leitmotif* be mistaken for a simple displacement of one emotion by another in a structurally continuous avant-garde programme. Rather, boredom's rise to prominence in the postmodern avant-garde marks the avant-garde's passage from a mode that enlists emotion as a catalyst to political action to a mode that enlists emotion as a "precious symptom" of a political situation in which the relation between emotion and action is moot.[49] In this respect, boredom's reputation as a worthless emotional waste-product is no misconception—and I have not, for this reason, sought to recuperate or rehabilitate an emotion that is not only morally problematic and politically effete but experientially unpleasant. Instead, I have argued that it is precisely *as* our emotional "trash" that boredom acquires its unique diagnostic traction for the avant-garde. Whereas shock's apparent political efficacy merely dissimulates what Heather Love calls "the conflicts in scale and political goals between psychic life and political power," boredom's conspicuous political impotence works to foreground that conflict, to underscore the gap between feeling and intervening, emoting and acting.[50] To say that the boring postmodern avant-garde decouples emotion and action is not, of course, to say that it somehow reifies diagnosis *over* action. Rather, as a measure of emotion's inadequacy to the scope of political action and the gravity of social injustice, *Gummo*'s tedium points up the need for a form of political action that does *not* rely on individual feeling as its ultimate catalyst and metric. For Bürger, the avant-garde's devolution from an emotional mechanism designed to heal the breach between art and politics to an emotional etiology that can only highlight or underscore that breach evinces the historical failure of the avant-garde. For *Gummo*, however, that devolution is a necessary first step toward a model of political life and social action that is not played out in the echo-chamber of feeling.[51]

As I've argued in this chapter, we seem to take it on faith that the scene of dispossession and poverty should galvanize both those who endure it, and those who witness it, to strong, oppositional emotion. The figure of the spontaneously animated, angered proletarian subject; the figure of the shocked, outraged avant-garde spectator who's compelled into action by a particularly potent piece of radical art—these figures seem to have an intractable hold on our political and aesthetic imagination. It's no surprise, then, that these are the two figures against which *Gummo*'s bored, apathetic characters and tedious, fatiguing effects have been repeatedly measured and found wanting by critics. Yet as I've shown, these figures need to be set against a host of postmodern criticism in the social sciences and humanities that demonstrates that emotions like shock and anger have been stitched into the fabric of postmodern late capitalism's ensemble of intellectual and affective

Boredom 181

commodities. Taking this as my theoretical backdrop, I've explored a film that, across its tonal, narrative, pro-filmic, cinematographic and character-ological registers, uses boredom to showcase one of the less well-elaborated effects of the new immaterial or affective economy, namely that if economic power buys strong feeling, economic dispossession yields only fatigue and boredom. If modernity marks a moment prior to what Hardt and Negri dub "the colonization of the affects," it may have been legitimate at this historical juncture to expect or even demand a correspondence between economic dispossession and forceful, animated negative emotion.[52] In foregrounding both shock's absorption into commodity culture, and boredom's ejection into the domain of the junk, however, *Gummo* makes a powerful case for the idea that it is high time to reconsider our assumptions about the relationship between injustice, emotion and political action.

And in doing so, it recasts these two figures, the angry proletarian and the shocked viewer, as fantasies—fantasies that disavow post-industrial Western society's congenital cross-implication of emotional animation and economic power. The problem with these fantasies is not just discursive: it's not, in other words, just the way they mandate a critical scene in which the poverty-stricken residents of a place like Xenia can be cast as emotionally and spiritually inimical to the avant-garde praxis that claims to operate in their name; nor is it just the way that those economically blessed with access to the emotional goods are routinely misrecognized, by contrast, as counter-cultural heroes; nor is it just the way the expectation that a scene of dispossession and poverty that stultifies those who suffer it should nevertheless stimulate those who watch it tends to perpetuate, at the level of form, the unequal distribution of resources that underpins the poverty it critiques at the level of content. The real problem, I suggest, is that to predicate political action on strong feeling is potentially to *license* the mundane, structural and all-too-familiar forms of inequality and marginalization that *Gummo* depicts. Jean-Francois Lyotard famously defined shock as *"par excellence, the sign of something happening, rather than nothing at all."*[53] In *Gummo's* emotional logic, however, shock is less the mark of something happening *per se* than the mark of something happening that—whether in the form of avant-garde art or mainstream consumer kitsch—is able to find mainstream recognition as a commodifiable event. Conversely, boredom is less the mark of nothing happening, than of something happening over and over and over again; something to which, precisely because it no longer excites or surprises us, precisely because it lacks both commercial and affective value, we may be ethically bound to pay attention.

## Notes

1. Eugene Levy, "Gummo," *Variety*, September 14, 1997, accessed July 10, 2011, http://www.variety.com/review/VE1117329547.html?categoryid=31&cs=1&p=.
2. Walter V. Addiego, "Portrait of Social Decay Flirts with Sensationalism," *San Francisco Examiner*, April 24, 1998, accessed June 25, 2012, http://www.sfgate.

## 182 *Boredom*

com/cgi-bin/article.cgi?f=/e/a/1998/04/24/WEEKEND10.dtl; David Denby, quoted in Unattributed, "The Loafer's Guide: Harmony Korine," *The Observer*, September 17, 2000, accessed July 10, 2012; http://www.guardian.co.uk/theobserver/2000/sep/17/life1.lifemagazine; Dennis Schwarz, "I found myself becoming bored and tuning the film out," *Ozus' World Movie Review*, August 22, 1999, accessed July 10, 2012, http://www.homepages.sover.net/ozus/gummo.html; Ed Scheid, "Gummo," *Box Office*, October 17, 1997, accessed July 10, 2012, http://www.boxoffice.com/reviews/theatrical/2008-08gummo.

3. Jonathan P. Eburne and Rita Felski, "Introduction" in *New Literary History* 41.4 (2010): v–xv, v; Bernado Bertolucci, cited in Craig McLean, "And the Ass Saw the Angel," *The Face*, July, 2000, 206; Gus van Sant, "Forward," Harmony-Korine.com, accessed April 25, 2012,http://www.harmony-korine.com/paper/int/hk/forward.html.

4. Hal Foster, *Return of the Real: The Avant-Garde at the End of the Century* (Cambridge, MA: MIT Press, 1996), 4; Michael O'Pray, *Avant-Garde Film: Forms, Themes and Passions* (London: Wallflower, 2003), 2. For Peter Bürger, for example, the essence of the avant-garde lies in its "question[ing of] the autonomous, self-referential status of art in bourgeois society" in an effort to "reintegrate art into the praxis of life"; this "questioning" entails "disengag[ing] ... from th[e] concept of beauty" through the use of techniques like "collage," which asks to be read not as part of an autonomous, organic "work" unrelated to the viewer's reality, but as a part of the viewer's own sensuous, material experience (Peter Bürger, *Theory of the Avant-Garde* (Minneapolis: University of Minnesota Press, 1984), cover blurb, 51, 103, 76). For Hal Foster, likewise, avant-garde art strives to "exceed [the] apparent autonomy [of modernist art]," whether through the "embrace of everyday objects and [a] pose of aesthetic indifference" that resists beauty, as in dada, or through the "use of industrial materials and [the] transformation of the function of the artist," as in Russian constructivism (Foster, *Return of the Real*, 4, 4–5). For Rosalind Krauss, meanwhile, the avant-garde effects a "disruption in the autonomy of the sign" that foregrounds the sign's lack of transparency, its dependence on social praxis; in instituting this disruption, the avant-garde typically deployed collage, as a strategy "in direct opposition to modernism's search for perceptual plenitude and unimpeachable self-presence" (Rosalind Krauss, *The Originality of the Avant-Garde and Other Modernist Myths* [Cambridge, MA: MIT Press, 1986], 205, 38).

5. Bürger, *Theory of the Avant-Garde,* 72; Foster, *Return of the Real*, 4.

6. Richard J. Williams, "Towards an Aesthetics of Poverty," in *Neo-Avant-Garde*, eds. David Hopkins and Anna Katharina Schaffner (Amsterdam: Rodopi, 2006), 200.

7. Peter Bürger, *Theory of the Avant-Garde* (Minneapolis: University of Minnesota Press, 1984), 80; Clement Greenberg, "Collage," in Idem., *Art and Culture: Critical Essays* (Boston, MA: Beacon Press, 1961), 70–83; Renato Poggioli, *Theory of the Avant-Garde* (Cambridge, MA: Belknap Press of Harvard University Press, 1968); Marjorie Perloff, *The Futurist Moment: Avant-Garde, Avant Guerre, and the Language of Rupture* (Chicago: University of Chicago Press, 2003); Fredric Jameson, *Postmodernism, or, The Cultural Logic of Late Capitalism* (Durham, NC: Duke University Press, 1990); Hal Foster, *The Return of the Real*. Indeed, many of those critics who argue for the continued purchase of avant-garde practice in postmodern art do so by arguing for postmodern art's ongoing ability to

Boredom    183

shock. For example, Hal Foster's effort to claim the work of Andy Warhol's for a latter-day avant-garde project turns on the argument that Warhol's simulacral repetitions are less "blank" than "shocked," less anaesthetized than traumatized (Foster, *The Return of the Real*, 130, 131.)

8. Jochen Shulte-Sasse, "Foreword," in Peter Bürger, *Theory of the Avant-Garde* (Minneapolis: University of Minnesota Press, 1984), xxxix; Bürger, *Theory of the Avant-Garde*, 80. The notion that avant-garde shock works to dissolve the illusion of aesthetic autonomy that usually blunts art's capacity for social transformation is key to most theorizations of the avant-garde (see Burger, *Theory of the Avant-Garde*, 51; Foster, *The Return of the Real*, 4; Krauss, *The Originality of the Avant-Garde*, 205).

9. Sianne Ngai, *Ugly Feelings* (Cambridge, MA: Harvard University Press, 2005), 262.

10. Ngai, *Ugly Feelings*, 262.

11. Thomas Carl Wall, "Dolce Stil Novo: Harmony Korine's Vernacular," *CR: The New Centennial Review* 4.1 (2004), 315.

12. Eugene Levy, "Gummo," *Variety*, September 14, 1997, accessed July 10, 2011, http://www.variety.com/review/VE1117329547.html?categoryid=31&cs=1&p= .

13. Haskell E. Bernstein, "The Ready-Made Life," *Social Research* 42.3 (1975): 512; The Situationiste Internationale, quoted in Laurie Langbauer, "The City, the Everyday and Boredom: The Case of Sherlock Holmes," *differences* 5.3 (1993), 86; Ngai, *Ugly Feelings*, 181. Admittedly, far from insisting on boredom's inappropriateness to the scene of political struggle, many critics have singled out boredom as an inherently radical emotion. For Siegfried Kracauer, for example, boredom is less the effect of a "culture of distraction" than a sign of its critical rejection, and thus a posture that we should cultivate by "tarrying for a while, without a goal, neither here nor there"; for Walter Benjamin, likewise, boredom is "the dream bird that hatches the egg of experience", providing fertile emotional soil for creativity and imagination; while for Martin Heidegger, boredom is a fundamental form of attunement, a mood that is capable of "look[ing] into our Da-sein ... penetrat[ing] us and attun[ing] us through and through." (Siegfried Kracauer, *Mass Ornament: Weimar Essays*, trans. Thomas Y. Levin [Cambridge, MA: Harvard University Press, 1995], p. 332; Walter Benjamin, *Selected Writings, Volume 3: 1935–38*, Michael W. Jennings, Howard Eiland, and Gary Smith [ed.] [Cambridge, MA: Harvard University Press, 2002], 149; Martin Heidegger, "Description of the Situation: Fundamental Attunement," in Gunter Figal [ed.], *The Heidegger Reader* [Bloomington, IN: Indiana University Press, 2007], 100). Yet in many cases, the attempted critical recovery of boredom depends on carving up the emotion into "good" and "bad" instantiations, where the qualities traditionally associated with the emotion are consigned to a devalued "bad" boredom, while a series of qualities more readily associated with ennui or melancholy are conferred upon a reified "good" boredom. Heidegger, for example, is careful to distinguish between "profound boredom" and "superficial boredom," between the boredom that is capable of "attun[ing] us through and through in the ground of dasein," and a "fleeting, cursory inessential boredom" that simply indexes the desire for some kind of stimulating external object; Bernstein, meanwhile, differentiates between boredom as transient "responsive feeling," and boredom as chronic "malaise." (Heidegger, "Description of the Situation," 103.; Bernstein, "The Ready-Made

## 184 Boredom

Life," 513.) The extent to which these distinctions between particular kinds of boredom ultimately perpetuate the critical devaluation of boredom in general becomes painfully clear in Patricia Spacks's effort to adjudicate the debate by suggesting that when we talk about an emotion that can have a broader, social bearing, we are talking not about "boredom" but about "ennui," since whereas "ennui implies a judgment of the universe; boredom [is] a response to the immediate." (Spacks, *Boredom*, 12.) Restless, irritable everyday boredom, then—as opposed to boredom distended into "chronic malaise," deepened into "profound boredom" or elevated as melancholic "ennui"—retains its status as critical anathema.

14. Elizabeth S. Goodstein, *Experience Without Qualities: Boredom and Modernity* (Stanford: Stanford University Press, 2005), 120.

15. John Richardson, *An Eye for Music: Popular Music and the Audiovisual Surreal* (Oxford: Oxford University Press, 2012), 57.

16. Spacks, *Boredom*, 138.

17. Peter Brooks, *Reading for the Plot: Design and Intention in Narrative* (Cambridge, CA: Harvard University Press, 1984), 40.

18. Otto Fenichel, "On the Psychology of Boredom," in Hanna Fenichel and David Rapaport (eds.), *The Collected Papers of Otto Fenichel, Vol 1*, (New York: W.W. Norton and Co, 1954), 293; Bernstein, "Boredom and the Ready-Made Life," 516. As Bernstein clarifies, "the inability to experience one's own feelings directly and intensely is the root cause of … boredom." (Ibid., 518.)

19. Fenichel, "On the Psychology of Boredom," 293; Bernstein, "The Ready-Made Life," 518.

20. From Clement Greenberg's classic essay "Avant-Garde and Kitsch," which situated "avant-garde culture" in direct opposition to "popular, commercial art and literature with their chromeotypes, magazine covers, illustrations, ads, slick and pulp fiction," to Bürger's *Theory of the Avant-Garde*, which counter-poses the literary avant-garde to a popular fiction that functions as "mere enticement, designed to prompt purchasers to buy what they do not need," theorists of the avant-garde have routinely appointed consumer culture as the avant-garde's foil and primary antagonist (Clement Greenberg, "Avant-Garde and Kitsch," 8, 9; Bürger, *Theory of the Avant-garde*, 54). According to Walter Adamson, for example, the avant-garde project is "above all, the effort to press art into the center of modern cultural life while resisting those tendencies that would reduce it to a commodity defined ultimately by its exchange value." (Walter Adamson, *Embattled Avant-Gardes: Modernism's Resistance to Commodity Culture in Europe* [Berkeley: University of California Press, 2007], 3.)

21. Mike Featherstone, *Consumer Culture and Postmodernism* (London: Sage, 2007), 88–9; Stephen Miles, *Consumerism: As a Way of Life* (London: Sage, 1998), 150.

22. From Baudrillard's work on "banality" as one of advanced capitalism's "fatal strategies"; to Jameson's analysis of boredom as "a precious symptom of our own existential, ideological, and cultural limits"; to Gianni Vattimo's argument that ennui is the presiding after-effect of modernity, with its logic of "novelty become obsolete and replaced by new novelty in a process that discourages creativity in the very act of demanding it"—boredom, often framed in terms of a rubric of cultural exhaustion and repetition, pervades the theoretical construction of postmodern consumerism. (Jean Baudrillard, *Jean Baudrillard: Selected Writings*, ed. Mark Poster [Stanford: Stanford University Press, 1988], 198; Fredric Jameson, *Postmodernism, or, The Cultural Logic of Late Capitalism*

Boredom 185

[Durham, NC; Duke University Press, 1991], 72; Gianni Vattimo, "*Verwindung*: Nihilism and the Postmodern in Philosophy," *Substance* 53 [1987]: 8.)

23. Gael Sweeney, "The King of White Trash Culture: Elvis Presley and the Aesthetics of Excess," *White Trash: Race and Class in America,* ed. Annalee Newitz and Matt Wray (New York: Routledge, 1997), 250.

24. Daniel Miller, "Introduction" in *Consumerism: Critical Concepts in the Social Sciences,* ed. Daniel Miller (London: Routledge, 2001), 2.

25. Reinhard Kuhn, quoted in Patrice Petro, *Aftershocks of the New: Feminism and Film History* (New Jersey: Rutgers University Press), 86.

26. Walter V Addiego, "Portrait of Social Decay Flirts with Sensationalism," *San Francisco Examiner*, April 24, 1998, accessed July 10, 2011, http://www.sfgate.com/cgi-bin/article.cgi?f=/e/a/1998/04/24/WEEKEND10.dtl.

27. Russell Smith, "Gummo," *The Austin Chronicle*, November 28, 1997, accessed July 10, 2011, http://www.austinchronicle.com/gyrobase/Calendar/Film?Film=oid%3a140777.

28. Paul Tatara, "Review: Proof that kids shouldnot play with cameras," *CNN Interactive*, November 7, 1997, accessed July 10, 2011, http://www.cnn.com/SHOWBIZ/9711/07/review/gummo.

29. Janet Maslin, "Cats, Grandmas and Other Disposables," *New York Times*, October 17, 1997, accessed July 13, 2011, http://movies.nytimes.com/movie/review?res=9907E6DA123FF934A25753C1A961958260&partner=Rotten%20Tomatoes.

30. Wall, "Dolce Stil Novo," 308.

31. Patricia Meyer Spacks, *Boredom: The Literary History of a State of Mind* (Chicago: University of Chicago Press, 1995), x. For another example of this assumption, see D. A. Miller's contention that "Far from the intrinsic reflex-response to banality, boredom hysterically converts into yawning affectlessness what would otherwise be outright panic." (D. A. Miller, *The Novel and the Police* [Berkeley: University of California Press, 1988], 145.)

32. Krysztof Ziarek, *The Force of Art* (Stanford: Stanford University Press, 2004), 88; Andreas Huyssen, *After the Great Divide: Modernism, Mass Culture, Postmodernism* (Bloomington, IN: Indiana University Press, 1987), 15; Fredric Jameson, *The Cultural Turn: Selected Writings on the Postmodern, 1983–1998* (London: Verso, 1998), 19.

33. Michael Hardt and Antonio Negri, *Empire* (Cambridge, MA: Harvard University Press, 2000), 293; Michael Hardt and Antonio Negri, *Reflections on Empire* (Cambridge: Polity Press, 2008), 62; Zygmunt Bauman, *Work, Consumerism and the New Poor* (Berkshire: McGraw-Hill International, 2004), 32. Bauman and Hardt and Negri form part of a legion of critics who have explored aspects of emotion's commodification in late capitalist economies, including Arlie Russell Hochschild, *The Managed Heart: Commercialization of Human Feeling* (Berkeley, CA: California University Press, 1983); Eva Illouz, *Cold Intimacies* (Cambridge: Polity Press, 2007); and Luc Boltanski and Eve Chiapello, *The New Spirit of Capitalism* (London: Verso, 2005).

34. Bauman, *Work, Consumerism and the New Poor*, 25.

35. Ngai, *Ugly Feelings*, 5.

36. Bauman, *Work, Consumerism and the New Poor*, 25.

37. Bauman, *Work, Consumerism and the New Poor*, 38.

38. Maslin, "Cats, Grandmas and Other Disposables"; Lisa Alspector, "Too Big to Ignore," *Chicago Reader*, April 9, 1998, accessed July 13 2011, http://www.

## 186  Boredom

chicagoreader.com/chicago/too-big-to-ignore/Content?oid=896013; Nathan Adams, "Harmony Korine Got Gross with *Kids*, but *Gummo* Saw Him Achieve Maximum Sleaze," *Film School Rejects*, March 26, 2013, accessed July 14, 2011, http://www.filmschoolrejects.com/features/harmony-korine-kids-gummo.php.

39. Peter Stallybrass, "Marx's Coat," in *Border Fetishisms: Material Objects in Unstable Spaces* ed. Patricia Spyer (New York: Routledge, 1998), 183.

40. Stallybrass, "Marx's Coat," 183.

41. Ken Fox, "Gummo," Tvguide.com, December 1, 2005, accessed December 17, 2012, http://movies.tvguide.com/gummo/review/132299.

42. Edward Guffman, "Gummo Stages a Freak Show of Kids and Rubs it In," *San Francisco Chronicle*, Thursday May 21, 1998, accessed December 17, 2012, http://www.sfgate.com/movies/article/Gummo-Stages-a-Freak-Show-of-Kids-and-Rubs-It-In-3005633.php.

43. Russell Smith, "Gummo," *The Austin Chronicle*, November 28, 1997, accessed June 10, 2012; http://www.austinchronicle.com/gyrobase/Calendar/Film?Film=oid%3a140777; Dennis Schwarz, "I found myself becoming bored and Tuning the film out," Ozu's World Movie Reviews, accessed June 11, 2011, http://www.sover.net/~ozus/gummo.htm.

44. Wall, "Dolce Stil Novo," 309–310.

45. It is worth noting that when Solomon attempts a similar work-out regime a little later in the film (he tries lifting home-made "weights," a set of forks tied together with masking tape, in front of the wall mirror in his basement, to the soundtrack of Madonna's "Like a Prayer"), he becomes an object of ridicule rather than admiration, his actions signs not of elevation above consumer culture but of a hopeless yearning to live up to an unachievable, commodity-driven ideal of masculinity. As his mother chides, "You're gonna stunt your growth with those things! You shouldn't lift while you're growing." Indeed, the presence of a full-length mirror in the scene, a mirror whose "point of view" the camera frequently occupies, relegates his actions to the realm of the imaginary, an exercise in vanity rather than vocation.

46. Mary Douglas, *Purity and Danger: An Analysis of Concepts of Pollution and Taboo* (New York: Routledge, 2003), 7.

47. Williams, "Towards an Aesthetics of Poverty," 200.

48. Mike Kelley, "From the Archives: Mike Kelley Interviews Harmony Korine," *Filmmaker Magazine*, February 13, 2012, accessed March 25, 2012, http://www.filmmakermagazine.com/news/2012/02/from-the-archives-mike-kelley-interviews-harmony-korine/.

49. Fredric Jameson, *Postmodernism*, 72.

50. Patrice Petro has acutely identified the critical potential latent in boredom in her suggestion that while an "aesthetics of boredom retains the modernist impulse of provocation and calculated assault ... it nevertheless abandons the modernist fiction of the self-contained aesthetic object, precisely by exploring the temporal and psychic structures of perception itself." (Patrice Petro, *Aftershocks of the New: Feminism and Film History* [New Brunswick: Rutgers University Press, 2002], 68.)

51. Bürger, *Theory of the Avant-Garde*, 94.

52. Hardt and Negri, *Empire*, 412.

53. Jean-Francois Lyotard, "The Sublime and the Avant-Garde," trans. Linda Liebmann, *Art Forum* 22 (1984), 40.

# 6 Knowingness
## Feeling Theory and its Other

### I

A whimsical coming-of-age story about one Max Fischer (Jason Schwartzman), a diminutive fifteen-year-old with sizeable ambitions, Wes Anderson's *Rushmore* (1998) was met by many critics as a sign that "knowingness"—an emotional or tonal quality that Philip Fisher evocatively glosses as "the feeling of 'getting it'"—had had its cultural day.[1] Setting the seeming "sincer[ity]" of a late-nineties *Rushmore* against the "knowing pastiche" and "winking familiarity" of a mid-nineties *Pulp Fiction* (Quentin Tarantino, 1994), Jesse Fox Mayshark, for one, contended that "having grown up on [a] wink-and-nod knowingness," Anderson, alongside a number of other directors of a similar ilk, had cast knowingness aside in favour of "a sort of self-conscious meaningfulness."[2] Mayshark was far from alone in revelling in *Rushmore*'s renunciation of the "winking," "nudges" and "knowing ... superiority" that had, as critics Lisa Schwarzbaum and Mark Olsen agreed, too long dominated cinematic culture, both as an intended spectatorial effect and as a primary "tone."[3] And nor, it seemed, was *Rushmore* alone in its eschewal of "knowing ... superiority."[4] On the contrary, if scholarly commentary is anything to go by, *Rushmore*'s note of "compassionate respect" and "sincerity" was part of a chorus of artistic, literary and cinematic voices that were sounding similarly "sincere" and "compassionate" refrains.[5] As far back as 1993, Jim Collins was heralding the arrival of what he called a "New Sincerity," diagnosing in film texts like *Dances with Wolves* (Kevin Costner, 2000), *Hook* (Steven Spielberg, 1991), and *Field of Dreams* (Phil Alden Robinson, 1989) a "sincerity that avoids any sort of knowing irony or eclecticism," and by 2010, Timotheus Vermeulen and Robin van den Akker had coined a novel periodizing term, the "meta-modern," to account for the demise of "knowingness" across the domain of contemporary art.[6] Significantly, for none of these critics was the idea that we were witnessing the end of knowingness an occasion for regret. As an emotion organized not just around a sense of "getting it" (as Fisher has it) but around a sense that "one has knowledge or awareness that is secret or known to only a few people" (as the Oxford English Dictionary has it), knowingness exudes an epistemic complacency and epistemic one-upmanship that would justify the emotion's inclusion among the very ugliest of the "ugly feelings" that

188    *Knowingness*

Sianne Ngai catalogues in her book of that title.[7] Unsurprisingly, then, these critical obituaries for the "wink-and-nod knowingness" whose rather smug, unpleasant mien had monopolized much earlier cultural activity were delivered with something like relief.

What bearing the demise of a decidedly "ugly" and unappealing minor emotion like knowingness might have on this book's wider argument about emotion and postmodernism is not immediately clear. Yet its significance comes into stark relief when we observe that the "wink-and-nod knowingness" whose absence Mayshark notes approvingly in *Rushmore* is specifically the "wink and nod knowingness of *postmodernism*."[8] While knowingness's relation to postmodern theory and aesthetics has never been explicitly elaborated or conceptualized, the term "knowingness" pops up so frequently in discourse within, about and against postmodern theory and aesthetics that it might easily lay claim to the status of postmodern textuality's signature emotion. Steven Connor defines postmodern architecture as that which "repeat[s] knowingly" a series of past styles; Linda Hutcheon draws on a "nudging" knowingness to describe postmodernism's "distinctive character" or "mode"; while Lawrence Grossberg argues that "postmodernity's statements exhibit an ironic, knowing distance."[9] Ubiquitous across postmodern theory as a way of approximating the general spirit or temper of postmodern cultural objects, the term occurs just as often—though far more pejoratively—in commentary *about* postmodern theory, perhaps most notably in the work of "anti-postmodern" defenders of traditional disciplinary practice. From Richard Rorty's comment on the "knowing theorizations" of postmodern ideology critique and Norm Levitt's insistence that postmodern theory "offer[s] the possibility of becoming an initiate ... authoriz[ing] a knowing (and often smug) attitude," the term "knowingness" became something of a critical projectile in the so-called "culture wars" of the 1990s, a sign of all that was false and fruitless about this then-novel critical enterprise.[10] So well-established is the identification between knowingness and postmodernism, in fact, that the two terms have become virtually synonymous, alternating with each other in a definitional circuit in which to call something "postmodern" implies its possession of a certain knowing tone, even as to call something "knowing" implies its membership of the group of cultural objects we deem postmodern.[11] In this sense, critical murmurs around the demise of "knowingness" in *Rushmore* and beyond encode—and often accompany—claims about the demise of postmodernism. And *Rushmore*'s appearance near the *end* of the decade from which *The Emotional Life of Postmodern Film* lifts its postmodern archive puts it at the beginning of a decade in which, as I have already argued, these covert murmurs about the displacement of postmodernism by a range of "post-postmodernisms" became overt manifestos.[12]

But just how have knowingness and postmodernism been critically laminated? What exactly are the postmodern textual practices whose displacement in this "post-postmodern" moment has come to "mean" the demise of knowingness? While the postmodern aesthetic and critical practices to which the scholars cited above yoke knowingness are somewhat motley (from architectural pastiche, to discursive irony and distance, to ideology critique), a broader survey of theories of and commentary on postmodernism suggests that the emotion can be lined up primarily with two key postmodern strategies. On the one hand, knowingness has tended to coalesce critically around practices of allusion, the "feeling of getting it" gelling in obvious ways with a device that—from *Pulp Fiction*'s glittery mesh of allusions and references to Cindy Sherman's immaculate reconstructions of iconic moments in Hollywood cinema—both participates in and invites the display of an elite cultural expertise. Thomas Elsaesser's ascription to postmodern or postclassical cinema of "a special sort of awareness of the codes that govern classical representation and its genre conventions, along with a willingness to display this knowingness" in the form of allusions exemplifies the critical tendency to ascribe knowingness, somewhat anthropomorphically, to the text itself, as a "special sort of awareness" that is then "display[ed]" in the form of allusion; while Alan Kirby's contention that "postmodernism prided itself on the 'media literacy,' the smartness of its ironic, knowing textual recipient" reminds us that knowingness is just as widely conceived as allusion's spectatorial effect.[13] On the other, the term knowingness has been widely applied to the practice of "postmodern critique"—a mode of ideology critique that, informed in part by poststructuralist theory, seeks to "foreground the productive, constructing aspects" of representation in order to facilitate the "de-doxification" or "de-naturalization" of established truths."[14] Whether in artistic form, as in postmodern feminist art's "scrutiny [of] patriarchal structures of culture," or in scholarly practice, as in Jean-Francois Lyotard's relentless interrogation of cherished modernist ideals like meta-narrative and social totality, the feeling of being privy to a "knowledge or awareness that is secret or known to only a few people" once more seems to square all too well with the postures indexed in and solicited by a practice organized around "exposing" the ideological, representational and social forces that govern the givens of our world.[15]

Despite the general consensus as to knowingness's typical textual loci, of course, knowingness's cultural, political and epistemic value has long been a matter of considerable controversy—a controversy whose terms break down rather neatly on either side of the "culture wars" divide. For Fisher, Levitt and Rorty, as well as psychoanalyst Jonathan Lear, and philosopher Raymond Tallis—all vocal defenders of traditional disciplinary practice against the incursion of postmodern scholarship—"knowingness" is less a sign of knowledge than a sign of postmodern critique's *resistance* to "what a philosopher [or a scientist for that matter] would call knowledge," the very "obverse of the anguished sense of uncertainty that drives ... epistemology, the scrutiny of knowledge itself."[16] For postmodern theorists, by contrast, knowingness took on a positive, euphoric value as a token of postmodern natives' historically unprecedented semiotic sophistication,

190 *Knowingness*

their laudable "competen[ce]" and "mastery" in the face of complex cultural and aesthetic codes.[17] And this critical difference on the question of knowingness's epistemic value is matched by a range of other differences. Whereas anti-postmodernist critics have represented the emotion as isolating and solipsistic (for Andrew Britton, for example, "the self-referentiality of cinema's clichés [in cinema after 1975] turns entertainment into a solipsistic totality of knowingness, [as] the community building-building roles of genres is replaced by 'a cosy conspiracy of self-congratulation and spurious familiarity'"), for most postmodern theorists, by contrast, knowingness is understood as facilitating and feeding into the construction of epistemic communities.[18] And finally, whereas for anti-postmodernist critics, knowingness is decidedly backward or even reactionary in its politics, for postmodern critics, knowingness carries a potentially "critical" or "subversive" charge.[19] As this suggests, then, between postmodernism's defenders and detractors there is little agreement as to the emotion's epistemic, social and political merits. The important points to be noted for the moment, however, are the points of basic critical consensus. It is widely agreed that knowingness converges chiefly around two specific critical and aesthetic practices, namely allusion on the one hand and critique on the other. It is widely agreed that—whether as a result of the singular historical "event" of 9/11, or for more diffuse and complex reasons—these practices began to fall out of favor around the end of the twentieth century, as both critical and cultural practitioners began searching for new artistic, methodological and social strategies.[20] And, finally, it is widely agreed that this turn away from postmodernism's trademark textual devices amounts, almost by definition, to a turn away from knowingness. The renunciation of postmodern "plenty, pastiche and parataxis," in other words, marks a renunciation of knowingness itself.[21]

This chapter will probe this last assumption further through an analysis of *Rushmore*, asking whether we are really through with knowingness after all. Yet the field whose agenda and aims will form the ultimate horizon of this analysis is not cinematic culture but feeling theory. For, perhaps unsurprisingly, given what we have shown to be the ongoing tension between feeling theory and postmodernism, the discourse in which this book is implicated has its own stake in the destiny of knowingness. As *The Emotional Life of Postmodern Film* has already established, feeling theory poses a powerful theoretical and methodological provocation to the strategies of ideology critique around which postmodern knowingness so often crystallizes. At the level of theory, the enterprise endows "affect" and "emotion" with the ability to exceed the hold of familiar social, historical and bodily regimes in a way that defies postmodern critique's tendency to treat the systems it analyzes as totalizing and all-encompassing.[22] At the level of methodology, feeling theory deploys analytical models that constitute a direct "challenge [to] the hermeneutics of suspicion and symptomatology," whose emphasis on exposure and demystification is displaced, as Ann Cvetkovich

## Knowingness   191

puts it, by an effort to "document ordinary life," to "represent global political conditions and the felt experience of everyday life," and to "depict ... 'ordinary affects.'"[23] What is significant for our purposes, however, is that for many in feeling theory, this methodological shift away from ideology critique is coded as a tonal shift away from knowingness—an emotion at once denounced as critically dangerous and dismissed as no longer of any threat. Brian Massumi's advocacy of asignifying intensities that elude or exceed "signification or coding," for example, appoints as its critical foil an older ideology critique whose mandate has long been to ensure that "from the moment a newness irrupts, [critical] procedures already ready-at-hand clamp down for the knowing capture."[24] Nigel Thrift's embrace of new, post-critical methodologies, likewise, is set against the backdrop of the conviction that "without [feeling theory's] kind of affective politics, what is left of politics will too often be the kind of macho program-making that emaciates what it is to be human—because it is so sure it already knows what that is or will be."[25] Sedgwick, meanwhile, includes knowingness in her inventory of the "negative affects" endemic to what she calls "paranoid reading," a mode of textual interpretation that, in Sedgwick's telling, shares a great deal of ground with postmodern critique.[26] According to Sedgwick, committing to the alternative, "reparative" model of reading she advocates entails "surrender[ing] the knowing, anxious, paranoid determination that no horror, however apparently unthinkable, shall ever come to the reader as new."[27] While marginally admitted to feeling theory's emotional canon, then, knowingness is barely worthy of its sustained attention, let alone avowal. For all three of these critics, in fact, knowingness is the critical tone or sensibility that must be relegated to the remote critical past if we are to pursue the more expansive and productive critical program that currently coalesces around the figures of affect and emotion.

It's easy enough to apprehend why feeling theorists—in a rather odd moment of congruence with champions of traditional disciplinary practice like Fisher, Lear and Rorty—would view knowingness with something close to distaste. While most feeling states can assume either emotional or affective form, knowingness's seeming dependence on knowledge not only ties it almost exclusively to emotion, but aligns it with all of the backward, reactionary qualities with which feeling theory has tended to burden "emotion." Indeed, in many ways, knowingness is everything that feeling theory decidedly is *not*. Consider, first, that, galvanized by the possibility of change, surprise and the new, feeling-oriented scholars maintain that "attending to elusory [sic], opaque spaces of affect orientates inquiry to the conditions under which new encounters, relations and events are produced."[28] Yet as what Raymond Tallis dubs "the obverse of the anguished sense of uncertainty that drives philosophy's primary discipline," as the abiding arch-enemy of the "wonder" or "awe" that Tallis, like Fisher and Rorty, installs at the heart of understanding, the emotional mechanism of knowingness seems designed precisely to fend off the possibility of surprise,

192 *Knowingness*

to ensure that, as Massumi puts it, "from the moment a newness irrupts, [critical] procedures already ready-at-hand clamp down for the knowing capture."[29] Consider, second, that feeling theory rallies around an ideal of scholarly community and exchange, striving to resist the forms of academic one-upmanship that see us, as Grossberg has put it, "build our reputations and our positions on the corpses of other scholars, condemning their inadequacies and their complicities with the dominant powers."[30] Yet as a state characterized by the OED as "Showing or suggesting that one has knowledge or awareness that is secret or known to only a few people," knowingness, as its signature smirk suggests, seems to involve a gloating pleasure in the exclusions and hierarchies that underpin the knowledge it displays.[31] And consider, finally, that as a field of study that has made affect and emotion its primary critical objects, feeling theory has long mandated an affective mindfulness that Ann Cvetkovich has dubbed an "openness to the richness of emotional experience ... [that will] create space for new understandings of happiness and utopia."[32] Yet as what Rorty calls "a state of soul which prevents shudders of awe [and that] makes one immune to romantic enthusiasm," knowingness is an emotion that—in an uncanny amplification of the dynamic that, for Massumi, marks the relationship between emotion and affect in general—actively shuts off and shuts down affect.[33] Knowingness's "self-protective project," in other words, is altogether paralysing to the strange, nameless "shudders" that feeling theorists have gathered together under the umbrella of affect.[34] Admittedly, knowingness is hardly alone in our emotional lexicon in its relation to normative regimes of power, to social hierarchy, or to the resistance to affect; it is readily admitted across feeling theory that *all* affect is available to being "captured by a subject ... tamed and reduced," caught up in a network that puts it to work in the service of social, economic and cultural praxis.[35] Yet while generally available to recruitment by established social and political regimes, most feelings are also endowed with "a certain surplus of affect that 'escapes confinement,'" a "surplus" that makes them equally available to unsettling, exceeding and even resisting those regimes.[36] Knowingness, by contrast, seems beyond the reach of recuperation or rehabilitation. Wedded to epistemic hierarchy, social exclusivity and theoretical sameness, the emotion is thoroughly incompatible with feeling theory's methodological ideals on virtually every level.

It should come as little surprise, then, that far from countenancing knowingness in its critical practice feeling theory has tended to catalyze critical enthusiasm for an emotional posture or position that doubles as knowingness' opposite: naïveté. Melissa Gregg and Gregory Seigworth's argument that critics in thrall to older, postmodern methodologies have tended to view feeling-oriented work "as naïvely or romantically wandering too far out into the groundlessness of a world's or a body's myriad inter-implication" implicitly installs this state of "naïveté" as a long-embattled but finally triumphant critical ideal.[37] Naomi Scheman's denunciation of postmodern

Knowingness    193

theorizing for "encourag[ing] an attitude of knowingness that insulates us from what are seen as naïve, even embarrassing encounters with texts," similarly, ascribes to this "naïve, even embarrassing encounter[]" a critical and epistemic productivity it denies the "attitude of knowingness."[38] Diverging from knowingness not just in its relation to the new (it is open), but in its relation to hierarchy (it aspires to none) and in its relation to feeling (it helps promote it), this "naïveté" seems in every way more appropriate to feeling theory's critical imperatives. Indeed, where the term "naïveté" does not make an appearance, the term "openness" seems to serve much the same critical purpose. Teresa Brennan prescribes "an openness ... to one's own sensations and feeling for the other"; in her introduction to *Political Emotions*, Cvetkovich suggests that an "openness to the richness of emotional experience ... marks the affective turn"; while Ben Anderson refers to "the ambiguous openness that the term affect names."[39] Naming less discrete, distinct feelings in themselves than species of a kind of "pre-feeling" underwriting the very possibility of feeling—and thus recalling Brennan's account of "living attention" or "feeling intelligence"—these receptive, pre-affective states of "openness" and "naïveté" are the new, affect-friendly critical postures that feeling theory routinely sets against an old, affect-resistant knowingness.[40]

A bad object or foreign body, a reprobate relic from the critical past, knowingness has little place, then, in feeling theory. Yet the cognitive-appraisal model of emotion that currently holds sway across the field makes staging the drama of knowingness's expulsion and eviction relatively easy. Not only shackled to "the domain of the personal and private," but shackled to specific appraisals or judgments, a cognitive-appraisal model of knowingness seems in little danger of slipping free of the aesthetic and critical strategies to which we have tended to tie it.[41] Heather Love's recommendation that cultural criticism relax its familiar posture of knowingness, for example, involves confidently splicing the emotion to a particular set of critical procedures—"familiar academic protocols like maintaining critical distance, outsmarting (and other forms of one-upmanship), [and] believing the hierarchy"—whose renunciation can thus be expected to terminate the emotion's flow between critic, reader and world.[42] Similarly, Scheman's association of knowingness with an outmoded postmodern form of reading, Massumi's elision of knowingness with the "old" cultural studies, and Sedgwick's conflation of knowingness with the techniques of ideological demystification she identifies with "paranoid" reading—all three accounts align knowingness with a discrete, specifiable critical practice whose rejection guarantees knowingness's disappearance. While this process seems fishy enough when we are broaching knowingness as a spectatorial or readerly emotion, it seems even fishier as a way of thinking about knowingness as a textual tone. A thoroughly diffuse phenomenon that encompasses a total network of relations within and around the text, the concept of "tone," as Sianne Ngai has argued, "'cannot be brought into an explicit correlation

194  *Knowingness*

with [a text's] component elements' ..[or] locate[d] in any isolated formal feature"—despite our tendency to read tone anthropomorphically as an emotion that, inhering mysteriously somewhere within the text, is then expressed or "displayed" in the form of allusion.[43]

This chapter, then, will take issue with the model of knowingness implicit in these arguments for its expiry. A far more mobile and insidious emotion than the argument that we might simply "surrender" it credits, knowingness, I will argue, is less a function of individual subjective judgments or specific textual devices than an effect of a social exchange—a form of exchange that becomes urgently expedient in the wake of the wider epistemic and cognitive crises that have been theorized not just under the sign of postmodernism, but across more recent accounts of globalization, network culture and bio-power. In arguing this, I will return to my initial cinematic example, Wes Anderson's coming-of-age classic *Rushmore*. While regularly marshalled as a sign both of the demise of knowingness, and of the emergence of what Mark Olsen dubs a cinema of "engagement and empathy," *Rushmore*, I will argue, is nevertheless a text in which knowingness possesses an abiding if unacknowledged power. Indeed, the film's claim to have severed itself from the circuits of knowingness that energize many a canonical instance of postmodern film merely strengthens its complicity in these circuits through the labour of what I will call a "knowing naïveté."[44] The critical reach of this argument, however, extends beyond the question of the continued existence of a particular tone or sensibility in popular cinema. For while I do not wish to efface the crucial political, institutional and generic differences between cinema and cultural studies, I do suggest that *Rushmore*'s status as the avatar of a "New Sincerity" places it in a relation to filmic postmodernism that is roughly equivalent to feeling theory's relation to critical postmodernism. *Rushmore*'s implication in the work of "knowing naïveté," then, suggests that feeling theory's efforts to immunize itself against the toxic presence of an insidious knowingness may not be as successful—or, indeed, as productive—as they initially seem.

## II

With its aura of quaint detachment from the contemporary cinematic landscape, *Rushmore* more than justified its critical uptake as a sign that an identifiably "knowing" postmodern cinema was on the wane. Shot in and around the tree-shadowed, neo-gothic limestone faculty buildings of Anderson's own alma mater, St. John's School in Houston, Texas, *Rushmore* plays out in what Kenneth Turan calls a "unique world," a dreamy, timeless prep school of the imagination in which particular historical markers and "hip references" have been replaced by a kind of picturesque, a-historical whimsy.[45] And the naïveté that suffuses the film's storybook locations and over-decorated interiors is sustained at the levels of the cinematography, dialogue and narrative. First, whereas more openly knowing postmodern films continually undercut or "establish their superiority over" their characters through a bristling display of their own mastery of filmic codes, style and intertexts, *Rushmore*'s cinematography tends not only toward clunky amateurism but toward a kind of historical backwardness.[46] Its rigid, frontal orientation amplified by the use of a cartoonishly wide-angle anamorphic lens, the camera seems to function less as mobile agent than as proscenium arch, as if, like many early films, *Rushmore* had not fully extracted itself from a model of cinema as filmed theatre.[47] Second, whereas one prominent strain of postmodern film, notably associated with the work of Quentin Tarantino, traffics in an insistently referential and allusive "talkiness" whose relation to character or narrative development remains moot, this "type of pop culture dialogue—a fixture of Nineties hip cinema—is ... absent from Anderson's feature," where dialogue functions primarily to reveal character rather than to reference other texts.[48] Third and finally, whereas classically postmodern films pride themselves on their knowing play with the codes of filmic narrative, *Rushmore* is a traditional, linear coming-of-age story, faithfully and even ploddingly documenting Max's maturation as he falls in love with a teacher and out of favor with his school before acquiring a humbled recognition of his own value.

While these formal tendencies alone would justify the film's inclusion in the critical logbooks of a "New Sincerity," the case for the film's relinquishment of knowingness is further reinforced at the level of theme, which codes the arc of Max's "coming of age" as a movement from the lonely, isolated knowingness limned by film critic Andrew Briton to a socialized naïveté. The boy we meet in the opening scenes is a boy making strenuous efforts to cultivate an aura of knowingness: captain of the fencing team, leader of the "model United Nations" and founder of the astronomy club—positions clearly articulated to a "knowledge or awareness that is secret or known to only a few people"—he is also openly and aggressively in love with a teacher twice his age.[49] The boy unveiled in the final scene of the film, by contrast, is a boy who has learned to act both his age and his station, embracing the public school system and dating a girl of roughly similar years. Supported by a spatial transition from the snobbish exclusivity of a tony private school to a public school gymnasium in which rich and poor, old and young mingle freely, this thematic statement is brokered in part through a striking shift at the level of visual style. The earlier sections of the film, which track Max's efforts to establish himself in a position of social and epistemic authority, rely on fixed shots that effectively isolate individual characters in lavishly art-decorated Cornell box-like tableaux. The final scene, by contrast, indulges in a series of leisurely pans and tracks whose sinuous movement locates characters previously rigidly segregated from each other, from Rushmore Prep's waspy principal to Max's lowly barber father, in a single, demotic cinematic space. Whereas Max's bids to gain acceptance from his upper-crust schoolmates by seeking unsuccessfully to replicate their social codes only succeeded in alienating him from them, his humbled embrace of

196  *Knowingness*

his own naïveté creates a unified, egalitarian space in which he effectively transcends class boundaries.

Cinematographically, too, *Rushmore* is alive to the social and historical shifts that have stripped the posture of "getting it" of its cultural premium. Exemplary here is the film's opening sequence, a classroom scene that initially sets up a classic circuit of knowingness only to devolve quickly into a cutting critique of it. When the teacher promises, rather extravagantly, that if one of his students can solve "the hardest geometry equation in the world," no one in the class will have to "open another math book for the rest of [their] li[ves]," the class falls into hushed, excited discussion, amidst which the repeated whispering of the name "Max" can be distinguished, prompting the teacher to inquire, "Max, care to try it?" Until now suspensefully off-screen, Max is finally unveiled in mid shot as a bespectacled boy with a gleaming bowl-cut. With a wry, knowing smile, he delivers with an ironic question—"I'm sorry, did someone say my name?"—that provokes the class to chuckles of knowing laughter. Resting on a reference to a certain shared knowledge—everyone knows, after all, "that someone [said his] name," and clearly everyone knows *why* they said it—this knowing exchange tends to cement the link, long established in postmodern film aesthetics, between knowingness and a kind of dense, information-rich allusion. This link is further consolidated when Max actually solves the problem and is held aloft by his classmates in a moment of scholarly congratulation. Importantly, however, the scene's seeming investment in the social and cultural profits of knowingness is quickly undercut when the entire sequence is revealed to be a dream: the image of Max being cheered by his fellow students is intercut with a looming, high-angle close-up of Max asleep, mouth open and head resting on the back of a pew, as the noise of classmates' applause fade into what we now realize is the "actual" sound of assembled students applauding the speaker during morning chapel. Indeed, this scene is just one of many scenes in *Rushmore* that pivot on the failure of Max's efforts to command either respect or intimacy through the kinds of epistemic display we have come to associate with knowingness. Alienating him from the very community he is trying to enter, Max's ostentatious displays of inappropriate, excessive or misplaced knowledge mark him out not as savvy but as try-hard, smart-arse or even criminal. In this sense, then, *Rushmore* not only casts knowingness as an unappealing and isolating trait, but equates postmodern theorists' investment in knowingness with a kind of dismal schoolboy fantasy.

Yet if *Rushmore* seems in this not only to abandon but actually to condemn knowingness, it should be remembered that we are working within the ambit of a very specific model of the emotion. In this model, knowingness registers as the emotional or tonal complement of a person or a text's possession of an "awareness that is secret or known to only a few people"—a feeling that is then subsequently "display[ed]" on the body of the text or person, whether through a knowing wink, nod or smile, or through reference or allusion. Despite its critical pedigree, however, this model of knowingness seems strikingly inadequate to the actual working of the emotion. While the analysis of the scene in the previous paragraph treated the shot of Max's knowing smirk as the record of a single emotional moment, closer attention to the shot reveals both its unusual length and its unusual visual-aural intricacy, suggesting that what initially seems like one emotional unit—the knowing smile—can be broken down into three separate stages. First, our eyes are drawn to Max's wry smile, as he asks, quizzically, "did somebody say my name?"; then, shifting from the visual to the aural register, we notice the noise-off of the class's responsively knowing laughter, indicating their own knowledge that his question was intended in jest; finally, returning to the visual register, we revisit the image of Max's face, its expression of gratified knowingness deepened this time, as he breaks into a knowing smile that logs the recognition manifest in their laughter. What this image yields, then, is not a single, uniform emotional bloc, but a complex set of emotional gestures whose workings and implications merit close critical attention.

*Figure 6.1* "Did somebody say my name?"

*Figure 6.2* The deepened grin of gratified knowingness.

198　*Knowingness*

Consider, then, that the first of these gestures, the "knowing" smile, is tentative and hesitant, less an expression of knowingness than an invitation to knowingness, and a long way from the smug, complacent sense of epistemic mastery with which the emotion is generally associated by both its advocates and its critics. In its tentativeness and its hesitation, in fact, Max's initial smile implies that while in this particular case a "knowledge that is secret or known only to a few people" *is* in circulation—in conjunction with his ironic, pseudo-naive question, Max's small, wry smile calls up their mutual understanding that yes, they did "say [his] name," and that this is because his undisputed genius makes him the only conceivable person in the class who could solve the problem—this smiling visual overture could equally be delivered *without* the sender's possessing any specifiable secret knowledge at all. As the OED's definition of "knowing" intimates, knowingness does not depend on *having* knowledge but rather on "*showing or suggesting* that one has knowledge" to another. In this light, it should come as little surprise that this initial moment is very quickly succeeded by a second moment, namely the class's warmly amused, embracing response, which indicates that Max's "showing or suggesting that [he] has knowledge" has been accepted. And it is only after all this rapid emotional two-step that we reach the third and final moment—only here that the tentative smiles deepens into the confident, gloating grin of knowingness.

Notwithstanding Steven Shaviro's insistence that emotion is affect "owned and mastered by the subject," then, knowingness is not a feeling that a spectator or text just "has" as a result of knowledge *possessed*, but a feeling that must be conferred upon her by others through forms of social feedback that signal knowledge *ascribed*.[50] As the triple ricochet performed by Max's knowing smile indicates, the knowledge, "competence" or "mastery" around which knowingness is so often supposed to crystallize are secondary in importance to both the wink or smile through we imply knowledge's presence, and the wink or smile through which an other affirms it. Far, then, from a feeling that arises in a subject as a result of a solitary, cognitive recognition of an allusion, knowingness is both completely independent of any necessary relation to any actual knowledge, and completely dependent on social cues and corroboration.[51] Indeed, this argument for the primacy of social feedback in emergence and evolution of knowingness might be best illustrated through reference to a hypothetical scenario in which Max's classmates did *not* respond warmly to his smile: leaving Max less smugly vainglorious than thoroughly embarrassed, this alternative scenario virtually epitomizes what Sedgwick means when she speaks of shame, an emotion that is in many ways knowingness's opposite number, as a state that arises when "the circuit of mirroring expressions … is broken."[52]

But there is more to say here, for to argue that knowingness can materialize in the absence of any kind of shared "knowledge" is not to say that there is no necessary evaluative content at all and thus that knowingness falls outside the purview of the cognitive appraisal paradigm altogether.

Notice that Max's final, gratified smile, the smile of knowingness, is very decidedly a smile *at* or *about* something. What is significant for our purposes, however, is that the cognitive object of Max's knowing grin is not the essentially dispensable *knowledge* he shares with his class-mates, but the knowing *relationship* he shares with them—a relationship deepened in light of their genial willingness to participate in this peculiar exchange. A metaleptic emotional effect of its own effect, a spectral after-light of the very wink or nudge that seems to flag its presence, knowingness, then, is a feeling of "getting it" that not only emerges through social feedback, but that takes social feedback as its object.[53] And the consequences of this re-reading of knowingness for the emotion's relation to specifically postmodern textual practices are far-reaching. For it suggests that while the strategies of allusion and critique associated with postmodernism aesthetics and scholarship enshrine very specific forms of knowledge, participating in the knowing circuits these texts set in motion depends not on the ability, as Kirby has it, to "identify the quotations, the sources, and allusions" inherent *in* these texts but on forming *around* these texts a feedback loop of mutual affirmation and belief.

This argument ramifies in significant ways on the reading of *Rushmore* we have already advanced. Before we go on to explore these ramifications, however, we should note that what is valuable about this account of knowingness as a social emotion in which knowledge is ascribed rather than possessed is not just that it seems more faithful to the emotion's relation to postmodern aesthetics, but that it helps us resolve some apparent anomalies within postmodern epistemology. For if, as we have seen, the great majority of work on postmodern aesthetics foregrounds the spectator's discursive mastery and competence, the great majority of work on postmodern social, cultural and technological life, by contrast, foregrounds the postmodern subject's sense of epistemic failure and inadequacy. On the one hand, we have Jameson on the failure of "cognitive mapping," Lyotard on the waning of meta-narrative, and Baudrillard on the extinction of reality in the simulation, all narratives of postmodernism that star not a masterful, knowing subject but a baffled, bewildered and overwhelmed one.[54] On the other, we have critics like Baudrillard, Jonathan Bignell, David Harvey and Douglas Kellner articulating the postmodern moment to the proliferation, dematerialization, speeding up and diversification of media and communications systems—a narrative in which, once again, the postmodern subject registers as overwhelmed by a dizzying array of cultural choices and a dizzying quantity of information.[55] Tracing knowingness to a social rather than epistemic relation, however, helps us account for this curious disparity between the figures of epistemic mastery that feature so heavily in theories of postmodern aesthetics, and the figures of epistemic loss that dominate across the rest of the field. For it suggests that, rather than conflicting, these two narratives may be intimately intertwined—with postmodern aesthetics' embrace of a posture of knowingness working to offset at the emotional and aesthetic level the confusion that afflicts postmodern subjects at the cultural, technological and social level. As a euphoric, pleasurable "feeling of getting" it with no necessary relation to *actually* "getting it" at all, knowingness affords us a provisional purchase on the incomprehensible by ensuring that if we cannot possibly know everything, then we can, at least, in the confirming if misrecognizing embrace of the knowing community, feel like we know something—something, moreover, that as the OED reminds us, is "secret or known to only a few people." As Carl Matheson observes in a philosophical account of knowingness that is remarkably rare in the literature on knowingness in the acuity with which it pinpoints this paradoxical process, "with the abandonment of knowledge came the cult of knowingness. That is, even if there is no ultimate truth (or method for arriving at it), I can at least show myself to be in a superior position for now on the shifting sands of the game we are currently playing."[56] Rather than either an emotional sign of semiotic mastery (as the postmodernists have it), or an emotional sign of philosophical complacency (as its critics have it), knowingness is a feeling of mastery to which we have compensatory recourse on both an individual and cultural level precisely when things are getting—as my chapter on bewilderment showed—bewildering.

Arguing this, however, does not just explain why a feeling so strongly articulated to epistemic certainty should emerge against a backdrop of epistemic failure. It also does something else. For if we have already contended that knowingness *can* survive the demise of postmodern aesthetic strategies, the argument in the previous paragraph supplies strong social and cultural reasons why it *must*. Few scholars would suggest that cognitive mapping's failure, meta-narrative's waning and simulations triumph are less relevant to today's world than they were at the time of writing, and even fewer would deny that, as N. Katherine Hayles puts it, we have only "plunge[d] even deeper into the infosphere of ubiquitous computing, global Internet culture, and information economies" that Baudrillard's theory of the communicational "obscene" anticipated in 1981.[57] If anything, the social, discursive and technological phenomena to which an aesthetics of knowingness is a response are more prominent now than ever. What, then, are the implications of this differently inflected model of knowingness's structure and impetus for both postmodernism itself and for the critical and aesthetic practices—of which *Rushmore* and feeling theory are my primary examples—that supposedly come "after" postmodernism? That the roster of postmodern aesthetic and critical strategies that ostentatiously foreground and solicit knowingness have lost some of their cultural clout is now a matter of critical consensus, and our analysis of *Rushmore*'s narrative, thematic and formal registers seems to bear this consensus out. Yet the assumption that the waning of postmodern aesthetics amounts to a transcendence of knowingness must be set against some of the arguments we have just advanced. If, in many circles, knowingness is now a critical and cultural anathema, it is also, as we have seen, both a valuable emotional salve in the face of impending epistemic and

*Knowingness* 201

technological crises, and a slippery, social emotion that cannot be locked down to specific textual practices.

To say that knowingness is a slippery and mobile emotion, however, is not to say that just any callow, half-baked or juvenile enterprise can come to function as a node in a social circuit of knowingness. How, then, *does* a text become a magnet for knowingness in the absence of the battery of aesthetic and critical devices that so ostentatiously and overtly solicits the emotion? One answer to this question, oddly, comes from Anderson himself, whose response to an interviewer's inquiry as to "how the current trend [among filmmakers like Quentin Tarantino] of incorporating tons of pop-culture references will hold up thirty years from now," is to declare that "in ten years, they're going to be passé," observing that his own films, by contrast, are "not topical and timely, and I don't want them to be. I want them to be the kind of stories you can go back to and they won't feel dated. It's also just what I'm drawn to. I don't want to have current, contemporary references in it. I want it to be something that's sort of self-contained."[58] For while Anderson champions the closure and self-containment by which his films remain faithful to the rich experiential reservoir of the authorial self ("it's just what I'm drawn to"), his constant circling back to the question of what he is *not* doing ("not topical and timely"; "I don't want to have current contemporary references in it") suggests that this naïve, self-contained and timeless model of filmmaking ("stories you can go back to and they won't feel dated") itself functions referentially, as a meta-allusion to very aesthetic practice that it denounces and displaces. And this rhetorical process by which the refusal of reference comes to read as a knowing meta-reference to knowingness's absence provides a useful heuristic for knowingness's percolation through a post-postmodern moment. Where the avowal of knowingness has become a social and critical anathema, but where the value of knowingness continues to reign supreme, knowingness comes to circulate not around grandiose displays of cultural mastery, but around those texts that have mastered the meta-knowledge that the grandiose display of cultural mastery has long since passed its use-by date. Those texts that have become vectors in contemporary circuits of knowingness, in other words, are texts that—like *Rushmore*—have learned to formalize and stylize naïveté into a set of aesthetic codes as recognizable in their way as the wink or the allusion. In doing so, these texts participate in the workings of what I will call a "knowing naïveté."

Returning, finally, to the film whose supposed naïveté I have already limned but which I would now like to convert into the paradigm for "*knowing naïveté,*" we might inaugurate our analysis with attention to the opening shot of the scene in the hotel room where Blume has booked himself an indefinite stay when his wife sues for divorce—a lingering close-up on a hotel welcome card with the calligraphic entreaty, "Enjoy Your Stay." For if a decades-long acquaintance with the codes of postmodern filmic practice has trained us to trawl a shot of this length for its allusive or referential yield, this shot delivers up only its own thunderous literalism, its only allusion to its own ostentatious

## 202  *Knowingness*

refusal to allude. Rather than simply refusing the kind of cultural sophistication traditionally enshrined in practices of allusion, pastiche and textual play, then, that is, *Rushmore* functions reflexively as a series of meta-allusions to sophistication's absence. Similarly, *Rushmore* doesn't just *not* meddle with traditional narrative structure: ringing in every point on its plodding, linear story arc with the parting of a red velvet stage curtain, the film explicitly foregrounds its naïveté by drawing on the appurtenances of the amateur stage production. Likewise, the film doesn't just *not* play with cinematography: the stubbornly frontal orientation of the camera, underscored by Anderson's obsessively symmetrical framing, tends both to foreground the very camera work it ostensibly elides and to render the activities of the characters within it oddly comical, like puppets whose emotional histrionics are bathetically restricted to the cramped frontiers of a miniature theatre. And finally, the film doesn't just *not* resist filmic convention: it follows them with a ponderous, gauche literalism. If it has long been standard filmic practice to ensure that the angle of a subjective point of view shots reflects the relative positions of the interlocutors in a shot-reverse shot exchange, *Rushmore*'s deployment of this device in the end-game encounter between Max and Mr Blume on a small hillock in a local park registers three height differentials rather than the two that the characters license, shifting from Blume's high-angle point of view shot, gazing upon a seated Max, to Max's low-angle point of view shot, looking at a standing Blume, to *a tree's* higher-angle point of view shot when Mr Blume turns to the remark on the pine tree that shadows the pair. If *Rushmore* is *knowingly* naïve, then, it is because it has learned to stylize and foreground its refusal of cultural competence in the very same way that earlier films worked to stylize and package their cultural sophistication.[59]

The power of knowing naïveté, however, lies not just in its ability to trump a more overtly knowing aesthetic mode, but in the carapace of quaintness that enables it to deny that it's playing the game of knowing one-upmanship in the first place. At stake here, I suggest, is the film's mastery of the critical and cultural games that Eve Kosofsky Sedgwick grapples with across her analyses of the logic of *it takes one to know one*.[60] Where, as Sedgwick shows, the act of critique invariably leaves a dubious critical residue on the critic, overtly attacking knowingness would leave *Rushmore* vulnerable to the charge of being knowing itself—thus putting it at risk of further knowing one-upmanship. What secures *Rushmore*'s knowing naïveté against reproach, then, is not only that it is not openly knowing, but that it is also not openly *anti*-knowing. Indeed, *Rushmore*'s effort to camouflage its complicity in a network of knowingness is promoted by Max himself, who becomes the fall-guy for any gestures of "knowingness-attribution" that might be set in motion by the knowing energies that circulate in and around the film.[61] The sneaking suspicion that *Rushmore* harbors its own social and cultural ambitions is overshadowed by the bombastic, cartoonish knowingness of Max himself, who—despite his appalling grades—claims Harvard as his "safety school," should he be rejected by the Sorbonne.

*Knowingness* 203

Of course, if Max's presence in the film helps to elide the film's investment in knowingness, it also risks exposing that investment. If, as a filmic paean to naïveté, the film can hardly be seen to endorse Max's knowingness, any attempt to mock that knowingness threatens, as Sedgwick has shown, to rebound doubly back on the film itself. Paradigmatic here is the early scene in which Max endeavors to create a verbal rapport with Mr Blume (Bill Murray), a prominent local businessman and the father of two students at the school, who has just delivered a less than rousing speech to the assembled students. Insinuating himself between Blume and the school Principal, Dr Guggenheim, Max declares: "I just wanted to say that I strongly agree with your views concerning Rushmore. Your speech was excellent." Yet while Max's own speech is quite as "excellent" as Blume's—his discourse and his manners flawless—he not only fails to secure a knowing parley between himself and Blume, but, on the contrary, becomes the *object* of a knowing exchange between Blume and Dr Guggenheim. Exploiting the lens's depth of field to hold Max and Dirk in the centre background of the frame while allowing Guggenheim and Blume, unbeknownst to Max, to exchange glances across their foregrounded positions flanking the frame, the film ensures that the knowing circuit that Max seeks to establish between himself and Blume through a display of verbal mastery is secured instead between Blume and Guggenheim at the level of the visual. And no wonder: for Max is practicing, unsuccessfully, exactly the kind of overt knowingness that the film's shrewdly naïve knowingness (usually) knows better than to try itself. There is just one catch here. For as the signature gesture of critique, the mechanism of "exposure" through which the film is able to disclose Max's knowingness implicates the film in just the kind of blatant—and thus unsuccessful—knowingness that a properly knowing naïveté might do well to avoid. Brutally stark, the film's wide-screen camera recalls not the callow fumblings of early cinema but the kind of unblinking acerbic gaze more closely associated with a Hal Hartley or Todd Solondz. The film's knowing exposure of Max's overt knowingness thus leaves *Rushmore* susceptible to further gestures of knowing one-upmanship, threatening to trigger an infinitely regressive chain of knowing antagonism in which every smart-aleck is simply a dope in the making.

It is significant, then, that the sequence that follows immediately on the heels of this one marks the film's abrupt retreat into a kind of ferment of naïveté. A top-shot of "The Rushmore Yankee," a red, hard-bound school yearbook, cues an extended montage sequence composed of staged tableaux, all of which centrally feature Max in scenarios intended to read as the book's "contents": the first features Max leading four fellow students across a grassy, tree-studded quadrangle, accompanied by the title "Rushmore Yankee: Publisher," in the film's canny red and white font; the next features Max at the center front row in a class full of listening booths with the title "French club: President"; and so on, running the gamut from Captain of the fencing team to Founder of the astronomy circle. Carefully rebuilding the rind of whimsy that will secure it against further chains of knowing one-upmanship, the film aligns itself here not only with an antiquated media form (the book), but with an obsolete cinematic practice, drawing heavily on the codes of a moment in film history in which movies were structured as a series of frontal tableaux. Indicating both the voracious range of Max's interests and his seeming ubiquity within the school community, the sequence offers important insights into Max's character and social standing. Yet its characterological force is clearly subordinate to its aesthetic function. And this tendency to retreat into a frenzy of cinematic atavism at the very point that it risks acquiring an overt or explicit relation to knowingness can be shown to be at work at crucial moments throughout the film.

Oddly, however, if a knowing Max tempts *Rushmore* with a reversion to all-too-explicitly knowing practices of mockery and exposure, a guileless and simple-minded Max seems to lay the film open to an even more dangerous fate—that of simply looking naïve. Denuded of his signature smirk, Max arrives at the film's final scene transfigured into precisely the kind of bland, amiable creature—precisely, that is, the kind of non-character—that the conventional coming-of-age story seems so committed to molding its protagonists into. Without Max's problematized knowingness against which to pit itself, however, the film's own knowing naïveté reads as a kind of naïve sentimentalism. Jonathan Rosenbaum is one of many critics to register the extent to which the final scene's almost ceremonial unveiling of Max's successful character transformation is matched by a less narratively explicable formal and tonal shift: "unlike the madder scenes" earlier in the film, this "optimistic ending bears some recognizable relation to the real world."[62] Yet for this clearer relation to "the real world," the film trades the adroit balance of full-blown knowingness and its psuedo-naïve disavowal that characterizes the most powerful moments in Anderson's films. As Olsen describes the final scene, in which all the players are brought together for a party to celebrate the exhibition of Max's new play, "all squabbles are forgotten and differences set aside … Anderson allows us a final, slow-motion look around the room, taking in every detail, reaffirming that these are the moments we remember—the laughter, the friendships, the triumphs, the successes."[63] If these scenarios sound painfully sentimental, this is because they are: deprived of the figure whose unsuccessful knowingness has continually enabled the transfiguration of its naïve pseudo-classicism into what I have called a "knowing naïveté," the final scene is weighed down by sentimentalism, an orgy of lessons heavy-handedly learned, relationships over-hastily healed and differences clunkily overcome.

## III

A number of voices, both popular and scholarly, have dismissed knowingness as an anachronistic vestige of the postmodern past, and vested their liberatory hopes in naïveté, openness or sincerity. This chapter, however, has argued that these critical and aesthetic efforts to vanquish knowingness may be less successful than many of us, rallying busily and optimistically around various instantiations of the "post-postmodern," may hope. For one thing, knowingness's emergence in postmodern aesthetics is a response to a range of discursive, social, technological and geopolitical pressures that exert just as much force today as they did in postmodernism's 1980s and '90s heyday. For another, knowingness is a mobile, social emotion or tone that circulates around and is conferred upon subjects and texts rather than expressed by them through specific textual strategies or bodily signs—so that while we can never be sure that we will be party to knowingness's satisfactions, we can also never fully extricate ourselves from or straightforwardly "surrender" the emotion, either. This is not to say, of course, that knowingness has not undergone something of a face-lift in a post-postmodern aesthetic moment in which the textual strategies conventionally associated with it have by and large been retired. Indeed, as my analysis of *Rushmore* has shown, the post-postmodern cinematic moment sees knowingness accrue not to sophisticated cinematic allusions but to moments of cinematic naïveté, formalized in *Rushmore* as a "knowing naïveté" that exaggerates and foregrounds its refusal of cultural sophistication as emphatically as postmodern aesthetic practice foregrounded its expertise. What is clear, however, is that the arrival of a "New Sincerity" in post-postmodern aesthetic practice indicates not the demise of knowingness, nor even just its persistence, but its second wind as an emotion that actually thrives on the kind of cultural backlash that has seen more ostentatiously knowing practices, like allusion and critique, stripped of their former cultural constituency. While, as Linda Hutcheon has put it bluntly of postmodernism, "it's over," and while few would deny that postmodern aesthetic and critical practice has fallen out of favor, one of its chief tonal hallmarks retains a powerful presence in our lives—in part because so many of the infrastructural, discursive and technological phenomena that have always energized the emotion do too.[64]

But if *Rushmore* has been the primary textual example on which this analysis has relied, it is feeling theory whose co-ordinates have formed its horizon and its stimulus. As we have seen, the spectre of knowingness is something of a *bête noir* for feeling theory: more than just riding roughshod over the field's foundational opposition between emotion and postmodern critique, knowingness is stamped by a spirit of complacency and competitiveness that seems thoroughly at odds with a critical practice committed to epistemic and social "openness." It thus comes as no surprise that, where feeling theory has addressed knowingness at all, it is only to dismiss it as the obsolete signature emotion of an equally obsolete critical practice. My reading of *Rushmore*, however, suggests that feeling theory's critical resistance to knowingness, evinced in part by its embrace of critical methodologies that seem immune to the emotion, is inadequate to keep knowingness at bay. To the very extent that it is "naïve" in its approach to narrative and characterization, *Rushmore* is a "knowing" text, its lack of allusion alluding knowingly

206  *Knowingness*

to its paranoid, postmodern, openly knowing predecessors; analogously, to the very extent that feeling-orientated criticism avows a post-knowing naïveté, it can be seen to perform an act of knowing one-upmanship that not only partially explains the critical prestige currently attendant upon it, but shows feeling theory to be fully enmeshed in the knowing critical paradigm it imagines itself to have escaped. Knowingness's secret, siren-like allure seems to capture even those most resistant to its implicit ideological cargo.[65] With this evidence of knowingness's persistence in mind, feeling theory's studious refusal to acknowledge the ways in which its practice reflects and resonates with an older postmodern enterprise seems unsustainable.

The fact that knowingness plays an ongoing role in feeling theory does not, of course, in itself oblige us to embrace or espouse it as an important critical term, for, as Sedgwick has made clear, the notion that a phenomenon is true "is, it turns out, separable from the question of whether the energies of a given ... intellectual or group might best be used in the tracing or exposure" of that phenomenon.[66] Yet I want to insist that in addition to its purely epistemic value in laying bare some of feeling theory's less estimable energies, knowingness may also harbor a latent strategic value for actually extending and enriching that field. On one level, this value lies precisely in the emotion's status as feeling theory's "other"—its relentless censure and disavowal across feeling theory bringing into relief some of the inexplicit presumptions and postulates that structure feeling theory as a field. As feeling theory's critical foil, that is, knowingness provides a much-needed reminder of the fact that, like any other critical practice, feeling theory authorizes a specifiable series of emotional and critical norms—perhaps the most prominent of which, "openness" and "naïveté," amount to a kind of denial that such norms exist. On another level, however, I would suggest that a deliberate, subjectivized practice of knowing critical self-scrutiny might counter some of the less productive effects of this naïveté and openness. Gregg and Seigworth's introduction to *Affect Theory* seeks to deny any kind of trackable uniformity in the thinking that congregates around feeling, arguing not only that feeling-orientated work is not propelled by knowingness, but that it could not itself become the object of knowingness. "There is," the writers argue, "no single generalizable theory of affect: not yet, and (thankfully) there never will be"—a "never" whose absoluteness contrasts sharply and symptomatically with their commitment both here and elsewhere to the open-ended logic of the "not yet."[67] Yet the point is not just that this denial seems inconsistent. Rather, it is that, while Sedgwick ascribes the epistemic blockages that began to afflict postmodern critique in the 1990s to the rigid pattern–recognition endemic to what she calls its "deadening pretended knowingness," such blockages may equally arise from a naïve refusal to acknowledge any patterns at all—especially those patterns into which our own work might find itself habitually falling.[68] According to Sedgwick, knowingness's "smooth, dismissive" tendency to flatten the new into the same, to assimilate the particular and strange to

Knowingness 207

broad, conventionalized social and linguistic categories, forestalls the sorts of epistemic openness necessary to reparative reading.[69] Yet it is the application of precisely that "knowing" capacity to see and hear "more of the same" that enables Sedgwick to identify the workings of knowingness in her own work, and thus to posit the possibility of modes of seeing that seemed less rigid or hidebound. Here it is worth recalling that there's a flipside to Fisher's reification of wonder, an emotion that doesn't seem far from feeling theory's naïveté. While on the one hand he scorns "a stupidity that never wonders because it never notices anything," he also scorns "the opposite: those who find everything amazing or striking, even the trivial differences of surface, monstrosity, oddness and the merely strange."[70] Just as, according to Walter Benjamin, cinema's latent "shock effect" can arise only in a state of distraction, so the ambient hum of a cynical knowingness may provide just the right emotional climate for something new to flourish.[71]

## Notes

1. Philip Fisher, *Wonder, the Rainbow, and the Aesthetics of Rare Experiences* (Cambridge, MA: Harvard University Press, 1998), 8. For another succinct definition of "knowingness," see Edith Hall's construction of the emotion as "feeling confidently in charge of information." (Edith Hall, "The Aesophic in Aristophanes," in *Greek Comedy and the Discourse of Genres*, ed. Emmanuella Bakola, Lucia Prauscello and Mario Telo [Cambridge: Cambridge University Press, 20130, 284).
2. Jesse Fox Mayshark, *Post-Pop Cinema: The Search for Meaning in New American Films* (Westport, CT: Praeger Publishers, 2007), 14, 1, 2, 5, 5.
3. Lisa Schwarzbaum, "*Rushmore*," *Entertainment Weekly*, February 12, 1999, accessed June 5, 2011, http://www.ew.com/ew/article/0,,274402,00.html; Mark Olsen, "If I Can Dream: The Everlasting Boyhoods of Wes Anderson," *Film Comment* 35.1 (1999): 12. Relying anthropomorphically on the expressive morphology of the "knowing wink" and the "knowing nudge" in a way that seemed to bear out Ngai's emotion-based model of "tone" as a "text's affective bearing, orientation or 'set toward' the world," Schwarzbaum maintained that *Rushmore* "treats eccentricity with compassionate respect: no winking, no nudges." (Sianne Ngai, "Tone," in Idem, *Ugly Feelings* [Cambridge, MA: Harvard University Press, 2005], 29); Schwarzbaum, "*Rushmore*.") Olsen, meanwhile, suggested that whereas Anderson's older contemporaries Gregg Araki and Hal Hartley "use a knowing stance to establish their superiority over characters and audience alike," *Rushmore* manifests a refreshing "sincerity largely absent from the contemporary youth picture." (Olsen, "If I Can Dream," 12.) Blogger Kenny Byerly agrees, maintaining that while "there's bad irony in movies, where smug knowingness is used to excuse intellectual laziness … Anderson's movies are extremely sincere emotionally." (Kenny Byerly, "Stevie Z," *Herbie the Love Blog*, December 16, 2004, accessed June 5, 2011, http://kbweb.blogspot.com/2004/12/stevie-z.html.).
4. Olsen, "If I Can Dream," 12.
5. Schwarzbaum, "*Rushmore*"; Olsen, "If I Can Dream," 12.
6. Jim Collins, "Genericity in the 90s," in *Film Theory Goes to the Movies*, ed. Jim Collins, Hilary Radner and Ava Preacher Collins (London: Routledge, 1993),

208  *Knowingness*

258, 257; Timotheus Vermeulen and Robin van den Akker, "Notes on Meta-modernism," *Journal of Aesthetics and Culture* 2 (2010): 6, accessed January 19, 2011, http://journals.sfu.ca/coaction/index.php/jac/article/view/5677. Contemporary cultural criticism, both inside and outside the academy, is scattered with similar claims, though not all of them are clothed in the rubric of knowingness. Announcing a "shift away from postmodernism in children's cartoons," philosopher Alan Kirby describes *Shrek The Third* as a deliberately "warm rather than knowing or ironic" riposte to the negative press and public reception that greeted *Shrek 2*'s dated use of "knowing irony." (Alan Kirby, *Digimodernism: How New Technologies Dismantle the Postmodern and Reconfigure Our Lives* [New York: Continuum, 2009], 17, 16.) Literary critic Jason Morris, meanwhile, maintains that contemporary poetic practice is marked by the rise of a "New Sincerity," an emotional posture of "honesty" and "immediacy" that seems starkly at odds with knowingness's smugly skeptical relation to truth. (Jason Morris, "The Time Between Time: Messianism and the Promise of a New Sincerity," *Jacket* 35 (2008), online edition, paragraph 1, accessed January 19, 2011, http://jacketmagazine.com/35/morris-sincerity.shtml.) Journalist Jonathan Jones points to similar transformations taking place in the art world, where new work is "sweep[ing] away the fag-end of postmodernism and renew[ing] faith in art" after what he calls the "world-weary intellectual climate of the late 20th century." (Jonathan Jones, "This Altermodern Love," *The Guardian*, April 8, 2009.)

7. Philip Fisher, *Wonder, the Rainbow, and the Aesthetics of Rare Experiences* (Cambridge, MA: Harvard University Press, 1998), 8; Concise Oxford English Dictionary, 2009 ed., s.v. "Knowing." Italics in original; Ngai, *Ugly Feelings*. Something of the disdain that circulates around knowingness is actually registered in the OED's entry for the term "knowing": *listed alongside its primary definition is a "chiefly derogatory" related meaning:* "experienced or shrewd, especially excessively or prematurely so." Note that the OED contains no entry for "knowingness," only for the adjective, "knowing," from which the noun "knowingness" is derived.

8. Mayshark, *Post-Pop Cinema*, 5 (my italics).

9. Steven Connor, *Postmodernist Culture: An Introduction to Theories of the Contemporary* (Oxford: Blackwell, 1989), 85; Lawrence Grossberg, *We Gotta Get out of this Place: Popular Conservativism and Postmodern Culture* (London: Routledge, 1992), 212; Linda Hutcheon, *The Politics of Postmodernism* (New York: Routledge, 1989), 1.

10. Richard Rorty, *Achieving Our Country: Leftist Thought in Twentieth Century America* (Cambridge, MA: Harvard University Press, 1998), 126; Paul R. Gross and Norm Levitt, *Higher Superstition: The Academic Left and its Quarrels with Science* (Baltimore: Johns Hopkins University Press, 1994), 73.

11. While Steven Connor has savagely disparaged the tendency to frame postmodernism primarily as "a sensibility or state of mind," there is no denying the primacy of tone or mood to our experience of postmodern texts. (Steven Connor, introduction to *The Cambridge Companion to Postmodernism*, ed. Steven Connor (Cambridge: Cambridge University Press], 10.) Indeed, in many ways, a tonal or emotional optic affords us a certain purchase on the phenomenon of postmodernism that stylistic or periodizing optics cannot. It is no accident, I suggest, that Ngai's wonderful account of tone draws heavily on the work

of Lawrence Grossberg, whose discussion of affect as "a socially constructed domain of cultural effects" that congregates around texts, institutions and social formations, while remaining quite distinct from them, was specifically developed in the context of an analysis of postmodern culture, in an effort to account for the fact that, as he puts it elsewhere, "something 'feels' different." (Lawrence Grossberg, *We Gotta Get out of This Place: Popular Conservatism and Postmodern Culture* [New York: Routledge, 1992], 80; Lawrence Grossberg, "Postmodernity and Affect: All Dressed Up with no Place to Go," *Communication* 10.3–4 [1988]: 277.) And if Grossberg is unique among theorists of postmodernism in the depth and detail with which he theorizes tone, he is not alone in framing postmodernism in a tonal or affective register. While "knowingness" is the tonal attribute most often identified with postmodernism, Jameson has famously pointed to what he calls postmodernism's "whole new [euphoric] emotional ground tone"; Cristopher Nash's *The Unravelling of the Postmodern Mind* describes the postmodern as the epoch of the "narcissant affective state"; while Ziauddin Sardar casts postmodernism as "the temper of our times," announcing that "postmodernism is *espiritu del tiempo*—the spirit of the 21st century." (Jameson, Postmodernism, 6; Cristopher Nash, *The Unravelling of the Postmodern Mind* (Edinburgh: Edinburgh University Press, 2001), 126; Ziauddin Sardar, *The A-Z of Postmodern Life: Essays on Global Culture in the Noughties* (London: Vision, 2002), 4.)

12. The body of critical literature heralding the demise of postmodernism understood as an aesthetic and critical practice is extensive. For three key texts see Jason Gladstone and Daniel Worden's introduction to their special issue of *Twentieth Century Studies* on the subject, "Introduction: Postmodernism, Then," *Twentieth Century Literature* 57.3–4 (2011): 291–308; Robert McLaughlin, "Post-Postmodern Discontent: Contemporary Fiction and the Social World," *Symploke* 12.1–2 (2004): 66; and Brian McHale, "What Was Postmodernism?" *Electronic Book Review*, December 20, 2007, accessed September 3, 2011, www.electronicbookreview.com/thread/fictionspresent/tense. This work sits alongside an array of scholarship exploring the demise of postmodernism as a social and historical moment. See Kirby, *Digimodernism*; Robert Samuels, "Automodernity After Postmodernism: Autonomy and Automation in Culture, Technology and Education," in *Digital Youth, Innovation, and the Unexpected*, ed. Tara McPherson (Cambridge, MA: The MIT Press, 2008), 220; Raoul Eshelman, *Performatism, or, the End of Postmodernism* (Aurora: Davis Group, 2008; Timotheus Vermeulen and Robin van den Akker, "Notes on Metamodernism," *Journal of Aesthetics and Culture* 2 (2010): 1–12.

13. Warren Buckland and Thomas Elsaesser, *Studying Contemporary American Film* (London: Bloomsbury Academic, 2002), 72; Kirby, *Digimodernism*, 155. Some key examples of critics who make this claim follow. For David Bordwell, who treats knowingness as an aesthetic practice typical of postclassical cinema, rather than as a tone or an emotion, knowingness and allusion are virtually identified, as in his reference to "Allusionism and knowingness" (David Bordwell, *The Way Hollywood Tells It: Story and Style in Modern Movies* [Berkeley: University of California Press, 2006], 16); for film critic Noel Carroll, Laurence Kasdan's deployment of allusion in *Body Heat* "tells us that for this very reason [the film] is to be regarded as intelligent and knowing" (Noel Carroll, "The Future of Allusion: Hollywood in the Seventies (and Beyond),"

## 210  *Knowingness*

*October* 20 [Spring, 1982]: 54); while for Jonathan Rosenbaum, postmodern films "depend on references and asides ... to convey a fashion-plate surface of knowingness" (Jonathan Rosenbaum, *Movies as Politics* [Berkeley: University of California Press, 1997], 173.) See also Marco Calavita, *Apprehending Politics: News Media and Individual Political Development* (Albany, NY: State University of New York Press, 2004), 183; Todd Gitlin, "Flat and Happy," *The Wilson Quarterly* 17.4 (1993): 47–55; and Eleftheria Thanouli, "To Be or Not to Be Post-Classical," in *Mind the Screen: Media Concepts According to Thomas Elsaesser,* ed. Jaap Kooijman, Patricia Pisters and Wanda Strauven (Amsterdam: Amsterdam University Press, 2008), 226.

14. Hutcheon, *The Politics of Postmodernism,* 22, 28, 2. Clearly, postmodernism and poststructuralism are very different enterprises. Yet as Hutcheon has written, "Umberto Eco ... considers postmodern 'the orientation of anyone who has learned the lesson of Foucault, i.e. that power is not something unitary that exists outside us.' He might well have added to this, as others have, the lessons learned from Derrida about textuality and deferral, or from Vattimo and Lyotard about intellectual mastery and its limits. In other words, it is difficult to separate the 'de-doxifying' of postmodern art and culture from the deconstructing impulse of what we have labelled postmodern theory." (Hutcheon, *The Politics of Postmodernism,* 3–4.) For examples of critical work that diagnoses a strain of knowingness in postmodern critique, whether in cultural or scholarly practice, see Hutcheon *Politics of Postmodernism,* 1; Chris Barker, *Cultural Studies: Theory and Practice* (London: Sage, 2000), 210; Alexia L. Bowler, "Postfeminism and Critique," in *Postfeminism and Contemporary Hollywood Cinema,* ed. Joel Gwynne and Nadine Muller (London: Palgrave Macmillan, 2013), 193; for specifically anti-postmodernist instantiations of this identification, see Rorty, *Achieving Our Country,* 126–7; Gross and Levitt, *Higher Superstition,* 70–73; Brian Massumi, *Parables for the Virtual: Movement, Affect, Sensation* (Durham, NC: Duke University Press, 2002), 236; Nigel Thrift, *Non-Representational Theory: Space, Politics, Affect* (New York: Routledge, 2008), 97; and Naomi Scheman, "To See it Feelingly: On Knowingness and (In)vulnerability," Emotions, Affects ... And Other Intimacies conference, Umeå, Sverige, 2011.

15. Hilary Robinson, introduction to *Feminism-Art-Theory: An Anthology, 1968–2000,* ed. Hilary Robinson (Oxford: Blackwell, 2001), 2; Eve Kosofsky Sedgwick, *Touching Feeling: Affect, Pedagogy, Performativity* (Durham, NC: Duke University Press, 2003), 124.

16. Fisher, *Wonder,* 8; Raymond Tallis, "Knowingness and Other Shallows," *Philosophy Now,* June, 2008, accessed March 13, 2011, http://philosophynow.org/issues/72/I_Kid_You_Not_Knowingness_and_Other_Shallows.

   *The quote from Fisher runs in full:* "The satisfaction of intelligibility ... is different from what a philosopher would call knowledge and it is even more remote from what Descartes called certain knowledge." See also *Norm Levitt, who argues, in an impassioned attack on postmodern science studies, "a fatal knowingness ... licenses practitioners to talk endlessly about science without ever talking about science."* (Norm Levitt, "The Science Wars: Deconstructing Science is Pseudo-Science," *The Skeptic Encyclopedia of Pseudoscience,* ed. Michael Shermer [Santa Barbara, CA: ABC-Clio, 2002], 757); Jonathan Lear, who argues that "there is a sickness in this 'knowingness'" in which "reason is being used to jump ahead to a conclusion" (Jonathan Lear, Open-Minded:

Working Out The Logic of the Soul [Cambridge, MA: Harvard University Press, 1998], 43); and Edith Hall, who suggests that "knowingness—feeling confidently in charge of information both technologically and intellectually—can prevent us all from understanding deeper emotional currents at work." (Edith Hall, "The Aesophic in Aristophanes," in *Greek Comedy and the Discourse of Genres*, ed. Emmanuella Bakola, Lucia Prauscello and Mario Telo (Cambridge: Cambridge University Press, 2013), 284.

17. Andrew Ross, *No Respect: Intellectuals and Popular Culture* (London: Routledge, 1989), 59; Umberto Eco, "*Casablanca*: Cult Movies and Intertextual Collage," *Substance* 14.2 (1985): 11. The notion that the postmodern spectator possesses an historically unprecedented mastery of film codes is widespread. If postmodern cinema as a "paramount laboratory for semiotic research in textual strategies," a cinema of "depthless pastiche," a "layering of cinematic references and in-jokes," the postmodern spectator is correspondingly defined by her "encyclopedic film competence," her ability to "draw on a repertoire of codes and references," and her "mastery of the process of decoding/deciphering." (Eco, "*Casablanca*": 3; Peter Brooker and Will Brooker, Introduction to *Postmodern After-Images: A Reader in Film, Television and Video,* ed. Peter Brooker and Will Brooker [London: Arnold, 1997], 6; Collins, "Genericity in the Nineties," 248; Eco, "*Casablanca*": 11; Jonathan Bignell, *Postmodern Media Culture* [Edinburgh: Edinburgh University Press, 2000], 52; Ross, *No Respect,* 59.).

18. Drehli Robnick, quoting Andrew Britton, in "Allegories of Post-Fordism in 1970s New Hollywood," in *The Last Great American Picture Show,* ed. Thomas Elsaesser, Alexander Horwath and Noel Kind (Amsterdam: Amsterdam University Press, 2004), 346. For examples of this view of knowingness as a means of establishing epistemic community see, Richard Smith, "Charles Dickens and the Problems of Knowingness," Philosophy of Education Society of Great Britain, Annual Conference, New College, Oxford, March 30-April 1, 2012; and Peter Bailey, "Conspiracies of Meaning: Music Hall and the Knowingness of Popular Culture," *Past and Present,* 144.1 (1994): 138–170.

19. Linda Hutcheon, *Politics of Postmodernism,* 1; Bran Nicol, "Postmodernism," in *A Companion to Modernist Literature and Culture,* ed. David Bradshaw and Kevin J. H. Dettmar (Malden, MA: Blackwell, 2006), 562. Rorty's *Achieving Our Country* blames, in part, the academy's turn to "knowing" postmodern critique for the failure of radical leftist politics in the late 20th Century, and in this sense he exemplifies the anti-postmodernist insistence on knowingness's political conservativism. (Rorty, *Achieving Our Country,* 126–129.).

20. Jason Gladstone and Daniel Worden provide some prominent examples of texts that seem to operate in a post-postmodern register, a catalogue that includes "*McSweeneys Quarterly Concern*'s emo-sincerity, the ethnic bilungsroman's emphasis on multicultural identity as upward mobility, Jonathan Franzen's social realism [and] *n+1*'s enthusiastic recuperation of 'high cultural critique." (Gladstone and Worden's "Introduction: Postmodernism, Then," 291.).

21. Vermeulen and van den Akker, "Notes on Metamodernism," 1. The shift away from postmodern aesthetic and critical practice is visible across a variety of contexts, from the scholarly, where a range of new methodological practices have eroded the status of postmodern critique; to the artistic, where practices informed by postmodern theory have given way to the earnest engagement with global cultural and economic flows enshrined in Nicholas Bourriaud's

## 212  Knowingness

"Altermodern" manifesto; to the literary and cinematic, where the "style without substance … language without meaning … cynicism without belief" associated with once-reified aesthetic practices of allusion, pastiche and self-reflexivity have been jettisoned in favor of a renewed investment in more traditional forms of storytelling. (Nicholas Bourriaud, *Altermodern: Tate Triennial 2009* [London: Tate Publishing, 2009]; McLaughlin, "Post-Postmodern Discontent": 66.).

22. Deborah Gould, "Affect and Protest," *Political Emotions*, ed. Janet Staiger, Ann Cvetkovich and Ann Reynolds (New York: Routledge, 2010), 32.

23. Naomi Scheman, "To See it Feelingly: On Knowingness and (In)vulnerability" (paper presented at the Emotions, Affects … And Other Intimacies conference, Umeå, Sverige, 2011); Janet Staiger, introduction to *Political Emotions*, ed. Janet Staiger, Ann Cvetkovich and Ann Reynolds (New York: Routledge, 2010), 4; Ann Cvetkovich, introduction to *Political Emotions*, ed. Janet Staiger, Ann Cvetkovich and Ann Reynolds (New York: Routledge, 2010), 8. This practice emphasizes texture and particularity over easy political judgments, and advises "going slowly," "noticing the details of the moment or the object" and "paying attention to the complexities of lived experience and cultural expression in ways that do not necessarily break down into convenient dichotomies between left and right, progressive and reactionary, resistance and containment." (Cvetkovich, introduction to *Political Emotions*, 11, 6.).

24. Brian Massumi, *Parables for the Virtual: Movement, Affect, Sensation* (Durham, NC: Duke University Press, 2002), 236.

25. Nigel Thrift, *Non-Representational Theory: Space, Politics, Affect* (New York: Routledge, 2008), 97.

26. Sedgwick, *Touching Feeling*, 145.

27. Sedgwick, *Touching Feeling*, 146.

28. Ben Anderson, "Modulating the Excess of Affect: Morale in a State of 'Total War,'" in *The Affect Theory Reader*, ed. Melissa Gregg and Gregory J. Seigworth (Durham, NC: Duke University Press, 2010), 220; Rorty, *Achieving Our Country*, 126; Oxford Dictionaries, definition: knowing (Oxford: Oxford University Press, 2011), http://oxforddictionaries.com/definition/knowing.

29. Raymond Tallis, "I Kid You Not: Knowingness and Other Shallows," *Philosophy Now*, March/April, 2014, accessed November 2, 2011, http://www.philosophynow.org/issue72/I_Kid_You_Not_Knowingness_and_Other_Shallows (italics mine); Fisher, *Wonder*, 1–10; Rorty, *Achieving Our Country*, 126. The aptly named Jonathan Lear also figures knowingness as a hindrance to the wonder and awe that is philosophy's true emotional accomplice: *"Philosophy, Aristotle says, begins in wonder, or awe. If so, Oedipus [whom Lear has earlier identified as an embodiment of knowingness] cannot get started: he is too busy figuring things out to have any such experience"* (Lear, *Open-Minded*, 51.).

30. Lawrence Grossberg, "Affect's Future," in *The Affect Theory Reader*, ed. Melissa Gregg and Gregory J. Seigwoth (Durham, NC: Duke University Press, 2010), 336.

31. *Concise Oxford English Dictionary*, 2009 ed., s.v. "knowing."

32. Cvetkovich, introduction to *Political Emotions*, 9.

33. Rorty, *Achieving our Country*, 126. My italics.

34. Ibid., 125, 126.

35. Steven Shaviro, *Post-Cinematic Affect* (Hants: 0-Books, 2010), 3. Clare Hemmings points, for example, to "the delights of consumerism, feelings of belonging attending fundamentalism or fascism," while Lauren Berlant has devoted

## Knowingness  213

considerable theoretical energy to demonstrating how "affective states—a desire to feel reciprocity and a sense of belonging, for example—can generate attachments to normativity and current social arrangements, even those that create the stressful conditions of one's life." Clare Hemmings, "Invoking Affect: Cultural Theory and the Ontological Term," *Cultural Studies*, 19.5 (September 2005): 551; Gould, "Affect and Protest," 32. See Lauren Berlant, *Cruel Optimism* (Durham, NC: Duke University Press, 2011).

36. Shaviro, *Post-Cinematic Affect*, 4.
37. Melissa Gregg and Gregory J. Seigworth, "An Inventory of Shimmers," in *The Affect Theory Reader* ed. Melissa Gregg and Gregory J. Seigworth (Durham, NC: Duke University Press, 2010), 4.
38. Scheman "To See it Feelingly."
39. Teresa Brennan, *The Transmission of Affect* (Ithaca: Cornell University Press, 2004), 134; Cvetkovich, introduction to *Political Emotions*, 6; Anderson, "Modulating the Excess of Affect," 167.
40. Brennan, *The Transmission of Affect*, 105, 128. See also Silvan Tomkins' notion of the "interest" that underlies all affect. (Silvan Tomkins, Affect Imagery Consciousness, Vol. I: The Positive Affects (New York: Springer Publishing Company, 2008), 188–190).
41. Ann Cvetkovich, "Public Feelings" (address to the local Public Feelings branch, University of Texas, Austin, January 2002), quoted in Janet Staiger, "Political Emotions, Everyday Genres," *Political Emotions*, ed. Staiger, Ann Cvetkovich and Ann Reynolds (New York: Routledge, 2002), 2.
42. Heather Love, "Truth and Consequences: on Paranoid Reading and Reparative Reading," *Criticism*, 52.2 (2011): 263.
43. Ngai, *Ugly Feelings*, 43. Ngai is quoting Otto Baensch. Buckland and Elsaesser's attribution to postmodern or postclassical cinema of "a special sort of awareness of the codes that govern classical representation and its genre conventions, along with a willingness to *display* this knowingness" is exemplary here. (Buckland and Elsaesser, *Studying Contemporary American Film*, 72.)
44. Olsen, "If I Can Dream," 12.
45. Kenneth Turan, "*Rushmore*: Pest-as-Hero Theme in Mountain of Eccentricity," *Los Angeles Times*, December 11, 1998, accessed November 10, 2011, http://articles.latimes.com/1998/dec/11/entertainment/ca-52764; Olsen, "If I Can Dream," 12.
46. Olsen, "If I Can Dream," 13.
47. Charles Musser, *The Emergence of Cinematic: The American Screen to 1907, Vol. I* (Berkeley: California University Press, 1990), 4.
48. Olsen, "If I Can Dream," 13.
49. Concise Oxford English Dictionary, 2009 ed., s.v. "Knowing."
50. Steven Shaviro, *Post-Cinematic Affect* (Hants: O-Books, 2010), 3.
51. It should be noted here, however, that if knowingness's social dimension places it outside the horizon of an orthodox cognitive-appraisal model of emotion that binds emotion to individual cognition, we cannot simply account for knowingness by "expanding" our cognitive-appraisal model of emotion—as many critics in the human sciences have—to "include" the social, whether as the object of the emotion, as a means of regulating the emotion, or as a prompt or cue for the emotion. For whereas these analyses can account for emotions that have social causes, effects or objects, knowingness is an emotion that depends upon the social in its very articulation. (Larissa Z. Tiedens and Colin Wayne

214  *Knowingness*

Leach, *The Social Life of Emotions* [Cambridge: Cambridge University Press, 2004). Yet if knowingness cannot be accounted for through an expanded, socialized instantiation of cognitive appraisal theory, it also diverges from the paradigm—currently in vogue across feeling theory—of affective "contagion" or "transmission." Often associated with the work of Teresa Brennan, the model of affective transmission suggests that it is possible for feeling to "pass" directly between bodies, such that, as Sara Ahmed puts it, "I feel sad because you feel sad; I am ashamed by your shame." (Brennan, *The Transmission of Affect*; Sara Ahmed, *The Cultural Politics of Emotion* [London: Routledge, 2004], 10.) Yet to the extent that this schema keeps in place the notion of an originary, subjective feeling—a feeling that is only subsequently circulated or transmitted to another—it seems inadequate to the challenge posed by the emotion of knowingness, which is only properly felt to the extent that its initial cues are reciprocated and confirmed. Unsettlingly enough, then, this feeling of "getting it," of having some special understanding that is "known only to a few people" is *neither* a subjective, personal emotion, locked down to individual cognition, nor a free-floating affect, able to migrate directly between organisms.

52. Sedgwick, *Touching Feeling*, 36.

53. To argue this is to suggest that the understanding of knowingness enshrined in the OED's construction of the state of being "knowing" as a state "suggesting possession of knowledge known only to a few people" has so far suffered from a misplacement of emphasis: whereas most critics have dwelt on the first part of the equation, in which knowingness a certain "possession of knowledge," the emphasis should have fallen on the second part *"known only to a few people"* namely the construction of the group itself, the people in the knowing circuit, the social bonds formed.

54. Fredric Jameson, "Cognitive Mapping," in *Marxism and the Interpretation of Culture*, ed. Cary Nelson and Lawrence Grossberg (Urbana and Chicago: University Illinois Press, 1988), 352; Jean-Francois Lyotard, *The Postmodern Condition: A Report on Knowledge* (Minneapolis: University of Minnesota Press, 1984); Jean Baudrillard, *The Ecstasy of Communication*, trans. Bernard Schutz and Caroline Schutz (Los Angeles, CA: Semiotexte/Foreign Agents, 2012). As Rosalind Gill puts it, "The notion of postmodernism is also widely usd to signal a crisis in the ability of philosophy to underwrite knowledge production." (Rosalind Gill, *Gender and the Media* [Malden, MA: Polity Press, 2007], 66).

55. Baudrillard, *The Ecstasy of Communication;* Jonathan Bignell, *Postmodern Media Culture* (Edinburgh: Edinburgh University Press, 2007); David Harvey, *The Condition of Postmodernity* (Oxford: Blackwell, 1989); Douglas Kellner, *Media Culture: Cultural Studies, Identity and Politics Between the Modern and the Postmodern* (London: Routledge, 1995).

56. Carl Matheson, "*The Simpsons*, Hyper-Irony, and the Meaning of Life," *The Simpsons and Philosophy: The D'Oh! Of Homer*, ed. William Irwin, Mark T. Conrad and Aeon Skoble (Peru, IL: Carus Publishing, 2001), 120.

57. N. Katherine Hayles, "Attacking the Borg of Corporate Knowledge: The Achievement of Alan Liu's 'The Laws of Cool,'" *Criticism* 47.2 (Spring 2005): 235.

58. Keith Phipps, "Wes Anderson," *A.V. Club.com*, February 10, 1999, accessed May 3, 2011, http://www.avclub.com/article/wes-anderson-13580.

59. This double-game is best indexed in the rhetorical manoeuvres of the director himself, whose revealing answer to an interviewer's inquiry as to "how the current

trend of incorporating tons of pop-culture references will hold up thirty years from now," is the declaration that "in 10 years, they're going to be passé," and the observation that his own stories, by contrast, are "not topical or timely, and I don't want them to be. I want them to be the kind of stories you can go back to and they won't feel dated. It's also just what I'm drawn to. I don't want to have current, contemporary references in it. I want it to be something that's sort of self-contained." (Keith Phipps, "Interview with Wes Anderson," *The Onion A/V Club*, accessed July 9, 2011, http://rushmoreacademy.com/1999/02/01/onion-av-club-interview-with-wes-anderson-archive.) Anderson's emphasis here, of course, is on a certain narrative closure and coherence, a kind of naivete; yet as the claim to avoid "current, contemporary references" suggests, this model of narrative naivete itself functions referentially, as a meta-allusion to more explicitly knowing texts. While purporting to emerge from the experiential reservoir of an auteurial self immune to the whims of cultural change ("it's just what I'm drawn to"), this "self-contained" world only gains its interest through knowing reference to forms of cinematic textuality that "incorporate tons of pop-culture references."

60. Sedgwick, *Epistemology*, 152.
61. Sedgwick, *Epistemology*, 156.
62. Jonathan Rosenbaum, "In a World of His Own: *Rushmore*," *Chicago Reader*, February 12, 1999, accessed December 9, 2010, www.jonathanrosenbaum.com?p=6501.
63. Olsen, "If I Can Dream," 17.
64. Hutcheon, *Politics of Postmodernism*, xi.
65. To this extent, postmodern theory's explicit avowal of knowingness might seem less an indefensible embrace of this most morally ambivalent of emotions, than a valuable candour about some of criticism's less-attractive tendencies.
66. Sedgwick, *Touching Feeling*, 124.
67. Gregg and Seigworth, "An Inventory of Shimmers," 3.
68. Sedgwick, *Epistemology*, 12.
69. Ibid., 53.
70. Fisher, *Wonder*, 47.
71. Walter Benjamin, "The Work of Art in the Age of Mechanical Reproduction," *Illuminations: Essays and Reflections*, ed. Hannah Arendt (New York: Vintage Digital, 2011), Kindle Edition, "The Work of Art in the Age of Mechanical Reproduction."

# Restlessness
## A Coda

### I

An inherently restless enterprise, critical theory has made the new, the surprising, the original and the strange its disciplinary mandates.[1] It should come as little surprise, then, that, whatever our consensus on knowingness, scholars have jumped at the chance to define the conceptual and terminological co-ordinates of what comes "after" postmodernism, a venture whose critical yield in manifestoes, special issues and conference topoi now rivals that of "postmodernism" itself. While scholars associated with feeling theory have been reluctant to endow this "post-postmodern" moment with a critical handle, those in other fields have been more ambitious in their coinage and conceptualization. For sociologist Gilles Lipovetsky, the post-postmodern period is a period of "hypermodernity" defined by "movement, fluidity and flexibility."[2] For philosopher Alan Kirby, the postmodern ends abruptly with the rise of digimodernism, as the development of digital technology reconfigures the roles of reader, writer, producer and text in ways that mere aesthetic shifts cannot.[3] For art critic Nicholas Bourriaud, postmodernism's "negativity," "depressiveness" and "essentialism" have been displaced by the emergence of "altermodernism," understood as a "synthesis between modernism and post-colonialism."[4] And for Timotheus Vermeulen and Robin van den Akker, the post-postmodern moment is best captured by the term "metamodernism," a period of symbiosis in which "postmodern irony" joins forces with "modern enthusiasm."[5] As this medley of monikers for a new, post-postmodern moment attests, feeling theory is far from alone in its insistence on relegating postmodernism to a moribund moment in the critical and cultural past.

Despite the obvious critical allure of these campaigns for a brave, new post-postmodern moment, of course, no scholar worth her deconstructive salt would greet them without skepticism. Indeed, it's easy enough to establish that many of the qualities with which these theorists wish to furnish the post-postmodern are lifted from the same old, shop-worn postmodern, upcycled and re-upholstered, perhaps, but hardly unprecedented. Confronted, for example, with Vermeulen and van den Akker's vision of a "metamodern" oscillation between "a modern enthusiasm and a postmodern irony, between hope and melancholy, between naivete and knowingness," a condition marked by a longing for an emotional and spiritual transcendence

218  *Restlessness*

that it simultaneously acknowledges as impossible, one would be hard put not to hear echoes of Lyotard's identification of postmodernism with the renewal of the aesthetics of the sublime—an aesthetico-affective response that, as we have seen, hinges on balancing representational *im*possibility against conceptual possibility.[6] This sense that the qualities now ascribed to the post-postmodern echo those long ascribed to the postmodern, then, cannot but temper some of the energy of this restless scholarly scramble for the new. And, in many ways, this book seeks to extenuate this energy still further. In an effort to counter the kind of futile, fidgety restlessness that galvanizes the dismissal of postmodernism, I have shown that while often represented as incompatible with or irrelevant to contemporary work on feeling, postmodern theory and aesthetics is structured around a series of peculiar, "posthumous" emotions, from bewilderment to boredom, that may actually enrich our appreciation of emotion's form and possibilities. In this light, feeling theory's critical arsenal might be better equipped by turning backward to a seemingly stale postmodernism than by jumping, reflexively and restlessly, on the next big critical thing.

Yet if a certain critical restlessness is something this book is calculated to resist, in many ways "restlessness" is actually exemplary of the bevy of emotional phenomena that have been its subject. Like many of the emotions this book has broached, restlessness is idiosyncratic in form, naming less a fixed, delimited condition than an open-ended emotional cycle in which states of attachment and disengagement are endlessly pursued by states of disgust and detachment. Also like the emotions in this book, "restlessness" is a term on high rotate across postmodern theory and aesthetics. And this should come as little surprise since—once again, like all the emotions in this book—restlessness shares a special affinity with the traits ascribed to the postmodern, cleaving neatly to what Leslie Paul Thiele identifies as postmodernity's "routinization of novelty," which sees the excitement of the dazzlingly new forever alternate with the boredom of the mundanely familiar. On the one hand, restlessness seems the emotion most germane to the state of perpetual desire demanded of the postmodern consumer, a consumer who, as Zygmunt Bauman notes, "seek[s] actively to be seduced."[7] On the other, restlessness is an emotion peculiarly felicitous to the constitutional "flexibility," that, as Luc Boltanski and Eve Chiapello have shown, is the attribute most sought after in the new labour market, in which workers must be "*adaptable* and *flexible*, able to switch from one situation to a very different one, and adjust to it; and *versatile*, capable of changing activity or tools, depending on the nature of the relationship entered into with others or with objects," in what Italian Marxist social theorist Paolo Virno calls restlessness's "agitation without end and without goal."[8] Restlessness, that is, names not just the emotional logic of a market driven by the urge to innovation, but the emotional signature of the consumer compelled to keep up with it and of the worker capable of adapting to the new labour markets developed around it. Yet restlessness's special calibration to postmodernism's distinctive economic and social climate is not without its attendant ironies. If restlessness is a peculiarly postmodern emotional mode, then the quintessentially restless gesture of consigning postmodernism to the critical and cultural past merely reaffirms, paradoxically, just how postmodern we remain. While we have already argued that the *content* of many claims made for the post-postmodern recapitulate the aesthetic and formal qualities traditionally ascribed to the postmodern, it should now be clear that so, in many ways, does their *form*.

More than just exemplifying the emotions that make up this book, however, restlessness has a unique, double-sided and even meta-emotional structure that allows it to reflect on and thematize them. For like restlessness—though in perhaps less clearly legible ways—all of the emotions I have examined crystallize around a dialectic of emotional deficiency and emotional intensity, exacting, as they each do, emotion out of the very crucible of its failure or absence. Whereas cognitive-appraisal models tend to project emotion as a visceral or cognitive entity that subjects unambivalently "have or possess," postmodernism introduces a moment of negativity or lack into the experience of emotion.[9] Fascination coalesces around the gleaming specter of an Other who is imagined to experience a depth and intensity of feeling ostensibly inaccessible to the subject; boredom is a dysphoric emotional registration of the absence of feeling, in which the moment of apathy and indifference itself engenders pain; while the peculiarly self-reflexive species of fear I have looked at in this book is energized by the spectacle of the end of fear, whether in the other or the self. Indeed, if it's possible to detect a certain "restlessness" in postmodern emotion's dialectic of emotional deficiency and emotional reanimation, the same restlessness can be detected in the logic of contagion that structures these emotions. Whereas the compass of an emotion like anger may be limited to the enraged subject and her inciting object, whether pet peeve or institutional injustice, postmodern emotions' fierce fixation on the question of emotion itself ensures that the question of what *you* are feeling is so close to the heart of what *I* am feeling that a restless process of emotional displacement, transfer, projection and mimicry between subjects becomes a structural imperative.[10] Itself predicated on a kind of projection of the other as unusually captivated by a surface in which I myself can see nothing, the posture of fascination generates an aura of emotional intensity fascinates others in turn; manifesting itself in the form of a "blank" face stripped of the familiar stamps of subjectivity, bewilderment's peculiar brand of subject-object inversion tends to instill the same bewildering sense of subject-object instability in others; boredom—as *Gummo* makes painfully clear—also tends to *be* boring, generating a kind of narrative and stylistic entropy that pervades the structure and reception of the film; while knowingness actually comes into being through the social feedback loop that the knowing wink or knowing glance sets in motion. Postmodern emotion's preoccupation with the precarity of its own existence, that is, spawns structures of projection and mimicry that allow it to

## 220   *Restlessness*

circulate restlessly between subjects in ways that cognitive-appraisal models of emotion neither allow nor can account for.

In addition to a certain phenomenological descriptive value, as an account of an emotional archive long neglected in feeling theory, however, these analyses also lay claim to a certain critical value, as an intervention in some of feeling theory's basic theoretical and terminological postulates. In particular, this book has argued that, while long dismissed as the rigid, subjective and non-progressive counterpart to a liberatory and mobile affect, "emotion" may be quite as valuable to feeling theory's theoretical and political programme as "affect." While all bearing some relation to the notions of cognition, subjectivity, judgment and intentionality that inform our still-dominant cognitive-appraisal models of emotion, the emotions that populate this book's motley emotional menagerie are neither "tamed and reduced," nor the "capture and closure of affect."[11] Indeed, postmodern theory's own, often virulent efforts to denounce or discipline the emotional life that animates it is just one measure of this dissident, radical edge. Fascination tends to be dismissed as a "zombie emotion" where it is acknowledged as an emotion at all; boredom is regularly condemned as a trivial, vapid consumer curio; and while routinely lauded for its purchase on key postmodern precepts, bewilderment is just as routinely quarantined to the body of the sexual and social other. And it's easy enough to understand what actuates this kind of critical anxiety. Fascination's triangulated structure brings emotion's foundational reliance on the other into stark relief; boredom's theatricalized relation to the commodity speaks all to clearly to the emotional economy in which postmodern feeling is implicated; and, under the pressure of postmodernism's insistent destabilization of the subjective and hermeneutic foundations that have conventionally underpinned emotion, bewilderment is a sign of the subject's enmeshment in a social universe she can neither control nor comprehend. In this light, "emotion" provides just as much theoretical grist to the effort to account for the moments of non-cognition, self-loss, failure and subjectedness that mark our relation to social and political life as "affect."

Indeed, if this book has a range of specifiable consequences for feeling theory's conceptual and terminological apparatus, it equally bears on feeling theory's methodological habits. Perhaps most prominently, *The Emotional Life of Postmodern Film* has sought to unsettle some of the field's familiar maps of the relation between "postmodern critique" and "feeling theory," by insisting that the relentless deconstructive labour identified with postmodern theory may inform our current critical thinking in more ways than we know. Yet this book's central gambit is that the ongoing influence and indebtedness that pertains between postmodernism and feeling theory might not be such a bad thing. On the contrary, *The Emotional Life of Postmodern Film* contends that postmodern aesthetics and theory yield some valuable lessons for the critical practice that in many ways marks their demise. In my discussion of euphoria, for example, I argued that Jameson's euphoric intensities function as a kind of prescient, proleptic critique of our critical investment in an organic, nonsubjective and noninterpretative "affect." In my discussion of knowingness, meanwhile, I argued that precisely to the extent that the emotion has emerged as a kind of critical "other" for those of us working in feeling theory, a reprobate reminder of everything we hope we've overcome, the emotion may have some ongoing value for the field in helping us delineate, and perhaps even defy, the field's methodological mandates. And, finally, in my discussion of bewilderment, I suggested that attention to the devastating, destructive fallout of postmodern theory's equivocal investment in bewilderment supplies an urgent note of caution for a contemporary critical apparatus itself invested in the diagnostic value of negative, dysphoric emotions like shame, anger, depression and loss.

*The Emotional Life of Postmodern Film* has advanced its arguments through a series of cinematic examples, treating cinema as a mode of vernacular postmodernism whose careful calibration to commercial demands ensures that the capacity to move the spectator is never very far from the surface. As Steven Shaviro puts it bluntly, "Cinema generates affect," and in this sense it should come as no surprise that, while standard film-theoretical accounts of postmodern cinema authorize a glacial, emotionless vision of the phenomenon, close attention to the warp and weave of postmodern aesthetics reveals a strange, borderline species of emotion hidden in plain sight.[12] Certainly is the fraught relation of emotion not to postmodern cinema but to digital technology—the gamut of technological innovations, from portable devices to 3D cinema and CGI, that have changed the way film is produced, distributed and experienced—that poses the more urgent theoretical challenge for film studies scholars today. Critics such as Thomas Elsaesser, Malte Hagener, Vivian Sobchack and Shaviro have taken up this challenge in their explorations of the "material and technological crisis of the flesh" associated with the incipient obsolescence of the material technology on which classic theories of cinema are based.[13] Yet by turning back to an earlier cinematic and critical moment, a moment whose present redundancy is intensified by its so-recent vogue, it is possible to throw new light on these debates about feeling in the context of new cinematic technologies. At once viscerally emotional and icily remote, the films in this study have yielded a range of examples of emotion's capacity to adhere to the very aesthetic practices that seem to militate against it, as allusion becomes knowingness, indeterminacy becomes bewilderment, a depthless plane becomes a gleamingly fascinating surface, and the absence of emotion become an occasion for abject fear. This book's recasting of familiar postmodern aesthetic strategies as vehicles not for "the absence of emotion but [for] a different emotional orientation" clearly enhances our understanding of postmodern cinema.[14] Yet in establishing a paradigm for thinking emotion in productive, dialectical relation to a genre or medium that resists it, it may also facilitate and feed into our effort to apprehend the structures of feeling that emerge in a "computer and network-based, and digitally generated, 'new media'"[15] By

## 222 Restlessness

tracing the emotional lineaments of an aesthetic and theoretical archive that so starkly foregrounds emotion's capacity to adapt and transform in the face of its own expiry, then, we may also go some way toward equipping contemporary film theory with an emotional lexicon germane to the cinematic experiences yielded both by newly digitized production and consumption practices, and by a newly reflexive and mobile relation to genre.

This book is less a "cartographic enterprise" than an "effort of renewal and transformation," less an exhaustive emotional map of a historical aesthetic and theoretical moment than an effort to excite a more recent body of literature into new ways of thinking.[16] At the heart of this book, that is, is a critical gambit rather than an empirical project: the hunch that feeling theory's development might be best aided not by groping for the new and shiny but by reassessing the old and shop-worn; not through an engagement with the more obviously radical "affect" but with the seemingly staid and stodgy "emotion." Yet while I hope this book has some worth as a critical provocation, I also hope it has merit as a descriptive and phenomenological chronicle of what it is like to engage with postmodern texts. After all, the emotions I have reviewed in these pages do not just suffuse postmodern theory and aesthetics but percolate through everyday journalistic and critical discourse, suggesting their purchase as figures that congeal a set of aspirations and anxieties, subject positions and social relations, that may be in many ways as relevant to us now as they were in the halcyon days of the postmodern.

## Notes

1. As Bill Brown has put it, critical theory has well and truly "internalized the fashion system (a system meant to accelerate the obsolescence of things." (Bill Brown, "Thing Theory," Critical Inquiry 28.1 [Autumn, 2001], 13.)
2. Gilles Lipovetsky, Hypermodern Times (Cambridge: Polity Press, 2005), 11.
3. Alan Kirby, Digimodernism: How New Technologies Dismantle the Postmodern and Reconfigure Our Lives (New York: Continuum, 2009).
4. Nicholas Bourriaud, Altermodern: Tate Triennial 2009 (London: Tate Publishing, 2009).
5. Timotheus Vermeulen and Robin van den Akker, "Metamodernism," Journal of Aesthetics and Culture 2 (2010), 6. See also the work of Robert Samuels, who has argued that our current moment is one of "automodernity," in which "instead of technological automation creating a sense of mechanical alienation and impersonal predetermination, digital youth turn to new media and technologies to increase their sense of freedom and individual control"; and Raoul Eshelman, who offers the term "performatism" to describe the mode of engagement invited by much contemporary art, in which a subject whose ontological foundations were dismantled within postmodernity is temporarily resurrected, as performance, through the application of transparent constraints and rules (Robert Samuels, "Automodernity After Postmodernism: Autonomy and Automation in Culture, Technology and Education," in Digital Youth, Innovation, and the Unexpected, ed. Tara McPherson [Cambridge, MA: The MIT Press,

*Restlessness* 223

2008], 220; and Raoul Eshelman, Performatism, or, the End of Postmodernism [Aurora: Davis Group, 2008].)

6. Vermeulen and van den Akker, "Metamodernism," 10. As Lyotard puts it, "The sublime ... takes place ... when the imagination fails to present an object which might, if only in principle, match a concept. We have he idea of the world (the totality of what is), but we do not have the capacity to show an example of it ... we can conceive the infinitely great, the infinitely powerful, but every presentation of an object destined to make visible this absolute greatness or power appears to us painfully inadequate." (Lyotard, "An Answer to the Question: What is Postmodernism?" in idem, The Postmodern Condition: A Report on Knowledge, trans. Geoff Bennington and Brian Massumi [Minneapolis: University of Minnesota Press, 1988], 78.)

7. Zygmunt Bauman, Work Consumerism and the New Poor (Maidenhead: Open University Press, 2004), 26.

8. Luc Boltanski and Eve Chiapello, The New Spirit of Capitalism (London: Verso, 2005), 112; Paolo Virno, "The Ambivalence of Disenchantment," in Radical Thought in Italy: A Potential Politics, ed. Michael Hardt (Minneapolis: University of Minnesota Press, 1996), 15.

9. Steven Shaviro, Post-Cinematic Affect (Hants: 0-Books, 2010), 3.

10. The contagious quality that I am here ascribing to the emotions this book has examined is not quite identical to the "emotional infection" that Norman K. Denzin imputes to feeling in general, or to the "affective transmission" that Teresa Brennan imputes to affect. (Norman K. Denzin, On Understanding Emotion [New Brunswick, NJ: Transaction Publishing, 2007], 150; Teresa Brennan, The Transmission of Affect (Ithaca, NY: Cornell University Press, 2004.) Rather, it refers to the sense that, oriented less around an object than around the question of (the other's) emotion itself, postmodern emotion seems to slide restlessly between subject and other, inside and outside, quite independently of any object-cause.

11. Steven Shaviro, Post-Cinematic Affect (Hants: 0-Books, 2010), 3; Brian Massumi, Parables for the Virtual (Durham, NC: Duke University Press, 2002), 35.

12. Steven Shaviro, The Cinematic Body (Minneapolis: University of Minnesota Press, 1993), 23.

13. Shaviro, Post-Cinematic Affect; Thomas Elsaesser and Malte Hagener, Film Theory: An Introduction Through the Senses (New York: Routledge, 2010); Vivian Sobchack, Carnal Thoughts: Embodiment and Moving Image Culture (Berkeley: University of California Press, 2004). Vivian Sobchack, Carnal Thoughts: Embodiment and Moving Image Culture (Berkeley: University of California Press, 2004), 161. Writing of new cinematic technologies, including the displacement of film stock by a dispersed and seemingly disembodied digital technology, Sobchack argues that "the electronic [media] is phenomenologically experienced not as a discrete, intentional, body-centered mediation and projection in space but rather as a simultaneous, dispersed, and insubstantial transmission across a network or web that is constituted spatially more as a materially flimsy latticework of nodal points than as the stable ground of embodied experience" (Sobchack, Carnal Thoughts, 154). This move, in turn, has met with a barrage of recuperative criticism insisting that the incipient obsolesence of the material technology on which classic theories of cinema are based has not evacuated our experience of movies of visceral power, and that in "the era of

## 224  *Restlessness*

digital cinema, the body and the senses are, if anything, even more central for an understanding of the film experience." (Elsaesser and Hagener, Film Theory: An Introduction Through the Senses, 171.) For another example of this argument, see Shaviro, whose Post-Cinematic Affect offers a stunning series analyses of the "structures of feeling" that emerge in a "computer- and network-based, and digitally generated, 'new media.'" (Shaviro, Post-Cinematic Affect, 2.)

14. Sara Ahmed, The Cultural Politics of Emotion (London: Routledge, 2004), 4.
15. Shaviro, Post-Cinematic Affect, 1.
16. Steven Connor, introduction to The Cambridge Companion to Postmodernism, ed. Steven Connor (Cambridge: Cambridge University Press, 2004), 5.

# References

Abbas, Ackbar. "On Fascination: Walter Benjamin's Images," *New German Critique*, 48 (1989): 43–62.

Abel, Marco. *Violent Affect: Literature, Cinema and Critique after Representation*. Lincoln, NE: University of Nebraska Press, 2007.

Adams, Parveen. "Death Drive." *The Modern Fantastic: The Films of David Cronenberg*. Edited by Michael Grant, 102–22. Wiltshire: Flicks Books, 2000.

Adamson, Walter. *Embattled Avant-Gardes: Modernism's Resistance to Commodity Culture in Europe*. Berkeley, CA: University of California Press, 2007.

Adorno, Theodor. *Minima Moralia: Reflections on a Damaged Life*. London: Verso, 2005.

Ahmed, Sara. *The Cultural Politics of Emotion*. London: Routledge, 2004.

———. *The Promise of Happiness*. Durham, NC: Duke University Press, 2010.

Altieri, Charles. "Constructing Emotion in Deconstruction." *Contemporary Literature*, 43. 3 (Autumn 2002): 606–614.

Altman, Rick. "Dickens, Griffith and Film Theory Today." *South Atlantic Quarterly* 88. (1989): 321–59.

Anderson, Ben. "Modulating the Excess of Affect: Morale in a State of 'Total War.'" *The Affect Theory Reader*. Edited by Melissa Gregg and Gregory J. Seigworth, 161–185. Durham, N.C.: Duke University Press, 2010.

Anderson, Perry. *The Origins of Postmodernity*. London: Verso, 1998.

Aristotle. *Nicomachean Ethics*. Chicago: University of Chicago Press, 2011.

Barker, Chris. *Cultural Studies: Theory and Practice*. London: Sage, 2000.

Barker, Jennifer. *The Tactile Eye: Touch and the Cinematic Experience*. Berkeley: University of California Press, 2009.

Barker, Martin, Jane Arthurs and Ramaswami Haindranath. *The Crash Controversy: Censorship Campaigns and Film Reception*. London: Wallflower Press, 2001.

Barthes, Roland. *Camera Lucida: Reflections on Photography*. Translated by Richard Howard. New York: Hill and Wang, 1981.

Barthes, Roland. *Mythologies*. Frogmore: Paladin, 1973.

Baudrillard, Jean. *America*. London: Verso, 1999.

———. *The Intelligence of Evil or the Lucidity Pact*. Translated by Chris Turner. New York: Berg, 2005.

———. *Fragments: Conversations with Francois L'Yvonnet*. Translated by Chris Turner. London: Routledge, 2004.

———. *Passwords*. Translated by Chris Turner. London: Verso, 2003.

———. *Fatal Strategies*. London: Pluto Press, 1999.

———. *Revenge of the Crystal: Selected Writings on the Modern Object and its Destiny, 1968–1983*. London: Pluto Classics, 1999.

———. *Simulacra and Simulation*. Translated by Sheila Faria Glaser. Ann Arbor: University of Michigan Press, 1994.

## 226  References

———. "Simulacra and Science Fiction." *Science Fiction Studies* 18.3 (November 1991): 309–313.

———. "Ballard's *Crash.*" *Science Fiction Studies* 18. 3 (November, 1991): 313–320.

———. *Ecstasy of Communication*. New York: Autonomedia, 1988.

———. *Jean Baudrillard: Selected Writings*. Edited by Mark Poster. Stanford: Stanford University Press, 1988.

———. *For a Critique of the Political Economy of the Sign*. St Louis, MO: Telos Press, 1981.

Bauman, Zygmunt. *Work, Consumerism and the New Poor*. Berkshire: McGraw-Hill International, 2004.

Beard, William. *The Artist as Monster: The Cinema of David Cronenberg*. Toronto: University of Toronto, 2006.

Beckett, Samuel. *Waiting For Godot: A Tragicomedy in 2 Acts*. New York: Grove Press, 1982.

Belazs, Bela. "Visible Man, or the Culture of Film." Translated by Rodney Livingstone. *Screen* 48.1 (2007): 91–108.

Benjamin, Walter. *Illuminations: Essays and Reflections*. Edited by Hannah Arendt. New York: Vintage Digital, 2011, Kindle Edition.

———. *Selected Writings, Volume 3: 1935–38*. Edited by Michael W. Jennings, Howard Eiland, and Gary Smith. Cambridge, MA: Harvard University Press, 2002.

Bergson, Henri. *Laughter: An Essay on the Meaning of the Comic*. Translated by Cloudesely Brereton and Fred Rothwell. Rockville, ML: Arc Manor, 2008.

Berlant, Lauren. "Cruel Optimism." *differences: A Journal of Feminist Cultural Studies* 17.3 (2006): 20–36.

———. "Structures of Unfeeling: *Mysterious Skin.*" Paper presented at Sydney Gay and Lesbian Mardis Gras: Queer Thinking, University of Sydney, Australia, February 19, 2011.

———. *Cruel Optimism*. Durham, NC: Duke University Press, 2011. Kindle Edition.

———. "Nearly Utopian, Nearly Normal: Post-Fordist Affect in *La Promesse* and *Rosetta.*" *Public Culture* 19.2 (2007): 273–301.

———. "The Subject of True Feeling: Pain, Privacy, Politics." *Left Legalism, Left Critique*. Edited by Wendy Brown and Janet Halley, 105–133. Durham, N.C.: Duke University Press, 2002.

———. "Love: A Queer Feeling." *Homosexuality and Psychoanalysis*. Edited by Tim Dean and Christopher Lane, 432–452. Chicago: University of Chicago Press, 2001.

———. *The Queen of America Goes to Washington City: Essays on Sex and Citizenship*. Durham, NC: Duke University Press, 1997.

Bernstein, Haskell E. "Boredom and the Ready-Made Life." *Social Research* 42.3 (1975): 512–537.

Best, Stephen and Sharon Marcus. "Surface Reading: An Introduction." *Representations* 108.1 (2009): 1–21.

Best, Stephen and Douglas Kellner. *The Postmodern Turn*. New York: The Guilford Press, 1997.

Best, Susan. *Visualizing Feeling: Affect and the Feminine Avant-Garde*. London: I. B. Tauris and Co., 2011.

Bignell, Jonathan. *Postmodern Media Culture*. Edinburgh: Edinburgh University Press, 2000.

## References 227

Blanchot, Maurice. *The Space of Literature*. Translated by Ann Smock. Lincoln: University of Nebraska, 1982.

Boggs, Carl, and Tom Pollard. *A World In Chaos: Social Crisis and the Rise of Postmodern Cinema*. Lanham: Rowman and Littlefield, 2003.

Boltanski, Luc and Eve Chiapello. *The New Spirit of Capitalism*. London: Verso, 2005.

Bonnycastle, Stephen. *In Search of Authority: An Introductory Guide to Literary Theory*. Ontario: Broadview Press, 2007.

Bora, Renu. "Outing Texture." *Novel Gazing: Queer Readings in Fictions*. Edited by Eve Kosofsky Sedgwick, 94–127. Durham, NC: Duke University Press, 1997.

Botting, Fred and Scott Wilson. "SexCrash," *Crash Cultures: Modernity, Mediation and the Material*. Edited by Jane Arthurs and Iain Grant, 79–90. Bristol: Intellect Books, 2003.

Bourke, Joanna. *Fear: A Cultural History*. Washington, DC: Shoemaker and Hoard, 2007.

Bourriaud, Nicholas. *Altermodern: Tate Triennial 2009*. London: Tate Publishing, 2009.

Brennan, Teresa. *The Transmission of Affect*. Ithaca: Cornell University Press, 2004.

Briefel, Aviva and Sam Miller. *Horror After 9/11: World of Fear, Cinema of Terror* Austin, TX: University of Texas Press, 2011.

Brinkema, Eugenie. "Laura Dern's Vomit, or, Kant and Derrida in Oz." *Film-Philosophy* 15.2 (2011): 51–69.

Brooker, Peter and Will Brooker. Introduction to *Postmodern After-Images: A Reader in Film, Television and Video*. Edited by Peter Brooker and Will Brooker, 1–19. London: Arnold, 1997.

Brown, Bill. "The Dark Wood of Postmodernity: Space, Faith, Allegory." *PMLA* 120.3 (2005): 734–750.

Brown, Judith. *Glamour in Six Dimensions: Modernism and the Radiance of Form*. Ithaca: Cornell University Press, 2009.

Browning, Mark. *David Cronenberg: Author or Film-maker?* Bristol: Intellect Books, 2007.

Buchanan, Ian. *Deleuzism: A Meta-Commentary*. Edinburgh: Edinburgh University Press, 2002.

———. *Fredric Jameson: Live Theory*. London: Continuum, 2006.

Buckland, Warren and Thomas Elsaesser. *Studying Contemporary American Film*. London: Arnold, 2002.

Bürger, Peter. *Theory of the Avant-Garde*. Minneapolis: University of Minnesota Press, 1984.

Butler, Judith. *Bodies That Matter: On the Discursive Limits of "Sex."* New York: Routledge, 1993.

Butler, Rex. *Jean Baudrillard: The Defence of the Real*. London: Sage, 1999.

Canning, Peter. "Indeterminacy." *The Encylopaedia of Postmodernism*. Edited by Victor E. Taylor, 189–190. New York: Routledge, 2001.

Carroll, Noel. *Beyond Aesthetics: Philosophical Essays*. Cambridge: Cambridge University Press, 2001.

———. "The Nature of Horror." *The Journal of Aesthetics and Art Criticism* 46.1 (1997): 51–59.

———. *The Philosophy of Horror, or, Paradoxes of the Heart*. London: Routledge, 1990.

## 228 References

———. "The Future of Allusion: Hollywood in the Seventies (and Beyond)." *October* 20 (Spring, 1982): 51–81.

Cartwright, Lisa. *Moral Spectatorship: Technologies of Voice and Affect in Postwar Representations of the Child*. Durham, NC: Duke University Press, 2008.

Cates, Diana Fritz. "Conceiving Emotions: Martha Nussbaum's *Upheavals of Thought*." *Journal of Religious Ethics* 31.2 (Summer, 2003): 325–341.

Cheng, Anne Anlin. "Shine: On Race, Glamour and the Modern." *PMLA* 126.4 (October, 2011): 1022–1041.

Chow, Rey. *Writing Diaspora: Tactics of Intervention in Contemporary Cultural Studies*. Bloomington: Indiana University Press, 1993.

Clarke, David B., Marcus A. Doel, William Merrin and Richard G. Smith. "Introduction: The Evil Genius of Jean Baudrillard." *Jean Baudrillard: Fatal Theories*. Edited by David B. Clarke, Marcus A. Doel, William Merrin and Richard G. Smith, 1–14. New York: Routledge, 2009.

Clough, Patricia. *The Affective Turn: Theorizing the Social*. Durham, NC: Duke University Press, 2007.

Clover, Carol. *Men, Women and Chainsaws: Gender in the Modern Horror Film*. Princeton, NJ: Princeton University Press, 1993.

Collins, Jim. "Genericity in the Nineties." *Film Theory Goes to the Movies*. Edited by J. Collins, H. Radner and A. Preacher Collins, 242–264. London: Routledge, 1993.

Connor, Steven. Introduction to *The Cambridge Companion to Postmodernism*. Edited by Steven Connor, 1–19. Cambridge: Cambridge University Press, 2004.

———. "Fascination, Skin and the Screen." *Critical Quarterly* 40.1 (1998): 9–24.

———. *Postmodernist Culture: An Introduction to Theories of the Contemporary*. Oxford: Blackwell, 1989.

Constable, Catherine. "Postmodernism and Film." *The Cambridge Companion to Postmodernism*. Edited by Steven Connor, 43–61. Cambridge: Cambridge University Press, 2004.

Corngold, Stanley. *Complex Pleasure: Forms of Feeling in German Literature*. Palo Alto, CA: Stanford University Press, 1998.

Craig, Pamela and Martin Fradley. "Teenage Traumata: Youth, Affective Politics, and the Contemporary American Horror Film." *American Horror Film: The Genre at the Turn of the Millennium*. Edited by Steffen Hantke, 77–102. Oxford, MS: University of Mississippi Press, 2010.

Craven, Roberta Jill. "Ironic Empathy in Cronenberg's *Crash*: The Psychodynamics of Postmodern Displacement from a Tenuous Reality." *Quarterly Review of Film and Video* 17.3 (2000): 187–209.

Creed, Barbara. "Anal Wounds, Metallic Kisses." *Screen* 39.2 (Summer 1998): 175–179.

Cvetkovich, Ann. *An Archive of Feelings: Trauma, Sexuality and Lesbian Public Cultures*. Durham, NC: Duke University Press, 2003.

———. Introduction to *Political Emotions*. Edited by Janet Staiger, Ann Cvetkovich and Ann Reynolds, 5–11. New York: Routledge, 2010.

Damasio, Antonio. *Descartes' Error: Emotion, Reason and the Human Brain*. London: Vintage, 2006.

Davis, Kimberly Chabot. *Postmodern Texts and Emotional Audiences*. West Lafayette: Purdue University Press, 2007.

de Sousa, Ronald. "Emotions: What I Know, What I'd Like to Think I Know, and What I'd Like to Think." *Thinking About Feeling: Contemporary Philosophers*

## References 229

*on Emotion*. Edited by Robert Solomon, 61–75. New York: Oxford University Press, 2004.

de Spinoza, Benedict. *Ethics*. Translated by Edwin Curley. London: Penguin Books, 1996.

Degli-Esposti, Cristina. Introduction to *Postmodernism in the Cinema*. Edited by Cristina Degli-Esposti, 3–18. London: Berghahn, 1998.

Deigh, John. "Primitive Emotions." *Thinking about Feeling: Contemporary Philosophers on Emotion*. Edited by Robert Solomon, 9–27. Oxford: Oxford University Press, 2004.

Deleuze, Gilles. *Difference and Repetition*. London: Continuum, 2004.

———. *Francis Bacon: The Logic of Sensation*. London: Continuum, 2003.

Deleuze, Gilles and Felix Guattari. *A Thousand Plateaus: Capitalism and Schizophrenia*. London: Continuum, 2004.

Denzin, Norman K. *Images of Postmodern Society: Social Theory and Contemporary Cinema*. London: Sage, 1991.

———. *On Understanding Emotion*. New Brunswick, NJ: Transaction Publishing, 2007.

Derrida, Jacques. *Aporias: Dying-Awaiting (One Another At) "The Limits of Truth."* Palo Alto: Stanford University Press, 1993.

———. *Writing and Difference*. London: Routledge, 2001.

Dika, Vera. *Recycled Culture in Contemporary Art and Film: The Uses of Nostalgia*. Cambridge: Cambridge University Press, 2003.

Doane, Mary Ann. "The Close-Up: Scale and Detail in the Cinema." *differences: A Journal of Feminist Cultural Studies* 14.3 (2003): 89–111.

———. *Femme Fatales: Feminism, Film Theory, Psychoanalysis*. New York: Routledge, 1991.

———. "Gilda: Epistemology as Striptease." *Camera Obscura* 4 (1983): 6–27.

Dolar, Mladen. *The Voice and Nothing More*. Cambridge, MA: M.I.T. Press, 2006.

Dosse, François. *Empire of Meaning: The Humanization of the Social Sciences*. Translated by Hassan Melehy. Minneapolis: University of Minnesota Press, 1999.

Douglas, Mary. *Purity and Danger: An Analysis of Concepts of Pollution and Taboo* New York: Routledge, 2003.

Ebert, Roger. *Roger Ebert's Movie Yearbook, 2009*. Kansas City: Andrew McMeel Publishing, 2009.

Eco, Umberto. "*Casablanca*: Cult Movies and Intertextual Collage." *Substance* 14.2, Issue 47 (1985): 3–12.

Edelman, Lee. *Homographesis: Essays in Gay Literary and Cultural Theory*. New York: Routledge, 1994.

———. "*Rear Window*'s Glasshole." *Out Takes: Essays on Queer Theory and Film*. Edited by Ellis Hanson, 72–96. Durham, NC: Duke University Press, 1999.

Eburne, Jonathan P. and Rita Felski. Introduction to *New Literary History* 41.4 (2010): v-xv.

Elden, Stuart. *Mapping the Present: Heidegger, Foucault, and the Project of a Spatial History*. New York: Continuum, 2001.

Elsaesser, Thomas and Malte Hagener. *Film Theory: An Introduction Through the Senses*. New York: Routledge, 2010.

Epstein, Jean. "Magnification and Other Writings." *October* 3 (Spring, 1977): 9–25.

Feagin, Susan. "The Pleasures of Tragedy." *American Philosophical Quarterly* 20 (1983): 95–104.

## 230  References

Featherstone, Mike. *Consumer Culture and Postmodernism*. London: Sage, 2007.

Felski, Rita. *The Uses of Literature*. Boston: Blackwell, 2008.

Fenichel, Otto. *The Collected Papers of Otto Fenichel, Vol 1*. Edited by Hanna Fenichel and David Rapaport. New York: W.W. Norton and Company, 1954.

Fisher, Philip. *The Vehement Passions*. Princeton, NJ: Princeton University Press, 2002.

———. *Wonder, the Rainbow, and the Aesthetics of Rare Experiences*. Cambridge, MA: Harvard University Press, 1998.

Flatley, Jonathan. *Affective Mapping: Melancholia and the Politics of Modernism*. Cambridge, MA: Harvard University Press, 2008.

———. *The Uncanny*. Translated by David McLintock. London: Penguin Classics, 2003.

Foster, Hal. *The Return of the Real*. Cambridge: MIT Press, 1996.

———. "What's Neo About the Neo-Avant-Garde?" *October* 7 (Fall, 1994): 5–32.

Foucault, Michel. *Discipline and Punish*. London: Vintage Books, 1979.

Freud, Sigmund. *Sexuality and the Psychology of Love*. Edited by Philip Rieff. New York: Touchstone, 1997.

Fuss, Diana. *Identification Papers: Readings on Psychoanalysis, Sexuality and Culture*. New York: Routledge, 1995.

Gane, Mike. *Baudrillard: Critical and Fatal Theory*. London: Routledge, 1991.

———. Introduction to *Symbolic Exchange and Death*. Edited by Mike Gane, viii–xiv. London: Sage, 1993.

Gaut, Berys. "Empathy and Identification in Cinema." *Midwest Studies in Philosophy* 34.1 (2010): 136–157.

Girard, Rene. *Deceit, Desire and the Novel*. New York: Continuum International Publishers, 1988.

Gledhill, Christine. "The Melodramatic Field: An Investigation." *Home is Where the Heart Is: Studies in Melodrama and the Woman's Film*. Edited by Christine Gledhill, 5–39. London: British Film Institute, 1987.

Gould, Deborah. "Affect and Protest." *Political Emotions*. Edited by Janet Staiger, Ann Cvetkovich and Ann Reynolds, 18–44. New York: Routledge, 2010.

Grace, Victoria. *Baudrillard's Challenge: A Feminist Reading*. London: Routledge, 2000.

Greenberg, Clement. "Avant-Garde and Kitsch," http://blog.lib.umn.edu/mulli105/1601fall10/Greenberg-AvGd%26Ktch.pdf.

Gregg, Melissa and Gregory J. Seigworth. *The Affect Theory Reader*. Durham, NC: Duke University Press, 2010.

———. "An Inventory of Shimmers." *The Affect Theory Reader*. Edited by Melissa Gregg and Gregory J. Seigworth, 1–28. Durham, NC: Duke University Press, 2010.

Grodal, Torben. *Moving Pictures: A New Theory of Film Genres, Feelings and Cognition*. Oxford: Oxford University Press, 1999.

Gross, Daniel M. *The Secret History of Emotion: From Aristotle's Rhetoric to Modern Brain Science*. Chicago: University of Chicago Press, 2006.

Gross, Paul R. and Norman Levitt. *Higher Superstition: The Academic Left and its Quarrels with Science*. Baltimore: Johns Hopkins University Press, 1998.

Grossberg, Lawrence. "Affect's Future." *The Affect Theory Reader*. Edited by Melissa Gregg and Gregory J. Seigworth, 309–338. Durham, NC: Duke University Press, 2010.

*References* 231

———. *We Gotta Get out of this Place: Popular Conservativism and Postmodern Culture*. London: Routledge, 1992.

———. "Postmodernity and Affect: All Dressed Up with no Place to Go." *Communication* 10.3–4 (1988): 271–293.

Gunning, Tom. "An Aesthetic of Astonishment." *Viewing Positions: Ways of Seeing Film*. Edited by Linda Williams, 114–133. NJ: Rutgers University Press, 1995.

Hantke, Steffen. "Academic Film Criticism, The Rhetoric of Crisis and the Current State of American Horror Cinema." *College Literature* 34.4 (Fall, 2007): 191–202.

———. "They Don't Make 'Em Like They Used To: On the Rhetoric of Crisis and the Current State of American Horror Cinema." *American Horror Film: The Genre at the Turn of the Millenium*. Edited by Steffen Hantke, vii-xxxii. Oxford, MS: University of Mississippi Press, 2010.

Hardt, Michael. "About Love." Paper presented at European Graduate School, Pennine Alps, Switzerland, 2007. http://www.youtube.com/watch?v=ndnkjnMxxLc& feature=relmfu.

Hardt, Michael and Antonio Negri. *Reflections on Empire*. Cambridge: Polity Press, 2008.

Harpold, Terry. "Dry Leatherette." *Postmodern Culture* 7.3. May, 1997.

Harris, Oliver. "Film Noir Fascination: Outside History, but Historically So." *Cinema Journal* 43.1 (Fall, 2003): 3–24.

Harvey, David. *The Conditions of Postmodernity: An Enquiry into the Origins of Cultural Change*. Malden, MA: Blackwell Publishing, 1990.

Hawkins, Gay. *Ethics of Waste: How We Relate to Rubbish*. Oxford: Rowman and Littlefield, 2006.

Heath, Stephen. "Notes on Suture." *Screen* 18.4 (1977): 48–76.

Heidegger, Martin. "Description of the Situation: Fundamental Attunement." *The Heidegger Reader*. Edited by Gunter Figal, 79–103. Bloomington, IN: Indiana University Press, 2007.

———. "The Question Concerning Technology." *Technology and Values: Essential Reading*. Edited by Craig Hanks, 99–113. Malden, MA: Wiley-Blackwell, 2010.

———. "The Origin of the Work of Art." *The Continental Aesthetics Reader*. Edited by Clive Cazeaux, 80–101. London: Routledge, 2000.

Hemmings, Clare. "Invoking Affect: Cultural Theory and the Ontological Term." *Cultural Studies*, 19.5 (September 2005): 548–567.

Hills, Matt. *The Pleasures of Horror*. London: Continuum, 2005.

Hoffman, E.T.A. *The Golden Pot and Other Stories*. Translated by Ritchie Robertson. Oxford: Oxford University Press, 1992.

Hudson, Jennifer A. "'No Hay Banda, and Yet We Hear a Band': David Lynch's Reversal of Coherence in *Mulholland Drive*." *Journal of Film and Video* 56.1 (Spring, 2004): 17–24.

Hume, David. *Essays and Treatises on Several Subjects*. London: A. Millar, 1809.

Humphries, Reynold. *The American Horror Film: An Introduction*. Edinburgh: Edinburgh University Press, 2002.

Hutcheon, Linda. *The Politics of Postmodernism*. New York: Routledge, 1989.

———. *The Politics of Postmodernism*. New York: Routledge, 2002.

Huyssen, Andreas. *After the Great Divide: Modernism, Mass Culture, Postmodernism*. Bloomington: Indiana University Press, 1986.

## 232 References

———. "Mapping the Postmodern." *A Postmodern Reader*. Edited by Linda Hutcheon and Joseph P Natoli, 105–156. Albany, NY: State University of New York Press, 1993.

Illouz, Eva. *Cold Intimacies: The Making of Emotional Capitalism*. Cambridge: Polity Press, 2007.

James, William. *The Principles of Psychology, Vol. II*. New York: Cosimo Classics, 2007.

Jameson, Fredric. *Archaeologies of the Future: The Desire Called Utopia and Other Science Fictions*. New York: Verso, 2005.

———. *The Political Unconscious*. London: Routledge Classics, 2002.

———. *The Cultural Turn: Selected Writings on the Postmodern, 1983–1998*. London: Verso, 1998.

———. *Signatures of the Visible*. New York: Routledge, 1992.

———. *The Geopolitical Aesthetic: Cinema and Space in the World System*. Bloomington, IN: Indiana University Press, 1992.

———. *Postmodernism, or, The Cultural Logic of Late Capitalism*. Durham, NC; Duke University Press, 1991.

———. "Cognitive Mapping." *Marxism and the Interpretation of Culture*. Edited Cary Nelson and Lawrence Grossberg, 347–357. Urbana and Chicago: University Illinois Press, 1988.

———. Foreword to *The Postmodern Condition: A Report on Knowledge*. Jean-Francois Lyotard. Translated by Geoff Bennington and Brian Massumi, xii–xxi. Minneapolis: University of Minnesota Press, 1984.

———. "Postmodernism, or, the Cultural Logic of Late Capitalism." *New Left Review* 146 (1984): 53–94.

Jameson, Fredric and Masao Miyoshi. *The Cultures of Globalization*. Durham, NC: Duke University Press, 1998.

Jancovich, Mark. *The Cultural Politics of the New Crticism* (Cambridge: Cambridge University Press, 1993.

Jentsch, Ernst. "On the Psychology of the Uncanny." Translated by Roy Sellars. http://art3idea.psu.edu/locus/Jentsch_uncanny.pdf.

Johnson, Barbara. *Persons and Things*. Cambridge, MA: Harvard University Press, 2008.

Jones, Alan. "*Crash*: David Cronenberg Turns S&M Injury to S.F. Metaphor." *Cinefantastique* 28.3 (October 1996): 8–9.

Kellner, Douglas. *Baudrillard: A Critical Reader*. Oxford: Basil Blackwell, 1994.

Kermode, Mark. "What a carve up!" *Sight and Sound* 13.12 (December 2003): 12–16.

Kirby, Alan. *Digimodernism: How New Technologies Dismantle the Postmodern and Reconfigure our Culture*. New York: Continuum, 2009.

Kracauer, Siegfried. *Mass Ornament: Weimar Essays*. Translated by Thomas Y. Levin. Cambridge, MA: Harvard University Press, 1995.

Kroker, Arthur and David Cook. *The Postmodern Scene: Excremental Culture and Hyperaesthetics*. Montreal: New World Perspectives, 1986.

Laine, Tarja. *Feeling Cinema: Emotional Dynamics in Film Studies*. London: Bloomsbury Academic, 2013.

Lacan, Jacques. *The Seminar of Jacques Lacan Book XI: The Four Fundamental Concepts of Psychoanalysis*. New York: W.W. Norton and Company, 1998.

———. *Ecrits: A Selection*. Translated by Bruce Fink. New York: W.W. Norton and Company, 2002.

## References    233

Langbauer, Laurie. "The City, the Everyday and Boredom: The Case of *Sherlock Holmes*." *differences* 5.3 (1993): 80–102.

Lasch, Christopher. *The Culture of Narcissism: American Life in An Age of Diminishing Expectations* New York: W.W. Norton and Company, 1979.

Latour, Bruno. "Why Critique Has Run out of Steam: From Matters of Fact to Matters of Concern." *Critical Inquiry* 30 (Winter, 2004): 225–48.

Lear, Jonathan. *Open-Minded: Working Out the Logic of the Soul.* Cambridge, MA: Harvard University Press, 1998.

Lentzer, Jay R. and Donald R. Ross. "The Dreams that Blister Sleep: Latent Content and Cinematic Form in *Mulholland Drive*." *American Imago* 62.1 (2005): 101–123.

Levitt, Norm. "The Science Wars: Deconstructing Science is Pseudo-Science." *The Skeptic Encyclopedia of Pseudoscience.* Edited by Michael Shermer, 750–762. Santa Barbara, CA: ABC-Clio, 2002.

Lewis, Barry. "Postmodernism and Fiction." *The Routledge Companion to Postmodernism.* Edited by Stuart Sim, 111–121. New York: Routledge, 2005.

Leys, Ruth. "The Turn to Affect: A Critique." *Critical Inquiry* 37.3 (Spring 2011): 434–472.

Lipovetsky, Gilles. *Hypermodern Times.* Cambridge: Polity Press, 2005.

Love, Heather. *Feeling Backward: Loss and the Politics of Queer History.* Cambridge, MA: Harvard University Press, 2006.

———. "Truth and Consequences: On Paranoid Reading and Reparative Reading." *Criticism*, 52.2 (2011): 235–241.

———. "Feeling Bad in 1963." *Political Emotions.* Edited Janet Staiger, Ann Cvetkovich and Ann Reynolds, 112–133. New York: Routledge, 2010.

———. "Spectacular Failure: The Figure of the Lesbian in *Mulholland Drive*." *New Literary History.* 35.1 (Winter, 2004): 117–132.

Lyotard, Jean-Francois. *The Differend: Phrases in Dispute.* Translated by Georges Van Den Abeele. Minneapolis: University of Minnesota Press, 1988.

———. *Discourse, Figure.* Translated by Antony Hudek and Mary Lydon. Minneapolis: University of Minnesota Press, 2011.

———. *Libidinal Economy.* Translated by Iain Hamilton Grant. London: Continuum, 2004.

———. *Lessons on the Analytic of the Sublime.* Translated by Elizabeth Rottenberg. Stanford, CA: Stanford University Press, 1994.

———. *The Inhuman: Reflections on Time.* Stanford, CA: Stanford University Press, 1991.

———. *The Postmodern Condition: A Report on Knowledge.* Translated by Geoff Bennington and Brian Massumi. Minneapolis: University of Minnesota Press, 1984.

———. "The Sublime and the Avant-Garde." Translated by Linda Liebmann. *Art Forum* 22 (1984): 36–43.

MacDonald, Scott. *Avant-Garde Film.* Cambridge: Cambridge University Press, 1986.

Malpas, Simon. *Jean-Francois Lyotard.* London: Routledge, 2003.

Markowitz, Sally. "Guilty Pleasures: Aesthetic Meta-Response and Fiction." *Journal of Aesthetics and Art Criticism* 50 (1992): 307–316.

Marks, Laura U. *Touch: Sensuous Theory and Multisensory Media.* Minneapolis: University of Minnesota Press, 2002.

## 234  References

Massumi, Brian. "The Autonomy of Affect." *Cultural Critique* 31 (Fall, 1995): 83–109.

———. *Parables for the Virtual: Movement, Affect, Sensation.* Durham, NC: Duke University Press, 2002.

———. Preface to *The Politics of Everyday Fear.* Edited by Brian Massumi, vii–x. Minneapolis: University of Minnesota Press, 1993.

Mayshark, Jesse Fox. *Post-Pop Cinema: The Search for Meaning in New American Film.* Westport, CT: Praeger Publishers, 2007.

McCarthy, Cameron and Alicia P. Rodirguez, Ed Buendia, Shuaib Meacham, Stephen David, Teriberto Godina, K. E. Supriya, and Carrie Wilson-Brown. "Danger in the Safety Zone: Notes on Race, Resentment and the Discourse of Crime, Violence and Suburban Security," *Cultural Studies* 11.2 (1997): 274–95.

McHale, Brian. *Postmodernist Fiction.* New York: Routledge, 1987.

———. "What Was Postmodernism?" *Electronic Book Review.* December 20, 2007, http://www.electronicbookreview.com/thread/fictionspresent/tense.

McGowan, Todd. "Lost on *Mulholland Drive*: David Lynch's Panegyric to Hollywood." *Cinema Journal* 43.2 [2004]: 67–89.

McLaughlin, Robert. "Post-Postmodern Discontent: Contemporary Fiction and the Social World." *Symploke* 12.1–2 (2004): 53–68.

McRobbie, Angela. *Postmodernism and Popular Culture.* London: Routledge, 1994.

McRoy, Jay and Guy Crucianelli. "I Panic the World: Benevolent Exploitation in Tod Browning's *Freaks* and Harmony Korine's *Gummo*." *The Journal of Popular Culture* 42.2 (2009): 257–272.

Meikle, Jeffrey L. *American Plastics: A Cultural History.* New Brunswick: Rutgers University Press, 1995.

Mestrovic, Stjepan Gabriel. *The Coming Fin de Siecle.* New York: Routledge, 1991.

Miles, Stephen. *Consumerism: As a Way of Life.* London: Sage, 1998.

Miller, D. A. *The Novel and the Police.* Berkeley: University of California Press, 1988.

Miller, Daniel. Introduction to *Consumption: Theory and Issues in the Study Consumption*, 1–14. Edited by Daniel Miller. London: Routledge, 2001.

Miller, Jacques-Alain. "Suture (Elements of the Logic of the Signifier)." *Screen* 18.4 (1977): 24–34.

Modleski, Tania. "The Terror of Pleasure: The Contemporary Horror Film and Postmodern Theory." *Film Theory and Criticism: Introductory Readings.* Edited by Leo Braudy and Marshall Cohen, 764–773. Oxford: Oxford University Press, 2004.

Morris, Jason. "The Time Between Time: Messianism and the Promise of a New Sincerity." *Jacket* 35 (2008), http://jacketmagazine.com/35/morris-sincerity.shtml.

Morris, Meaghan. *The Pirate's Fiancee: Feminism, Reading, Postmodernism.* London: Verso, 1988.

Muir, John Kenneth. *Wes Craven: the Art of Horror.* Jefferson, NC: McFarland and Company, 2004.

Mulvey, Laura. *Fetishism and Curiosity.* London: British Film Institute, 1996.

Munt, Sally. "Shame/Pride Dichotomies in *Queer as Folk*." *Textual Practice* 14.3 (2000): 531–46.

Murphy, J.J. "Harmony Korine's *Gummo*: The Compliment of Getting Stuck with a Fork." *Film Studies* 5 (Winter, 2004): 92–105.

Nathensen, Donald L. *Shame and Pride: Affect, Sex and the Birth of the Self.* New York: W.W. Norton and Company, 1992.

## References   235

Natoli, Joseph P. and Linda Hutcheon. "Representing the Postmodern." *A Postmodern Reader*. Edited by Natoli and Hutcheon, 193–202. Albany, NY: State University of New York Press, 1993.

Newman, Kim. *Nightmare Movies: Horror on Screen Since the 1960s*. London: Bloomsbury, 2011.

Ngai, Sianne. *Ugly Feelings*. Cambridge, MA: Harvard University Press, 2005.

Nussbaum, Martha. *Upheavals of Thought: The Intelligence of the Emotions*. Cambridge: Cambridge University Press, 2001.

O'Pray, Michael. *Avant-Garde Film: Forms, Themes and Passions*. London: Wallflower, 2003.

Olsen, Mark. "If I Can Dream: The Everlasting Boyhoods of Wes Anderson." *Film Comment* 35.1 (1999): 12–17.

Oudart, Jean-Pierre. "Cinema and Suture." *Screen* 18.4 (1977): 35–47.

Pawlett, William. *Jean Baudrillard: Against Banality*. London: Routledge, 2007.

Pellegrini, Ann and Jasbir Puar. "Affect." *Social Text* 27.3 (2009): 35–38.

Perloff, Marjorie. *Radical Artifice: Writing Poetry in the Age of Media*. Chicago, IL: University of Chicago Press, 1991.

Pfeil, Fred. "Revolting Yet Conserved: Family Noir in Blue Velvet and Terminator." *Postmodern Culture* 2.3 (May 1992).

Phillips, Kendall. *Projected Fears: Horror Films and American Culture*. Westport, CT: Praeger Publishers, 2005.

Pisters, Patricia. *The Matrix of Visual Culture*. Stanford, CA: Stanford University Press, 2003.

Plantinga, Carol R. and Greg M. Smith. *Passionate Views: Film, Cognition and Emotion*. Baltimore: Johns Hopkins University Press, 1999.

Poggi, Christine. *Inventing Futurism: The Art and Politics of Artificial Optimism*. Princeton, NJ: Princeton University Press, 2009.

Polan, Dana B. "Eros and Syphilization: The Contemporary Horror Film." *Planks of Reason: Essays on the Horror Film*. Edited by Barry Keith Grant and Christopher Sharret, 142–152. Oxford: Scarecrow Press, 2004.

Probyn, Elspeth. "Shaming Bodies: Dynamics of Shame and Pride." *Body and Society* 6.1 (2000): 125–35.

———. "Teaching Bodies: Affects in the Classroom." *Body and Society* 10.4 (December 2004): 21–43.

Readings, Bill. *Introducing Lyotard: Art and Politics*. London: Routledge, 1991.

Reevy, Gretchen M. *Encyclopedia of Emotions*. Santa Barbara: Greenwood, 2010.

Robinson, Hilary. Introduction to *Feminism-Art-Theory: An Anthology, 1968–2000*. Edited by Hilary Robinson, 1–8. Oxford: Blackwell, 2001.

Robinson, Jenefer. "Emotion: Biological Fact or Social Construction?" *Thinking about Feeling: Contemporary Philosophers on Emotion*. Edited by Robert C. Solomon, 28–43. Oxford: Oxford University Press, 2004.

Rockoff, Adam. *Going to Pieces: The Rise and Fall of the Slasher Film, 1978–1986*. Jefferson, NC: McFarland and Company, 2002.

Rorty, Richard. *Achieving Our Country: Leftist Thought in Twentieth Century America*. Cambridge, MA: Harvard University Press, 1998.

Rosenbaum, Jonathan. *Movies as Politics*. Berkeley: University of California Press, 1997.

Ross, Andrew. *No Respect: Intellectuals and Popular Culture*. London: Routledge, 1989.

## 236   References

Samuels, Robert. "Automodernity After Postmodernism: Autonomy and Automation in Culture, Technology and Education." *Digital Youth, Innovation, and the Unexpected*. Edited by Tara McPherson, 219–240. Cambridge, MA: The MIT Press, 2008.

Sardar, Ziaudden. *Postmodernism and the Other: The New Imperialism of Western Culture*. London: Pluto Press, 1998.

Scheman, Naomi. "To See it Feelingly: On Knowingness and (In)vulnerability." Unpublished paper. Emotions, Affects … And Other Intimacies conference, Umeå, Sverige, 2011.

Schmid, Heiko, Wolf-Dietrich Sahr and John Urry. *Cities and Fascination: Beyond the Surplus of Meaning*. Farnham: Ashgate Publishing, 2011.

Schwalbe, Michael L. "Goffman Against Postmodernism: Emotion and the Reality of the Self." *Symbolic Interaction* 16.4 (Winter, 1993): 333–350.

Sconce, Jeffrey. "Indecipherable Films: Teaching Gummo." *Cinema Journal*, 47.1 (Autumn, 2007): 112–116.

Sedgwick, Eve Kosofsky. *Touching Feeling: Affect, Pedagogy, Performativity*. Durham, NC: Duke University Press, 2003.

Sedgwick, Eve Kosofsky and Adam Frank. "Shame in the Cybernetic Fold: Reading Silvan Tomkins." *Shame and its Sisters: A Silvan Tomkins Reader*. Edited by Eve Kosofsky Sedgwick, Adam Frank and Irving E. Alexander, 1–28. Durham, NC: Duke University Press, 1995.

Shannon, Sonya. "The Chrome Age: Dawn of Virtual Reality." *Leonardo* 28.5 (1995): 369–380.

Sharrett, Christopher. "The Problem of *Saw*: Torture Porn and the Conservativism of Contemporary Horror Film." *Cineaste* 35.1 (Winter 2009): 32–37.

Shaviro, Steven. *The Cinematic Body*. Minneapolis: University of Minnesota Press, 1993.

———. "Post-Cinematic Affect." *Film Philosophy* 14.1 (2010): 1–102.

———. *Post-Cinematic Affect*. Hants: O-Books, 2010.

———. "The Life, After Death, of Postmodern Emotions." *Criticism* 46.1 (2004): 125–141.

Sim, Stuart. *Lyotard and the Inhuman*. London: Icon Books, 2001.

Sinclair, Iain. *Crash*. London: British Film Institute, 1999.

Singh, Greg. *Feeling Film: Affect and Authenticity in Popular Cinema*. London: Routledge, 2014.

Sipos, Thomas M. *Horror Film Aesthetics: Creating the Visual Language of Fear*. Jefferson, NC: McFarland and Company, 2010.

Slade, Andrew. *Lyotard, Beckett, Duras and the Postmodern Sublime*. New York: Peter Lang Publishing, 2007.

Sloterdijk, Peter. *Critique of Cynical Reason*. Minneapolis: University of Minnesota Press, 1987.

Smith, Gregg M. *Film Structure and the Emotion System*. Cambridge: Cambridge University Press, 2003.

Sobchack, Vivian. *Carnal Thoughts: Embodiment and Moving Image Culture*. Berkeley: University of California Press, 2004.

Solomon, Robert. *The Passions: Emotion and the Meaning of Life*. Indianapolis: Hackett Publishing Company, 1993.

Spacks, Patricia. *Boredom: The Literary History of a State of Mind*. Chicago: University of Chicago Press, 1995.

# References  237

Stacey, Jackie. *The Cinematic Life of the Gene*. Durham, NC: Duke University Press, 2010.

Staiger, Janet. Introduction to *Political Emotions*. Edited by Janet Staiger, Ann Cvetkovich and Ann Reynolds, 1–4. New York: Routledge, 2010.

Stallybrass, Peter. "Marx's Coat." *Border Fetishisms; Material Objects in Unstable Spaces*. Edited by Patricia Spyer, 183–207. New York: Routledge, 1998.

Stearns, Peter. *American Cool: Constructing a Twentieth Century Emotional Style*. New York: New York University Press, 1994.

Stewart, Kathleen. *Ordinary Affects*. Durham, NC: Duke University Press, 2007.

Sutton, John and Doris McIlwain, Wayne Christensen and Andrew Geeves. "Applying Intelligence to the Reflexes: Embodied Skills and Habits between Dreyfus and Descartes." *Journal of the British Society for Phenomenology* 42.1 (January, 2011): 78–103.

Sweeney, Gael. "The King of White Trash Culture: Elvis Presley and the Aesthetics of Excess." *White Trash: Race and Class in America*, 249–266. Edited by Annalee Newitz and Matt Wray. New York: Routledge, 1997.

Terada, Rei. *Feeling in Theory: Emotion after the Death of the Subject*. Cambridge, MA: Harvard University Press, 2001.

Thiele, Leslie Paul. "Postmodernity and the Routinization of Novelty: Heidegger on Boredom and Technology." *Polity* 29.4 (Summer, 1997): 489–517.

Thompson, Krista. "The Sound of Light: Reflections on Art History in the Visual Culture of Hip-Hop." *Art Bulletin* 91.4 (2009): 481–505.

Thrift, Nigel. *Non-Representational Theory: Space, Politics, Affect*. New York: Routledge, 2008.

Tiedens, Larissa Z. and Colin Wayne Leach. *The Social Life of Emotions*. Cambridge: Cambridge University Press, 2004.

Tietchen, Todd F. "Samplers and Copycats: The Cultural Implications of the Postmodern Slasher in American Film." *Journal of Popular Culture* 26.3 (1998): 98–107.

Toles, George. "Auditioning Betty in Mulholland Drive." *Film Quarterly* 58.1 (2004): 2–13.

Tomkins, Silvan S. *Affect, Imagery, Consciousness, Volume 1: The Positive Affects*. New York: Springer Publishing Company, 2008.

Torres, Sasha. "Televising Guantanamo: Transmissions of Feeling During the Bush Years." *Political Emotions*. Edited by Janet Staiger, Ann Cvetkovich, Ann Reynolds, 45–65. New York: Routledge: 2010.

Tudor, Andrew. *Monsters and Mad Scientists: A Cultural History of the Horror Movie*. Blackwell: Oxford, 1989.

Urbano, Cosimo. "'What's the Matter with Melanie?' Reflections on the Merits of Psychoanalytic Approaches to Modern Horror Cinema." *Horror Film and Psychoanalysis: Freud's Worst Nightmare*. Edited by Steven J. Schneider, 17–34. Cambridge: Cambridge University Press, 2004.

Vattimo, Gianni. "*Verwindung*: Nihilism and the Postmodern in Philosophy." *Substance* 53 (1987): 7–17.

Vermeulen, Timotheus and Robin van den Akker. "Notes on Metamodernism," *Journal of Aesthetics and Culture* 2 (2010).

Villarejo, Amy. "The Halting Grammar of Intimacy: Watching *An American Family*'s Final Episode." *Political Emotions*. Edited by Janet Staiger, Ann Cvetkovich, Ann Reynolds, 193–214. New York: Routledge: 2010.

## 238   References

Virno, Paolo. "The Ambivalence of Disenchantment." *Radical Thought in Italy: A Potential Politics*. Edited by Michael Hardt, 12–29. Minneapolis: University of Minnesota Press, 1996.

Waldenfels, Bernard. "Levinas and the Face of the Other." *The Cambridge Companion to Levinas*. Edited by Simon Critchley and Robert Bernasconi, 63–81. Cambridge: Cambridge University Press, 2002.

Wall, Thomas Carl. "Dolce Stil Novo: Harmony Korine's Vernacular." *CR: The New Centennial Review* 4.1 (2004): 307–321.

Wallace, Lee. *Lesbianism, Cinema, Space: The Sexual Life of Apartments*. New York: Routledge, 2009.

Weber, Brenda. *Makeover TV: Self-hood, Citizenship and Celebrity*. Durham, NC: Duke University Press.

Wee, Valerie. "The Scream Trilogy, Hyperpostmodernism, and the Late Nineties Teen Slasher Film." *Journal of Film and Video* 57.3 (Fall, 2005): 44–61.

Wells, Paul. *The Horror Genre: From Beelzebub to Blair Witch*. London: Wallflower Press, 2004.

Wexler, Philip. *Critical Theory Now*. London: The Falmer Press, 1991.

Willet, Cynthia. "Baudrillard, 'After Hours,' and the Postmodern Suppression of Socio-Sexual Conflict." *Cultural Critique* 34 (1996): 143–161.

Williams, Linda. "Film Bodies: Gender, Genre and Excess." *Film Quarterly* 44.4 (Summer, 1991): 2–13.

———. "Melodrama Revised." Refiguring American Film Genres: Theory and *History*. Edited by Nick Browne, 42–88. Berkeley: University of California Press, 1998.

———. *Hard Core: Power, Pleasure and the Frenzy of the Visible*. Berkeley: University of California Press, 1989.

Williams, Raymond. *Marxism and Literature*. Oxford: Oxford University Press, 1977.

Williams, Richard J. "Towards an Aesthetics of Poverty," *Neo-Avant-Garde*. Edited by David Hopkins and Anna Katharina Schaffner, 197–222. Amsterdam: Rodopi, 2006.

Wood, Robin. "An Introduction to the American Horror Film." *The American Nightmare*. Edited by Richard Lippe and Robin Wood, 7–28. Toronto: Festival of Festivals, 1979.

Woods, Tim. *Beginning Postmodernism*. Manchester: Manchester University Press, 1999.

Woodward, Kathleen. "Global Cooling and Academic Warming: Long-Term Shifts in Emotional Weather." *American Literary History* 8.4 (Winter, 1996): 759–779.

———. *Statistical Panic: Cultural Politics and Poetics of the Emotions*. Durham, NC: Duke University Press, 2009.

Zizek, Slavoj. "Introduction: Alfred Hitchcock, or, The Form and its Historical Mediation." *Everything You Always Wanted to Know about Lacan, But Were Afraid to Ask Hitchcock*. Edited by Slavoj Zizek, 1–14. London: Verso, 1992.

———. *The Zizek Reader*. Edited by Elizabeth Wright and Edmond Leo Wright. Oxford: Blackwell, 1999.

———. *Looking Awry: An Introduction to Jacques Lacan Through Popular Culture*. Cambridge, MA: MIT Press, 1992.

———. *The Sublime Object of Ideology*. London: Verso, 1989.

Zylinska, Joanna. "'Nourished … on the Irremediable Differend of Gender': Lyotard's Sublime." *Gender After Lyotard*. Edited by Margaret Grebowikz, 155–170. Albany, NY: State University of New York Press, 2007.

# Index

Abbas, A. 71 n. 56
Adams, P. 78
Adorno, T. 104 n. 31
affect: definition of 3, 12; and
    postmodern theory 1–3, 8, 23,
    38–52, 55–68; and feeling theory
    1–5, 8–16, 23, 40–43,
    46–51, 57–9, 61–8, 91, 100–101,
    190–3, 206; and emotion 3–5,
    12–16, 23, 34 n. 66, 39–42, 44–50,
    55, 59, 62–8, 82, 91–2, 100–101,
    190–93, 198, 206, 220–1; in film
    studies 17–20, 22; "the waning of"
    1–2, 23, 27 n. 8, 39–42, 102 n. 6,
    110, 113–16, 127–8
affective turn, the *see* feeling theory
affectlessness *see* numbness
Ahmed, S. 10, 37 n. 106, 214 n. 51
Anderson, B. 193
Anderson, W. 21, 25, 187–207,
    214–5 n. 59
anger 4–5, 10, 15, 19, 24, 27, 29,
    34 n. 68, 38, 54, 165, 168–9, 171, 180
avant-garde, the 24–5, 60–61, 166–71,
    173–5, 178–81, 182 n. 4

Barker, J. 17–18
Barthes, R. and the punctum 83–5, 94;
    and the face 147, 154
Bauman, Z. 173–4, 218
Baudrillard, J. and boredom 170,
    184 n. 22; and the demise of the
    real 3; and ecstasy 23, 38,
    54–58; and the end of emotion
    in postmodernism 2, 22, 52–3;
    and the obscene 53, 200; and
    postmodernism 7, 51, 143,
    161 n. 37; and reversibility 71–2,
    n. 65; and the simulation 23, 52,
    82, 199
Beckett, S. 127

Belasz, B. 101 n. 2
Benjamin, W. 35 n. 72, 168, 183 n. 13,
    207
Bergson, H. 9
Berlant, L. 3, 10, 14, 19, 40, 49,
    73 n. 85, 91, 100, 212–13 n. 35
Bernstein, H. 168–9
Best, S. (Stephen) 32 n. 47
Best, S. (Susan) 32 n. 52
bewilderment 4–6, 19, 21–2, 24, 26,
    134–58, 160 n. 20, 162 n. 50,
    163 n. 55, 216–221
Bignell, J. 199
Blanchot, M. 104 n. 31
Boltanski, L. 218
Bonaventure hotel, the 87–8, 139–41,
    157, 160 n. 20
Botting, F. 92, 94, 97
Bora, R. 83, 103 n. 18
boredom 4–6, 16, 21–2, 24–6, 56,
    165–81, 183–4 n. 13, 184 n. 22,
    218–220
Bourriaud, N. 211–12 n. 21, 217
Brennan, T. 105 n. 47, 193, 214 n. 51,
    223 n. 10
Brinkema, E. 2, 17, 22, 42, 69 n. 22,
    137
Brown, B. 141, 144, 160 n. 33, 222 n. 1
Brown, J. 84
Browning, M. 81
Buchanan, I. 41–4, 48
Burger, P 167, 180, 184 n. 20
Butler, J. 154

Carroll, N. 17–19, 22, 110, 113, 117,
    122, 124, 126, 129 n. 3, 130 n. 18
Cheng, A. 80, 89
Chiapello, E. 218
Chow, R. 143, 152, 163, 55
Chute, H. 8
Clough, P. 26, 29, 58

240  *Index*

Clover, C. 19, 22, 123
cognitive-appraisal theory: and affect 3–4, 13, 82; and bewilderment 138–9, 141; and boredom 168; definition of 12–13, 19 n. 13, 30 n. 27, 84; and ecstasy 54–5; and the euphoric intensity 44–5; and fascination 82, 84–7, 89, 91, 100, 101; and fear 110, 117–8, 121, 125, 128; and feeling theory 3, 13; and knowingness 193; limitations of 4–7, 9–10, 14–16, 68, 82, 84–7, 89, 91, 100, 101, 121, 125, 128, 138–9, 141, 168, 193; and the obscene 53; and postmodernism 3, 41, 82; and the simulation 52–3; and the sublime 62, 65
cognitive mapping 19, 142–4, 157, 199–200
Collins, J. 20, 187
Connor, S. 28 n. 9, 188
Constable, C. 2, 20–21
consumerism 24–5, 170–1, 173–8, 181, 218
*Crash* (Cronenberg) 4, 20–1, 23, 77–83, 85–101, 102 n. 7
Craven, W. 21–4, 108–117, 122–28, 130 n. 22, 132 n. 53
Creed, B. 97–8
Cvetkovich, A. 4, 32 n. 46, 80, 189–190, 192–3

Davis, K. 11–12
Davis, M. 161 n. 34
Deigh, J. 139
Deleuze, G. and affect 9, 11, 13, 16, 40; and faciality 145; and the scream 108
depthlessness *see* postmodernism
Derrida, J. 11, 83, 142, 161 n. 35
Doane, M. 137–8, 152
Dolar, M. 108
Douglas, M. 178

Ebert, R. 130, 131
Eco, U. 21, 210 n. 14
ecstasy 4, 22–3, 28, 51–8, 68, Edelman, L. 135, 137, 153
Elsaesser, T. 16, 189, 221
emotion 4–6, 11, 15–16; devalued status of 5, 12, 15, 50, 222; and feeling theory; 1–5, 7–17, 19, 22–6, 38–42, 46–7, 50, 54–5, 57–9, 61–8, 78, 81, 89, 91, 99, 100–101, 190–194, 200, 205–6, 218, 220–2; in

film studies 16–20, 22, 136, 145–6; recursivity of 6, 16, 21, 23, 38, 45–6, 68, 116, 121, 125, 128, 165, 167, 168. *See also* anger; bewilderment; boredom; ecstasy; euphoria; fascination; fear; knowingness; postmodernism
Epstein, J. 156
euphoria 4, 6, 22–3, 38–51, 65, 83, 220–1

faciality 24, 127, 134–8, 140–1, 144–58, 162 n. 50
fascination 4–8, 21–3, 54, 77–101, 104 n. 31, 105 n. 33, 146, 219–220.
fear 6, 8, 10, 15, 17–19, 21–4, 38, 54, 63, 68, 84, 100, 108–128, 129 n. 11, 165, 219, 221
Featherstone, M. 170
feeling theory 1–19, 22–3, 25–6, 27 n. 8, 32–6, 38–42, 46–8, 50–1, 54–5, 67–9, 61–71, 73–5, 78, 81, 89, 91, 99–103, 187, 189–94, 200, 205–7, 210–15, 217–18, 221–2
Felski, R. 10
Fenichel, O. 189
Fisher, P. 5, 15, 34, 84, 122–3, 133, 133 n. 55, 169, 187, 189, 191, 207
Flatley, J. 10
Foster, H. 157, 167, 173, 182 n. 4, 183 n. 7
Foucault, M. 19, 143
Frank, A. 4, 27 n. 8
Freud, S. 24, 51, 116–121,
Frow, J. 6
Fuss, D. 153

Gane, M. 51
Gaut, B. 17–18, 22
Guattari, F. 9
Girard, R. 89
Gledhill, C. 17
Gould, D. 14, 65, 76 n. 124
Grace, V. 53, 57, 70
Greenberg, C. 167, 184 n. 20
Gregg, M. 9, 14, 44, 58, 69 n. 16, 70 n. 29, 192, 206
Grossberg, L 25, 33 n. 57, 40–2, 188, 192
*Gummo* (Korine) 21, 24–5, 165–81
Gunning, T. 109–110, 147

Hantke, S. 113, 131 n. 25
Hardt, M. 10, 31 n. 40, 173, 181
Harris, O. 101

# Index    241

Harvey, D. 2, 7, 84–5, 161 n. 37, 199
Hawkins, G. 178
Heidegger, M. 89, 168
Hemmings, C. 10, 33 n. 60, 42, 69 n. 21
Hills, M. 111
Hoffman, E. T. A. 117–121, 128
Hume, D. 102 n. 31, 122
Hutcheon, L. 7, 27 n. 9 , 83, 188, 205, 210 n. 14
Huyssen, A. 83, 173

Jameson, F. and affect 39–42, 65; and the avant-garde 167, 173; and bewilderment 139–144, 148, 157–8, 160–1, n. 34; Bonaventure hotel 87–89, 139–141, 157, 160–1, n. 34; and cinema 20–1; and cognitive mapping 142, 157–8, 199; and depthlessness 77–8; and euphoric intensity 23, 31 n. 37, 38—51, 62, 64–66, 209, 220–1; and glossiness 82, 84–5, 87–88, 94; and postmodernism 7, 38–9; and the and the "waning of affect" 1–2, 22, 39, 110, 116; boredom 170, 184 n. 22
Jancovich, M. 96
Jentsch, E. 24, 116,  118–21, 125, 128
Johnson, G. 94
Jones, A. 78

Kellner, D. 70 n. 52, 143, 199
Kirby, A. 189, 199, 208 n. 6, 217
Knowingness 4, 6, 19, 21–2, 25, 68, 122, 126, 187–207, 207–8 n. 6
Korine, H. 21, 24–5, 165–81
Kracauer, S. 35 n. 72, 168, 183 n. 13
Kroker, A. 137

Lacan, J. 43, 89, 136, 143, 154
Laine, T. 10, 17–18, 22, 125
Latour, B. 32
Lear, J. 189, 191, 212 n. 29
Levitt, N. 188–9
Leys, R. 9, 42, 69 n. 22
Lipovetsky, G. 217
Love, H. 10, 31 n. 43, 32 n. 45, 153, 180, 193
Lynch, D. 21, 24, 134–8, 144–58, 159 n. 15, 162 n. 51, 163 n. 55
Lyotard, J.-F. 22, 37, 189; and affect 40, 58–65; and the avant-garde 173, 181; and meta narrative 3, 7, 199; and the sublime 22–23, 31 n. 37, 38, 58–68, 218, 223 n. 6

Malpas, S. 67
Markowitz, S. 5
Marks, L. 17–18
Massumi, B. 9, 58 , 61; and affect 2–4, 13–14, 26 n. 7, 40–2, 44, 49, 50, 58, 63, 65–6, 92, 116, 1; and emotion 7, 63, 65–6, 92; and fear 126; and knowingness 191–3
Mayshark, J. 21, 77, 187–8
McHale, B. 7, 27 n. 9
McRobbie, A. 83
Miller, D. 170
Modleski, T. 114
Morris, M. 54, 57
*Mulholland Drive* (Lynch) 21, 24, 134–8, 144–58, 159 n. 15, 162 n. 51, 163 n. 55
Mulvey, L. 83, 149

Natoli, J. 83
Newman, K. 115–6, 128
Ngai, S. and the avant-garde, 167; and emotion 3, 15, 69 n. 16, 187–8; and tone 193–4
Nussbaum, M. 12–13, 29, 39, 54, 65
numbness 22–4, 32, 110–111, 114–7, 116, 119–128, 131 n. 25

Olsen, M. 187, 194, 204,
Oudart, J-P. 137, 141–2, 145,

Pellegrini, A. 1
Perloff, M. 167
Pisters, P. 16
Plantinga, C. 17–18
postmodernism 1–16, 19–26, 28–68; and cinema 19–25, 77–9, 81–3, 85, 87, 89–96, 99, 109–116, 123–8, 137–8, 144, 147–8, 151–3, 155–8, 178, 189–90, 194–6, 201, 204–5, 209; demise of 1–3, 27–8 n. 9, 32 n. 47; and depthlessness 77–78, 80–5, 87, 89, 99–100; and texture 79–101
Puar, J. 1
Probyn, E. 27 n. 8

Rockoff, A. 116,
Rorty, R. 33, 188–9, 191–2, 211 n. 19
Rosenbaum, J. 204, 210 n. 13
*Rushmore* (Anderson) 21, 25, 187–207, 214–5 n. 59

242   *Index*

Sardar, Z. 83, 209 n. 11
Scheman, N. 192–3
Sedgwick, E. 3–4, 9–10, 12, 14, 27
  n. 8, 80–1, 84, 100, 191, 193, 198,
  202–03, 207
Seigworth, G. 9, 14, 44, 192, 206
Shannon, S. 80
Shaviro, S. 4, 16, 20, 36 n. 66, 42, 52,
  62, 198, 221
Sinclair, I. 90
Singh, G. 17, 26
Sipos, T. 113–4
Slade, A. 60, 74
Sloterdijk, P. 7
Smith, G. 16–17
Smith, R. 57
Sobchack, V. 17, 36 n. 80, 52, 221,
  223 n. 13
Solomon, R. 12–3
Spacks, P. 168, 172, 184 n. 13
Stacey, J. 152
Staiger, J. 34–5 n. 72
Stallybrass, P. 175
Spinoza, B. 9, 163 n. 55

*Scream* (Craven) 21–4, 108–117,
  122–28, 130 n. 22, 132 n. 53
*Scream, The* (painting) 110–1, 124

Terada, R. 3–4, 6, 11, 15, 63, 69 n. 16
texture  8, 78–85, 91–2, 95–6, 100
Thiele, L. 218
Thrift, N. 3, 10, 14, 19, 80, 191
Toles, G. 136
Tomkins, S. 4, 9, 13, 87, 135
Torres, S. 119

Urbano, C. 125

Virno, P. 218

Wall, T  168, 172, 176
Wallace, L. 153, 163 n. 55
Weber, B. 151
Williams, L. 16–17, 19, 22, 130 n. 18, 155
Williams, R. 70 n. 32
Wood, R. 114–116
Woodward, K. 1–2, 15, 161 n. 37

Zizek, S. 89, 104 n. 26, 126, 159 n. 14